MEDIASCAPES

SECOND EDITION

MEDIASCAPES

New Patterns in Canadian Communication

Edited by

Paul Attallah
Carleton University

Leslie Regan Shade
Concordia University

THOMSON

NELSON

Australia   Canada   Mexico   Singapore   Spain   United Kingdom   United States

THOMSON
NELSON

Mediascapes: New Patterns in Canadian Communication, Second Edition

by Paul Attallah and Leslie Regan Shade

Associate Vice President, Editorial Director:
Evelyn Veitch

Executive Editor:
Anne Williams

Senior Marketing Manager:
Wayne Morden

Developmental Editor:
Elke Price

Permissions Coordinator:
Terri Rothman

Senior Production Editor:
Bob Kohlmeier

Copy Editor:
Margaret Crammond

Proofreader:
Sandra Braun

Indexer:
Dennis A. Mills

Production Coordinator:
Ferial Suleman

Design Director:
Ken Phipps

Interior Design:
Peter Papayanakis

Cover Design:
Eugene Lo

Cover Image:
January, by Janice Wong

Compositor:
Integra

Printer:
Quebecor World

Library and Archives Canada Cataloguing in Publication

Mediascapes : new patterns in Canadian communication / edited by Paul Attallah and Leslie Regan Shade — 2nd ed.

Includes bibliographical references and index.
ISBN 0-17-640652-2

1. Mass media—Canada—Textbooks.   I. Attallah, Paul, 1954–
II. Shade, Leslie Regan, 1957–

P92.C3M46 2005   302.23'0971
C2005-902453-4

CONTENTS

P R E F A C E

The future of communication in Canada does not look like its past. There are three main reasons for this fact. The first has to do with the rate and nature of technological change. Anyone who has observed technology even superficially in the past decade will realize that the rise of digitization and the Internet has profoundly altered the way in which media content is produced, distributed, and consumed. Formerly separate technologies such as the telephone, publishing, and music are now converging around a common technological infrastructure. Furthermore, the technological convergence is driving business or corporate convergence as companies merge or form alliances and partnerships. The world in which telephones were regulated separately from music distribution has been challenged by convergence and mergers, and has thus produced interesting policy debates.

The second main reason for our new communication future is related to what is very broadly called "globalization." The flow of capital, people, and knowledge around the world has both accelerated and altered our expectations about which types of information, entertainment, and knowledge should be available, and to whom. The worldwide reach of the Internet, for example, has severely challenged the ability of governments and corporations to control information for their own advantage. It has also underlined the necessity for forms of regulation or law that are not simply entertainment. As a new global culture emerges, new trade regimes and trade organizations such as NAFTA, the European Union, and the World Trade Organization have also come into existence. So, too, have new expectations about appropriate and desirable communication. Communication rights have come to be seen as an intrinsic element of ensuring diversity and equity in an information society.

The third main force driving our new communication future is the changing public or audience for media. Canadian society is becoming increasingly multicultural in its demographic composition. The old world in which everyone was united around a single culture or cultural representation no longer exists. Technology has made us more open to diverse cultures, interests, and tastes. This openness has been accompanied by an increasing sophistication on the part of audiences. Nowadays, no one consumes the media innocently. As we become increasingly skilled in decoding their messages and meaning, we demand media content as sophisticated as we are.

We now experience the media not as a national phenomenon, but as a global phenomenon. Consequently, this is a book about media in Canada, not specifically about Canadian media. The old world in which we used media to protect ourselves against the world is being replaced by a new future in which access to global media makes up the world. This book is concerned with that future.

FEATURES OF THE TEXT

Each of the five major parts of the book opens with an introduction that identifies salient themes addressed in the chapters. Each chapter concludes with *questions* that reinforce the main ideas presented in the chapter, a *references* list, a selected *bibliography*, and/or a *further reading* list. Some chapters also include end-of-chapter *notes*.

MEDIASCAPE ON-LINE RESOURCES (WWW.MEDIASCAPES2E.NELSON.COM)

The book support Web site contains student and instructor resources. Students and instructors can link directly to relevant Web sites associated with each of the book's chapters, and they can also access a variety of media profiles and updates, as well as a glossary of media terms.

ACKNOWLEDGMENTS

We thank the reviewers who commented on draft versions, among them David Black, Royal Roads University; Pascal Michelucci, University of Toronto; Roman Onufrijchuk, Simon Fraser University; Alexandre Sévigny, McMaster University; David Skinner, York University; Serra Tinic, University of Alberta; and James Wong, Wilfrid Laurier University. We would also like to thank various people at Thomson Nelson who have made our editing experiences a pleasure: Senior Production Editor Bob Kohlmeier; Executive Editors Rod Banister and Anne Williams; Developmental Editor Elke Price; Marketing Manager Wayne Morden; and Copy Editor Margaret Crammond. We also would like to thank our many contributors from all across Canada, who have made this book be "as Canadian as possible."

Part I
Institutional Context

Introduction

Paul Attallah
Carleton University

It is very easy to assume that **communication** has always been with us since people have always "communicated." And while it is true that people have always used language and other symbols to create meaning, what they have understood as communication has, unfortunately, never been simple or straightforward.

For example, if we consider two people talking—which for many observers is the most fundamental communication situation—we immediately run up against some rather daunting difficulties. How do the two people manage to agree that their words will mean the same thing for both of them? Would it not depend on the context of their conversation rather than on the content of the words themselves? Merely to attach the same meanings to words, then, the two people would have to share not only the same language but also an entire universe of cultural and other assumptions about which words to use when, about who speaks and in which order, about the proper way to demonstrate sincerity or to ensure the truth of one's statements, and so on. Indeed, two people can share all of that and still manage to misunderstand one another.

As a result, for one person to say something that another will understand, the speaker must imagine what the listener is likely to understand even before speaking. The speaker must try to imagine the world from the point of view of the listener and from the listener's set of abilities in order to say something that will even seem reasonable. Upon closer examination, therefore, even the most fundamental communication situation proves not to be very straightforward.

Plainly, then, it is frequently useful to take into account the *context* in which communication occurs. The context provides many of the cues on how to interpret meanings, when to use meanings, when meanings are appropriate or inappropriate, etc.

Consequently, we tend to examine *communication in context*. This is one of the important meanings of the phrase *mass communication*. It means not just that communication affects lots of people or that it occurs on a grand scale but also that the *context* in which it happens—the nature of our *mass* society—has a determining influence on the nature of communication.

The chapters that follow are concerned precisely with trying to understand the relationship between communication and the context in which it occurs. Needless to say, there are many ways of approaching that relationship. At the most basic level, the chapters ask certain questions: Is Canada like or unlike the United States, or other modern countries? Is communication defined the same way here as it is in other places? Is it carried out in the same manner or style? Is it organized— by the media, the state, individuals—in the same way?

It is fair to say that communication became a problem worthy of study only within the last 200 years or so. Before then, people certainly communicated, but the activity was second nature to them. They did not pause to consider it as a problem, as something outside themselves that merited attention. It was simply part and parcel of everyday culture, an aspect of individual identity, something that just happened.

With the rise of *modernity*, however, communication became a problem. Modernity refers to that state of affairs, beginning roughly around the time of the democratic revolutions—the American Revolution (1776), French Revolution (1789), and European Revolutions (1830–1844)—when people suddenly had to take responsibility for the organization of society. It describes contemporary mass society. The ancient monarchies were overthrown and along with them their social structures and modes of thought. Indeed, even where the monarchies were not overthrown, as in Britain, new deliberative bodies—parliament, congress, national assembly—that represented the will of the people gained in prominence and authority.

As a result, virtually nobody nowadays believes that rulers are chosen by God or that they rule by divine right. However, this was the dominant social belief prior to modernity. Since modernity, we are much more inclined to agree that rulers are chosen, however imperfectly, by the people and that the rules they enact and social arrangements that result—for both good and ill—are ultimately the responsibility of the people. Modernity marks that moment when people come together and use reason to determine consensually the rules of social organization and collective behaviour.

And that is precisely why communication has become such a problem in modern society. In order to determine the rules by which society would be organized, we have had to communicate with each other, to share ideas, to engage in debate, to exchange models, to reach consensus, and so on. But in order to do *that*, we have had to reflect long and hard on communication.

What is appropriate to say to others? How should it be said? Should someone have more authority? How will we know when a true idea has been expressed? How can we ensure that everyone has access to the ideas and a chance to participate in the general debate?

It would be unfair and inaccurate to claim that we have found perfect answers to all these questions, but we have at least found ones that are serviceable and reasonable. In order to guarantee that everyone can speak, we have instituted such notions as freedom of speech. We have even enshrined it in institutions such as parliament. We attempt, however imperfectly, not to disenfranchise anyone from the debate and even create events, such as elections, referenda, and consultations, at which people are specifically called upon to express themselves and assume responsibility for social organization. And to ensure that knowledge and information are widely shared and easily accessible, we have created the media. This is why arguments over such issues as freedom of the press, concentration of ownership, and privacy are so fierce and indispensable. They go directly to the heart of the type of society we wish to make.

Modernity, then, led to the creation of institutions of communication: free speech, elections, parliament, and the media. But the mere existence of the institutions does not mean that everything said in them will be transparently true, morally uplifting, or intellectually enlightening. It is easy to use the institutions poorly.

Furthermore, the institutions have generated new sets of unanticipated problems. For example, while the original function of the mass media was to widen the sphere of public debate by making information widely available, it is clear that the media have also acquired unexpected characteristics. They tend to be industries with their own internal requirements for efficiency, profit-generation, and operation. Indeed, their autonomous development often means that it is in their best interest to shape or handle information in ways that will enhance their own operations rather than serve the public good. A central question, therefore, is the extent to which our institutions of communication actually widen the sphere of public debate or whether they merely manipulate and shape public opinion.

There are significant differences between the ways communication has been institutionalized in Canada and in the United States. The media are organized differently, and we have distinct cultural and political traditions. Indeed, the central fact of Canadian public life—the existence of two dominant language groups with their own cultural perspectives—has itself resulted in a different range of questions about communication. Generally, it seems that in the United States communication has been understood *instrumentally*, as a means to convey content. This has resulted in questions about the effectiveness of the conveyance and the impact of the content. In Canada, less attention has been devoted to the means of conveyance and more to the way in which the very existence of the means may have shaped public life. Canadian research has therefore tended to identify communication with culture—with a whole way of life—and has tended to ask how it embodies values or shapes long-term views or excludes possibilities as well as includes them.

Whether this has resulted in greater truth is itself one of the questions within the Canadian tradition. It is unlikely that a single, definitive, and conclusive answer will ever leap off the page. It is likely, however, that we can understand the strands that make up the tradition and so place ourselves in a position to offer our own views on it.

Between the early 1950s and the present, communication emerged in Canada as *a problem worthy of attention* under a number of guises. During this time period, (a) both federal and provincial governments established departments of communication and began to intervene in culture; (b) universities began to teach communication as an academic discipline; (c) journals and books devoted to communication began to appear; (d) the concept of *cultural industries* acquired currency and communication began to designate both popular culture and the means of its delivery; and (e) thinkers such as Marshall McLuhan and Neil Postman became famous for their ideas about communication.

The process by which a field such as communication emerges can be called its *institutionalization*. This means that communication ceases to be merely a generalized concept to which anyone can refer and becomes instead rooted and located within specific institutions and structures whose singular purpose is to study, propagate, refine, and apply it. Once institutionalized, the study of communication develops its own language, tools, and questions. The institutionalization of a field is always an important event, and in Canada, beginning in the early 1950s, communication underwent institutionalization as an object of academic study (the universities, publishing), an area of state and policy intervention (governments, royal commissions, ministries), an economic force (the cultural industries), a technological phenomenon (new and old communications technologies), a social problem (what communication does to us, to our children, etc.), and the bearer of modern culture (entertainment, information).

Significantly, though, in Canada, the process of institutionalization (i.e., the institutions in which communication came to be rooted) tended to define communication in opposition to the way it had been institutionalized in the United States. Furthermore, it also tended to ask itself certain questions characteristic of the Canadian experience, questions which, perhaps paradoxically, come to preoccupy most other modern societies decades later.

The most important of these questions concerns Canada's relationship with the United States. Living next to the United States is like standing in gale force winds. Everyday a storm of information, ideas, styles, trends, and fashions sweeps northward from New York, Los Angeles, Washington, and other American locations. That experience led Canadian communication scholars to reflect upon the relationship between technology and culture, the differences between cultures, the nature of identity, and alternative forms for the organization of communication. Eventually, as American culture reached further and further afield, the rest of the world would also come to ask similar questions, thereby giving Canadian communication scholarship an unanticipated echo and international impact.

We should avoid the trap, however, of believing that the institutionalization in Canada is somehow superior, inherently good, or beyond reproach. It is not. First, it incorporates not just noble motives but also self-interest, the fear of modernity, reactionary impulses, and so on. Second, it results not only in good outcomes but also in counterproductive, silly, undesirable, or pointless outcomes.

We wish not to *celebrate* communication in Canada but to *understand* it. One of the main tasks for communication scholars, therefore, is to assess institutionalization, not merely to cherish or defend it.

The most decisive influence on communication studies was exercised by the Canadian state. Governments at both federal and provincial levels not only established departments of communication but also commissioned reports, studies, and inquiries. Additionally, the state supported its activities with financial resources and lent them an unusually high degree of public visibility. In essence, then, the Canadian state has set the public agenda of communication research in this country. It employed a generation of communication scholars, indicated to them valuable areas and types of study, and supported research directions. And its influence continues to be felt in granting agencies, the establishment of research themes, and the endowment of university chairs.

The state, though, has not been alone. One of the best places to observe the interplay of factors shaping communication studies in Canada is in our universities (see Table 1). Since 1965, when Concordia University established the first communication studies department, interest in the field has literally exploded.

Table 1 also illustrates some of the main structuring themes of communication research. Broadly speaking, the field is divided between a *political economic* orientation and a *cultural studies* orientation. It is extremely easy to overstate the degree of opposition between them, to overlook their affinities, and to reduce each to caricature. Indeed, both claim to be *critical* rather than *administrative*, both can oppose or guide the state, both can espouse nationalism, and both see a link between structures of power and social outcomes.

In Canada, *administrative* or mainstream research tends to be overshadowed by *critical* research. This is one way for Canadian universities to distinguish themselves from their American counterparts. It may, however, have led, very *uncritically*, to the assumption that Canadian communication research is critical *per se*, thereby leaving underdeveloped much fundamental research associated with a more administrative approach. Indeed, one of the persistent problems of Canadian communication research is the perennial lack of hard data and up-to-date information that an administrative orientation would be more likely to produce.

A smaller, though increasingly important, theme revolves around technology—especially new information technologies, digitization, and the Internet. We have already seen the full panoply of methods applied to cyberspace, whose study increasingly breaks down between the two major political economic and cultural studies orientations. Significantly, the professors who teach communication tend to have reached intellectual maturity in an era before video games, the Internet, computer processors, and so on. There is a gap between them and the spontaneous experiences of students with whom they come into contact. While such generational gaps are hardly new, they do point to a likely shift over time in the overall configuration of the field of communication in Canada away from such classic questions as communication and cultural identity and towards questions such as the formation of taste groups, the internationalization of culture, virtual communities, and so on.

Another strand of communication research in Canada derives from the cognitive sciences and is closer to psychology. This strand, which finds expression in interpersonal and organizational communication and in some forms of audience research, focuses less on the societal dimension of communication and more on its perceptual dimension. A good example of this may be found in the work of Marshall McLuhan, especially in relationship to the perceptual impact of technologies such as television or the telephone. McLuhan studied this dimension under the terms *hot* and *cool* media.

TABLE 1   Major Canadian Communication Studies Programs

University	Faculty	Degrees Offered	Home School	Area of Focus
Alberta	Extension	M.A.C.T.		Communication and technology
Brock	Social Sciences	B.A., M.A.	Department of Communications, Popular Culture and Film	Business; media and culture; policy; information technology
Calgary	Communication and Culture	B.A., M.C.S., M.A., Ph.D.	Communication Studies	Cultural industries; interpersonal; intercultural; organizational; law
Cape Breton	School of Arts and Community Studies	B.A., BACS	Department of Communication	Interpersonal; rhetoric; media studies
Carleton	Public Affairs and Management	B.A., B.J., M.A., M.J., Ph.D.	School of Journalism and Communication	History and theory; policy and political economy; socio-aesthetics; technology; journalism
Concordia[a]	Arts and Science	B.A., B.J., Graduate Diploma, M.A., Ph.D.	Department of Communication Studies	Mass media; media practice; broad communication application; cultural studies
Laval	Lettres	B.A., M.A., Graduate Diploma	Département d'information et de communication	Industries culturelles; médias; communication publique; journalisme
McGill	Arts	B.A., M.A., Ph.D.	Department of Art History and Communication Studies	Visual culture; new media; image technology; social semiotics; social contextualization; culture
McMaster	Humanities	B.A.	Communication Studies Program	Language and social life; cultural studies; performance studies; mass media
Montréal[a]	Arts et Sciences	B.A., B.Sc., M.Sc., Ph.D.	Département de communication	Médias de masse/nouvelles technologies; aspects sociaux, culturels, juridiques, et institutionnels des médias; organisationnel
Ottawa	Arts	B.A., M.A.	Department of Communication	Organizational; communication and media studies

University	Faculty/School	Degrees	Program	Focus
Royal Roads	School of Communication and Culture	B.A. and M.A. in Applied Communications, M.B.A. in Public Relations and Communication Management, Graduate Certificate in Public Relations Management	Program in Communications	Applied communication; organizational; public relations; intercultural; international
Ryerson[b]	School of Graduate Studies	B.J., M.A., Ph.D.	Program in Communication and Culture	Media and culture; politics and policy; technology in practice; applied perspectives
Simon Fraser	Applied Science	B.A., M.A., Graduate Diploma	School of Communication	Media; social; journalism; political economy; technology; cultural industries
Toronto	Graduate Studies – Faculty of Information Studies	M.I.S., Ph.D. (in Information Studies)	McLuhan Program in Culture and Technology	Media; culture; technology
New Brunswick at Saint John	Interdisciplinary Studies	B.A.	Information and Communication Studies	Information and communication technologies and practices
Québec à Montréal[a]	Lettres, langues et communications	B.A., B.J., M.A., Ph.D.	Département de communication	Médias; culture; communication de groupe; sociopolitique; psychosociologique; sémiotique; anthropologique; ergonomie cognitive
Western Ontario	Information and Media Studies	M.A., M.L.I.S., M.A.J., M.S., Ph.D.	Media Information and Technoculture/Journalism	Critical; institutions, practices, and cultural meanings associated with technologies of communication, information, knowledge, learning, and entertainment
Wilfrid Laurier	Arts	B.A.	Communication Studies	Media industries and contemporary culture; theory and criticism; visual communication
Windsor	Arts and Social Sciences	B.A., M.A.	Department of Communication Studies	Media practices; theory and criticism; policy and systems; social justice
York[b]	Arts	Diploma, B.A., M.A., Ph.D.	Division of Social Sciences – Communication Program	Traditional forms of mass communication (print, radio, film, television); emerging interactive telecommunications networks and computer systems; new media

Note. This is an overview of communication programs; any omissions are unintentional. [a]The Ph.D. is offered jointly by Concordia University, Université du Québec à Montréal, and Université de Montréal. [b]The M.A. and Ph.D. are offered jointly by Ryerson and York.

Finally, a minor strand in Canadian communication is rhetoric, the use of language for persuasion and public presentation. It is often said that public discourse in Canada is atrophied, and this is apparently reflected not just in political speech-making but also in the institutionalization of communication. Rhetoric is much more important in American universities, and the reasons for its marginalization in Canada deserve to be studied in their own right. Dorland and Charland (2002) argue that the weakness of a Canadian rhetorical tradition is due to the weakness of Canadian civil society (the sphere of social relations ungoverned by the state) and to the disposition of our political institutions. Nonetheless, the rhetorical tradition may perhaps be observed in the role that schools of journalism play in Canada. Significantly, depart-ments of linguistics are also frequently concerned with rhetoric, broadly conceived, and frequently study phenomena such as *discourse* and sociolinguistics. The interest of these approaches for communication should not be overlooked.

This first section of this book contains two important chapters. Sheryl Hamilton's "Considering Critical Communication Studies in Canada" addresses specifi-cally the question of why Canadian communication studies are considered to be critical and evaluates the worth of that claim. After describing the essential features of the *critical* approach, Hamilton concludes that, in the Canadian context, it may gloss over as many problems as it solves.

Anne-Marie Kinahan's "From British Invasions to American Influences: Cultural Studies in Canada" examines the role and status of the cultural studies approach. Unlike Britain, the United States, Australia, and New Zealand, where cultural studies has flourished, Canada has witnessed a relatively atrophied version of this approach. Part of the reason is that communication predated cultural studies and already did many of the things that cultural studies claims to do. Another part of the problem is that the development of popular culture in Canada, so strongly influenced by the United States, made it relatively difficult to point to any straightforward alignment between cultural formations and indigenous social classes. Finally, a third part of the problem is the lively and vigorous antagonism of political economy, itself very well entrenched in the Canadian academy, to anything that smacks of cultural studies.

Together, these two chapters form an important overview of the two dominant tendencies in Canadian communication research. A project for the future might be to examine how they could be integrated and the reasons which might prevent their integration. Indeed, they may both separately and jointly point in the direction of entirely new questions that they themselves cannot really handle.

REFERENCES

Dorland, Michael, and Maurice Charland. (2002). *Law, rhetoric, and irony in the formation of Canadian civil culture.* Toronto: University of Toronto Press.

1

Considering Critical Communication Studies in Canada

Sheryl N. Hamilton[1]
Carleton University

It is often claimed that Canadian communication studies is *critical* whereas American studies is merely *administrative*. With our proud legacy of Harold Innis, Marshall McLuhan, George Grant, and Northrop Frye, we seek answers to the big questions. We look patronizingly on American communication studies and the way it seems to promote **corporate media** interests. We chuckle knowingly at the repeated folly of seeking to understand the effects of media messages on individuals. There may certainly be a kernel of truth to the claim that Canadian communication studies is critical, but it also contains numerous blind spots. If we want to argue that Canadian communication studies is critical, we must first stop assuming it is so, and start articulating what it might mean.

CRITICAL VERSUS ADMINISTRATIVE

Any attempt to define "critical" inherits the troubled distinction between administrative and critical communication research from the United States. Despite its inaccuracy and simplicity, "critical versus administrative" continues to be one of the central underlying frames through which scholars have aligned, organizations have developed, and the history of the field is taught and understood.

How did we come to divide the field into these two camps? There are two American communications events that establish the distinction between critical and administrative. The first is Paul Lazarsfeld's 1941 article, "Remarks on Administrative and Critical Communication Research," which first named the distinction. The second event is the special issue of the *Journal of Communication*, published in 1983, which exposed tensions within the field, created the frames in which subsequent debate would take place, and set them in conflict.

Paul Lazarsfeld is considered to be one of the "founding fathers" of communication studies. With his colleagues, he pursued quantitative research using large-scale surveys and statistical analysis to explore the effects of media on people's behaviour. The research was funded through alliances between philanthropic foundations, universities, and interested corporations. Their ultimate goal was to make media more effective.

In the late 1930s, this approach was challenged by a group of émigré Jewish scholars who fled Nazi Germany to settle in the United States and came to be known as the **Frankfurt School.** Trained in European schools of thought, heavily influenced by Marxism, and deeply concerned about what they saw as the industrialization of culture, scholars such as Max Horkheimer, Theodor Adorno, and Herbert Marcuse both enriched and came into conflict with the approach of Lazarsfeld and his colleagues.

This conflict, and his desire to resolve it, motivated Lazarsfeld to write his 1941 article. He could not have realized that he would make a distinction about types of communication research that would organize professional and intellectual practice in the field for at least the next 50 years. In grappling with the clash of approaches, he labels his own *administrative* and the Frankfurt School's *critical*.

Administrative research, he suggests, is "carried through in the service of some kind of administrative agency of public or private character" (Lazarsfeld, 1941, p. 8). Viewing media as useful tools, administrative researchers pose such questions as "Who are the people exposed to the different media? What are their specific preferences? What are the effects of different methods of presentation?" (Lazarsfeld, 1941, p. 3). Lazarsfeld (1941) recognizes the limitations of administrative research approaches, noting that they may not take full account of history and that "they solve little problems, generally of a basic character, when the same methods could be used to improve the life of the community if only they were applied to forward-looking projects related to the pressing economic and social problems of our time" (p. 8).

In contrast, **critical research** assumes that "prior and in addition to whatever special purpose is to be served, the general role of our media of communication in the present social system should be studied" (Lazarsfeld, 1941, p. 9). It therefore differs from administrative research in two respects: "it develops a theory of the prevailing social trends in our times, general trends which yet require consideration in any concrete research problem; and it seems to imply ideas of basic human values according to which all actual or desired effects should be appraised" (Lazarsfeld, 1941, p. 9). Thus, critical research begins with social theory, contains normative values, and places communication in the larger social context. The concern of critical research with threats to human dignity and values is evident in the research questions it raises: "How are these media organized and controlled? How, in their institutional set-up, is the trend toward centralization, standardization and promotional pressure expressed? In what form, however disguised, are they threatening human values?" (Lazarsfeld, 1941, p. 10).

Lazarsfeld is suggesting that the purpose and methodologies of the research, the moral commitment of the scholar, the relationship between theory and empirical reality, and the place of values in research are crucial lines of distinction between critical and administrative research. In his view, critical research assumes the task of revealing how media function in order to reproduce dominant **ideology** in their given social context. Further, he recognizes that such an approach is essentially theoretical because it makes certain assumptions (e.g., about the power of media, the susceptibility of audiences, the nature of the media-audience contact) that are not always empirically verifiable. Finally, it is this very embrace of theory without concern as to its "prove-ability" that Lazarsfeld sees as the primary weakness of critical approaches (Lazarsfeld, 1941, pp. 12–13).

Lazarsfeld's identification of these two research traditions—critical and administrative—has formed a part of the field ever since. And while the administrative tradition certainly emerged as the "dominant paradigm" (Gitlin, 1981) in the United States until at least the 1980s, the debate did not end there.

Tensions between critical and administrative approaches were spurred on by the translation of the work of European Marxist thinkers such as Antonio Gramsci and Louis Althusser, the development of cultural studies, and the radical shifts in the social, economic, and cultural context of the mass media and their study in the United States after World War II.

The 1983 publication of a special issue of the *Journal of Communication*, titled *Ferment in the Field*, marked another watershed event in the dialogue between critical and administrative research. The editor, George Gerbner, gathered 35 original articles from 41 international scholars from both traditions to reflect on the distinction that Lazarsfeld had advanced 42 years earlier. As Gerbner (1983a) wrote in his introduction, "This volume represents the first time that so many internationally prominent scholars have examined and commented upon communications as a field of study in one publication" (p. 4).

Ferment in the Field remains one of the most significant reflections on the state of the field in the history of communication studies. It also reflects the tensions within professional communications circles in the United States. While the distinction between critical and administrative research is accepted rather than challenged by most authors in the issue, the validity of the two approaches is roundly debated. The result is a detailed exposition of the parameters and implications of what constitutes critical research. And while there is no agreed upon definition of critical communication studies, we can recognize a set of ontological, epistemological, and methodological commitments shared by scholars who identify themselves as critical communication researchers. These commitments can inform discussions in both the United States and Canada.

DEFINING CRITICAL COMMUNICATION STUDIES

While a number of scholars have attempted to define critical communication, there is no one widely accepted definition. There is agreement, however, on some of its attributes. It includes approaches from political economy, cultural studies, Marxist sociology, semiotic analysis, institution studies, dependency theory, international communications, and more. It offers a range of different ways to study communication—all of which are in opposition to administrative research (Slack and Allor, 1983, p. 208).

Schiller (1983) suggests that critical research includes a focus on production rather than individual consumption; an examination of the sources and exercise of power; and an assumption of continuous change in social processes and institutions. According to Smythe and Van Dinh (1983), critical research sets as its problem how to re-shape or create institutions to better serve the needs of a greater number of people; uses historical, materialist research techniques; and is ideological in the sense that it links critical problems and tools "with interpretations that involve radical changes in the established order" (p. 118). Commonalities identified by Carey (1983) include a less **positivist** approach to research; diverse methods; a sceptical view of the media; the occasional influence of pragmatism or symbolic interactionism; the inevitable influence of Marxism; and an interest in questions of culture and politics as they relate to communications and mass media.

The following sections examine these shared characteristics of critical communication research in the following categories: research problem, understanding of social power, methodology, researcher orientation, theoretical influences, and knowledge claims.

THE RESEARCH PROBLEM

How does critical communication studies define its research problem? Critical communication scholars have generally focused on the relations between communication and social power. This focus has been variously framed as a question of (1) social control and power (Halloran, 1983); (2) concern with structures of power (Gerbner, 1983b); or (3) an investigation into domination, contradiction, and struggle (Mosco, 1983). The central unit of knowledge is society rather than the individual, and communication practices are considered within their various social contexts.

Simply stated, critical communication research takes on the "big questions." As Rogers (1982) notes, "Critical scholars believe that a theory of communication is impossible without a theory of society, so their scope of analysis is much wider than that of empirical scholars" (p. 125). Therefore, critical researchers ask such questions as who controls the media? How can media be used by a greater diversity of people? How do we negotiate our roles within and between social groups through practices of communication? How do communication structures work with other social, economic, and cultural structures to order society?

Generally, this focus has meant a shift in emphasis from the effects of media on individuals to analyses that are more historically grounded and socially situated. Critical communication research has concentrated on ownership and control of media systems, the linking of media structures to other larger social structures, and analyses of the institutional aspects of communication. When considering individuals, critical scholars view them as members of groups already partly determined by social power arrangements. They then study these groups' resistance and domination. As Slack and Allor (1983) note,

> The communication process . . . is no longer defined in terms of the effects of messages on individuals but on the effectivity (or social role) of communication (as both institutional structures and symbolic constructions) in maintaining, enhancing, or disrupting the social formation (the existing interrelationship of politics, economics, and culture). (p. 214)

UNDERSTANDING SOCIAL POWER

Critical researchers ask the questions they do because they hold a different understanding of the relationship between communication and power. Bailie (1997) suggests that "[c]ritical communication scholarship is rooted in the assumption that social institutions and human relations are relations of history, power and struggle" (p. 33). Critical scholars therefore view social power as unequally distributed and generally subscribe to a conflict-based model of social relations that focuses on struggle and difference rather than on agreement and consensus. Indeed, critical communication studies rejects the linear model of causality at work in administrative research and replaces it with more complex forms of social determination. Consequently, administrative research is content to study, for example, the impact that radio advertising might have on listeners. Critical research, in contrast, wants to investigate the historical origin of radio advertising, the type of interest that tends to use radio advertising, the ways in which the advertising binds listeners to the capitalist system, and so on. It is precisely because the study of complex forms of social determination can lead in so many directions that distinctions among critical scholars have emerged. However, despite their differences, all critical thinkers share an opposition to the *liberal pluralist notion* of social power, which sees power as neutral and potentially equally shared.

In advancing a more diverse and less idealistic understanding of social power and how it intersects with communication structures and practices in society, critical scholars have been criticized for *assuming* rather than *demonstrating* that social power really works as they claim. The theory is powerful and seductive but not always easy to demonstrate. As well, *postmodernist* and *poststructuralist* conceptions of power pose a challenge to the critical understanding. Does it always operate from the top down (i.e., from an elite to a **mass**)? Is it always coercive or can it also be productive? Are there opportunities for resistance? The answers to these questions involve high stakes. Depending on one's definition of power, one will also draw different conclusions about what types of actions to take, what types of outcomes are appropriate, how power should be wielded, and who should wield it.

METHODOLOGY AND METHODS

As a result of the two preceding assumptions—(1) the appropriate object of study is the relation between power and communication, and (2) social power is unequally distributed—critical communication scholars use different methodologies and **methods** than administrative researchers.

Much of the debate between the critical and administrative approaches plays itself out in disputes over **methodology.** In fact, the administrative approach is sometimes called the **empirical** approach because it studies immediately observable phenomena using "scientific" methods. In contrast, critical research is often seen as methodologically unrigorous because it rejects empirical approaches to knowledge and is not concerned with demonstrating its theoretical claims through scientifically verifiable data.

Critical researchers have pointed out, however, that critical research frequently uses empirical methods (Mosco, 1983). As well, a number of scholars have observed that critical research is compatible with empirical methods (Allen, 1999; Elasmar, 1999; Gerbner, 1964; Halloran, 1983; Rogers, 1982). The framing of the debate between critical and administrative approaches, as between qualitative and quantitative research methods or between science and the humanities, has resulted in three unproductive lines of discussion. First, it has led to claims of moral superiority by both sides of the debate. For critical scholars, the moral superiority derives from a sense of the importance of the work being done; according to Halloran (1983), "[W]e have to accept that it is more important to be important than to be impeccable" (p. 278). For administrative scholars, claims to moral superiority are grounded in science and "pure" knowledge untainted by ideology.

The second unproductive debate results from the fact that no distinction is being made between *empirical* and *positivist*. Empirical methods seek to describe, through the application of established procedures, an aspect of material reality; positivist methods emerge out of a belief that objective truth can be rendered through the **scientific method.** Although the methods employed by critical researchers can certainly produce empirical results, critical researchers make no claim to produce positivist (i.e., objective) results. On the contrary, they would argue that the claim to objectivity or *value neutrality* is itself an ideological claim.

Third, debates about methodology have led to attempts to find a "middle ground," a strategy that often favours the empirical perspective. This approach fails because the debate has never really been about methodology—everyone can use the same methods. The debate has really been about differing ontologies and epistemologies (what does the world consist of and how can we know it?). These cannot be brought together onto a middle ground.

This reduction of more important issues to disputes about methodology has limited critical communication studies. In rejecting positivism, too often critical researchers do not reflect adequately on methodological rigour. However, the solution is not to be found in a turn to positivist or quantitative methods, but rather in a more sustained exploration of the relationship between theory and our ability to describe lived reality.

RESEARCHER ORIENTATION

The first three assumptions of critical research are (1) the appropriate object of study is the relationship between communication and power; (2) social power is unequally distributed; and (3) theory is more important than methods. Following from these is the fourth assumption advanced by critical researchers, which addresses the relationship between the researcher and who or what is being researched. It describes the orientation of the researcher to his or her work. It asks what it means to do ideological research. Interestingly, both proponents and critics of the critical approach to communication research have labelled critical approaches "ideological." For critics, this label means that critical research is unscientific, polemical, and simply reflective of the beliefs of the researcher. One scholar offers a classic formulation of the criticism when he suggests that critical scholars often "mistake ideology for sociology" (Lang, 1979, p. 92).

For its proponents, however, the term "ideological" is a way to show that research not only *analyzes* ideology as an object (i.e., it demonstrates the symbolic traces of social power) (Sholle, 1988) but is *also* political in itself because it is committed to the disruption of the status quo (Blumler, 1983; Mosco, 1983, 1996; Smythe and Van Dinh, 1983). Both sides of the debate therefore agree that critical communication research is not value-free; it is guided by its values in its selection and treatment of research questions. Critical researchers feel that applying values is an inevitable part—and, indeed, a positive aspect—of doing research. Administrative scholars, on the other hand, feel that values corrupt the objectivity of research. A critical approach counters that even if the administrative school of thought does not acknowledge its values (objectivity, truth, science, utility, pluralism), those values are still reflected in the choice of research questions and methods.

While critical scholars have been willing to acknowledge the existence of values in their research, they have become increasingly circumspect about what those values are. It is often assumed that critical researchers are on the "left" in political terms, but this orientation is not often defined. Hence, critical research can affirm certain ideological and political norms even without intentionally articulating, considering, and discussing them.

THEORETICAL INFLUENCES

A fifth basis on which to understand critical communication research is to ask what are its theoretical influences. The theoretical legacies of critical communication research that are acknowledged within the field include European critical theory, American pragmatism and the **Chicago School** of symbolic interactionism, and Marxist thought.

One of the distinguishing aspects of critical approaches is their recognition of the influence of European critical theory—specifically, the Frankfurt School. European critical theory includes the work of first-generation Frankfurt School members such as Theodor Adorno, Max Horkheimer, and Herbert Marcuse, as well as second-generation thinkers such as Jürgen Habermas. The influence of European critical theory has been to frame critical communication research in relation to larger critiques of modernism, to explore the specificity of commodity culture, and to offer a stinging critique of the industrialization of the cultural domain. It also advocates for greater democratization of the means of communication and their divorce from industrial production.

The theoretical influence of American pragmatism and Chicago School symbolic interactionism comes from the work of John Dewey, Kenneth Burke, George Herbert Mead, and Herbert Blumer. Emerging from this work is a concern with the practice of communication in relation to progressive social change and a shift from one-way models of communication to interactive models of meaning-making and identity formation.

The third major theoretical influence on critical communications is Marxist theory. This can be mapped through the shifting theorization of ideology and culture from more simple deterministic models ascribed to Marx to approaches from Althusser and Gramsci. The influence of Marxist thought is also strongly apparent in the political economy stream of critical communication thought. As a result, critical communication attaches great importance to ideology, to debates about questions of determination with the related question of where to locate culture, and to a shared recognition that one cannot consider communication messages and practices outside of their socioeconomic contexts.

All three theoretical influences have enriched the field of communication studies, but critical communication scholars have been slower to recognize the value of other critical approaches not growing directly out of class-based or political economic analysis. For example, both feminism and post-colonialism have produced deeply interesting critical theory that could enrich the field of critical communication studies as a whole. While this work has been accepted within the field, its applicability has tended to be seen as specific to gender, race, and ethnicity, as opposed to offering rich theoretical resources for critical communication studies more broadly.

KNOWLEDGE CLAIMS

The sixth shared assumption answers the question: what kinds of knowledge claims can and do critical communication researchers make? Critical communication seeks both to engage critically with existing social relations and to change those relations. Critical communication scholars work to produce "research that both advances criticism of the existing world system and promotes the 'critical state' that would transform it" (Mosco, 1983, pp. 245–246). Research should therefore offer resources to effect positive social change (Halloran, 1983).

Whether seen as creating conditions for free (or freer) communication, social democracy, or unfettered expressions of self, critical research sets as one of its central objectives the production of intellectual and political resources for social transformation and individual and collective emancipation (Bailie, 1997; Gerbner, 1964; Haight, 1983; Halloran, 1983; Jansen, 1983). Consequently, not only must communication be thought about more critically, but so too must the place of the researcher and his or her work in society. In this way, critical research is often considered "political" or activist. Many critical researchers have political commitments outside the university as well. However, it should be noted that the normative standard that is implicitly at work in these claims is often not clearly articulated. Who is to determine what counts as *positive change* and whose vision of emancipation is at work are questions that merit further reflection.

From this discussion of the American debates, a set of shared ontological and epistemological assumptions emerges through which we can begin to see what a critical approach to communication studies looks like. Critical communication studies (1) takes as its primary question the relationship between communication and social power; (2) understands social power as a dynamic structuring force and recognizes that power is unequally distributed within society; (3) privileges theory over method and is more concerned with producing social critique than objective knowledge; (4) embraces the role that values play in producing knowledge; (5) has its theoretical roots in American and European radical thought; and (6) seeks to produce knowledge that will effect positive social change.

CRITICAL COMMUNICATION STUDIES IN CANADA

The story of what constitutes critical communication studies in North America has primarily been defined as an American encounter with European theory, framed as an ongoing conflict between critical and administrative approaches. This section considers where Canada fits into this story. In a sense, Canada has functioned as a structuring absence in the debates. This is in part because of its instrumental **marginality** to American communication scholarship, but more significantly because Canadian communication studies sees itself as always already critical. It sees itself as beginning where the American debates end.

The status of Canadian communication studies as critical does not arise from "ferment in the field," but rather from its history. "Critical" functions as an underlying and often uninvestigated *assumption* in Canadian communication studies.

In Canada, the question has not been whether or not Canadian communication studies is critical, but rather in what ways communication studies in Canada is distinctly Canadian.

THE GHOST OF INNIS: CRITICAL-NESS ASSUMED

Babe (2000a), writing that "Canada has a rich heritage of communication thought" (p. 19), traces the foundations of Canadian communication thought through the work of ten scholars: Graham Spry, Harold Innis, John Grierson, Dallas Smythe, C.B. Macpherson, Irene Spry, George Grant, Gertrude Robinson, Northrop Frye, and Marshall McLuhan. At its very foundations, he states, Canadian communication thought is **dialectical,** holistic, ontological, oriented to political economy, and concerned with mediation. Most significantly for our purposes, he argues it is critical.

Babe sees Canadian communication thought as operating within the critical tradition, in opposition to administrative or pluralist approaches. By critical research he means "evaluative research, presuming enduring criteria for enduring goals towards which we should strive judging policies, activities, events, human relations, institutions and so forth" (Babe, 2000a, p. 16). It is this ability to evaluate critically that marks Canadian scholars as critical in the American sense of the term. Indeed, there is general agreement that, in its historical origins, Canadian communication thought, and particularly the work of Innis, is critical (Acland and Buxton, 1999; Carey, 1975, 1983; Grosswiler, 1996; Hardt, 1992; Kroker, 1984; Robinson and Theall, 1975).

What has been the legacy of these foundational thinkers in terms of understanding what critical communication studies means in Canada? According to the few scholars considering it, the question, like its American counterpart, takes as its central concern larger questions about the ways in which power and communication intersect. As Babe (2000a) notes, "Power considerations figure prominently in Canadian communication thought" (p. 310). Power in the Canadian context is understood with an attention to history and the interplay of historical forces (Kroker, 1984; Theall, 1975; Tremblay, 1981). It shares assumptions with other critical communication approaches about the nonlinear nature of social power, but theorizes that power in a specifically dialectical model (Babe, 2000a; Kroker, 1984; Theall, 1975). In other words, history is produced through the encounter of contradictory social forces. Furthermore, the historical legacy of foundational communication thought has offered some significant attempts to think through the place of technologies of communication (rather than only mass media) in processes of modernization (Carey, 1983; Kroker, 1984). Finally, it has placed at the forefront values having to do with human emancipation and exploring the conditions of a better life (Babe, 2000a; Kroker, 1984).

Interestingly, a majority of the thinkers identified as foundational were developing their communication ideas before the **institutionalization** of the field of communication studies in Canada. While most observers would agree that they were critical thinkers who contributed to the foundation of Canadian communication thought, it is less clear how their ideas have played out in communication studies as a discipline in Canada since the 1960s. According to Robinson (2000), "While the general outlines of Innis' and McLuhan's work are known, whether they have inspired a unique kind of Canadian scholarship is much more difficult to determine" (p. 122). In examining what critical communication studies might mean in Canada, can we escape the ghost of Harold Innis? Is the discipline of communication studies still critical?

HURDLES TO UNDERSTANDING THE FIELD

Part of the difficulty in knowing if Canadian communication studies is critical is knowing the field at all. Any appraisal of Canadian communication scholarship as a field of study or discipline is hindered by the striking lack of a well-detailed map of its emergence. When and how did communication studies become institutionalized within Canadian universities? When were the first professional associations established and with what effect? What journals serve this academic community? How can one characterize the work done in the field? Can we identify generational patterns? Is there a canon that emerges after Innis, McLuhan, et al.?

The first hurdle in answering these questions is the diffuse nature of Canadian communication scholarship. In the early 1980s, Salter (1981b) noted that much work in communication studies was appearing in the journals of other disciplines or was being published in communication journals in the United States or Europe. More than two decades later, Salter's claim remains true. In 2000, the then editor of the *CJC* expressed regret that Canadians cannot look to the ***Canadian Journal of Communication*** (Canada's only English-language academic journal devoted to communication) to map the history, development, and trends of communication studies in Canada (Lorimer, 2000a). Canadian communication scholars continue to publish in international journals or in contexts outside of the discipline altogether, and many do not identify strongly with Canadian communication studies (Lorimer, 2000a). This diffusion of scholarship is visible in the conference participation of scholars in university communication departments where many attend conferences for film studies, cultural studies, sociology, technology studies, interdisciplinary studies, and so on.

In addition to the diffuse nature of Canadian communication scholarship, another hurdle in mapping the field is the lack of a comprehensive and accepted historical account of its development. Lorimer had hoped the special issue of the *CJC* published in 2000 might accomplish this. Instead, individual scholars offered reflections on the institutionalization of the discipline in their particular university (Tate, Osler, Fouts, and Segal, 2000). As well, one might look to undergraduate communication textbooks in Canada for such an overarching narrative. Yet a review of current undergraduate texts in use in Canada over the last decade comes up empty (a fact recognized by others, e.g., Tate et al., 2000).

Without a recorded history, myths of origin are weak. Perhaps it has been this lack of well-established, historical narratives that has structured the attempts to define Canadian communication studies into its predictable identity crisis: Is Canadian communication uniquely Canadian? It is through this issue that the critical elements of Canadian communication studies have been negotiated, articulated, and ultimately limited.

UNIQUELY CANADIAN

The debate about Canadian national identity, which is at the heart of so much substantive Canadian communication research and policy, also plays itself out in the consideration of the discipline as a whole. For example, the third goal of Babe's (2000a) book is "to discern whether there exists a mode of communication inquiry that might be termed 'quintessentially Canadian'" (p. 4). He is not alone in this pursuit. Kroker (1984) attempts to map a distinctly "Canadian mind," while Robinson and Theall (1975) suggest that Canada can claim a "unique communications philosophy" (p. 1).

Claims to a specific Canadian approach to communication studies rest on two central arguments. First, Canadian communication studies is unique because it is critical. Critical functions as a largely undefined marker of distinction from the American administrative approach. It also casts Canadian communication studies research as morally superior to its American counterpart. Second, Canadian communication studies is framed as unique because of its distinctive epistemological position—one of in-betweenness or marginality.

On his return to Simon Fraser University in the mid-1970s, communication scholar Dallas Smythe, disheartened by his experience in communication studies in the United States, called for Canadian communication thought to distinguish itself from American approaches through its critical stance. He clearly hoped that Canadian communication research would not reproduce what he considered to be the errors of many American scholars. This notion of defining Canadian uniqueness through criticalness took hold in the field. Babe (2000a) argues that it is the values of Canadian scholarship that make it critical: "the fact that most of these theorists are able to contemplate a superior human nature, that is, to compare things as they should be with things as they are, qualifies them as critical theorists in the tradition acknowledged by Lazarsfeld" (p. 316). He recognizes the role of religion in foundational Canadian communication thought and suggests that it may be responsible for the "high moral standard" of these thinkers (Babe, 2000a, p. 308). The overtones of moral superiority or a location outside of ideology are also present in Kroker's (1984) claims that "the Canadian discipline . . . represents a courageous, and creative struggle to think outside of and against the closed horizons of technological society" (p. 13).

These claims abound in Canadian communication conferences, analyses, and classrooms. The chain of reasoning proceeds as follows. Canadian communication thought is unique (i.e., non-American) because it is critical. It is critical now (in the present) because it was critical then (when Innis was writing). And because it is critical, ultimately it is better than communication studies in the United States.

Unfortunately, these assumptions can have unanticipated consequences for knowledge. First, there is a lack of considered attention to what critical might mean now, as opposed to when Innis was writing. The concept became fixed in history. Second, it sets as the standard the distinction between critical and administrative research articulated by Lazarsfeld, rather than the complex history of debates within American and European communication studies. Therefore, it does not engage with a more sophisticated understanding of what critical communication studies might be. Finally, it reduces the important question of what critical might mean to the less interesting question of how we are different from our American counterparts.

Canadian communication studies research is assumed to be *already* within a critical paradigm, and the paradigm itself is assumed to be necessarily and essentially a political economic one. Unfortunately, such assumptions do not do justice to the diversity of work being produced under the name "critical," including policy studies, institutional analyses, feminist research, industry analysis, post-colonial studies, **queer theory,** and technology studies. Indeed, an examination of the graduate communication theses deposited in Canadian universities quickly shows that the field is both broader and more vital than is imagined even by its proponents.

The second major defining characteristic of Canadian communication studies that has been identified is in its in-betweenness and marginality. Canadian political, social, geographic, and economic marginality (mostly in relation to the United States) is seen as producing an **epistemology** of the margins. A number of scholars identify Canadian communication scholarship as unique in that it draws on both European and American traditions. Hence, while it is concerned with social rather than individual effects and is theoretical like European approaches, it is also more grounded like American approaches (Salter, 1981a). Kroker (1984) sees Canadian communication thought as an oppositional mode between European and American perspectives; he feels it is characterized by its location "in-between." He defines this as "a restless oscillation between the pragmatic will to live at all costs of the American and a searing lament for that which has been suppressed by the modern, technical order" (p. 7). From this position of in-between, Canadians offer a unique, critical perspective.

Some scholars go further than in-betweenness and claim that a defining characteristic of Canadian communication thought—and, indeed, of all Canadian intellectual and cultural development—is its marginality (Babe, 2000a, 2000b; Carey, 1975; Robinson and Theall, 1975; Theall, 1975). The belief that a critical stance emerges from a sense of marginality is echoed in claims made by American and British critical scholars (Carey, 1982; Garnham, 1983; Hardt, 1992; Smythe and Van Dinh, 1983). According to Robinson and Theall (1975), "Canada's geopolitical marginality on the fringe of the North American continent seems to have given rise to two distinct outlooks: a particular perception of this country's cultural mission and a unique communication studies philosophy" (p. 3). Babe (2000a) argues that "[p]eople at the margins can see things differently, that is, dialectically: unable to escape exposure to dominant discourses, they nonetheless understand that these discourses are not their own" (p. 23).

Yet what are the limits of this epistemological positioning on the margins? The claim to criticality through marginality again rests on the examples of the canonical Canadian communication thinkers: Harold Innis, Marshall McLuhan, George Grant, and Northrop Frye. But how pertinent is the sense of geographical marginality expressed by a few great thinkers to our definition of "the margins" today? How does marginality play itself out in relation to the globalizing context of the early 21st century? Furthermore, how can marginality function as a self-conscious characteristic? Theall (1975) claims that "[t]his phenomenon of marginality provides a natural negative perspective" (p. 20). But how can a phenomenon that has been thus articulated be considered natural? Perhaps, as Canadian musician Bruce Cockburn suggests, the trouble with normal is it always gets worse.

THE TROUBLE WITH NORMAL

What can be seen from the foregoing discussion is that the critical-ness of Canadian communication studies has been mapped onto discourses of the ongoing search for a unique Canadian national identity. Indeed, the search for Canadian uniqueness has derailed a sustained interrogation of what a critical approach to communication might entail and whether or not it is even present in the Canadian field. In short, the field has not been critical enough. Lorimer (2000b) criticizes generations of communication scholars in Canada for not moving past Smythe's limited "political economy" understanding of critical communications; he suggests, as have others, that as the discipline has matured, its critical edge has dulled (see also Salter, 1987). Has there ever been enough ferment in our field?

The mapping of a critical disciplinary identity onto a national identity has also produced certain blind spots. As Meisel (1987) notes, "[T]he questions asked by researchers—and the questions not asked—are greatly conditioned by their societal and national setting" (p. 57). The cultural nationalist position, for example, has always accepted a strong, legitimate state presence. Yet is approval of an interventionist state consistent with an approach that defines itself as critical and therefore as being in opposition to the normalizing power of any state? Although communication studies in Canada did not become institutionalized in the university system as a result of a close relationship with media industries (as in the United Sates), it might be that it has done so in a close relationship with government. In fact, a significant number of scholars attribute the rise of communication studies in Canada to the needs of royal commissions studying media (Robinson, 2000; Salter, 1987; Tate et al., 2000). Tate et al. (2000) regard this as a positive development:

> What tends to be invisible in the equation is precisely the impor-
> tant role which royal commissions and other government-
> created study groups and task forces have tended to play in
> our scholarly life. Focused stimulus, funding, and collegiality
> are generated that tend to give structure to new and emerging
> areas of organized scholarship. Arguably, it is not coinci-
> dental that the CCA [Canadian Communication Association]
> and the *CJC* (in its evolved form as a peer-reviewed scholarly
> journal) were established in the wake of the LaMarsh
> Commission. (p. 86)

Lorimer (2000b) also calls for more such research: "We . . . must maintain the role of collecting information and providing analyses of those industries so that government has a sound foundation on which to act" (p. 14).

Yet one of the hallmarks of critical research, even as Lazarsfeld framed it, was its intellectual independence. Gerbner (1983b) reminds us that "[c]ritical inquiry is the distinguishing feature of a discipline and the hallmark of independent scholar-ship" (p. 355). Others have urged more caution regarding this close relationship with the government's research agenda (de la Garde, 1987). Salter (1987) suggests that "[t]he influence of government funding on the research programs of a disci-pline should never be underestimated" (p. 35). She goes on to remark that "there are some dangers in relying upon the needs of government to create the research foci within a discipline" (p. 41). If we are to follow Gerbner's call for critical inquiry, it would seem that this relationship with the interests and agenda of the Canadian state requires more scrutiny—a scrutiny that will not take place if we do not recog-nize our institutional history and if we do not abandon the assumption that we are *already* critical.

NOT ENOUGH FERMENT IN THE FIELD

Critical communication studies in Canada situates itself in relation to debates within American communication studies, and specifically the distinction between critical and administrative approaches. Critical communication studies in the United States can be described through a series of commitments to the question of the intersection of communication and power in society, to a recog-nition of social inequity, to non-quantitative methods, to an epistemological position that recognizes the place of values in research, to theoretical roots in radical thought, and to the production of knowledge that contributes to a broader project of human emancipation.

When Canadian scholars have directed their minds to their own discipline, they have tended to focus on questions of national identity, assuming that Canadian communication studies is already critical (as defined above) and mobilizing as their evidence the work of foundational thinkers such as Harold Innis, Marshall McLuhan, and George Grant. Insufficient attention has been paid to writing, understanding, and engaging critically with the history of the field. Current claims about critical-ness rest on the relationship of many scholars to political economy or critical cultural studies approaches, or generally to a leftist/humanist/cultural nationalist orientation. If a critical approach is going to mean something, and not be just a normal—and normalizing—label, then we need to think about the ways in which our work is truly critical. One way to do this would be to map out a broader critical approach to communication studies. Such an approach should draw upon, rather than smugly ignore, the American experience. At the same time it should incorporate the specific Canadian contributions of a focus on history, a dialectical approach to power, a concern with technology and culture, an awareness of non-dominant epistemological positions, and the inclusion of specific values.

Bailie (1997) suggests that "critical communication studies are intricately linked to a project that promotes a critical imaginary: the ability to think beyond present social, political, and economic conditions to participate in the construction of alternative futures" (p. 33). Carey, too, uses the language of imagination when he argues that "a critical theory of communication must affirm what is before our eyes and transcend it by imagining, at the very least, a world more desirable" (1982, p. 33). To echo and paraphrase C. Wright Mills, who was addressing the discipline of sociology in the 1950s, perhaps what we need in Canada is a more active critical communication imagination—the kind that might be sparked through both honouring our ghosts and encouraging more ferment in the field.

QUESTIONS

1. What are the major differences between administrative and critical research as defined by American communication studies?
2. What are the six shared assumptions of critical communication research?
3. Why is it difficult to determine if Canadian communication studies is critical?
4. How does Canadian communication studies define itself as unique (i.e., distinct from U.S. communication studies)?
5. Discuss the ways in which Canadian communication studies is and is not critical.
6. Select a current communication phenomenon. How would you analyze it as a critical communication scholar? What kinds of questions would you ask?

NOTES

1. The author wishes to thank Jessica Wurster for her invaluable research assistance and McGill University for its support of this research. The anonymous reviewers' comments were constructive and informed and the assistance of editors Paul Attallah and Leslie Regan Shade has been invaluable.

REFERENCES

Acland, Charles R., and William J. Buxton. (1999). *Harold Innis in the new century: Reflections and refractions.* Montreal and Kingston: McGill-Queen's University Press.

Allen, Mike. (1999). The role of meta-analysis for connecting critical and scientific approaches: The need to develop a sense of collaboration. *Critical Studies in Mass Communication, 16,* 373–379.

Babe, Robert E. (2000a). *Canadian communication thought: Ten foundational writers.* Toronto: University of Toronto Press.

———. (2000b). Foundations of Canadian communication thought. *Canadian Journal of Communication, 26,* 19–37.

Bailie, Mashoed. (1997). Critical communication pedagogy: Teaching and learning for democratic life in democratizing communication? In M. Bailie and D. Winseck (Eds.), *Democratizing communication? Comparative perspectives on information and power* (pp. 33–56). Creskill, NJ: Hampton Press.

Blumler, Jay G. (1983). Communication and democracy: The crisis beyond and the ferment within. *Journal of Communication, 33*(3), 166–173.

Carey, James. (1975). Canadian communication theory: Extensions and interpretations of Harold Innis. In G.J. Robinson and D.F. Theall (Eds.), *Studies in Canadian communications* (pp. 27–60). Montreal: Graduate Program in Communications.

———. (1982). The mass media and critical theory: An American view. In Michael Burgoon (Ed.), *Communication yearbook 6* (pp. 18–34). Beverly Hills, CA: Sage.

———. (1983). The origins of the radical discourse on cultural studies in the United States. *Journal of Communication, 33*(3), 311–313.

de la Garde, Roger. (1987, Winter). The 1987 Southam lecture: Mr. Innis, is there life after the "American Empire"? *Canadian Journal of Communication,* 7–21.

Elasmar, Michael G. (1999). Opportunities and challenges of using meta-analysis in the field of international communication in critical studies. *Mass Communication, 16,* 379–384.

Garnham, Nicholas. (1983). Toward a theory of cultural materialism. *Journal of Communication, 33*(3), 314–329.

Gerbner, George. (1964). On content analysis and critical research in mass communication. In Lewis Anthony Dexter and David Manning White (Eds.), *People, society and mass communication* (pp. 476–500). New York: Free Press.

———. (1983a). Introduction. *Journal of Communication, 33*(3), 1–4.

———. (1983b). The importance of being critical—In one's own fashion. *Journal of Communication, 33*(3), 355–362.

Gitlin, Todd. (1981). Media sociology: The dominant paradigm. In G. Cleveland Wilhoit and Harold E. Bock (Eds.), *Mass communication review yearbook 12* (pp. 73–121). Beverly Hills, CA: Sage.

Grosswiler, Paul. (1996). The dialectical methods of Marshall McLuhan, Marxism, and critical theory. *Canadian Journal of Communication, 21*(1), 95–124.

Haight, Timothy R. (1983). The critical researcher's dilemma. *Journal of Communication, 33*(3), 226–236.

Halloran, James D. (1983). A case for critical eclecticism. *Journal of Communication, 33*(3), 270–278.

Hardt, Hanno. (1992). *Critical communication studies: Communication, history & theory in America*. London and New York: Routledge.

Jansen, Sue Curry. (1983). Power and knowledge: Toward a new critical synthesis. *Journal of Communication, 33*(3), 342–354.

Kroker, Arthur. (1984). *Technology and the Canadian mind: Innis/McLuhan/Grant*. Montreal: New World Perspectives.

Lang, Kurt. (1979). The critical functions of empirical communication research: Observations on German-American influences. *Media, Culture and Society, 1*, 83–96.

Lazarsfeld, Paul Felix. (1941). Remarks on administrative and critical communication research. *Studies in Philosophy and Social Science, 9*(1), 2–16.

Lorimer, Rowland. (2000a). Editorial: The genesis of this issue—Twenty-five years of the *CJC. Canadian Journal of Communication, 25*, 3–7.

———. (2000b). Introduction: Communications teaching and research—Looking forward from 2000. *Canadian Journal of Communication, 25*, 9–17.

Meisel, John. (1987, Winter). Some Canadian perspectives on communication research. *Canadian Journal of Communication, 55*–63.

Mosco, Vincent. (1983). Critical research and the role of labour. *Journal of Communication, 33*(3), 237–248.

———. (1996). *The political economy of communication: Rethinking and renewal*. London and Thousand Oaks, CA: Sage Publications.

Robinson, Gertrude J. (2000). Remembering our past: Reconstructing the field of Canadian communication studies. *Canadian Journal of Communication, 25*, 105–125.

Robinson, Gertrude Joch, and Donald F. Theall (Eds.). (1975). Introduction. In G.J. Robinson and D.F. Theall (Eds.), *Studies in Canadian communications* (pp. 1–6). Montreal: Graduate Program in Communications.

Rogers, Everett M. (1982). The empirical and critical schools of communication research. In M. Burgoon (Ed.), *Communication yearbook 5* (pp. 125–144). New Brunswick, NJ: Transaction Books.

Salter, Liora (Ed.). (1981a). *Communication studies in Canada/Études Canadiennes en communication*. Toronto: Butterworths.

————. (1981b). Editor's introduction. In L. Salter (Ed.), *Communication studies in Canada/Études Canadiennes en communication* (pp. xi–xxii). Toronto: Butterworths.

————. (1987, Winter). Taking stock: Communication studies in 1987. *Canadian Journal of Communication*, 23–45.

Schiller, Herbert I. (1983). Critical research in the information age. *Journal of Communication*, *33*(3), 249–257.

Sholle, David J. (1988). Critical studies: From the theory of ideology to power/knowledge. *Critical Studies in Mass Communication*, *5*, 16–41.

Slack, Jennifer Daryl, and Martin Allor. (1983). The political and epistemological constituents of critical communication research. *Journal of Communication*, *33*(3), 208–218.

Smythe, Dallas W., and Tran Van Dinh. (1983). On critical and administrative research: A new critical analysis. *Journal of Communication*, *33*(3), 117–127.

Tate, Eugene D., Andrew Osler, Gregory Fouts, and Arthur Segal. (2000). The beginnings of communication studies in Canada: Remembering and narrating the past. *Canadian Journal of Communication*, *25*, 61–103.

Theall, Donald F. (1975). Communication theory and the marginal culture: The socio-aesthetic dimensions of communication study. In G.J. Robinson and D.F. Theall (Eds.), *Studies in Canadian communications* (pp. 7–26). Montreal: Graduate Program in Communications.

Tremblay, Gaëtan. (1981). Préface. In L. Salter (Ed.), *Communication studies in Canada/Études Canadiennes en communication* (pp. vii–x). Toronto: Butterworths.

2

From British Invasions to American Influences: Cultural Studies in Canada

Anne-Marie Kinahan
Carleton University

Talking about culture in Canada is something of a national pastime. Whether the topic of discussion is nationalism, the popularity of American television, or government support of the CBC, everyone has something to say. Canadian culture, communication, and mass media are fundamentally linked, and these links have provided the basis for the government's approach to cultural and media policy. But talking about Canadian culture involves more than a discussion of state involvement in the arts or the presence of mass-mediated, American popular culture. When we talk about Canadian culture, we are engaged in a process of defining ourselves and our relationship to the world.

Cultural studies first emerged in Britain as an attempt to understand the role of culture in everyday life. Expanding the definition of culture from "high" forms like opera and classical music, cultural studies asserts that popular culture—television, magazines, newspapers, etc.—also deserves scholarly attention. Cultural studies analyzes the ways in which meaning is constructed in media texts, how audiences engage with popular culture, and the social role of the media. Developed in Britain in the 1950s and 1960s, cultural studies was adopted by Canadian, American, and Australian scholars in the 1980s and 1990s. Within the Canadian context, cultural studies approaches culture in two ways. The cultural policy approach critically analyzes the government's attempts to foster Canadian identity through culture and media industries. The popular culture approach investigates the forms and varieties of popular culture in Canada, and our engagement with, and negotiation of, mass-mediated culture.

DEFINING THE TRADITION: BRITISH CULTURAL STUDIES

The late 1950s and early 1960s was a formative era for what would later become British cultural studies, or simply, cultural studies. The rise and spread of television and other mass media was accompanied by an interest in popular and mass-mediated culture. Scholars such as Raymond Williams, Richard Hoggart, and E.P. Thompson analyzed the emergence of media and popular culture and the relationship between society, media, and culture.

Hoggart's *The Uses of Literacy* (1958), Williams's *Culture and Society, 1780–1950* (1958) and *The Long Revolution* (1961), and Thompson's *The Making of the English Working Class* (1963) each offered a critical approach to the study of mass media, culture, and society. Collectively, these books signalled the emergence of cultural studies and an approach that engaged with popular culture critically and thoughtfully.

Cultural studies defines culture as a whole way of life, as lived experience and patterned interaction among individuals, their communities, and society at large. Additionally, it offers a critical assessment of the role of culture in sustaining class and social inequalities. British cultural studies specifically seeks to explain how culture participates in the maintenance and reproduction of social norms, codes, and traditions. Cultural studies contends that, in the process of transmitting content, mass media also transmit attitudes, ideologies, and beliefs that obscure the operation of power in everyday life. In addition to transmitting **entertainment**, sports, and information, mass media transmit a view of the world: they order social life, categorize social groups, define issues of concern, and assert a normative worldview. This focus on the ideological content of mass media is accompanied by a theoretical approach that views audiences as active participants in media reception. Hence, cultural studies also analyzes how audiences can challenge, resist, or negotiate the dominant meanings of media texts.

Not limited to the study, condemnation, or celebration of popular forms of culture, cultural studies seeks to understand the means by which individuals and groups participate in society, how they make sense of their lives, and how culture informs a sense of belonging to or dislocation from contemporary life. In this sense, cultural studies also engages with the legacy of Marxism and its relevance for contemporary society. Cultural studies is connected to a left-wing intellectual and political project that not only seeks to explain the operation of power and domination in contemporary society but also looks for strategies for intervention and a transformation of social relations. These political and cultural concerns also characterize Canadian cultural studies; however, Canadian society offers a host of issues and problems quite distinct from those in Britain.

FROM COMMUNICATION AS CULTURE TO CULTURE AS COMMUNICATION: CULTURAL STUDIES IN CANADA

While British cultural studies was shaped by historically specific forces, it bequeathed a variety of theoretical and methodological approaches, social and political concerns, and analytical methods that influence cultural studies in the United States, Australia, and Canada. The practice and development of cultural studies in Canada has progressed along two paths.

The first of these practices—cultural studies in Canada—is represented by the adoption of cultural studies methods and theories by scholars in Canadian universities. Hence, while British cultural studies is specifically concerned with the study of British working-class and popular culture, its theoretical approaches have been expanded upon by scholars in other countries. Canadian scholars, however, did not merely import British cultural studies. Rather, they applied the theoretical frameworks of cultural studies to explain Canadian concerns and contexts. Hence, the second practice of cultural studies in Canada—Canadian cultural studies—is the deployment of these theoretical models in order to assess, criticize, and analyze the varieties of Canadian cultural experience.

Regardless of its specific location, cultural studies aims to unmask the operation of power in everyday life. It is, therefore, an inherently political project that attempts to transform social relations. Within a Canadian context, this political focus is not as explicitly concerned with working-class culture, as in Britain, but examines instead the varieties of cultural expression and experience in Canadian life. Blundell, Shepherd, and Taylor (1993) suggest that

> the problem goes further than that of identifying "culture" and "society" and attempting to understand the relationship between them. It lies rather in trying to grasp what it feels like to live within particular cultural and social circumstances, and how that feeling . . . is embedded within and acts upon wider social practices. (p. 3)

Admittedly, the attempt to explain how it feels to live in a given place at a specific historical, cultural, and political moment is a vast project. We might legitimately ask: What are the means by which we make sense of culture and society? What methods, theories, or arguments are best suited to launching such an analysis? One of the defining characteristics of cultural studies stemming from these questions is that it is not limited to any particular discipline. It draws on disciplines as varied as communication, history, sociology, film studies, art history, and English literature.

As a result of its inter- and multi-disciplinarity, cultural studies has not become a specialized practice. Indeed, cultural studies in Canada is not solely limited to the academy. In fact, to date there is only one Department of Cultural Studies in Canada, located at Trent University. However, the critical study of culture is a concern for scholars in communications, Canadian studies, English literature, and film studies, and has resulted in multi-disciplinary programs at several Canadian universities: the Department of Communications, Popular Culture and Film at Brock University; the joint program in Communication and Culture at York/Ryerson; the focus on Cultural Studies and Critical Theory at the Department of English of McMaster University; and the School for Studies in Art and Culture, which offers degree programs in film studies, art history, and music, at Carleton University.

But equally significant is the attempt to move beyond academic audiences. Popular journals such as *CinéACTION* and *Border/Lines*, scholarly journals such as

Topia, and publications such as *Capital Culture* (Berland and Hornstein, 2000) and *Theory/Rules* (Berland, Straw, and Tomas, 1996) are collaborations between academics, critics, visual artists, and authors exploring the interrelation between critical and cultural theory and artistic practice. This refusal to locate cultural studies within a specific discipline or institution means that it is understood less as a specific academic discipline and more as an informed, critical, and engaged perspective on lived experience and everyday life.

Within the context of communication, cultural studies helps to assess the specificities of culture and communication in Canadian society. The fact that cultural studies straddles both the social sciences and the humanities means that it lends itself well to an assessment of communication and media studies, which have been similarly situated in the gap between these two disciplines.

Straw (1993) argues that cultural studies in Canada was shaped by two developments in the study of media and society: (1) the advent of media policy studies, concerned with "economic dependence and government complicity in the development of Canadian broadcasting and **cultural industries**"; and (2) the increasing academic interest in questions of identity, subjectivity, critical social theory, and Marxism (pp. 94–95). For Straw, the value and promise of cultural studies is that it affords the opportunity to bridge the gap between these two perspectives (p. 95). The explicitly political project of cultural studies—the attempt to transform social relations—gave intellectuals a specific role in the policymaking process. Armed with an appreciation of the role of popular culture in everyday life, scholars would be able to make informed interventions into the realm of cultural policy.

The attempt to understand the connection between "culture as policy" and "culture as a whole way of life" is a central concern in discussions about culture in Canada, and it characterizes two approaches to Canadian cultural studies. Applied to the Canadian context, cultural studies critically assesses not only governmental attempts to construct Canadian culture through specific practices and policies, but also the ways in which individuals participate in the creation and consumption of culture and media.

Canadian cultural studies, then, can be separated into two branches of cultural and critical inquiry. One branch of inquiry is specifically concerned with the role of the state in the cultural realm and the development of cultural policy in Canada. Scholars in this branch have assessed the history of Canada's cultural industries, the connections between nation-building and Canadian culture, and how the state has linked culture to national defence. Additionally, they have studied Canada's cultural industries in the era of globalization. The second branch is the analysis of popular culture within Canada. This branch maps out the domain of Canadian popular culture, taking into account the ubiquity and popularity of American popular culture. Additionally, this branch analyzes how Canadian audiences negotiate, engage with, and resist dominant forms of American culture and media.

THE "PROBLEM" OF CULTURE IN CANADA

Cultural studies in Canada emerged from questions, issues, and problems entirely different from those of British society in the second half of the 20th century. Generally speaking, Canadian culture is the product of a variety of cultural, historical, and political forces. Historically, Canada became a colony of Britain and represented the extension of the British Empire into the "New World." But the two "founding" nations, Britain and France, are representative of two different cultures, languages, and political traditions. The tension between English and French cultures is still a prevalent concern, as articulated in debates about Quebec sovereignty and its recognition as a "distinct society."

Canadian history and culture is also marked by the legacy of the displacement of Aboriginal people. Questions about the "place" of Aboriginal culture in Canadian society are paramount concerns in discussions of Canadian politics, history, and culture (Valaskakis, 1988). For example, the **Broadcasting Act** of 1991 specifically acknowledges the importance of Aboriginal culture in Canada, and encourages the Canadian broadcasting system to reflect the "special place" of Aboriginal people. The attempt to ensure the participation of Aboriginal people in Canadian broadcasting is captured in various policies and culminated in the licensing of the Aboriginal Peoples Television Network (APTN) in 1999 (see Roth, Chapter 19 of this volume).

The attempt to construct a strong and unified Canadian culture is further problematized by the regional and multicultural characteristics of Canada. A defining characteristic is the extent to which Canada has attempted to construct unity out of diversity. Often described as a "cultural mosaic," Canada claims to be a nation that allows for the expression of regional and localized cultures as well as a variety of ethnic and national heritages. The attempt to define what it means to be Canadian often invokes the ways in which Canada can claim to be a compilation of diverse, multiple, and different cultures. But this understanding of Canada as a benevolent multicultural nation also belies and masks a latent racism. Walcott (1999) argues that multiculturalism policy, through establishing England and France as "founding" nations and articulating the "special place" of Aboriginal people, constructs and reinforces distinctions between "real" and "Other" Canadians (p. 31).

These internal characteristics of Canadian culture—English/French, Aboriginal people, regionalism, multiculturalism—are compounded by the fact that we share the world's longest undefended border with the United States. This proximity has enabled the free flow of American films, television programs, novels, and magazines into Canadian theatres, newsstands, and, most significantly, into Canadian homes. Indeed, one of the central concerns of Canadian cultural policy is the impact of the influence and proximity of the United States.

These internal and external tensions have historically been used to justify the involvement of the federal government in cultural matters. Since the 1920s, the

Canadian government has been involved in using the potential of the communications industry to further the development of a "distinct" Canadian identity. This government intervention has been enabled and supported by various cultural critics, academics, and arts groups, resulting in the creation of a "nationalist" approach to culture. This **cultural nationalism** supports and encourages government intervention in the cultural realm as a means of maintaining the sovereignty of the Canadian nation.

[margin note: How does this cultural nationalistic approach help?]

[margin note: they encourage government support as it continues to maintain Canada's sovereignty]

Within the cultural nationalist approach, Canadian culture is significant for two reasons: (1) it provides imagery, symbols, and materials to unify a culturally diverse and spatially dispersed population; and (2) it protects our culture from the impact and influence of American culture (Blundell, Shepherd, and Taylor, 1993, p. 11). One of the most striking aspects of Canadian society is its reliance on government rather than upon civil society or industry to ensure the continuance of Canadian culture through cultural policy, government subsidies, and the creation of cultural industries.

[margin note: (a) using symbols, images etc to unite all]

[margin note: (b) It protects Canadian culture from American culture.]

STATE INTERVENTION, NATION-BUILDING, AND CULTURAL POLICY

Canadian culture has a complicated, problematic, and political history. Indeed, Canadian culture is often considered to be virtually nonexistent. Taras (2001) suggests a number of reasons behind this perceived lack of Canadian identity: "Lacking a great historical moment or a common language, and having few national institutions, heroes, or symbols that provide unity, Canadians have little of the 'hardwiring' that can be found in other countries" (p. 185). Our own cultural weakness is cause for greater concern in light of the cultural dominance of the United States. Manning (1993) has argued that the central problem of Canadian culture is that it is perceived as constantly under threat from American culture. The political characteristics of Canadian culture stem from the necessity of fending off this perceived threat through protectionist or promotional policies (p. 5).

[margin note: Why is there a perceived lack of Canadian identity...]

[margin note: (1) Lacking a great historical moment or a common language]

[margin note: (2) Having a few national institutions, heroes, or symbols of unity]

[margin note: (3) Little hardwiring as other countries.]

Cultural policy in Canada developed under the assumption that, in order to encourage the articulation of a distinctively Canadian identity, and to stave off cultural absorption by the United States, it was necessary for the state to intervene in the cultural realm. Not only would this intervention serve the nationalist goal of fostering Canadian identity, it would also provide for the emergence of a vibrant cultural community. "Cultural policy was founded on the assumption that building national, publicly owned cultural and media infrastructures dedicated to presenting alternatives to American mass media would guarantee an expansion of creative, commercially unimpeded cultural space and public sphere" (Berland, 1995, p. 517). Hence, the dominant approach to culture in Canada is administrative and political and defines culture as a necessary element in the attempt to ward off the detrimental effects of American popular culture.

[margin note: This intervention served the too NATIONALIST GOAL OF]

[margin note: The]

[margin note: By building our own identity & saving Canada from the American Identity this would guarantee an expansion of creative, economically unimpeded cultural space & public sphere.]

Cultural Nationalist approach is concerned with nation building which involves forging a strong nationalism in order to ward off continentalism.
It also gives canadian culture a defensive & protectionist role.

Cultural nationalist approaches to culture in Canada have been explicitly concerned with nation-building, which involves forging a strong nationalism in order to ward off continentalism. The forces of American influence through culture and economy must be mitigated through the provision of outlets (both cultural and economic) for Canadian artistic expression. This approach gives Canadian culture a defensive and protectionist role. While Canadian culture is acknowledged as the expression of Canadian identity and experience, it is not seen as the organic, spontaneous expression of a community. Rather, it is created and enabled through government support of cultural industries involved in the production of Canadian film, television, sound recording, magazines, and literature. In this sense, culture in Canada becomes a political construct, a means through which identity and nationhood are created and maintained.

Thus culture in canada becomes a political construct a place whereby identity + nationhood are created

Canadian cultural studies has offered critical perspectives on the government's cultural role. Charland (1986) coined the phrase **technological nationalism** to explain the government's reliance on technology to unify the country. This reliance began with the construction of the Canadian Pacific Railway and continued with the reliance on communication technology to provide symbolic links between Canadians. This faith in technology is ultimately self-defeating because "it ties a Canadian identity, not to its people, but to their mediation through technology" (Charland, p. 197). Furthermore, there is a central irony since communication technologies also provide the means through which Canadians are routinely exposed to American popular culture. Technological nationalism results in the imposition of American culture "through the very technologies which should be constitutive of the Canadian experience and essence" (Charland, p. 213).

For Rutherford (1993), state intervention in the arts also constructs Canadian culture as a high culture alternative to crass Americanism. Similarly, Gasher (1997) argues that the various royal commissions that investigated mass media and culture in Canada—the Aird Commission (1928), the Massey Commission (1951), and the Fowler Commission (1955), specifically—were motivated not only by a concern for Canadian identity, but also by a distrust of commercialism and an endemic anti-Americanism (p. 15). Through these inquiries, and through various approaches to support of the arts in Canada, Canadian culture is constructed as an artistic domain separate and distinct from "popular" (i.e., American) forms of cultural expression. This approach may help to explain why Canadian films and television programs are often deemed "unpopular" by Canadian audiences.

canada as an artistic domain seperate & distinct from popular

Various forms of cultural policy, and support for artists and artistic expression, not only create a specific type of Canadian culture, they construct that culture as necessarily educational, edifying, and patriotic. Government inquiries such as the Massey Commission tacitly argued that a strong, vibrant nation of the type imagined by cultural elites depended on a strong cultural life. Hence, "culture would provide the bulwark to construct a strong nation with all its critical faculties intact, and to ward off the potentially harmful effects of creeping continentalism in the form of American mass culture" (Dowler, 1996, p. 337).

cultural policy that supports artist & its expressions create a Can. culture as well as construct culture as necessarily educational, edifying + patriotic

Canadian policy makers,
popular culture closely
associated w/ the
US represents
an insidious OR

threat to our
values, belief &
attitudes.

Mass/of transmissm

It may be said that for Canadian politicians and policymakers, popular culture, closely associated with the United States, represents an insidious threat to Canadian values, attitudes, and beliefs. Along with the transmission of American cultural products there is the fear of the transmission of American political, economic, and cultural values. Hence, Canadian culture is saddled with the responsibility of ensuring that cultural expression is not motivated by profit, popularity, or commercialism. Mass communication is certainly concerned with the transmission of messages, programs, and advertisements to audiences. Yet it is also a ritual that communicates traditions and values and can contribute to a sense of community. Within the Canadian context, the media of mass communication are by and large involved with the transmission of American content to Canadian audiences. This reality breeds the fear that American values and traditions are also being transmitted, threatening both the expression of Canadian identity and the formation of a Canadian community.

It is for these reasons that Canadian culture, supported by the government and enabled by cultural industries, is viewed as an essential element in the expression and maintenance of Canadian identity. Historically, the media of mass communication were thought to provide the technological and cultural material that would unify the country. In the current context, Canadian culture must provide a voice for the expression of Canadian experience. Attempts to support Canadian culture aim to ensure markets for Canadian products and a Canadian audience for homegrown cultural expression.

CANADIAN CULTURE IN A GLOBAL CONTEXT

Contemporary research on Canadian communication technology and mass media is concerned with the position of Canadian culture in North America and in international markets. Babe (1988) rejects the common perception that Canadian mass media have served to offset the detrimental effects of American culture:

> In Canada, techniques, systems and industries specializing in the diffusion of messages have most generally resided, even from the outset, under American control, and have been deployed consistently rather to further Canadian political, economic and cultural absorption into the U.S.A., to such an extent that it can be said with confidence that Canada persists despite, not because of, media of communication. (p. 59)

The study of mass communication evinces concerns about Canada's cultural industries and government support of these industries, about the arts in general, and about globalization. Underlying these concerns are the assumptions that culture is a reflection of society and a means by which we express a national identity, and that the prevalence of American popular culture in Canada poses a serious threat. These perspectives are essential to study the increasing role of economics in the cultural realm. Furthermore, institutionally focused analyses of the industrial structures of mass media, the dependency on American cultural output, and the impact of international trade agreements on Canadian cultural industries attest to the global reach of American culture.

For some, however, globalization also raises a central contradiction at the heart of the attempts to put culture in the service of a "national" identity on the one hand, and the need to compete in international markets, on the other (Straw, 2002; Dowler, 1999). Canadian culture is saddled with the difficult task of relating stories relevant to Canadians, while simultaneously negating any distinct markers of Canadian-ness which might hinder international exportability. Straw (2002) argues that globalization and trade in cultural goods have resulted in a situation in which the "distinctive" qualities of Canadian films or television programs exist not because they express Canadian identity, but because they provide an alternative to the standard fare routinely produced by the United States, Great Britain, or France (p. 104).

Canadian cultural studies offers a critical discussion of the tensions, contradictions, and difficulties that accompany any talk about "Canadian" culture. In light of various free trade agreements, globalization, and the general trend toward deregulation, Canada's protectionist approach to culture is increasingly open to challenge. Many critics have argued that we need to think of the production and reception of Canadian culture as bound up with the international circulation of cultural goods (Dowler, 1999; Acland, 2001; Straw 2002). Likewise, Gasher (1997) contends that the nationalist approach to cultural production and protection is no longer valid: "cultural policy . . . is always also finance, trade and industrial policy, a state of affairs which demands consistency" (p. 27). To that end, Gasher argues contemporary cultural policy should focus on removing obstacles and enlarging opportunities for Canadian cultural producers, a perspective that is echoed in cultural policy documents such as the Applebaum-Hébert report (p. 28).

POPULAR CULTURE IN THE CANADIAN CONTEXT

Media and policy scholars have argued that there is an important gap between the way culture is defined officially by governments and cultural elites and the way it is experienced by Canadians (Acland, 2001). Canadian policymakers have historically defined popular culture as the product of American media industries. This has meant that there is a difficulty in defining Canadian popular culture. Instead, policy **discourse** has defined Canadian culture as distinctive, non-commercial, and, by extension, not very popular with Canadian audiences. But one of the problems with this policy approach is that it ignores the fact that Canadians have participated in the creation of popular culture. As Dorland and Walton (1999) point out, "Canadians have not simply been acted upon but have been active participants in the construction of North American mass culture" (p. 205).

culture neglects the fact that canadian popular culture is always mediated in + through American Culture

The cultural nationalist attempt to carve out a unique expression of Canadian experience through culture neglects the fact that Canadian popular culture is always mediated in and through American media culture. As Dorland and Walton (1999) note, "Canada's is profoundly a border culture, across which interactions, patterns of influence, and exchange have always been more ambiguous and fluid than unmistakably one thing or another" (p. 204). Similarly, Manning (1993) contends that "Canadian culture is less the product of its own separate evolution than of its interactive relationship with an American Other . . . Canadian popular culture 'makes sense' only in relation to American alternatives with which it has a counteractive but reversible relationship" (p. 9).

Indeed, Canadian popular culture producers have managed to inflect a "Canadian" sensibility into well-established American cultural expressions. Miller (1993), Nicks (2002), and Leach (2002) have all illustrated the ways in which Canadian television both relies on and subverts the conventions of American television programming. Since popular culture products like television are intended for "mass" audiences, they must contain dominant messages that the majority of audience members will accept. However, they must also provide the opportunity for negotiated, or resistant, readings of their dominant messages if they also want to appeal to marginal audiences (Leach, 2002). Canadian dramas, they suggest, provide alternatives to the neat resolution and predictability of American genres. Often dealing with contemporary social and political issues, programs like *DaVinci's Inquest* (CBC), *This Is Wonderland* (CBC), or *The Eleventh Hour* (CTV) often resist narrative closure, address ethical issues, and leave difficult issues unresolved. Canadian dramas still rely on generic conventions, but "inflect" a Canadian sensibility that appeals to Canadian as well as international viewers.

Discussing the presence of American films in Canadian theatres, Feldman (1993) argues

> It is not just that cinema in Canada has always meant Hollywood cinema, but film, like television, is distinguished by the fact that Canadians not only watch but actually make the American product. We do so literally in productions that highlight American talent and disguise Canada as Anytown, U.S.A. (p. 209)

In addition to the ubiquity of Canadian locations standing in for "Anytown, U.S.A," Canadian actors, directors, and musicians have enjoyed successful careers producing American content. One need only think of filmmakers Norman Jewison (*Moonstruck, Hurricane*) and James Cameron (*The Terminator, Titanic*), television shows *C.S.I.* and *24*, or singers Céline Dion, Shania Twain, Alanis Morrisette, and Avril Lavigne to realize that Canadians are and have been involved in the production of "American" popular culture. This short list of Canadian "success stories" is not intended to trumpet the accomplishments of a few Canadians south of the border, but rather to suggest ways that we may begin to talk about Canadian popular culture as created through processes of exchange and engagement with American cultural forms.

NEGOTIATION AND RESISTANCE: CULTURE AND CANADIAN AUDIENCES

Canadian cultural studies has proceeded along two critical and analytical paths. The first has been an interrogation of cultural policy in Canada, and the legacy of state intervention in the cultural realm. This field of study has analyzed the government's role in the creation of official Canadian culture. The second has been an informed and engaged analysis of Canadian popular, regional, and folklore culture. Attempting to discuss culture as "a whole way of life," Canadian cultural studies has approached topics as diverse as weather (Berland, 1993), masculinity and professional sports (Burstyn, 1999; Abdel-Shehid, 1999), hockey (Genosko, 1999; McSorley, 1999; Earle, 2002), female audiences and magazines (Korinek, 2000; Currie, 1999), and second wave feminism (Freeman, 2001). Each of these studies points to the centrality of mediation in our experience of popular culture, and also offers insight into how Canadian audiences negotiate their involvement with mass-mediated culture.

Canadian cultural studies demonstrates the ways in which Canadians participate in, resist, challenge, and engage with popular culture. Manning (1993) sees Canadian popular culture as indicative of **reversible resistance** through which Canadian audiences knowingly and ironically negotiate American popular culture. He argues that we must pay attention to the complex ways in which meaning is constructed and negotiated in media texts. To do so focuses attention not only on the prevalence of American culture in Canada, but also on the "response of the Canadian audience to that enormous influence, along with the significance of that response in the creation of Canadian popular culture" (p. 4). Indeed, despite our avid consumption of American popular culture, we still retain a sense of ourselves as Canadian. A central characteristic of Canadian popular culture is its engagement with, and resistance to, American cultural forms. In contrast to governmental perspectives that view the popularity of American "mass" popular culture as a threat to Canadian identity and sensibilities, Canadian cultural studies maintains that "mass culture in itself does not pose, and never has posed, a direct threat to Canadian identity, because consumers have 'read' its messages through a special lens made in Canada" (Rutherford, 1993, p. 280).

Our experience as neighbour to the world's most prodigious producer of popular entertainment has resulted in a unique, and contradictory, cultural experience. We are located within that popular culture at the same time that we are increasingly alienated from it. A minority figure within a majority popular culture, Canadian experience is one of being both inside and outside. Indeed, Pottie (1999) draws a correlation between Canada's experience within North American culture and the experiences of gays and lesbians within a predominantly heterosexual society:

> As Canadians, and as Canadian lesbians and gays, we live both within and outside popular culture, shifting between majority and minority viewpoints, among international, national, local, and community levels of identity, assimilating, rejecting, and negotiating the images and commodities of contemporary culture. (p. 229)

Walton (1999) suggests that Canadians employ strategies of resistance, irony, and parody in their engagement with American mass media. While the construction of a Canadian identity is necessarily dependent on our proximity to the United States, this proximity also serves to define our difference. The engagement with Canadian culture almost necessarily demands a discussion of the impact and influence of American culture, but scholars such as Walton (1999) and Manning (1993) assert that such engagement is often ironic, playing on the assumption of Canada's supposed cultural inferiority. Furthermore, the success of Canadian actors and comedians in the United States, as well as the popularity of such films as *Wayne's World*, suggest that cultural influence is not a one-way street:

> The construction of Stan Mikita's doughnut shop in *Wayne's World* (a parodic play on Tim Horton's and a play that I would venture to suggest most Canadians "got" and most Americans missed) . . . [is] just as representative of Canada as National Film Board documentaries. (Walton, 1999, p. xii)

This attention to the ways in which popular culture expresses and reflects distinctly Canadian sensibilities is an important contribution to the interrogation of culture in Canadian society. Canadian cultural studies represents a significant movement away from perspectives that assume the detrimental effects of our proximity to the United States. The adoption of a cultural approach to the study of communication in Canada foregrounds discussion of culture as a social process—a negotiation between a text and its audience, between theory and practice, between policy and cultural consumption. Canadian cultural studies aims continually to interrogate the processes by which artists, producers, critics, and audiences actively engage with a variety of cultural forms.

THE RELEVANCE OF CANADIAN CULTURAL STUDIES: CULTURE AND EVERYDAY LIFE

Acland (2001) argues that what is significant about our popular culture practices is that we are routinely engaged in consuming popular culture products that are not our own. "The experience of moviegoing in Canada can be a frustrating one," he states. "Though it offers a view to an exhilarating world movie culture, cinema-going essentially takes you away from your national home" (p. 279). But, he contends, if we are to understand the everyday practices of Canadian cultural reception and production, we need to take account of our engagement with international, mass-mediated, popular culture. Through focusing on Canadian participation in and appreciation of an international popular culture, Canadian cultural studies allows us to talk about culture without condemning the popular choices of Canadian audiences. Indeed, discussing culture as a "whole way of life" necessarily entails the realization that media consumption and popular culture reception are never just about listening to a certain type of music, seeing a specific film, or reading a particular magazine. Rather, these processes are part and parcel of a larger participation in public life which involves negotiating our relationship with popular media that are predominantly not of our own making.

For Canadian cultural studies, discussing culture as a whole way of life represents a movement away from cultural nationalist perspectives that condemned the products of mass-mediated popular culture, and condemned the choices of the majority of Canadians. Significantly, Canadian cultural studies sees the operation of power not only in media texts but also in the cultural policy discourses that construct official Canadian culture as an antidote to the perceived harm of American culture. It also provides a way to talk about Canadian popular culture as the product of a complex, ironic, and playful engagement with an internationally circulating popular culture. In this sense, Canadian cultural studies illustrates the ways in which Canadian audiences are active producers of meaning, and active participants in the creation of culture.

QUESTIONS

1. Why is culture such an object of concern and debate in Canada?
2. Why did Canadian cultural studies emerge from communication studies?
3. Why does the Canadian government intervene in the cultural realm? What is the legacy of this involvement?
4. What is the relationship between Canadian and American popular culture?

REFERENCES

Abdel-Shehid, Gamal. (1999). "Who got next?" Raptor morality and Black public masculinity in Canada. In Lynne Van Luven and Priscilla L. Walton (Eds.), *Pop can: Popular culture in Canada* (pp. 128–139). Scarborough, ON: Prentice-Hall Allyn and Bacon Canada.

Acland, Charles. (2001). From the absent audience to expo-mentality: Popular film in Canada. In David Taras and Beverly Rasporich (Eds.), *A passion for identity: Canadian studies for the 21st century* (pp. 275–291). Scarborough, ON: Nelson.

Applebaum, Louis, and Jacques Hébert. (1982). Federal Cultural Policy Review Committee: Summary of Briefs and Hearings. Ottawa: Department of Communication.

Babe, Robert. (1988). Emergence and development of Canadian communication: Dispelling the myths. In Rowland M. Lorimer and Donald C. Wilson (Eds.), *Communication Canada: Issues in broadcasting and new technologies* (pp. 58–79). Toronto: Kagan and Woo.

Berland, Jody. (1993). Weathering the North: Climate, colonialism, and the mediated body. In Valda Blundell, John Shepherd, and Ian Taylor (Eds.), *Relocating cultural studies: Developments in theory and research* (pp. 207–225). London: Routledge.

———. (1995). Marginal notes on cultural studies in Canada. *University of Toronto Quarterly, 64*(4), 514–525.

Berland, Jody, and Shelley Hornstein. (Eds.). (2000). *Capital culture: A reader on modernist legacies, state institutions, and the value(s) of art.* Montreal and Kingston: McGill-Queen's University Press.

Berland, Jody, Will Straw, and David Tomas (Eds.). (1996). *Theory rules: Art as theory/theory and art.* Toronto: University of Toronto Press and YYZ Books.

Blundell, Valda, John Shepherd, and Ian Taylor. (1993). Editors' introduction. In Valda Blundell, John Shepherd, and Ian Taylor (Eds.), *Relocating cultural studies: Developments in theory and research* (pp. 1–17). London: Routledge.

Burstyn, Varda. (1999). *The rites of men: Manhood, politics, and the culture of sport.* Toronto: University of Toronto Press.

Charland, Maurice. (1986) Technological nationalism. *The Canadian Journal of Political and Social Theory, X*(1–2), 196–220.

Currie, Dawn H. (1999). *Girl talk: Adolescent magazines and their readers.* Toronto: University of Toronto Press.

Dorland, Michael, and Priscilla L. Walton. (1999). Untangling Karla's web: Postnational arguments, cross-border crimes, and the investigation of Canadian culture. In Lynne Van Luven and Priscilla L. Walton (Eds.), *Pop can: Popular culture in Canada* (pp. 195–206). Scarborough, ON: Prentice-Hall Allyn and Bacon Canada.

Dowler, Kevin. (1996). The cultural industries policy apparatus. In Michael Dorland (Ed.), *The cultural industries in Canada: Problems, policies and prospects* (pp. 328–346). Toronto: James Lorimer & Co.

———. (1999). Cultures, borders and free trade. In Lynne Van Luven and Priscilla L. Walton (Eds.), *Pop can: Popular culture in Canada* (pp. 195–206). Scarborough, ON: Prentice-Hall Allyn and Bacon Canada.

Earle, Neil. (2002). Hockey as Canadian popular culture: Team Canada 1972, television and Canadian identity. In Joan Nicks and Jeannette Sloniowski (Eds.), *Slippery pastimes: Reading the popular in Canadian culture* (pp. 321–343). Waterloo, ON: Wilfrid Laurier University Press.

Feldman, Seth. (1993). Our house, their house: Canadian cinema's coming of age. In David H. Flaherty and Frank E. Manning (Eds.), *The beaver bites back?*

American popular culture in Canada (pp. 209–221). Montreal and Kingston: McGill-Queen's University Press.

Freeman, Barbara M. (2001). *The satellite sex: The media and women's issues in English Canada, 1966–1971.* Waterloo, ON: Wilfrid Laurier University Press.

Gasher, Mike. (1997). From sacred cows to white elephants: cultural policy under siege. In Joy Cohnstaedt and Yves Frenette (Eds.), *Canadian cultures and globalization/Cultures canadiennes et mondialisation* (pp. 13–39). Montreal: Association for Canadian Studies/Association d'études canadiennes.

Genosko, Gary. (1999). Hockey and culture. In Lynne Van Luven and Priscilla L. Walton (Eds.), *Pop can: Popular culture in Canada* (pp. 140–150). Scarborough, ON: Prentice-Hall Allyn and Bacon Canada.

Hoggart, Richard. (1958). *The uses of literacy.* London: Penguin.

Korinek, Valerie J. (2000). *Roughing it in the suburbs: Reading* Chatelaine Magazine *in the fifties and sixties.* Toronto: University of Toronto Press.

Leach, Jim. (2002). Reading Canadian "popular" television: The case of *E.N.G.* In Joan Nicks and Jeannette Sloniowski (Eds.), *Slippery pastimes: Reading the popular in Canadian culture* (pp. 111–126). Waterloo, ON: Wilfrid Laurier University Press.

Manning, Frank E. (1993). Reversible resistance: Canadian popular culture and the American other. In David H. Flaherty and Frank E. Manning (Eds.), *The beaver bites back? American popular culture in Canada* (pp. 3–28). Montreal and Kingston: McGill-Queen's University Press.

McSorley, Tom. (1999). Of time and space and hockey: An imaginary conversation. In Lynne Van Luven and Priscilla L. Walton (Eds.), *Pop can: Popular culture in Canada* (pp. 151–156). Scarborough, ON: Prentice-Hall Allyn and Bacon Canada.

Miller, Mary Jane. (1993). Inflecting the formula: The first seasons of *Street Legal* and *L.A. Law.* In David H. Flaherty and Frank E. Manning (Eds.), *The beaver bites back? American popular culture in Canada* (pp. 104–122). Montreal and Kingston: McGill-Queen's University Press.

Nicks, Joan. (2002). *Straight Up* and youth television: Navigating dreams without nationhood. In Joan Nicks and Jeannette Sloniowski (Eds.), *Slippery pastimes: Reading the popular in Canadian culture* (pp. 141–157). Waterloo, ON: Wilfrid Laurier University Press.

Pottie, Lisa. (1999). Canadian queer identities: Cross-border shopping for politics and fun. In Lynne Van Luven and Priscilla L. Walton (Eds.), *Pop can: Popular culture in Canada* (pp. 224–230). Scarborough, ON: Prentice-Hall Allyn and Bacon Canada.

Rutherford, Paul. (1993). Made in America: The problem of mass culture in Canada. In David H. Flaherty and Frank E. Manning (Eds.), *The beaver bites back? American popular culture in Canada* (pp. 260–280). Montreal and Kingston: McGill-Queen's University Press.

Straw, Will. (1993). Shifting boundaries, lines of descent: Cultural studies and institutional realignments. In Valda Blundell, John Shepherd, and Ian Taylor (Eds.), *Relocating cultural studies: Developments in theory and research* (pp. 86–102). London: Routledge.

————. (2002) Dilemmas of definition. In Joan Nicks and Jeannette Sloniowski (Eds.), *Slippery pastimes: Reading the popular in Canadian culture* (pp. 95–108). Waterloo, ON: Wilfrid Laurier University Press.

Taras, David. (2001). Surviving the wave: Canadian identity in the era of digital globalization. In David Taras and Beverly Rasporich (Eds.), *A passion for identity: Canadian studies for the 21st century* (pp. 185–199). Scarborough, ON: Nelson.

Thompson, E.P. (1963). *The making of the English working class.* London: Penguin.

Valaskakis, Gail Guthrie. (1988). Television and cultural integration: Implications for Native communities in the Canadian north. In Rowland M. Lorimer and Donald C. Wilson (Eds.), *Communication Canada: Issues in broadcasting and new technologies* (pp. 124–138). Toronto: Kagan and Woo.

Walcott, Rinaldo. (1999). "Keep on movin' ": Rap, Black Atlantic identities and the problem of nation. In Lynne van Luven and Priscilla L. Walton (Eds.), *Pop can: Popular culture in Canada* (pp. 27–41). Scarborough, ON: Prentice-Hall Allyn and Bacon Canada.

Walton, Priscilla L. (1999). Introduction. In Lynne van Luven and Priscilla L. Walton (Eds.), *Pop can: Popular culture in Canada* (pp. ix–xii). Scarborough, ON: Prentice-Hall Allyn and Bacon Canada.

Williams, Raymond. (1958). *Culture and society, 1780–1950.* London: Penguin.

————. (1961). *The long revolution.* London: Penguin.

Part II
Audiences and Markets

Introduction

Paul Attallah
Carleton University

Every communicative act presupposes an audience. Every mass medium and every media text already contains within it a theory of who should watch, read, or consume it. Indeed, if no one is listening to what we say, there's little point in saying it. Conversely, the very fact that we communicate at all indicates an enduring hope that we will indeed find someone to listen, to understand, to respond.

Communication always hopes for a response. Sometimes we hope for a response of submission or obedience or predetermined behaviour. But just as often we hope for responses of dialogue and understanding that will extend and amplify the game of communication.

However, to achieve a response—for the ideas in one mind to enter another as they were intended, without distortion or misunderstanding—requires an enormous imaginative effort. Not only must we speak, we must also speak from the point of view of the intended listener.

Successful communication requires therefore that we inhabit the mind and the context of the other. As such, the audience is always present at the very beginning of every communicative act.

Unfortunately, we tend to dismiss the audience and to assume that we know all about it and its responses. As a result, audiences tend to be understudied and poorly understood.

The television audience—the most studied of all audiences—may serve as an example. The television audience is widely held to be passive and vulnerable to manipulation. Hence, television violence provokes great anguish and advertising is routinely condemned. Furthermore, it is commonly believed that television targets the lowest common denominator, thereby deserving its nicknames of "idiot box" and "boob tube"—nicknames which also describe the audience's presumably low intelligence. Naturally, many people seek to distinguish themselves by proclaiming that they do not own a television set or do not watch it or watch only certain shows.

Unfortunately, observation of real television audiences reveals a staggering array of factors that contradict the belief in passive absorption. Television is rarely an isolated activity and people are usually doing other things while watching: eating, reading, talking on the telephone, instant messaging, playing with the dog, etc. Consequently, the conditions for the imperious takeover of the mind are rarely united.

Additionally, studies of how audiences interpret television show some rather striking inconsistencies. For example, researchers have examined how audiences interpret public affairs programs and prime-time dramas. Their results could hardly be more disorienting. It was as if their test subjects had not even watched the same programs.

Of course, we cannot conclude from this that every audience sees something different for the simple fact that many books, movies, news reports, and television programs do indeed result in broadly shared agreement as to their meaning, value, or impact. We are rarely faced with a situation of total breakdown in which the intended meaning of a media message is always or necessarily or systematically misunderstood, evaded, or ignored. On the contrary, we are very often faced with situations in which there is at least some agreement on the meaning of messages.

Nonetheless, one of the characteristics of the contemporary age is the literal explosion of communication. We wander through cityscapes plugged into private soundtracks, advertising reaches us over our cell phones, instant messaging systems connect us permanently to our peer groups, and television splinters into a thousand channels. Furthermore, formerly unsuspected media of communication—sound, colour, gesture, odour, speed, intensity—now also beckon to us.

Our communication experience is therefore richer, more intense, and more constant than ever before. Everyone and everything speaks to us. And as a result, we have become highly sophisticated—perhaps even cynical—audiences.

It is extremely common for people to make fun of messages. Advertising, movies, TV, and music are regularly treated ironically; they are subjected to jokes, dismissal, parody, contradiction, and so on. Indeed, with the exception of very young children, nobody nowadays approaches the world of messages, news, entertainment, or communication innocently. We approach it with savviness and cynicism and are as likely to reject as to accept it.

This is a problem for anyone who wants to reach an audience. How can audience cynicism or distrust or irony be built into a message in order to make it acceptable to its intended audience? A standard strategy is to flatter the audience by casting actors who can function as idealized versions of the intended receivers. This is why rock videos feature hip young people who are idealized versions of the intended audience. But it is also true of sitcoms, movies, advertising models, and so on. Another strategy is to make the message funny, thereby indicating that it can safely be watched because even its makers know that it should not be treated seriously. This is an attempt to disarm criticism. Producers also try to incorporate the cultural codes of their intended audience into messages. This is extremely common in advertising but is also characteristic of productions such as *South Park* or *Late Night with Conan O'Brien*. They deliberately incorporate their audience's perceived attitudes into their visual style and narrative structure. They shock or amuse not for the sake of shocking or amusing but as a strategy to reach a target audience.

Of course, even the best laid plans do not always work, and the relationship between message makers and audiences remains fraught with difficulty and contradiction. Indeed, it raises the intractable question of where meaning lies. Is meaning to be found in the intentions of those who make the messages or in the interpretations of the audiences who receive and use the messages?

It is often assumed that meaning lies with the producers of messages. This is why there is so much agitation over "media impacts" and "media effects." The assumption is that the meaning is contained within the message, which therefore has the ability to impose itself on all audiences everywhere. This approach views meaning as being highly stable—it is in the message and does not change—and already decided—there is no debate upon reception as to what the message really means. However, this type of imposition rarely happens.

If meaning lies with audiences, however, then it becomes undecidable and open to debate. The makers of a message might have intended a certain meaning but there is no guarantee that the audience will take that meaning. The end point of this line of reasoning, of course, is that every message acquires a new meaning as it is received by new audiences. This process is endless because there are always new audiences, and meaning is therefore never stable. However, that rarely happens, either.

It is in fact much more likely that meaning is a negotiation—the result of the encounter between the intentions of producers and the interpretations of audiences. It results from what producers imagine audiences to know and want and understand and from what audiences already know about how producers try to reach them. No producer reaches audiences naively and no audience is naive in its reception of messages. Both have histories. The audience in particular has a history of the media, of how they operate and the strategies they use, of how others have reacted to the media, of how they should act now in order to mark their individuality over and against messages.

Every message is, therefore, a theory of the audience, and every audience is an instruction on how to produce messages. We can therefore begin with audiences and ask which strategies media use to reach them, or we can begin with messages and ask how the intended audience is already embedded within them. Messages will contain markers that orient audiences appropriately, and audiences will respond to messages that contain appropriate markers. It becomes highly significant, therefore, to ask what type of message will be produced if we assume that the audience is, for example, female or young or poor. Likewise, it becomes significant to ask what audiences are imagined by messages that contain markers that are indicative of gender, age, or social status.

The chapter by Paul Attallah offers a general introduction to the problem of the audience in communication studies. It compares the audience to other types of human groups, notably the mass and the public, and reflects upon the paradoxical fact that while media may seek to target audiences, audiences also acquire knowledge of and sophistication toward the media.

Charlene Elliott's chapter expands the notion of medium well beyond the traditional technological devices (radio, TV, film, etc.) usually covered by that term to include the five senses (touch, sight, smell, hearing, taste). The chapter reflects upon the way in which cultural artifacts—in this case the space of Starbucks coffee shops—construct audience attitudes by orchestrating existing cultural references, beliefs, and behaviour patterns.

The chapter by Eileen Saunders addresses specifically the question of how we have traditionally imagined children and youths as audiences. Assumptions of the fragility and innate innocence of children have long been with us and have informed a very wide array of communication approaches. But such assumptions may also prevent us from asking other equally important questions. For example, while it is widely believed that children should be protected from advertising, the rush to do so may blind us to the fact that children are also citizens in the marketplace and that they, too, develop attitudes, responses, and strategies toward the messages directed at them.

Josh Greenberg and Brian Wilson examine the way in which media texts seek to shape the beliefs and attitudes of their audiences—their hegemonic function—by containing authoritative statements that assume their own naturalness. This invites audiences to identify and agree with the statements while simultaneously making it very difficult to disagree with them. In this sense, media messages can be persuasive not because they make logical arguments that cannot be defeated but because they construct a universe of perception that cannot be escaped.

The last chapter in this section, by Rebecca Sullivan, looks at the ways in which feminist research has approached questions of the audience. It explicitly sees representation as a locus of struggle over meaning. Different groups seek to construct media messages differently because they hope for different types of outcomes. The question here is not only who gets to imbed cultural markers within messages but also which types of markers will best achieve the desired outcome.

The general themes of the audience section are that audiences are not passive or easily manipulable, though neither are they heroic or indomitable. Instead, audiences are permanently caught up in systems of representations, in their own experiences and memories of the media, in social and political projects, and with their own ability to act, to reflect, to joke about, to embrace, and to ignore.

3

The Audience

Paul Attallah
Carleton University

The **audience** is an indispensable though often neglected aspect of communication studies. All mass media want an audience. They contain within them—in their organization, their content, their style—a *theory* about who should consume them, and how, and why. Indeed, every medium of communication—from an interpersonal conversation to global webcasts—represents an attempt or strategy to reach an audience. And every theory of the audience—every way of imagining what people do, and how, and why—points in the direction of an appropriate means or mechanism of reaching the audience.

MEDIA AND AUDIENCES

Media imply audiences and audiences imply media. Indeed, without an audience, there's no real point to the media's efforts. The audience confers meaning upon the activities of the media. We can often measure the success, relevance, or importance of a particular medium by examining the type or composition and size of its audience.

For example, media are often judged to be successful when they attract large audiences. Hence, *Spider-Man* films and reality TV shows are deemed successful because of the enormous audiences they generate.

But audience size is not the only criterion of success. Sometimes we scorn a large audience. For example, although a musical performer such as Britney Spears generates extremely large audiences, she tends not to receive critical praise or respect. The important element here is not the size of the audience but rather its composition. We assume that some audiences, no matter how large, are less sophisticated or more easily pleased and therefore not worth much attention. This is certainly the case with the audience for daytime soap operas. Although soap operas typically generate gigantic and fanatically loyal audiences, they and their audiences generally have a low status.

The same phenomenon works with newspapers. If a newspaper is little read, we might first conclude that it is not very important. However, if its small readership includes all the leading decision-makers, then we are likely to conclude that despite its small circulation, it may in fact be a very important newspaper. Again, the important criterion in our judgment is the *composition* of the audience.

But beyond audience size and composition—two common ways of determining the success and importance of a medium—is another factor which can be called **audience competence**. This is more difficult to grasp, but it is a very valuable concept. Some media seek to address not large audiences but very specific and specialized audiences. This has always been the case with specialist forms such as science fiction or horror comics or jazz. People who do not appreciate these forms often make harsh judgments about those who do, dismissing them as nerds, poseurs, wannabes, and so on. Whether these judgments are valid or not hardly concerns us. More significant is the fact that whether we belong to a specialized audience or not, we all recognize that the cultural form involved addresses not a mass but a specialist audience. Consequently, in order to enjoy the specialized form fully, the audience members must develop an expertise or *competence* that allows them to make fine distinctions within the form.

Audience competence is obvious in specialized forms such as jazz or experimental film, but *all* audiences tend to develop competence. Indeed, the more time they spend with a particular cultural or media form, the more sophisticated audiences become. The process of increasing competence and sophistication can be illustrated by the DVD. Until the late 1990s, virtually no one owned a DVD player, but now they are extremely common. Their primary use, obviously, is to watch movies and, increasingly, old television shows. DVDs contain not just the most recent films and television shows but virtually the entire Hollywood back catalogue. As a result, even casual viewers can become acquainted with the entire history of Hollywood or the whole output of a particular television producer. The DVD, therefore, is a device through which even casual viewers gain ever increasing sophistication about the history and particularities of film and television in general or of particular genres in which they are most interested. This was never planned but it happened. The DVD has given moviegoers and television viewers the same sort of background competence that voracious novel readers have always possessed. And the process will undoubtedly be repeated with whatever new technology comes next.

Furthermore, the new sophistication of film audiences, for example, now feeds back into the types of films that Hollywood makes. It is becoming increasingly difficult to end films with classic "happy endings" precisely because audiences know that this is the classic way to end a film. The knowledge that such an ending is a cliché impels Hollywood to look for new ways of bringing films to a close, or for novel types of motivations so that even a "happy ending" might seem fresh and new. Similarly, every new blockbuster needs bigger effects, more spectacular action, something fresher and newer, precisely because audiences know all about the predecessors.

The process of increasing sophistication is even more evident with television because the production cycle is so much faster than with film. A program such as *The Daily Show with Jon Stewart* depends crucially upon a high degree of audience sophistication with the styles, manners, and rhythms of news programming. A viewer unfamiliar with the history of television, with other TV programs, or with popular attitudes toward television is unlikely to find it very funny. Likewise, a program such as *Trailer Park Boys* is a deliberate parody of our expectations about "good" acting and camerawork, proper moral tone, socially acceptable behaviour, and so on. Even much gentler programs such as *Scrubs* or *Corner Gas* are constructed around the presumption of audience familiarity with the styles and genres of television itself.

One of the most striking examples of audience sophistication is to be found in so-called *fan fiction*, stories written by fans but based on characters and situations provided by the media. Jenkins (1992) calls this "textual poaching." Among the earliest examples of fan fiction were the K/S stories written by fans of the original *Star Trek*. These stories involved the characters of Kirk and Spock (hence K/S, pronounced "K slash S") and developed what the fans believed were the unspoken sexual tensions between them. Since then, numerous television programs and movies have given rise to fan fiction, stories told by fans that will never appear elsewhere than in the fiction they write for each other.

Finally, technology such as P2P software also depends upon a very high degree of musical background knowledge among its users. To know which songs you want and how you want to mix them up with other songs—in what order, with what mood, etc.—is to possess a very high degree of background knowledge about what exists, a fairly articulate set of aesthetic judgments (what's good and what's bad), an insight into the impact the music will or should have (what order to give the songs), and so on. This is not to say that all P2P users are musical sophisticates but that for such a technology to work and be valuable to its users, those users must possess a degree of musical sophistication.

There is, however, an interesting criticism of audience sophistication. Some media critics such as Todd Gitlin (1990) argue that so-called "knowing" or "savvy" audiences are actually unwitting prisoners of the media. They argue that to be savvy about the media is actually to be drawn ever more firmly into their orbit and to take ever more delight in precisely the things the media make available. Rather than challenge the media, sophistication may therefore be the sign of one's permanent lapse into an unshakable media embrace. In other words, sophistication may not be an index of audience intelligence but of the media's ability to breed further loyalty. Are the fans of *Big Brother* savvy about the media and human behaviour or merely faithful audiences whose sense of sophistication blinds them to the media's hold on them?

MASS VS. FRAGMENTED AUDIENCE

The very fact of audience competence, however, raises another question. It is often assumed that the modern audience is a mass audience. The view of the audience as an undistinguished mass, in which everyone more or less enjoys the same content and draws the same meanings from the content, is often called the **mass society** hypothesis or the **stimulus-response** view of modern society.

However, more recently, the view has emerged that audiences are in fact highly fragmented. The view that they are multiple, interlocking, and driven by highly differentiated interests and desires is often called the functionalist view of society. The fact of the matter is that a permanent tension exists between these two poles and that we can find examples of both types of audience. Indeed, it may be the case that both types exist only on condition of the other also existing.

For example, it is certainly true that the television audience has become highly fragmented over the past 20 years. This is reflected in the organization of the television industry. Where once there were only a few channels, there are now hundreds. The major networks that used to dominate audience ratings have seen their shares decline precipitously. Television is a clear example of a formerly mass medium confronting the fact of the **fragmentation** of its audience. Indeed, television has discovered that it does not have an audience but rather *multiple audiences*.

Television is moving toward the model of book publishing, magazines, and newspapers. In these media, numerous offerings are quite common, and it is easy for the reader of one type of content to know little or nothing about other types of content. This is the same transformation that confronted radio 50 years ago when television itself was first introduced.

However, some media—including television—are still capable of generating quite massive audiences. Every summer, blockbuster films generate staggering audience figures and television events such as Janet Jackson's appearance at the Super Bowl, the premiere of *Survivor,* or the finale of *Friends* are still capable of attracting huge audiences. The same is true of a song that everyone has heard or a best-selling novel about which everyone knows.

It seems that while audiences enjoy the ability to consume private pleasures in small, fragmented groups, they also measure the quality and desirability of those pleasures against a common cultural standard. For example, while some people may greatly enjoy the all-romance or all-wrestling channel, their ability to *know* that this is their preferred content depends upon their ability to locate that content within a broad range of other content types. After all, if we only ever know one thing—country music or green clothes—then we can never know whether we like those things a lot or only a little, whether we might find ways to intensify our enjoyment of them or of avoiding them altogether. To know what we like demands that we know what others like, too. It is only in that confrontation with the tastes of others that we can actually come to understand something about our own tastes.

It seems therefore that specialized interests can only emerge after exposure to generalized interests or in relationship to them, even if that relationship consists in denigrating and avoiding those other interests. And as audiences, we clearly tend to fluctuate between the two states of mass and fragmentation (see Neuman, 1991).

As a result, many millions of people will see a blockbuster film but from that common *mass* experience different audience *fragments* will develop an increased liking for the star of the film, for the type of special effects in the film, for the type of story advanced in the film, and so on. Common experiences can spin off into specialized interests, and specialized interests are shaped in relation to common experiences.

Finally, there are certain events that seem to *demand* that we come together as a mass audience. These are often events of significant public life, such as a general election (on election night we constitute a mass audience for television), the death of a leader (the funerals of Pierre Trudeau and Princess Diana formed mass audiences), a big sporting event (the Olympic Games, hockey playoffs, the World Cup), unusual events (high-profile televised trials), acts of war (the Gulf War), and so on.

All of these events call us together as a *mass* audience and usually assume that we all draw the same meanings from them. They can also be the basis for us spinning off into specialized or fragmented audiences. We do not have to be together all the time, and being with our fragmented groups is fun most of the time. But it may be the case that we do have to be together at least some of the time.

AUDIENCE ADDRESS AND BEHAVIOUR

Different media address the audience in different ways. Hence, while we might be fans of a specific television show, prefer certain types of movies, and enjoy particular types of music, all of these media address us as audiences in quite different ways (see Marshall, 1997). For example, there are some fairly obvious differences in the ways we consume media. Film has traditionally been a special event, requiring us to leave the home, pay money for the privilege of watching the film, and sit in a darkened theatre with a group of other people we have never met. The situation is sufficiently strange that, if we did not enjoy the experience, we might never go to another movie. Film, therefore, attempts to instill the sense of a special experience in the hope that we will want to go back to see more films. As a result, everything about a film usually signals itself as "special." Film stars are the biggest stars, distant and mysterious. Film audiences are typically left wanting to know more about them and therefore turn to gossip columns, fan magazines, autographed pictures, and so on. Film budgets are regularly touted as an indicator of just how "special" the event is. So are the box office grosses, the advertising campaigns, the promotional tie-ins, and so on. Everything about film, therefore, suggests it is special and seeks to make the audience want more. But films do this by maintaining a distance between themselves and the audience.

This is the opposite of television. Because television is typically consumed in the home and is available virtually all the time, it tends not to be a special event. On the contrary, it is familiar. Consequently, television stars are quite different from film stars: they are not as big, as special, or as distant. In fact, they offer themselves almost as family members. We therefore tend to feel we know much more about TV stars. For example, Oprah Winfrey is a huge television star who seems to have revealed everything to her audience, from her weight to her literary preferences! In order to make us want more, television strives not to be a special event that we crave but a friend whose company we expect. Therefore, whereas films maintain distance and impose themselves as special, television closes the gap and offers itself up as friendly and familiar. Indeed, it is also why Dr. Phil can be a huge television star but is unlikely ever to have comparable success in film.

The music industry addresses us in yet another way. It tends to be directed more at emotions and at setting moods. It is therefore commonplace for people to associate particular songs with particular events in their lives (hence, the saying, "They're playing our song!"). People tend not to remember television programs or movies with the same degree of intensity or emotional attachment. Music tends to evoke not just strong feelings in the present but also strong feelings about the past, about attitudes and attachments, and so on. As a result, music stars tend to have a charismatic authority. They tend to attract an audience interested not so much in the star's appearance or personal life but in the whole set of emotions and values that the star represents.

It is, of course, possible to be a fan—to be a part of the audience—of film, television, and music despite the different modes of address. Indeed, it is extremely common for a person who likes jazz also to like a certain type of film and perhaps even to enjoy a specific type of television. It is quite common for our tastes to be relatively *coherent* across media. In fact, part of our maturing as adults consists in constructing a coherent attitude and set of judgments across a multitude of media events and experiences. The judgments we form of these events are very closely tied to the life cycle. For example, no one is surprised that very young children have typically "childish" tastes. Nor is it surprising that old people seem to have a more restricted range of preferences, often harkening back to when they themselves were young. Nor is it especially surprising that young adults consume a tremendous range of cultural and media artifacts and tend to invest strongly in a small cross section of them. It is also likely that people's media menu evolves through life as well, with television being heavily consumed by both the young and old, and music and film by young adults. These are not hard and fast rules to which no exceptions may be found. They are indicators of the broad and strangely shifting contours of the audience.

However, because film tends to cultivate an aura of specialness, television an aura of familiarity, and music one of charisma, they also tend to produce different types of responses in their audiences. It is quite common in the music industry to stage concerts that bring together in a single location very large numbers of people. In that moment of the concert, the audience typically celebrates the co-presence of all its members and affirms the symbolic values they believe the music represents. The most extreme example of this phenomenon may have been provided by the "Deadheads," the hardcore fans of the Grateful Dead who virtually toured with the band and developed their own subculture. The music was linked to a set of beliefs that translated itself into a lifestyle. The same phenomenon, though in a less intense way, also occurs at raves. People come together for a good time but also to affirm the values they believe the music represents and to translate those values into collective behaviour. Indeed, clothing styles—a visible marker of one's value—are much more closely linked to music than to television or to movies. Music, therefore, tends very much toward intensity, the co-presence of its members, and the collective affirmation of values. This is one of the reasons music concerts can also be dangerous venues; it is easy for something to go wrong when large numbers of people gather. In this sense, then, concerts share considerable similarities with sporting events and the way in which sports crowds can veer suddenly from happiness to anger.

It is relatively uncommon, on the other hand, for television audiences to be roused to action. Indeed, it is more frequently said of television that it makes its audiences lazy and dull. But there are clear differences in the manner of television's reception. A television audience is almost never co-present. People—except perhaps for a few friends or family members—very rarely gather to watch TV together. The television audience is, by definition, dispersed, and its members are generally unknown to each other. They are usually only represented as ratings statistics. Under those conditions, people are unlikely to celebrate their co-presence or to translate their shared values into a visible behaviour pattern. What television does do, however, is cultivate familiarity. It is not just that talk-show hosts are familiar to us; a huge amount of television content is explicitly concerned with the ordinary and the everyday. Situation comedies are typically set in very ordinary, everyday locations. The news is specially concerned with the day's events. Soap operas take as their subject matter the most banal of daily occurrences. Much prime-time drama is located in real locations or locations that we are invited to understand as real and believable. Hence, because so much of television is ordinary and everyday, it generates the belief that whatever is everyday and ordinary *deserves* to be on TV. As a result, television tends to establish an equivalence between its spectacle and reality. It is therefore easy to assume that *because* TV stars are familiar and friendly then friendly and familiar people can also be TV stars. As a result, people tend to want to *be on TV* and to achieve a sense of fame—of well-knownness and status—in that way. Viewers line up to be contestants on game shows, to express their most intimate secrets on talk shows, to outlast everyone on *Canadian Idol*, and so on. Television is oriented toward making the famous ordinary and the ordinary famous, rather than toward the affirmation of collective values.

Film tends to propose models of individual behaviour. This is obvious in the status of the film star and in the attention paid to the star's private life. Film does not so much rouse people to action, as music does (though of course films can be rousing and exciting), or cultivate a desire for self-exposure, as television does, but sets forth examples of highly desirable behaviour that are to be envied and emulated. The physical beauty of the film star, the star's lavish lifestyle, the star's personal pursuits and hobbies become cultural ideals of elevated behaviour. Of course, it is precisely because stars are unavailable, and because the film industry constructs itself as a distant yet special event, that the behaviour of stars becomes such an object of fascination. Consequently, it is hardly surprising to observe that many social trends have been represented first in movies and in the behaviour of movie stars. The cult of youth and of the well-tanned body, a felt need for plastic surgery, various outdoor activities, wearing sunglasses, and so on, are all derived from behaviour patterns associated with the glamour of the movie star.

AUDIENCE SWAPPING

Nonetheless, whatever the particular mode of address, it is quite possible for audiences to be coherent *across* media. We have already seen that it is highly likely for a person who likes a particular type of music also to like particular types of TV and film. Because of the relative coherence of audience tastes, the various media frequently undertake to swap audiences back and forth among themselves and to use audience success in one area in order to build it in another.

For example, *The X-Files* was sufficiently popular on TV to be made into a movie. The hope was that its success could be translated from one medium to another and that its TV audience would follow the characters into film. Indeed, it was also hoped that film audiences unfamiliar with the program or its characters might be introduced to them through the film, thereby augmenting the television audience. The phenomenon could also happen in the opposite direction; TV audiences unfamiliar with the film experience might be introduced to it through the film of the television program.

But crossovers between TV and film are hardly new. The best known example is probably the *Star Trek* films and television shows, all produced by Paramount Pictures with the specific intention of building audiences in both media for the greater profit of the corporation. There are also, of course, crossovers between music and other media. Elvis Presley became a movie star, and innumerable musical groups have appeared in films. The tradition has continued down to Will Smith, who began as a rapper, had a hit TV show (*Fresh Prince of Bel Air*), then became a movie star who also recorded the hit songs based on his movies. At one time, film stars even tried to launch music careers, and a few were successful (for example, Judy Garland).

The most enduring form of crossover is probably between a novel and the film based upon it. And there have also been crossovers between comic books, TV, film, music, and almost any other combination one cares to imagine.

Cross-media tie-ins—the novelization of the movie, toys and games given away at fast food restaurants, the soundtrack of the movie, merchandise bearing the logo of the film—are also attempts to capitalize on existing audiences and to bring new people into the audience. It is not at all uncommon for children to learn about the existence of a movie, and to want to watch it, from seeing colouring books based on the movie or from receiving a free toy of one of the characters. Movie sequels and prequels serve the same function of extending old audiences and capturing new ones.

Industries swap audiences back and forth. The greatest danger of this strategy is that the product will become overexposed and audiences will tire of it. A second and more insidious danger is that they will reach the wrong audience, thereby alienating their original audience. For example, it often happens when a book is made into a movie that the fans of the book are disappointed because the movie somehow fails to match what they had imagined. It alienates them. Likewise, many fans of the comic book *Batman* were displeased by the 1989 *Batman* movie. Much the same thing appeared to have happened to John Travolta, who after initial success, seemed to make a number of bad and unmemorable films. Performers are often accused of "selling out" or "betraying their audience" when this happens. Later, however, especially after *Pulp Fiction* (1994), Travolta regained favour by apparently rediscovering and re-connecting with his audience.

MASS, PUBLIC, AUDIENCE

We have already seen that a particular audience member's tastes can be coherent across media, despite different modes of address and behaviour. A larger question, however, poses itself. *Why* do audiences come together in the first place? *How* do we account for the existence of a group of people as an audience?

There are many types of groups, not all of which qualify as audiences. A group of people walking downtown hardly constitutes an audience, though its members are co-present and can be in very large numbers. To be an audience, therefore, is not to be just any random group of people.

An audience is a group of people united for a particular purpose or around a common goal. However, a group of people can come together for the specific purpose of protesting the government or raising a barn or praying for the dead. These groups of *purpose-oriented* individuals would also not likely be called an audience. The mere fact of having a purpose does not make an audience.

An audience, therefore, must be a nonrandom group and the purpose guiding its formation must be of a particular type. The purposes driving the groups mentioned above—protesting, barn raising, prayer—all seem to be the wrong type of purpose. It is fair to say that the purpose that unites audiences is an *experience*. Audiences come together not to *do* something but to *experience* something. This is one of the main differences between political rallies and movies or television, for example. Political rallies are usually oriented toward the purpose of *achieving a goal* or *effecting change* or *implementing a program*. Their goal is to bring about a particular type of action among those attending, not principally to make them feel good. Movies and television do not usually seek to bring about action but to provide an *experience* which they hope will be sufficiently enjoyable as to cause a desire for a repetition of the experience.

Audiences, therefore, are nonrandom groups of people united around a desire for an experience. Significantly, the hope is also that the experience will be repeatable. Many other types of groups—such as political rallies—can be one-time affairs. Since the point of political meetings is not to instill an enjoyable experience that members will wish to repeat, the purpose of the rally can frequently end once the goal has been achieved. For experience-seeking audiences, however, an experience that happened only once would be a failure. A good experience is one that can be repeated.

We can state, therefore, that the type of experience most frequently sought by audiences is an *entertainment experience*. The examples of protesting, barn raising, and prayer are clearly not entertainment experiences. They are goal-oriented activities whose duration can be quite limited. Indeed, the groups that engage in these activities can cease to exist once their goal has been achieved. An audience, however, will tend to be an ongoing phenomenon. Each particular experience will be valuable in itself but will also instill the desire for a repetition of the experience. In that sense, then, the process of forming an audience is never complete. The audience can always be re-formed, and frequently *wants* to be re-formed, around another experience, at another time, in another place.

Furthermore, audiences need not be co-present, even if sometimes they are. The audiences for film and television are typically highly dispersed in time and space. The audience for a sporting event *can* be co-present, all its members concentrated in a particular location at a specific time to witness the event, but that co-present audience can be supplemented by other, more distant audiences following the event on television or on radio. Some will read about it in the newspaper the next day. Some will re-create the event as part of a computer game. Hence, while the audience *can* be co-present, it need not be. This is another of the factors distinguishing audiences from other types of groups. However, it also means that when politics, for example, addresses the public via the media, it tends to turn the public into an audience. Likewise, when rock concerts address their audience directly and in a co-present manner, they start to veer toward public action. Entertainment can bleed into public action and public action into mass behaviour.

The fact that audiences are usually associated with entertainment experiences often leads to a devaluation or dismissal of their activity, to the conclusion that what they do is unimportant. While this may sometimes be accurate, it may also be an overstatement. To be concerned with experiences and entertainment is not necessarily to be unconcerned with rational judgment or behaviour. On the contrary, as we have seen above in discussing the question of audience competence, there can be a high degree of rationality and sophistication involved in the act of being an audience member.

Nonetheless, the audience is usually compared unfavourably to the *public*. Whereas the audience is an entertainment or consumer concept, the public is held to be a political concept. Whereas the audience refers to preferences and enjoyment, the public refers to reason and judgment. Whereas the audience can be fickle and ephemeral, the public is usually held to grow out of principles, which it expresses with constancy.

The audience, therefore, is often treated as a degraded form of the public. It is often said to involve consumerism whereas the public involves citizenship. Indeed, the media are often condemned specifically for treating people as *consumers* rather than as *citizens*, for doling out entertainment instead of information, and for transforming information *into* entertainment.

However, the fact of audience competence may require that we temper such judgments. There are similarities between the audience and the public. Both are nonrandom groups and both are oriented toward a goal. The fundamental distinction between them concerns the nature of the goal, experience vs. action, with action being judged the superior goal. Both also require the use of rationality, albeit in different ways. The public uses its reason to determine the nature of social life and the limits of personal behaviour. The audience uses reason to determine the nature and quality of its experience. Neither is more nor less rational than the other though they clearly use their reason for different ends.

Nevertheless, an important distinction separates them. While both the audience and the public are nonrandom groups, their internal coherence springs from different sources. The members of an audience come together and understand themselves as members of the same audience not because some external agency forces them to, but out of a spontaneous sense of individual preference. When they are together as an audience, it is because they share a common experience or a common judgment on the nature, value, and desirability of the experience. In short, audiences come together on the basis of *elective affinities*, self-chosen reasons for coming together. A public *can* come together on the basis of elective affinities but its goal is not to prolong the pleasure of the experience or to repeat it. Its goal is to establish an external norm—a law, a rule, a method of procedure—that would itself set the parameters under which people can come together. It seeks to institute a state of affairs that indicates appropriate and inappropriate activity or behaviour. A public, therefore, seeks to prescribe limits on behaviour whereas an audience does not. An audience sees individual preference as the precondition of its existence. A public sees individual behaviour as a problem to be controlled.

These distinctions and similarities may be brought into even sharper focus by comparing both the audience and the public to yet another type of group, the *mass*. The mass is certainly not the public; nor is it the audience. The mass is like them in that it is also a nonrandom group of people oriented toward a purpose; however, the purpose of the mass is usually externally given (i.e., members of a mass do not assemble on the basis of elective affinities), and the mass tends not to exercise reason in achieving its purpose. Hence, it is very often the case that members of a mass (or mob or crowd) are given over to spontaneous and extreme actions, often of a violent or destructive nature. The members of a mass do not originally come together with the intention of forming a mass. Usually, a mass occurs suddenly when a large group of people has assembled for some other reason; an unexpected incident occurs, and the group turns into a mass. This is why riots, for example, are rarely planned. They tend to be spontaneous events whose origins are very difficult to explain, whose course is unpredictable, and whose end is likewise almost impossible to foresee. Furthermore, the members of a mass typically set aside their conscious judgment and allow themselves to be guided by the spirit or mood of the crowd. That is why members of a mass find themselves doing things that they would never do on their own. Conscious judgment tends to be replaced by a group mind.

The mass, therefore, is a type of accidental though nonrandom group who is oriented toward a goal that is not self-chosen, and whose actions in accomplishing the goal are not rational but emotive, spontaneous, and unconscious.

The mass, the public, and the audience describe, therefore, three modes of being that human groups can assume. It would be an error to claim that they are completely separate and distinct states. They form a fluid continuum such that we can inhabit any of those states. Indeed, it is likely that we can inhabit them all simultaneously and that one state can easily morph into another.

For example, while political groups can exercise reason, it is equally possible for any large gathering of people to turn into a mass. Indeed, many have observed that the Nazi movement was specifically of this type. On the one hand it was a political party, a nonrandom grouping organized around a goal; but the behaviour of the members at mass rallies, in giant public spectacles, and elsewhere, exhibited all the traits of mass behaviour. Individual judgment seemed to have been replaced by a group mind.

Likewise, entertainment can be merely a pastime, but it can also instill beliefs and values. Many a book has been written, for example, with the specific purpose of teaching moral lessons. Many a story has been filmed in order to make the viewer *feel* an emotion or a situation from which lessons are to be learned and rational action undertaken. Indeed, much entertainment deals with complex issues and situations that invite audiences to be tolerant, to suspend judgment, to try to understand the other's point of view. Does the television program *The Daily Show with Jon Stewart* belong to the category of entertainment or of politics?

The mass—the sheer fact of people coming together in large numbers and being able to undertake action—is probably the basis of both the audience and the public. And sometimes mass behaviour results in outcomes that we judge to be entirely laudable and desirable: revolts of the oppressed, spontaneous resistance to outmoded rules and norms, rejections of intolerable conditions, and so on. The mass should not be condemned automatically or out of hand.

As communication scholars, though, our role is first to understand the shifting and fluid relationships among mass, public, and audience, and always to resist quick and easy judgments about any of them.

QUESTIONS

1. How is an audience different from a mass?
2. Describe a group that shifts between being an audience, a mass, and a public.
3. Can audiences undertake "political" action?
4. Is audience sophistication a sign of audiences' ability to think as they wish or media's ability to convince audiences to stick closely to the media?
5. How is an audience different from a public?
6. How do different media address us differently as audiences?

REFERENCES

Gitlin, Todd. (1990, Winter). Blips, bites and savvy talk: Television's impact on American politics. *Dissent*, 18–26.

Jenkins, Henry. (1992). *Textual poachers, television fans and participatory culture.* New York: Routledge.

Marshall, P. David. (1997). *Celebrity and power.* Minneapolis/London: University of Minnesota Press.

Neuman, W. Russell. (1991). *The future of the mass audience.* Cambridge, England: University Press.

4

Sipping Starbucks: (Re)Considering Communicative Media

Charlene Elliott
Carleton University

Colour, objects, scent, sound, and taste are vibrant communicators in cultural life, signifying a dizzying array of meanings. Yet in a culture preoccupied with new technologies and mass media forms, these "communicators" often become relegated to the background. At best, they are overlooked; at worst, they are considered unworthy of analysis.

This is unfortunate, for communication is more than media, and the communication field is far richer when viewed through a panoramic lens. Regarding communication solely as *mass* communication is reductionist, and some scholars have lamented the field's current "mediacentric perspective" (Mattelart, 1996, p. x) and its "unduly limited dialogues of media research" (Golding and Harris, 1997, p. 9). We would be wise to heed these concerns and, as a result, to consider communication that might be less "wired," but of equal importance.

Consider, for instance, the communicator of colour. Colour *per se* has been successfully used by a range of interest groups to convey particular messages to equally particular audiences. Breast cancer survivors and supporters rally around pink as a sign of their struggles, and as a visual cue for the need to raise breast cancer awareness around the world. Red, in the form of a ribbon, has been adopted by Mothers Against Drunk Driving, and is also used in AIDS awareness campaigns. From a commercial standpoint, marketers have used colour to distinguish goods and "refresh" stale brands. We are all familiar with the red=Coke and blue=Pepsi heuristic, but might be surprised to realize the seriousness with which certain corporations treat their "signature" colours. Starbucks, for example, once threatened to sue an independent coffee company for selling its coffee in plain green cups (which Starbucks felt communicated the Starbucks brand to consumers). Similarly, Lyons Partnership, owner of Barney the Dinosaur, has sued costume companies for renting out, among other things, purple hippopotamus and purple dragon costumes—because the purple in the costume might cause individuals to confuse it with Barney.

What proves shocking to many about the communication of colour is that its signification increasingly is being codified and granted legitimacy by our legal regimes. In March 1995, the United States Supreme Court sent shock waves through legal circles by granting, for the first time, a **trademark** to colour alone or colour *per se*. Australia followed suit the following year, and in March 1999, Germany's Supreme Court also ruled that colour *per se* could be owned. Although Canada's Supreme Court has yet to rule on this issue, the basis for a similar decision is certainly in place, for the Canadian Trademark Act is worded such that there is no reason in *law* why colour trademarking should not be possible.

The implications of owning colour are far-reaching. But why should this matter to communication students? It matters because it reveals that communication is brighter and louder and smellier, more flavourful—and also more subtle—than often realized. And it matters because marketers are increasingly recognizing the power of these unique communicators to influence an audience. Hence we have efforts to own a colour, a shape, a scent, or a sound. For instance, Coca-Cola's bottle and the shape of the Toblerone chocolate bar have been trademarked, as have NBC's three "signature" chimes, ABC's characteristic musical notes, and the fragrance of plumeria blossoms on sewing thread (Carraway, 1995, p. 246ff; James, 1996, p. 422ff). In Germany, the Flensburger Pils brewery even tried to trademark the sound of a beer bottle opening! ("Germany Overturns," 1999, p. 6). Since we are not only surrounded but also *influenced* by these communicators, it proves necessary to explore how they are being used to target, build, and persuade an "audience."

FLAVOURFUL BRANDS: ATTRACTING THE AUDIENCE

Other chapters of this book discuss the ways in which media such as film, television, newspapers, and Web sites relate to the vast numbers of people who make up the audience. However, audiences exist in several forms. Not merely moviegoers and music fans or viewers of reality TV, an audience comprises the grocery shoppers choosing President's Choice cookies over Nabisco Chips Ahoy! and the coffee drinkers sipping Starbucks in trendy corner cafés.

If colour, scent, tastes, and objects are communicative media, then the channelling of their meanings (often at the hands of marketers) is done with the audience in mind. As such, the mass media concerns of audience composition and competence, diversity and fragmentation also play out in these less overtly *media*ted forms. Marketers of fragrance, food, and drink—and Barney purple—all begin with ideas about the audience and theories of what will be persuasive. *How* these symbolic forms of communication are marketed proves particularly fascinating, and the following case study illustrates how something as simple as a coffee bean can be transformed into something symbolically exciting in order to attract an audience of coffee drinkers whose experience is based in the consumption experience itself.

STARBUCKS AND HAUTE-CAFFEINE: CREATING THE COFFEE SNOB[1]

Coffee is one of the most valuable commodities in world trade and a key export product for developing countries. Accounting for over 80 percent of total export earnings for some of the least developed countries (ICO, 2004), coffee has clear economic and political import. But coffee is also the preferred beverage of Canadians (second only to water), and its sociocultural significance is equally remarkable. Sixty-three percent of Canadians drink coffee daily (Coffee Association, 2003) and specialty coffeehouses adorn the urban landscape like bright confetti. Starbucks Coffee Company, the ubiquitous purveyor of specialty coffees, has retail stores throughout North America, Latin America, Europe, the Pacific Rim, and the Middle East. It competes with a host of other popular specialty retailers—including the Canadian-owned Second Cup Coffee Company, Timothy's World Coffee, and Blenz Coffee. Even companies such as Procter & Gamble, Kraft, and Sara Lee seek to capitalize on our growing affinity for premium coffee, by marketing "café quality" coffees for the home (Foster, 2004, p. 26).

Clearly, coffee is big business. Yet it is also a symbolic business, dealing with the production, packaging, and consumption of meaning—a meaning repeatedly ingested by Starbucks' patrons. The cultural "text" of coffee is particularly interesting, for it is multilayered; meaning resides in the form itself (i.e., the "artifact" of the bean/beverage) and in the discourses surrounding that form (i.e., in its packaging and marketing). These discourses "blend" within the cup and are literally and figuratively consumed.

Furthermore, coffee is a unique artifact for analysis because the commodity flow is from south to north. While coffee has from the outset been stamped with a European thumbprint, there is no question that this ancient, foreign beverage has radically re-shaped the social relations and complexion of both work and leisure within the consuming countries. Historically, coffeehouses served as forums for political discussion and learning (Naiman, 1995, p. 52; Pendergrast, 1999, pp. 7–15); they have transformed over the years into "retail theatres" used primarily for socializing (MacLeod, 1997, p. B4). The beverage itself has become integral to working and professional culture: it is simultaneously a pick-me-up that provides greater productivity and a pause (in the form of the coffee break). Arguably, coffee has transformed Western society through a kind of tempered coffee colonialism, in which an imported commodity has been wholly embraced to become a fixture of Western consumer society and a marker of (Western) identity.

Consuming caffeine, then, entails more than brewing or buying. "Going for coffee" has social and global implications. Coffee beans, physically removed from their place of origin, have been conceptually repackaged, and the resulting discourse operating both through and about coffee targets a particular audience interested in a cosmopolitan, sophisticated, and distinctive consumption experience. While it is possible to explore coffee's packaging and marketing from various perspectives, this chapter follows Arjun Appadurai's lead in focusing on the commodity itself—the "thing that is exchanged" (Appadurai, 1986, p. 3)—and how it relates to the consumer audience. Since an audience (on a fundamental level) comes together to *experience* something, often *repeatedly*, it is crucial to note how the coffee bean is transformed into a distinct social experience. As Starbucks illustrates, identical commodities do not necessarily brew into identical products; because of this, the audience of Tim Hortons is far different from the clientele of Starbucks' specialty coffees.

THE WORLD OF STARBUCKS

Starbucks is the world's largest retailer, roaster, and brand of specialty coffee. With over 7,500 stores operating in 32 countries (Starbucks, 2004; "Finance and Economics," 2004, p. 75), Starbucks' coffee discourse circulates widely and is quaffed copiously. In 2003, Starbucks was recognized as one of the "Most Trusted Brands" by *Ad Week* magazine, and proudly claimed eighth place in *Brandweek*'s "Super Brand List." Each week, more than 30 million customers visit a Starbucks (Bhatnagar, 2004), and the resulting consumer buzz has generated more than $4 billion (U.S.) in annual revenue for the company (Starbucks, 2004). Given its global reach and tremendous success, Starbucks provides a meaningful illustration of how one simple commodity has been costumed for Western consumption. Starbucks' messages are steeped in the beverage itself, the names of the coffee blends, and the labelling of the beans. This construction, packaging, and presentation of coffee works to create and appeal to a particular audience, where the "entertainment" experience is literally consumed and where Starbucks patrons are distinguished from "regular" coffee drinkers. But first, it is important to explore how the coffee bean *itself* has come to acquire this meaning.

In their extensive study on the social role of advertising, communication scholars William Leiss, Stephen Kline, and Sut Jhally reiterate the Marxist perspective of commodity fetishism, whereby all traces of production are erased from the object produced. "Goods reveal or 'show' to our senses their capacities to be satisfiers," they affirm, while "draw[ing] a veil across their own origins" (1990, p. 324). Since goods "do not bear the signatures of their makers," only the most astute shoppers realize the components of things and who made them (1990, pp. 324–325). Fredric Jameson's analysis of postmodernity voices similar concerns, in which "the point" of consumerism, arguably, is to

> forget about all those innumerable others for awhile; you don't want to have to think about Third World women every time you pull yourself up to your word processor or all the other lower class people with their lower class lives when you decide to use or consume your other luxury products. (1991, p. 315)

Traditional coffee marketing does not belie these ideas. Starting from the 1920s, when coffee became a major consumer product, national corporations like Standard Brands and General Foods advertised the stimulant as a regular part of the workaday world. By 1950, coffee was the favorite beverage of the American middle class (Pendergrast, 1999, p. xviii), and in the decade that followed consumers could select from an array of coffees that masked their origins completely. Maxwell House, Folgers, Nescafé, Sanka, and the inaptly named Chock Full o' Nuts certainly did little to connote their source or those producing the beans.[2] Origins were insignificant. As an American roaster of the 1960s claimed, U.S. consumers simply wanted "normal" coffee in paper cups and "diluted to the tastes of the time, along with a hamburger and fries" (Pendergrast, p. 271).

Arguments for commodity fetishism prove less convincing in the year 2005, where fairly traded coffee and "environmentally friendly" coffee (such as shade-grown and organic) are readily available—for an added price, of course. TransFair and Quality Mark labels highlight conditions within the producing countries both to raise, and to acknowledge, public awareness: these labels guarantee interested consumers that coffee producers have received fair prices and a stable market for their crop. Shade-grown and organic coffee marketing, in contrast, focus on the ecological impact of coffee harvesting, emphasizing either the alternatives to pesticides or water and soil conservation initiatives. Rather than veiling the wearisome information on where and how coffee is produced, then, fair trade, organic, and shade-grown products foreground such considerations. Shoppers know the coffee bean's "history" and can deliberately choose the coffee "experience" of labels they support.

In Starbucks, the interplay between global/local and producer/product is much more intricate—and ironic. Starbucks introduced organic and shade-grown coffee into its product line in 1999, and proudly displays the TransFair logo in its stores. But only about 2 percent of the coffee sold at Starbucks is fair trade, prompting some consumers and coffee retailers to criticize Starbucks for exploiting the movement for marketing purposes (Rogers, 2004; Linn, 2004; "Trouble Brewing," 2004).[3] And while the global/producer aspect of coffee is foregrounded by Starbucks Commitment to Origins coffee line (which supports fair trade and conservation initiatives by coffee farmers in developing countries, as well as organic and shade-grown coffees), the most significant "space" in this worldly harvesting of beans is reserved for the local consumer. "Through your purchases of Starbucks® coffees, you're also making a difference, helping to improve people's lives, and encouraging conservation where our coffee is grown," affirms a Starbucks promotional flyer titled *Commitment to origins* (2003a). This personal role is further reinforced on the company's Web site and on its Fair Trade coffee packages, which inform customers that their local coffee consumption helps "those who grow it—one cup at a time."

Starbucks' current packaging firmly supports this connection between producer, purveyor, and consumer—and consequently rejects Leiss, Kline and Jhally's sweeping claim that goods are made to "veil" their origins in order to sell (1990, p. 324). Starbucks certainly does not veil its coffee's origins—but it is worth emphasizing that the *audience*, not the source (i.e., producers/origins) remains of primary concern. Consider, by way of illustration, Starbucks' coffee packages. Until quite recently, every Starbucks package affirmed a maxim that was particularly dismissive of producing countries: "Whether this Starbucks came from Africa, Arabia, Indonesia or Latin America, its destination is your cup." While Starbucks' current packaging is less dismissive, it proves equally focused on its audience. The "destination is your cup" has been replaced by a careful script that, again, is more concerned with the consumer (and the purveyor) than the producer:

> For more than 30 years, Starbucks coffee buyers have traveled the globe in search of the treasure you now hold in your hands. To bring you the finest beans the world has to offer— the top one percent—our experts taste over 150,000 cups of coffee each year. Transformed by the distinctive Starbucks roast, this Arabica coffee is guaranteed to provide you an exceptional taste experience.
>
> Through our participation in origin country community projects and our purchase of sustainable coffees, we contribute to the people and places that produce coffee.

Although Starbucks positively "contributes" to the places that produce coffee, it is clearly more interested in transforming the bean to provide a treasured "taste experience" to its audience. It is the nature of this taste experience to which we now turn.

CAFFEINATED CARTOGRAPHY[4]

Although Starbucks proudly serves its coffee around the world, the company's sense of geography is refracted through a commodified Western lens—a lens meant to appeal to a mass audience. Reflecting on his Starbucks experience, one journalist carped that unsuspecting Starbucks consumers must select "beans from countries that college graduates cannot find on a map" (cited in Pendergrast, 1999, p. 371).

Indeed, Starbucks' coffees embrace a range of growing locations, from Mexico, Guatemala, Colombia, Indonesia, and New Guinea to Kenya, Ethiopia, and Yemen. That consumers are not *expected* to find these places, but merely to consume them symbolically, is reflected in the way in which the brand creates and deals with the audience. While a particular type of audience might come to Starbucks for a taste experience, it is important to emphasize that the *experience* outranks the taste. Consumers may have little knowledge of the coffee bean's birthplace, yet this is insignificant. What matters (to Starbucks, at least) is the appeal that comes from labelling and "constructing" the coffee *differently*, for it makes the buying experience that much more entertaining.

Proof of both the *symbolic role of place* and the *acknowledgment of taste* is found in Starbucks' Coffee Categories, which arrange the beans according to flavour, not origin. In this categorization, Mild beans provide the "perfect introduction to Starbucks coffees" (Starbucks, 2002) and subsume coffees from all of Latin America under the Starbucks greeting. Smooth selections, in contrast, offer "richer, more flavourful" tastes from sources as diverse as Java, Guatemala, and Ethiopia. Finally, Bold selections—"intriguing and exotic coffees"—stem from Yemen, Sumatra, and Kenya (among other places). These "categories" speak to the consumers' desire for a particular taste and utterly discount the reality of the world's spaces. And while Starbucks' cartography of coffee may initially appear to substantiate Harvey's (1992) view that global culture makes people "much more sensitized to what the world's spaces contain" (p. 294), the sensitivity is rather superficial. "Sensitivity," in this case, is an awareness that the "world's spaces" of Java, Sulawesi, New Guinea, or Guatemala "contain" one thing of import: the Starbucks coffee bean.

Starbucks' cartography of coffee is further problematized by its array of trade-marked blends. Shoppers curious about a blend's origin can learn, through Starbucks' edifying brochures, that the company's "master roasters" create these flavourful brews by combining various coffee beans to attain a desired "tasteprint." In this way, Starbucks seeks to create a level of *audience competence*—a specialized audience that will appreciate the finer details of the coffee "experience" and consequently return to experience it again and again. But how is this done and *what does it mean?* Starbucks' Web site explains that a commodity of Yemen is ground with a commodity of Indonesia to "create" Arabian Mocha Java, while the beans of East Africa mix with those of Latin America to become Serena Organic Blend. In this way, the world's coffees are "relocated" just like the other non-Western commodities imported into North American society—just like the Costa Rican bananas, Indonesian sweet potatoes, and Chilean grapes housed in the local supermarket.

Starbucks' relocation, however, has greater symbolic power. The commodity, iden-tified by its location, has been fused with another; the country of Indonesia is symbol-ically annexed with Yemen. Even this is beguiling, for the coffee label fails to identify Yemen as a source. Rather, it refers to the geographically vague Arabia, a place with no defined borders. And while there are, to be sure, Starbucks coffees that clearly identify a single origin—Conservation Colombia, Organic Shade Grown Mexico, New Guinea Peaberry, or Kenya (to name a few)—Starbucks blends are commonly packaged under vague or misleading names. Yukon Blend, for example, is actually composed of Indonesian and Latin American coffees. Gold Coast Blend has the same distant ingre-dients, only in different proportions. Gazebo Blend, quite surprisingly, contains beans from East Africa. And Caffè Verona, made up of Indonesian and Latin American cof-fees, has nothing to do with the romantic label that evokes the city in Italy.

Starbucks' "master roasters" thus function as modern *bricoleurs*, playing with commodity pieces to construct a tasty—and trademarked—text for consumption. Symbolically, the play is highly charged in that the beans identified by their origins are more than pieces—they index places. The *audience competence* encouraged by

Starbucks is based, then, not on a reality but on a brand image. This image captivates audiences and creates the Starbucks "experience." Moreover, as an audience participates in Starbucks' "culture" by gaining coffee competence and developing personal tastes, Starbucks' image too becomes part of their own identity.

PLAYING WITH THE MAP

Geographic recombination also occurs within Starbucks' menu and in its store, where language, country, and commodity all provide symbolic grist for the Starbucks mill and where Starbucks' retail theatre promises a worldly experience for its audience. Customers do not purchase from servers, they order from *baristas*. Cup sizes do not come in small, medium, or large, but in the equally Italian *tall, grande,* and *venti.* Popular espresso-based drinks such as cappuccino and café latte can be ordered *con panna* or as *macchiato.* Consumers with a certain competence are thus encouraged to display their expertise. For those *without* the knowledge, Starbucks readily provides the information necessary to participate. In this way, the Starbucks audience continually expands as the coffee novice, with little effort, transforms into a coffee aficionado.

As Starbucks' customers sip their grande cafés au lait in a Seattle-based coffeehouse, they also partake in a cultural experience: they imbibe a style of coffee (espresso) that was invented in France, perfected in Italy, and sourced from Latin America and Indonesia. Tellingly, Starbucks chooses not to identify the bean "origins" in the *name* of Espresso Roast, the blend used in every espresso drink on the menu. Described simply as "dense" and "caramelly-sweet" (Starbucks, 2002), this roast, which forms the heart of most Starbucks drinks, is thus identified mostly by its corporate origin. This is also true of Starbucks' signature and most popular coffee, Starbucks House Blend, which, by name alone, reveals nothing of the Latin American coffees that it comprises. Here, the cloaking of origins seems deliberate and supports the "veiling process" Leiss, Kline and Jhally (1990) deem as characteristic of Western advertising. With this kind of naming and marketing, Starbucks reveals that "space" or "place" is merely a style to be utilized for semantic purposes and discarded when not wanted.

As consumers of Starbucks and participants in the coffee experience, we must ask *why* the marketing masks certain countries of origin and articulates others; only by answering this question will we have true "audience competence" when sipping our lattes and coffee blends. The question is difficult, and must be answered from a more theoretical perspective. Studies in anthropology and advertising theory prove very helpful, for the evocation of difference has both a strong cultural function and marketing value. Anthropologist Sidney Mintz (1985) reveals that today's "commonplace" imported commodities have shifted in meaning over time. Sugar, for instance, was first introduced to European society as a luxury item and coveted precisely *because* of its distant origins. This is also true of tea and chocolate, which only gradually became integrated (through increased use and availability) into wider society (Mintz, 1985).

These foreign goods ultimately transformed into staples and markers of both European and Western cultures; the physically de-territorialized commodities became conceptually re-territorialized into the realms of the familiar and the local. Thus for years consumers jump-started their mornings with the trusted, quotidian brands of Maxwell House, Folgers, or Nescafé. But the rise of specialty coffee worked to refresh this common staple, to make the banal better, and to add what marketing guru Rosser Reeves calls a "Unique Selling Proposition" (cited in Macrae, 1991, p. 36)—the special perk that the competitors do not offer. Hence the evocation of the exotic. Foreign beans, made common, are traced back to their roots to heighten coffee's consumer appeal. As Howes (1996) notes, "[I]n general, the only time when the foreign nature of an imported product is emphasized in the West by its marketers . . . is when part of its appeal to Westerners lies in its exotic nature" (p. 186).

"Foreignness" within the specialty coffee market allows consumers to conceptually partake of exotic locales. Coffee aficionados use geography to illustrate their knowledge and taste preferences by ordering Brazil Ipanema Bourbon, Kenya, Sumatra, Kona, New Guinea Peaberry, or Colombia Narino Supremo. In short, they order a place in a cup. And since the coffee beans' origins are only a "spice" within Starbucks' marketing, they can be tinkered with. Kenya, the country, is a coffee name, but so is Kona, a region in western Hawaii. Ethiopia Sidamo, which Starbucks offers as a beverage, is both a place and a people: Sidamo refers to the Cushitic-speaking inhabitants of southwestern Ethiopia. Starbucks' Guatemala Antigua coffee is an inversion of the capital and country of Antigua, Guatemala.

Finally, as merely a "spice," coffee's exotic origins can be omitted from the marketing at will. Reference to the foreign is used to make products appealing rather than threatening (Howes, 1996, p. 187), and marketers strive to ensure that their products (even those positioned as exotic) maintain a strong pull of familiarity so that they appeal to consumer lifestyles or lifestyle aspirations (Leiss, Kline, and Jhally, 1990). This explains why the country of origin does not feature in the names of Starbucks' House Blend and Espresso Roast. Of course, there is the practical reason of wanting to appeal to the largest-possible audience by offering both exotic and familiar fare— but the logic extends deeper. Starbucks has established itself as an upscale, worldly, but pointedly American chain. Accuracy with regard to global details (such as geographical and source identification, or coffee names) proves secondary to Starbucks' marketing and image. As Starbucks' 1998 promotional flyer affirmed: "Starbucks works backwards from a cup of coffee. It proudly considers the product first."

THE RHETORIC OF STARBUCKS; OR "SPEAKING OF COFFEE . . ."

Starbucks' "world of coffee" reaches beyond naming the beans. Coffee descriptors used in the company's marketing literature reveal Starbucks to be more than geographically challenged: it is steeped in a semantically charged rhetoric that the audience, perhaps unwittingly, participates in while supporting the brand. Not surprisingly, the Starbucks blends that target the widest possible audience—Espresso Roast and House Blend—are described in positive and comforting terms. They are "dense" and "caramelly-sweet"; they are "lively" and "well balanced" (Starbucks, 2002). Starbucks' Web site goes on to explain that its signature House Blend coffee was chosen "because of its versatile temperament and wide appeal. You can drink it all day long." Coffees with designed or entirely created names, such as Yukon Blend, Lightnote Blend, Caffè Verona, Gold Coast Blend, or Breakfast Blend present equally laudatory descriptors: Yukon Blend is "mellow" and "well rounded"; Lightnote Blend is "smooth" and "round"; Caffè Verona is "complex" and "sweet"; Gold Coast Blend is "rich" and "sophisticated"; and Starbucks Breakfast Blend promises to wake up drinkers with its "bright" and "sparkling" flavour (2002).

Contrast these descriptors with certain "exotic" coffees, which have laudatory but certainly more loaded terms. Arabian Mocha Java is "satisfying" yet "spicy," Komodo Dragon Blend is "refreshing" but "unanticipated," and Arabian Mocha Sanani is "wild" and "exotic." As consumers, we would do well to recognize that many of these words and phrases are consistent with what Said (1978, pp. 1–4) would classify as Orientalist discourse—the ethnocentric and stereotypic means of viewing, describing, restructuring, and ultimately dominating Muslim lands in Africa and Asia. Orientalism pivots on the notion of the "mysterious East" (Said, 1993, p. x) and often portrays the foreign as primitive. Starbucks conveys those very categories with its reference to the "unpredictable," "intriguing," "wild," and "earthy" in its coffee selection descriptors. In fairness, the company has made great strides in tempering this ethnicized rhetoric over the past few years: Sulawsi, previously promoted as "exotic but approachable" (Starbucks 1998), now stands as "smooth" and "elegant"; Arabian Mocha Java's "exotic and wild" label has transformed into the more controllable "spicy and satisfying."

Certain Starbucks descriptors, however, still describe coffee with Orientalist rhetoric: as something primitive, to be controlled and consumed by the West. Colombia Narino Supremo, for example, is explained on Starbucks' Web site as "the best coffee we've tasted from this area of South America, and it's exclusively ours. . . . Many Starbucks blends are enriched by [its] apparent simplicity."

Arabian Mocha Sanani's description similarly brings together many of these threads, combining Starbucks' sense of the exotic and its Western gaze with the mysterious to create a coffee profile with multiple meanings—one that is both familiar (in terms of the taste of port, blackberries, and cocoa) *and* targeted to the bold audience:

> Arabian Mocha Sanani—Here's our most exotic and unpredictable coffee—laden with flavors of deep port wine, juicy ripe blackberries, warm earthen spices and arid cocoa. To some, the intensity is overwhelming; it's perfect for the daring coffee connoisseur.

Starbucks accentuates its ethnicized rhetoric by presenting, for those who seek adventure in their coffee experience, the "wild side" of coffee. Said (1978) notes that "a principal dogma" of Orientalism is that the East is unpredictable, savage even, and "something to be feared" (p. 301). These random and savage elements emerge in the three Starbucks coffees labelled "Arabian"—they are the only coffees profiled in Starbucks' (2002) flyer that are deemed either "spicy" or "wild."

To keep these elements under control, Starbucks offers on its Web site The Coffee Taster—a service that acknowledges that particular tastes exist in the wider coffee audience, and that helps consumers find their niche within Starbucks' universe. Customers who answer the following seven questions can receive a personal-taste profile and a list of matching Starbucks coffees.

1. What does coffee do for you?
2. What taste characteristic do you look for in a cup of coffee?
3. How do you like your coffee brewed?
4. Which best describes you as a coffee drinker?
5. How do you drink your coffee?
6. What sort of flavors do you generally enjoy?
7. What do you usually order in a restaurant?

The answers, from a semantic perspective, are complex. Again, Starbucks subordinates the commodity to personal taste in order to foreground the audience, but even its taste profiles are symbolically charged. If consumers identify themselves as coffee-nervous or coffee-novice by answering in preference of mild flavours, consistent tastes, and coffee with added cream and/or sugar, then The Coffee Taster affirms that Starbucks House Blend or Lighthouse Blend—in short, the non-exotic coffees—are a "sure thing." For these consumers, it would be "adventurous" to try Colombia Narino Supremo, and "daring" to try Guatemala Antigua. For those consumers who identify themselves as coffee risk-takers and who enjoy experimenting, "extremes," and the "wild," The Coffee Taster recommends Arabian Mocha Java, Arabian Mocha Sanani, and other exotic-sounding coffees. Regardless of the answers given, Starbucks' signature coffees never appear under the "daring" category; Starbucks House Blend is listed either as a "sure thing" or not at all.

CREATING THE CONNOISSEUR

With all of these choices, the Starbucks audience is urged to consume caffeine. The "Starbucks Experience" (as the company describes it) is promised to be both sophisticated *and* unique, addressing the individual consumer's needs while providing consistent, exceptional quality to a broader taste public. As we have seen, the "Starbucks Experience" is premised on style and image. Yet it utterly relies on the knowledge and preferences of the individual coffee snob—a knowledge base that the company is more than willing to cultivate.

How does Starbucks "market" audience competency and coffee sophistication? Look no further than the pocket-sized "Make It Your Drink: A Guide to Starbucks Beverages"—a 22-page booklet intended to help customers "build confidence in beverage ordering" (Starbucks, 2003b). This handy guide begins by listing 38 key terms (presumably) necessary to order gourmet coffee. "Learning the lingo," for Starbucks, requires knowing the difference between a *doppio* and a *double*, a *misto* and a *quad*. It means knowing that a *skinny* is made with nonfat milk and an *Americano* contains two shots of espresso. And it means knowing even the ridiculously obvious details: a *To-Go Cup* is "the white Starbucks paper cup used for enjoying a drink outside the store" and a *For-Here Cup* is "a ceramic cup for enjoying your drink inside the store." Moreover, if one orders a beverage *With Room*, then it means that the barista will leave "space to add milk in a drink."

Particularly interesting about this "education" is that it provides another illustration of how Starbucks targets a sophisticated audience—all while supporting the notion of individual needs. "Make it *your* drink," Starbucks urges, and goes on to provide various suggestions for "personalizing" a coffee: "choose your espresso" (i.e., regular, decaf, extra shots); "try a syrup flavour" (e.g., vanilla, caramel, almond); "choose your milk" (e.g., whole, nonfat, 2 percent, soy); and "add other modifiers" (including whipped cream or sugar substitute). "There are so many ways to put your personal stamp on a drink," enthuses the guide, although few might be nonplussed to learn that this "personalization" can be as trivial as determining a preference for the "many different, creative ways to take your milk in a drink."

CONSUMING CAFFEINE

To truly experience the richness of communication, we need to understand communication as something that is fully sensorial (i.e., full of tastes, colours, sounds, and smells). We also need to understand that "audience" extends beyond moviegoers and television viewers. The audience—defined as a group of people who seek, and hope to repeat, an experience (often an entertainment experience)—can equally be found in coffeehouses, sipping their "communication" while sharing it with others.

In the case of Starbucks, the audience is targeted with reference to representations that while global in part, are predominantly local. Coffee beans, distanced from their origins, have been relocated in an American chain, and while Starbucks seemingly respects the imported commodity, it re-fashions it completely to appeal to an audience desiring sophistication, a personalized experience, and the signs of worldly taste. While coffee may be commonplace, specialty-coffee purveyors have reintroduced its global dimension and transformed the banal bean into something symbolically exciting.

The resulting issues of the palate are not confined within a grande cappuccino or venti Starbucks House Blend. While Starbucks offers the audience a "unique" and distinctive coffee experience, it accomplishes this experience by re-mapping world geography and appropriating Third World spaces. Kenya and Estate Java coffees *claim* to substantiate Africa and Indonesia respectively, but what Starbucks is actually substantiating is the audience's taste for the exotic. Coffee's commodity form has been made and remade in Western society, and while Starbucks' current marketing blends within its semantic coffeepot the exotic and familiar, as well as the local and global, the resulting brew is poured from a Western perspective. Despite Starbucks' marketing of global culture to attract sophisticated consumers, what the audience *really* consumes are local and often stereotyped representations. This fact is confirmed, albeit unintentionally, by Starbucks' key slogan: "Starbucks—The World of Coffee." Indeed, it is Starbucks' world of coffee—and not the world's coffees—that is being packaged for consumption.

QUESTIONS

1. How does Starbucks construct audiences?
2. Should we ask different questions of a Starbucks "audience" than a media audience? Why or why not?
3. How does Orientalism play out in the marketing of Starbucks?
4. The audience is not homogeneous; rather, it is made up of individuals with different preferences and needs. How is this addressed in the contemporary marketing of coffee?
5. Identify and describe how other non-mediated, symbolic forms of communication have been used to target a particular audience.

NOTES

1. Portions of this analysis are drawn from Elliott (2001).
2. The exception is Juan Valdez, the mule-escorted, sombrero-wearing coffee grower invented by the National Federation of Coffee Growers of Colombia in the 1960s to laud Colombian coffee. This highly successful advertising campaign focused on Colombia's rich growing conditions and its picked-by-hand harvesting methods, which assured consumers of a better-tasting coffee (Pendergrast, 1999, p. 284).
3. In fairness, Starbucks pays an average price of $1.20 per pound for *all* its beans—almost twice the current market price and very close to the Fair Trade "fixed price" of $1.26 per pound ("Starbucks Validates," 2004; Rogers, 2004; Linn, 2004). Starbucks has also spearheaded a program called Coffee and

Farmer Equity Practices (CAFE Practices) to promote positive environmental, economic, and social conditions for coffee farms.

4. Much of the descriptive information in the following sections is drawn from Starbucks' packaging, Web site, and promotional brochures. Specific references will be provided where appropriate.

REFERENCES

Appadurai, Arjun. (1986). *The social life of things.* Cambridge, England: Cambridge University Press.

Bhatnagar, Parija. (2004, April 21). Starbucks trumps forecasts. *CNN/Money.* Retrieved from http://money.cnn.com/2004/04/21/news/fortune500/starbucks/index.htm

Carraway, C. (1995). Color as a trademark under the Lanham Act: Confusion in the circuits and the need for uniformity. *Law and Contemporary Problems, 57*(4), 243–279.

Coffee Association of Canada. (2003). *Coffee in Canada.* Retrieved from http://www.coffeeassoc.com/coffeeincanada.htm

Elliott, Charlene. (2001). Consuming caffeine: The discourse of Starbucks and coffee. *Consumption, Markets and Culture, 4*(4), 369–382.

Finance and economics: Burgers or beans? The Starbucks index. (2004, January 17). *The Economist, 370*(8358), p. 75.

Foster, Lauren. (2004, March 26). Battles brew in clash of the coffee makers. *Financial Times*, p. 10.

Germany overturns colour practices. (1999, July/August). *Managing Intellectual Property, 91*, 6.

Golding, Peter, and Phil Harris. (Eds.). (1997). *Beyond cultural imperialism.* London: Sage.

Harvey, David. (1992). *The condition of postmodernity.* Cambridge, England: Blackwell.

Howes, David (Ed.). (1996). *Cross-cultural consumption: Global markets, local realities.* New York: Routledge.

ICO (International Coffee Organization). (2004, September 9). *The story of coffee.* Retrieved from http://dev.ico.org/coffee_story.asp

James, R. (1996). Trademark Law—Lanham trademark act of 1946. *Duquesne Law Review, 34*(2), 419–434.

Jameson, Fredric. (1991). *Postmodernism; or, the cultural logic of late capitalism.* Durham, NC: Duke University Press.

Leiss, William, Stephen Kline, and Sut Jhally. (1990). *Social communication in advertising.* Scarborough, ON: Nelson.

Linn, Allison. (2004, April 25). When beans must be best: Rapid growth forces chain to pursue more sources of quality coffee. *Houston Chronicle*, p. 3.

MacLeod, Ian. (1997, May 7). Beans with a premium: Rich exotica of specialty coffees sweeps continent. *Hamilton Spectator*, p. B4.

Macrae, Chris. (1991). *World class brands*. Workingham, England: Addison-Wesley.

Mattelart, A. (1996). *The invention of communication*. Minneapolis: University of Minnesota Press.

Mintz, Sidney. (1985). *Sweetness and power*. New York: Viking.

Naiman, Sandy. (1995, February 26). Spilling the beans. *Toronto Sun*, p. 52.

Pendergrast, Mark. (1999). *Uncommon grounds*. New York: Basic Books.

Rogers, Tim. (2004, April 13). Small coffee brewers try to redefine fair trade. *The Christian Science Monitor*.

Said, Edward. (1978). *Orientalism*. New York: Vintage.

———. (1993). *Culture and imperialism*. New York: Vintage.

Starbucks Coffee Company. (1998). *The world of coffee* [Brochure].

———. (2002). *The world of coffee: A guide to Starbucks whole bean selections* [Brochure].

———. (2003a). *Commitment to origins* [Brochure].

———. (2003b). *Make it your drink: A guide to Starbucks beverages* [Promotional booklet].

———. (2004, March 30). Starbucks recognized as one of the most valued global brands. [Press release]. Retrieved from http://www.starbucks.com

Starbucks validates commitment to transparency in new corporate social responsibility annual report. (2004, April 7). *Business Wire*.

Trouble brewing for "fair trade" coffee. (2004, April 21). *Voice of America Press Releases and Documents*.

5

Good Kids/Bad Kids: What's a Culture to Do?

Eileen Saunders
Carleton University

Contemporary culture is characterized by a strong ambivalence toward children. On the one hand, as David Buckingham (2000) notes, "children are increasingly seen as threatened and endangered" (p. 3). We find recent evidence of this in Canada, in round-the-clock reporting on the abduction and murder of schoolgirls Cecilia Zhang and Holly Jones and in provincial inquiries into cases in which the social services system failed to protect children at risk. What underlies this perception is generally an image of the child as innocent, vulnerable, uncontaminated, and, most important, in need of adult protection. Indeed, the child represents the archetypal innocent and the archetypal victim.

On the other hand, "children are also increasingly perceived as a threat to the rest of us as violent, anti-social and sexually precocious" (Buckingham, 2000, p. 3). In Canada, there have been public calls for tougher measures to curb crime by young people and for more punitive approaches to dealing with young offenders.

This second construction is accompanied by an underlying image of the uncontrollable, uncivilized child—the child who lacks internal discipline, feelings, or empathy and therefore requires external controls. Such a perception is fuelled by events like the 1999 Columbine massacre, in which two teenagers killed 12 classmates and a teacher in their Littleton, Colorado, high school before taking their own lives. In response to the Columbine massacre and other murders committed by teens that followed it, we have become increasingly fearful of the "terror of adolescence" (Schissel, 1997, p. 11).

Interestingly, as Oswell (1998) points out, we shift our language depending on the particular "construction" of the child that we are employing:

> Whereas those in danger are constituted as "children," those deemed dangerous are quite clearly constituted as "youth." The category of "youth" is deployed when young people are seen to no longer perform the proper modes of conduct of "childhood." (p. 38)

In a similar fashion, children are also constructed as either "victims" or "threats." Oswell cites the infamous and tragic 1993 murder, in Britain, of a toddler named James Bulger at the hands of two 10-year-old boys. Press coverage of the case consistently referred to the boys as "youths," despite their age. One might compare this with the outcry against Calvin Klein Inc. in 1995, when the company launched a controversial ad campaign for CK jeans that featured scantily clad young models in a sexually provocative context. A storm of criticism ensued, and the company was eventually forced to withdraw the $6-million campaign. As Tucker (1996) has shown, the frame used to "define" the controversy was that of child pornography; the ads were framed as being exploitative of innocent victims, despite the fact that all the models were over 18.

So, youths become children or children become youths not based on any firm or fast biological definition of childhood or adolescence, or because of any fixed cultural meaning of either concept. There is a broader set of interests and concerns at play.

The "constructionist" understanding of the categories of childhood and youth stands in opposition to earlier "naturalistic" understandings that relied on markers such as biological age or were linked to stages of physical and cognitive development. This approach posited a universal model of childhood. Ariès (1962) and other historians laid the foundation for questioning such a model by demonstrating that the "idea" of childhood did not emerge in Europe until after the 15th century—a claim that challenged both the biological understandings of childhood and the cross-cultural implications of naturalistic models. Ariès also argued that the idea of *adolescence* appeared even later. It is only during the 18th century that we begin to detect a period of transition between childhood and adulthood.

If we start to think of childhood or adolescence as something "constructed," inevitable questions arise: Constructed how? By whom? Where? The notion of construction is quite simple. At different times and in different contexts, we think about and speak about children and youths in different ways. These ways then connect to how we respond to children as individuals, how we codify our understanding of them in law and in social policy, and how we represent them in public imagery. These ideas are found in different places. For example, psychology is one location in which ideas about childhood emerge, and from which they are circulated through academic journals, advice books for parents, and even daytime talk shows. The family is another location; how parents think about children or teens might differ quite dramatically from what a child psychologist would say, and we might find considerable differences in families across different class, racial, or ethnic communities. Each offers a constructed form of knowledge about childhood and adolescence.

The different discourses circulating in society about childhood and adolescence are not independent of one another. Academic or scholarly discourses exist alongside and interconnect with other public discourses. For example, there has been much media attention of late to the increase in childhood obesity and the decrease in the amount of time young people devote to physical activity. Worried parents, teachers, public health officials, and daytime talk-show hosts point with escalating alarm to the signs of a generation gone to fat. In such "media-enhanced social 'crises,' educators and parents, governments, the public, and advocacy groups look to scientific research to explain and solve social problems" (Luke, 1990, p. 1). Medical practitioners are called upon to provide "expert" advice to worried parents; sociologists are asked to describe the effect of decreased "family time" on children's physical activity; and communication researchers are sought out to provide the link between television or video games and decreased physical activity. Each offers an outline of the problem and a solution to the "crisis" (e.g., reducing high-fat snacks or setting time limits on television viewing).

KIDS AND MEDIA: CONTEXTUALIZING DISCOURSES

The idea of linking popular culture to widespread concern about children is hardly new. It has become commonplace to point out that 6000 years ago, the Greek philosopher Plato cited the threat posed to vulnerable young people by poets. Many researchers have noted the tendency to treat each new technology and each emergent cultural innovation with alarm, and to predict dire consequences for the young and for society. In an interesting historical investigation, Springhall (1998) details the public outcry in Victorian England against penny theatre (cheap, unlicensed entertainment for working children usually held in empty warehouses or workshops) and the association drawn between this form of entertainment and juvenile crime (pp. 11–37). In the early part of the 20th century, social concerns focused on the "movie problem"—the perception that children were spending too much time at daytime cinema (see Luke, 1990, pp. 31–44). Educators worried about the effect on academic performance, while parents were anxious about the "moral health" of their children. This concern was followed in subsequent decades by a succession of "scares" linked to radio, comic books, television, music videos, video games, Internet chat rooms, action animation series—the list could go on. While each scare has its own unique characteristics and its own predictions of dire consequences for the youthful audience, all of them share a strong moralistic argument about how popular culture threatens the moral fibre of the young. However, as Springhall (1998) pointedly suggests, "Media or **moral panics** often tell us a great deal more about adult anxieties, fear of the future, of technological change and the erosion of moral absolutes than about the nature of juvenile misbehaviour" (pp. 160–161).

The intersecting and shifting discourses of the "child in danger" and the "dangerous child" are reflected across a range of popular culture forms, from film and television news to talk shows and raves. These two opposing constructions of the child as both innocent and dangerous can be understood in greater detail by examining two specific communication debates. The first concerns advertising and children; the second is about media violence and children.

THE CONSUMING CHILD

Picture this typical scene. Six-year-old Sarah exits her school bus at the end of a busy school week. Happy that the weekend lies ahead, she pauses to straighten her SpongeBob SquarePants sweatshirt, then picks up her Teletubbies lunch box in one hand and her Harry Potter knapsack in the other. As she heads up her front steps, she spots her bright pink Barbie skipping rope and Bart Simpson sidewalk chalk on the driveway. Once inside she heads upstairs to her Tigger-wallpapered room with the Winnie-the-Pooh duvet. Later she and her mother head out to their local theatre to see the Disney hit, *Tarzan*. They stop on the way for supper at McDonald's, where Sarah is delighted to find a plastic Jane figurine along with her hamburger.

What's the problem with this seemingly innocent scenario? For critics of such scenes, the problem comes down to one simple charge: the commercial exploitation of children in their role as consumers. The idea of children as consumers, and the active targeting of them by advertisers who see them as a potential audience is relatively recent. As Kapur (1999) notes, "The most significant change in the cultural notion of childhood in the last decades of the twentieth century has been the construction of children as consumers" (p. 124). This is not to suggest that children did not constitute a market prior to this period; rather, "they were not sold to directly. Instead they were imagined as untainted receivers of gifts" (Kapur, 1999, p. 125). Their value to advertisers and product manufacturers was in the influence they brought to bear on parents and extended family members in purchase decisions. They constituted, in other words, an important "market of influence," possessing what Buckingham (2000) calls "pester power" (p. 147).

While this aspect of children as a market continues, there has also been a shift toward targeting children directly. Several factors were involved in the recognition of children as an important "primary market" (see McNeal, 1992, pp. 22–36). The economic and demographic expansion of the postwar 1950s gave teenagers real spending power. The identification of a preteen market came soon after, and by the late 1960s trade publications began to identify children as a separate market (McNeal, 1992, p. 5). The first ad agency to specialize in targeting children, Helitzer, Waring and Wayne, opened in the United States in 1963 (Pecora, 1998, p. 17). Other sociological changes contributed to a new appreciation of the child consumer. Fewer children per family, an increase in discretionary incomes, the emergence of dual-income families, and more single-parent families have all increased the influence of children in consumer decisions (McNeal, 1992, p. 7). Finally, technological innovations ranging from television to the **Internet** have increased the access of advertisers to the child audience.

POLITICAL ECONOMY AND THE CHILD CONSUMER

Despite the fact that advertisers had discovered the importance of children to product manufacturers long before, little attention was given to this area by communication researchers until the 1970s. When communication research did turn its attention to this issue, it was largely framed within the context of the *effects tradition*. In this approach, then dominant within North American social science, the research conducted was primarily concerned with television advertising. The short-term behavioural effects of the child–media relation were the focus, with research conducted on such issues as patterns of attention, capacity for comprehension, and behavioural and attitudinal influences. In addition, such research characterized children as being more vulnerable than adults to the effects of advertising.

Political economic discourse is different from the effects tradition while maintaining strong ties to it. It focuses on a different order of questions but, like the effects tradition, still frames the "child as consumer" debate in a way that views the child as victim.

Political economic analyses generally begin with an attempt to understand popular culture as an industry that is driven by economic forces and that has important consequences for how we think about the world. Analysis of advertising and children is framed in terms of understanding the particular economic forces that shape the relations of children to consumption, with a view to determining the economic and cultural causes and consequences of this relation. Some political economic work in this field is focused more on the institutional and economic forces that structure children's culture (see, for example, Englehardt, 1986; Pecora, 1998), while other work (notably Kline, 1993) focuses on the cultural consequences.

One of the first arguments made by critics who adopt a political economic approach is that children and their spending power have become an increasingly important force in the market. When combined with influence spending (the "pester" effect), the direct purchasing power of children adds up to considerable profit. Research conducted by James McNeal suggests that the under-14 age group accounts for $600 billion in annual influence spending (cited in Graydon, 2003: F8). Not surprisingly, advertisers have responded with increased investment in the kiddie sector. As Graydon notes, they have increased their spending on advertising to young people from $6.9 billion in 1992 to $12 billion in 2003 in the U.S. alone (Ibid.). One of the most recent niche markets to emerge and capture the eye of advertisers is the "tween" market (children aged 9–14), who number over 2.4 million in Canada; according to research conducted by YTV, "today's tweens represent almost $1.4 billion worth of spending power" and "[their] financial clout will continue to grow" (Steinberg, 1998, p. 60). In addition to profiting from the consumer choices made by this group, advertisers are keen to develop their brand loyalty and secure them as future consumers as well. Successful companies are those that can "capture" the consumer as early as possible: Baby Gap grows into GapKids and, once a teen, graduates to The Gap. The challenge for advertisers is to target the child audience in a manner that transforms market potential into consumer spending.

A second argument links the role of children as consumers to two key industries: toys and television. Briefly, the argument is that transformations in the marketing of toys to children go hand in hand with transformations in the nature of television programming for children—and both are subject to the economic imperatives of the marketplace. As Pecora (1998) succinctly notes:

> Over time these two industries have come together in a symbiotic relationship that blurs the lines between program and product. On television, programs offer the toy industry advertisements for characters and the toys present the entertainment industry with readily identifiable characters. (p. 40)

Most critics agree that the factors involved in this shift are both economic and political in nature. The increased competitiveness of the television industry, brought about by the emergence of cable networks and independent stations alongside the major networks, meant more competition for children's audiences, programming, and advertising dollars. In Canada, this increased competition developed toward the end of the 1980s when Shaw Cablesystems Inc. was given a licence to develop YTV, a new cable channel that styled itself on the U.S. cable channel Nickelodeon and was to enjoy future success. "By the mid-1990s, YTV was often winning the ratings war in the 2–14 age group, and established broadcasters (especially Global) were playing catch-up, imitating the station's look and style in their kid-vid time slots" ("TV Advertising," 1996, p. C2).

In the early 1980s, there was an effective deregulation of children's advertising and programming by the U.S. Federal Communications Commission (FCC). The relaxation of earlier restrictions on the amount of ad time on children's television and the use of promotional toys for product tie-ins made children's television a much more attractive site for advertisers. Canadian regulators, however, kept such restrictions in place for Canadian networks. According to Kline (1993), "Canadian policy makers blithely ignored what was happening, overlooking the new infrastructure (satellite, cable, video) which transformed the distribution of children's culture in Canada" (p. 272).

In the same period, the toy industry was shifting in a number of ways. Toy manufacturing, through mergers and acquisitions, became increasingly consolidated in the hands of a small number of large, multinational corporations. In 1980, three manufacturers—Hasbro, Mattel, and Coleco—controlled only 20 percent of the market; by 1992, the market was effectively controlled by five or six companies (Pecora, 1998, p. 48). At the same time, there were changes in the way toys were marketed. Toy buying became "deseasonalized" in the sense that "toy purchases became a weekly or monthly occurrence rather than a twice-a-year event occurring at Christmas and birthdays" (Seiter, 1993, pp. 196–197). Pecora (1998) adds that the emergence of large transnational retail outlets like Toys "R" Us aids this constant cycle of toy consumption by providing a stable outlet for year-round purchasing; annual revenues went from $200 million (U.S.) in 1975 to $7.2 billion in 1992 (p. 50). Finally, as part of a strategy to increase sales, the toy industry adopted "line extensions." So Barbie acquires a new sister or a new career, while Spider-Man gets a new villain to vanquish. According to Seiter (1993), line extensions offer a simple and effective way of building on children's established taste preferences.

The crucial link between shifts in the children's television industry and those in the toy industry is found in the development of character licensing, a technique Englehardt (1986) has dubbed "the strawberry shortcake strategy." The deregulation of the television industry, in conjunction with a search for ever-increasing expansion in the toy market, created an environment ripe for changes in marketing techniques aimed at children. The Strawberry Shortcake doll, first produced in 1980, was merely one of the early products introduced to take advantage of this new marketing environment. The parent company behind the doll's introduction, American Greeting Cards Ltd., created for the doll and its companions a marketing plan that involved everything from the actual dolls, to bedsheets and clothes, to (most important of all) a series of animated televisions programs that effectively served as 30-minute commercials for the range of licensed goods (Englehardt, 1986). Imitators quickly followed, and children's television was flooded with program-length commercials for a wide range of toys, including My Little Pony, the Care Bears, Teenage Mutant Ninja Turtles, and She-Ra. The annual revenues raised through licensing **royalties** skyrocketed from $9.9 billion (U.S.) in 1980 to about $70 billion in 1990 (Pecora, 1998, pp. 56–57).

The licensing of popular characters from children's popular culture is not a new phenomenon. From Raggedy Ann to Shirley Temple to Davey Crockett, there has been a history of successful "characters" (and, indeed, Walt Disney was a master at licensing his own characters). What is new is both the extent to which children's culture is dominated by licensed characters/toys—from books, to movies, to video games—and the manner in which they are introduced. As Kline (1989) notes, "This combination of television and playthings in a comprehensive and integrated market gambit reversed the time-honored marketing approaches of spin-offs and changed the way kids' cultural products are developed" (p. 307). Toys are now introduced at the same time as or before the television series and movies on which they are based. Before the latest kid's movie is released, the toys, clothing, and books based on the movie are already on store shelves.

One effect of this new marketing approach is the squeezing of non-licensed toys from the market. As Leonhardt and Kerwin show, in 1997 about 50 percent of all toys sold were licensed products from film or television (cited in Kapur, 1999, p. 128). Consider as well the licensed-toy sales projections in 1995 for three U.S. "characters": $300 million (U.S.) for Power Rangers toys, $130 million for Batman merchandise, and $100 million for products related to the Disney film *Pocahontas*. The difference between those figures and the projected $50 million in sales for the most popular non-licensed toy that year—the flying doll, Sky Dancer—demonstrates the profits at stake for toy companies and the entertainment industry (Pereira and Bannon, 1995). It should come as no surprise, then, that toy companies have come to exert more control over the production of children's popular culture, whether through commissioning animated television series directly or through influencing the kinds of characters developed. Here is an example:

> A Disney animator says one scene in *Pocahontas*—when the raccoon Meeko briefly braids the star's hair—was created after a suggestion from Mattel, which wanted to be able to make Braided Beauty Pocahontas dolls. . . . For *Batman Forever*, Kenner got Warner Bros. to put the Riddler in tights because baggy pants don't look good on action figures, said Rick Watkins, a former Kenner toy-development manager. (Pereira and Bannon, 1995, p. A21)

SELLING INNOCENCE?

One might ask, where is the harm? According to political economists of communication, the problem lies in the colonization of children's play and children's imaginations (Kline, 1993). Toy culture and entertainment industries are dominated by megacorporations that seek to lower risk and enhance profit margins. The result is that the shaping of children's popular culture—from story lines, to personality characteristics, to production quality—is at the mercy of business interests. According to Pecora, "Mutually beneficial arrangements bring about a culture of play driven by characters available at Toys "R" Us, not creative imagination" (1998, p. 60).

Children's play, Kline argues, is shaped by marketing factors that lead to a highly "ritualized" form of play and a prepackaged set of scripts; both what children play with and how they play is a consequence of market forces. In the end, this arrangement threatens the very innocence of childhood.

The view of the child as innocent prey and the market as an all-powerful and manipulative corrupter translates into a policy position that seeks to restrict access of commercial interests to children. Political economy suggests a discourse of protection, a call to adults to shield their young from the market. The self-regulatory codes already in place in the industry[1] are seen as largely ineffective and easily circumvented. While policy alternatives are seldom directly detailed, there is a generalized call for radical change in favour of noncommercial arrangements—what Kline labels "a new framework for the culture industries" (1993, p. 350).

At first glance, such initiatives appear persuasive. But they depend on some problematic assumptions about the *child* and about *children's culture*. Regarding the child, political economic analyses imply a passive and vulnerable viewer who has no cognitive defences against the powerful tactics of advertisers. Also implicit in this model is a more traditional, behaviourist view of how children react to advertising. The vulnerable child is exposed to the powerful machinery of toy marketing in conjunction with popular culture industries and the unmediated effect is found in a spiral of escalating consumerism and diminished childhoods.

Yet the evidence is not conclusive. We know from developmental research that even very young children can distinguish ad content from program content and understand the persuasive intent of an ad (see John, 1999). Also, as Buckingham (2000) points out, the available research does not support the link between exposure to advertising and cultivation of "consumerist" values; one's family and friends appear to have more influence in that respect (p. 151). Finally, as Seiter (1993) notes from her work with children, children are more active than we give them credit for in the way they interact with cultural objects; they do not simply *react* but instead "create their own meanings from the stories and symbols of consumer culture" (p. 10).

Regarding the conception of children's culture, an underlying theme of political economic work is a moral condemnation of mass culture for children. Kline (1993), for example, suggests that "[t]he marketplace will never inspire children with high ideals or positive images of the personality, provide stories which help them adjust to life's tribulations or promote play activities that are most help to their maturation" (p. 350). But, as Seiter (1993) notes of such arguments, "intellectuals tend to exclude the categories of 'quality' toys and 'creative' play, that is, the kinds of goods and services targeted at their own children" (p. 194). In other words, there is a line drawn between "good" toys sold in independent specialty toy shops (think Playmobil sets) and "bad" toys sold in retail chains like Toys "R" Us (think Barbie). In fact, Seiter (1993) argues, they are simply different segments of the same market, reflecting class differences rather than consequences for creativity and imagination.

Finally, in conjunction with the assumption of the child as vulnerable and the market as corrupting, the policy discourse of restricting children from the marketplace seems shortsighted at best. As Buckingham (2000) notes:

> Attempting to create a "safe space" for children, in which they will remain uncontaminated by commercial influences as is the case in current moves to ban advertising from children's television is to retreat into an unreal fantasy world. Rather than seeking to protect children from the marketplace, we need to find ways of preparing them to deal with it. (pp. 166–167)

In Buckingham's view, children can be so prepared through a combination of education and media literacy as well as by safeguarding their "rights" as consumers. This view represents a shift in conceptions of the child, from hapless victim to active participant in popular culture. With the change in conceptions of the child, the solution shifts from tougher controls on cultural producers to education of the child consumer, or, more specifically, providing the tools he or she needs to be a critical consumer.

THE VIOLENT CHILD

Headlines on youth and violence over the past decade have had the same undertones of menace. To cite but a few examples: "The Columbine Effect" (*Time*, March 19, 2001); "Kids Who Kill" (*Maclean's*, August 1994); "The Dark Side of Teen Culture" (*Chatelaine*, May 1993); "The Trouble with Teens" (*Maclean's*, March 2004). The manifestations of increased violence among the young appear to be everywhere.

Yet, there is considerable debate over the issue of whether contemporary youths are, in reality, more or less violent than their predecessors. On the one hand, the official crime statistics reveal a steady drop in youth crime and violence over the past decade. On the other hand, some might argue that the official crime rate fails to register many incidents, either because victims are too scared to report them or because they are handled through informal channels. Whatever one's position on the facts, it is clear that the *perception* of greater youth violence is growing, and that the media have an important role to play in this outcome. The result is that, at some point, the appearance of youth violence is linked to media violence, and a public outcry for the media to "clean up their act" soon follows. Commissions of inquiry are formed, public hearings are held, and the entertainment industry is pitted against regulators and parents in a battle to define the "youth problem." Public calls to action are usually followed by government promises to get tough on media violence and by threats to impose new codes of conduct for media.[2] Overwhelmingly, the relationship between media violence and violent children has been approached through a single model, the effects tradition, which proposes that "bad media = bad kids."

BEHAVIOURISM, LEARNING, AND VIOLENT KIDS

The debate about the effects of media violence on children can be traced to some of the earliest communication research. Writing in 1923, psychologist Joseph Geiger concluded that children learned both amoral messages and antisocial behaviour from movies (cited in Luke, 1990, p. 33). This link was further explored in the **Payne Fund Studies**, 12 volumes of research (published in 1933) on the effects of cinema on the child viewer. The link between media violence and real violence among the young became firmly established and was often resurrected over the decades, receiving even more support with the appearance of each new medium. It is not an exaggeration to suggest that more work has been published on this question than any other single issue in media research, and that questions about media/youth violence have been the subject of more government commissions of investigation than any other area.

The approach to the media/youth violence question was established early on. Indeed, the Payne Fund Studies were important in cementing the kinds of questions that were asked, or not asked, about children and media violence. This research "articulated particular concerns, conceptualized effects and produced a construct of the child" (Luke, 1990, p. 36), and in so doing established the parameters for later research. What is interesting about the Payne Fund Studies is that while questions were asked about such things as frequency of movie attendance, violent content, perception and retention, and emotional and behavioural response, nothing was asked about the economic structures of film or the social and historical context of the period. Rather, the research agenda is reflective of the more general effects tradition, in which media content is conceived of as "stimuli" and children are "measured" for their behavioural or attitudinal responses. As noted earlier, the effects tradition has been the dominant paradigm of most media research in North America throughout most of the last 75 years.

An effects model of media violence generally begins with the assumption that one can isolate and measure behavioural, attitudinal, and emotional variables and link them in a causal or correlative way to messages carried by media content. In other words, it offers some variation or refinement of the stimulus-response model, or *behaviourist* approach, in which media offer stimuli to which children respond. Over the years, the crude notion of *direct* or unmediated effects of media, which characterized much of the early work, was overtaken by concern with *indirect* or mediated effects.

A direct-effects approach (famously labelled the **hypodermic needle model** by Harold Lasswell) reflects the "classic" behaviourist approach that dominated North American psychology in the prewar period. Violent media messages were seen to serve as dangerous stimuli that had the same effect on all children who might be exposed to them.[3] This crude **behaviourism** was gradually replaced by social behaviourism, an approach that seeks mediating variables between the media and the receiver. Research in this area focuses on the factors that might qualify the power of the media over individuals, the kinds of individuals who are more susceptible to violent images, and the social categories (class, race, gender, etc.) that are more likely to become violent after media exposure. The object of research is to isolate these mediating variables so that one might predict the kinds of media situations and the types of children in which violence would be likely to be found. Nevertheless, the originating media message is still seen as the key factor in explaining why a child thinks, reacts, or behaves in a violent manner.

Various models have emerged over the years, under the general rubric of an effects tradition, to explain the process by which violent children emerge out of contact with violent media. All retain a focus on human experience as something that can be measured, quantified, predicted, and ultimately controlled if the right external factors are put in place. The details of the models are less important here than the general conclusions they offer about the impact of media in fuelling violence. The effects tradition continues to have a hold on the field of communication and on public discourse about violence and children. Some research has focused on the "aggressive cues" model. Pioneered by Berkowitz and his colleagues, this model seeks to find various factors, including cognitive skill differences among children, that stimulate children to acts of violence (see, for example, Berkowitz and Green, 1966). Other work adopts a "social learning" model, based on the early work of Bandura (1973), and attempts to isolate the variables that enhance or minimize the probability that a child will imitate or model aggressive behaviour seen in media. "Reinforcement" models analyze the extent to which violent media can strengthen existing predispositions to aggressive behaviour among certain types of children (see, for example, Josephson, 1987).

Some of the most widely known research is that of George Gerbner and his colleagues at the University of Pennsylvania. They propose a "cultivation" approach that attempts to link the quantity of violence on television to particular cultural attitudes toward violence. The gist of the argument is that a steady diet of media violence has consequences for how different groups think about violence; that is, television "cultivates" feelings and attitudes about violence in terms of who commits it, when it is legitimate, who the likely victims are, and so on. (See, for example, Gerbner, Gross, Morgan, and Signorielli, 1986.) To demonstrate the volume of violence children receive, Gerbner and his associates developed a "violence index" that tabulates the frequency of violent acts on television; the index is used annually to evaluate media performance in the United States. Though not a behaviourist explanation in the manner of the other models (Gerbner does not argue, for example, that media violence will fuel individual violence), this work does share an emphasis on the empirical measurement of both violence in the media and cultural attitudes.

Another factor to consider is the kind of evidence used by effects research to substantiate claims about media producing violent children. Two broad bodies of evidence are usually offered as "proof." The first type of evidence concerns the content of media, while the second type concerns the behaviour and attitudes of children. Content research generally focuses on establishing the volume and degree of violence found in different media sectors. This work is linked to audience research on the time children spend consuming media. The shock value of the statistics means they are regularly reported in the media: for example, we are told the average child will witness 8000 murders and 100,000 violent acts on television before leaving elementary school (Hamburg, cited in Bok, 1997, p. 188).

Evidence of children's behaviour and attitudes is gathered either through controlled laboratory experiments, which measure immediate short-term effects of violent stimuli under controlled conditions, or through field studies, which measure such things as viewing patterns and responses in more "natural" environments such as homes, daycare centres, and schools. Listed below are some of the key arguments made in the research:

- Children are exposed to heavy doses of media violence, and exposure increases with age.
- High exposure to violence is correlated with higher levels of violent behaviour and higher acceptance of violence as a legitimate response.

- The probability of imitating television violence increases when the violent role model is not punished.
- The probability of imitating violence increases when the child identifies with the violent hero.
- Heavy viewing of violence among young children is associated with a range of antisocial behaviour at later ages.
- Adolescent boys are more likely than adolescent girls to be affected by media violence.
- Some groups of children have been identified as more susceptible to the effects of media violence (in particular, visible-minority and immigrant children, low-income children, emotionally disturbed children, and abused children).

The link between public and academic discourses is particularly close in the case of media violence. Public-opinion polls regularly report parental concern over the amount of violence in media, and the public's belief that it contributes to violence in society.[4] The effects tradition has been closely aligned with calls for stricter controls on violent content. In almost all the commissions of inquiry established in the United States and Canada over the decades, effects research provided the "expert" evidence to support government action. In general, the policy positions aligned with an effects approach involve attempts to curb violence in children *by restricting their access* to violent media content, with the parent serving as the primary "enforcer" of controls. Among the policy measures aligned with this research are industry codes of conduct; ratings systems that evaluate violent content and display ratings through on-screen icons, package warnings, and viewer advisories; and technological devices designed to block access (**V-chips** installed in television sets, software blockers for computers, etc.). Whether these measures are actually effective is another matter. For example, a 1999 survey conducted in the United States found that parental supervision of television viewing has declined since 1997, and that only 38 percent of parents use television ratings to guide program selection.

FUELLING VIOLENCE?

The linking of bad kids with bad media has been repeated so often over the years—whether in government reports, press coverage, or talk shows—that it has almost achieved the status of "common sense." Yet, the assumptions on which this link is based are problematic. First, there are methodological problems in the research, including an overemphasis on short-term effects (which may not last over the long term), the artificial and hence unrealistic nature of the laboratory as a setting to predict violence in real life, and the confusion of correlation with causation.[5]

Second, this research tradition adopts a view of the child as "passive" and open to suggestion and manipulation in the face of the enormous power of the media, an assumption that stands in contradiction to the view of the child, held in cultural studies, as an active participant in interpreting media and constructing meaning. Meaning is not simply reducible to messages; it is not something "transmitted directly into the mind and thence the behaviour of the viewer" (Buckingham, 1993, p. 7). Rather, the child engages in a series of interpretive processes through which he or she constructs meaning (rather than just receiving messages) about the violence on the screen. Most important, children do not construct this meaning in some universal, predictable fashion.

A third key weakness is found in the way violent representations are selected for measurement and with the relative lack of attention to the contexts in which they appear (Kinder, 1999, p. 3). The idea that one can simply extract a violent act from the overall text and assume it is equivalent to other violent acts is seriously flawed. Does a violent act by a cartoon Spider-Man in vanquishing a villain equal a violent act by a character in *Kill Bill?* One cannot, in other words, easily identify violence as a simple and quantifiable attribute of media messages.

Finally, the most damning critique is that despite decades of research and repeated government commissions of inquiry, the evidence is neither definitive nor conclusive. In an exhaustive, and controversial, study published in 2002, Jonathan Freedman reviewed *all* of the previous research examining a "causal hypothesis" between exposure to film or television violence and increased aggression. His conclusion is that contrary to popular wisdom, the research evidence demonstrates that "exposure to media violence does not cause aggression, or if it does the effects are so weak that they cannot be detected and must therefore be vanishingly small" (2003, pp. 200–201).

And yet, despite the failure to find evidence of the link, and despite dropping rates of violent crime by the young, we continue to clamour for tighter controls on media violence. As Buckingham (2000) points out, "to seek evidence of 'the effects of media violence' is to persist in asking simplistic questions about complicated social issues" (p. 130).

CONCLUSION

There are two opposing constructions of the child in cultural discourse: one sees the child as pure, innocent, vulnerable, and in need of adult protection; the other sees the child as threatening, potentially violent, open to manipulation, and in need of adult control. These constructions are manifested across a range of debates in communications studies and can be illustrated by looking at two different theoretical perspectives: the political economic approach and the effects approach. Political economic work has focused on the corrupting influences of the market and their impact on childhood innocence, while effects research has detailed the ways in which violence in the media can unleash real violence by the young. One approach posits the child as victim, the other as threat. Each demonstrates the point that a theoretical position frames the way we look at any social issue; it leads us to make certain assumptions about individuals and audience behaviour, about causality and evidence, and about social policy.

There is overlapping ground between the political economic and effects constructions. Each begins with the assumption that there is something different about children and young people. In the case of political economy, children lack the cognitive skills or defences available to adults that would protect them from the effects of consumerism. In the case of violence effects research, there is something about media power over the young audience that makes them especially susceptible to violent "cues." Buckingham (2000) would argue that both views reflect a *pre*-social" definition of children (p. 14); in other words, the child is not yet fully formed or civilized. Furthermore, thinking of children as pre-social "effectively prevents any consideration of them as social beings, or indeed as citizens" (Buckingham, 2000, p. 15). This view is linked as well to a conception of the child as a passive receptor. According to this conception, children and young people are reactors rather than actors in popular culture.

It is interesting that both these approaches to communication research lead to policy positions that require exerting more control over children and youths. Through mechanisms that restrict access to cultural products or programming deemed offensive and/or exploitative, we attempt to limit the choices available to children and youths. Control is both centrally located in institutions of regulation (censor boards, licensing bodies, watchdog agencies, etc.) and dispersed in the form of parental controls (software blockers, V-chips, etc.).

Finally, we need to recognize that discourses about "children as innocent" and "children as threat" need to be connected also to questions of class, race, and gender. Media studies scholar Henry Jenkins characterizes the "innocent child" as follows:

> In our culture, the most persistent image of the innocent child is that of a white, blond-haired, blue-eyed boy and the markers of middleclassness, whiteness, and masculinity are read as standing for all children. (cited in Giroux, 2000, p. 5)

When we consider the "dangerous child," however, the markers of race, class, and gender work differently. As Giroux argues, "the notion of innocence does not apply to certain children and is being renegotiated for others" (2000, p. 8). In other words, the myths of innocence and danger that pervade our culture are not equally distributed across all sectors of childhood. This in itself is perhaps the best evidence for the argument that childhood as a separate developmental stage is a social concept that is constantly being constructed and reconstructed.

QUESTIONS

1. Identify a recent example of a media-induced "social crisis" about children or youths other than those cited in the chapter. What questions would you ask? How would you analyze it?
2. What are the major differences between Buckingham and Berkowitz in their characterizations of children?
3. If you were writing a code of ethics for children's television programming, what would it entail and why?
4. According to many critics, the global marketing of toys and popular culture by corporations like Toys "R" Us and Disney results in the disappearance of national cultures and a homogenization of children's play around the world. Do you agree or disagree? Give reasons for your answer.

NOTES

1. In English Canada, television advertising is governed by the voluntary Broadcast Code for Advertising to Children. In 1980, Quebec imposed tighter restrictions by banning, under the Consumer Protection Act, all advertisements directed at children under 13. Cable and satellite distribution, of course, undermine this type of measure.
2. In Canada, a crystallizing moment came in November 1992 when a petition against television violence was submitted to the House of Commons. Virginie Larivière, a Quebec teen whose younger sister had been murdered, was convinced that television violence was a key factor in this tragedy, and she collected over 1.3 million signatures on a petition calling for tougher government legislation.
3. An example of this type of research can be found even in the postwar period. Fredric Wertham's *Seduction of the Innocent* (1954) argued that comic book violence stimulated violent acts and attitudes in children who read them. A useful review of his arguments can be found in Lowery and Defleur (1995).
4. One U.S. poll reported that 80 percent of Americans think television violence is harmful to society, while in Canada four out of five women think television fuels more violence in society (cited in Media Awareness Network, Statistics and Public Opinion, at http://www.media-awareness.ca).
5. In other words, proving that aggressive kids also consume heavy doses of violent media tells us nothing about the *cause* of their aggression.

REFERENCES

Ariès, Philippe. (1962). *Centuries of childhood: A social history of family life*. New York: Knopf.

Bandura, Albert. (1973). *Aggression: A social learning analysis*. Englewood Cliffs, NJ: Prentice-Hall.

Berkowitz, L., and R.G. Green. (1966). Film violence and the cue properties of available targets. *Journal of Personality and Social Psychology, 3*, 525–530.

Bok, Sissela. (1997). TV violence, children and the press. In Pippa Norris (Ed.), *Politics and the press* (pp. 185–216). London: Lynne Rienner Publishers.

Buckingham, David (Ed.). (1993). *Reading audiences: Young people and the media*. Manchester, England: University Press.

———. (2000). *After the death of childhood*. Cambridge, England: Polity Press.

Englehardt, Tom. (1986). The strawberry shortcake strategy. In Todd Gitlin (Ed.), *Watching television* (pp. 68–110). New York: Pantheon Books.

Freedman, Jonathan L. (2002). *Media violence and its effect on aggression: Assessing the scientific evidence*. Toronto: University of Toronto Press.

Gerbner, George, Larry Gross, Michael Morgan, and Nancy Signorielli. (1986). Living with television: The dynamics of the cultivation process. In J. Bryant and D. Zillman (Eds.), *Perspectives on media effects* (pp. 17–39). Hillsdale, NJ: Lawrence Erlbaum.

Giroux, Henry A. (2000). *Stealing innocence: Youth, corporate power and the politics of culture*. New York: St. Martin's Press.

Graydon, Shari. (2003, November 29). Pester Power: Marketing's new weapon. *The Globe and Mail*, p. F8.

John, Deborah Roedder. (1999). Through the eyes of a child: Children's knowledge and understanding of advertising. In C. Macklin and Les Carlson (Eds.), *Advertising to children: Concepts and controversies* (pp. 3–36). London: Sage.

Josephson, Wendy L. (1987). Television violence and children's aggression: Testing the priming, social script and disinhibition predictions. *Journal of Personality and Social Psychology, 53*, 882–890.

Kapur, Jyotsna. (1999). Out of control: Television and the transformation of childhood in late capitalism. In Marsha Kinder (Ed.), *Kids' media culture* (pp. 122–136). Durham, NC: Duke University Press.

Kinder, Marsha (Ed.). (1999). *Kids' media culture*. Durham, NC: Duke University Press.

Kline, Stephen. (1989). Limits to the imagination: Marketing and children's culture. In Ian Angus and Sut Jhally (Eds.), *Cultural politics in contemporary America* (pp. 299–316). London: Routledge.

———. (1993). *Out of the garden*. Toronto: Garamond Press.

Lowery, Shearon and Melvin L. Defleur. (1995). *Milestones in mass communication research* (3rd ed.). White Plains, NY: Longman.

Luke, Carmen. (1990). *Constructing the child viewer.* New York: Praeger.

McNeal, James U. (1992). *Kids as customers.* New York: Lexington Books.

Oswell, David. (1998). A question of belonging: Television, youth and the domestic. In Tracy Skelton and Gill Valentine (Eds.), *Cool places: Geographies of youth cultures* (pp. 35–49). London: Routledge.

Pecora, Norma. (1998). *The business of children's entertainment.* New York: Guilford Publications.

Pereira, Joseph, and Lisa Bannon. (1995, September 12). Hollywood is major source of inspiration for new lines of toys. *The Globe and Mail*, p. A21.

Schissel, Bernard. (1997). *Blaming children: Youth crime, moral panic and the politics of hate.* Halifax, NS: Fernwood.

Seiter, Ellen. (1993). *Sold separately.* New Brunswick, NJ: Rutgers University Press.

Springhall, John. (1998). *Youth, popular culture and moral panics.* New York: St. Martin's Press.

Steinberg, Shawna. (1998, May 13). Have allowance; will transform economy. *Canadian Business*, 60.

Tucker, Lauren R. (1996). Calvin Klein jeans advertising: Kiddie porn or media ado about nothing? In Murray Pomerance and John Sakeris (Eds.), *Pictures of a generation on hold: Selected papers* (pp. 195–204). Toronto: Media Studies Working Group.

TV advertising for kids is like shooting fish in a barrel. (1996, December 7). *The Globe and Mail*, p. C2.

6

Youth Violence, Moral Panic, and the Canadian Media: News Coverage of School Shootings in the United States and Canada

Josh Greenberg
Carleton University

Brian Wilson
University of British Columbia

INTRODUCTION

> Whether Canadians like to admit it or not, Canada's war on crime, like the war on crime in many other countries and in other eras, is quickly becoming a war against youth ... we are on the verge of an acute "moral panic" in this country that, if allowed to continue, will result in the indictment of all adolescents.

—Schissel (1997, pp. 9–10)

Researchers interested in the study of youth and media typically contend that news portrayals of young people are unfair and inaccurate. The usual argument is that depictions of teenage violence, drug use, sexuality, and other adolescent social behaviours are overly dramatized and exaggerated, and are seldom accompanied by commentary about the complex circumstances within which these behaviours occur. These critiques are especially prominent following media coverage of spectacular incidents such as school shootings or bullying-inspired murders and suicides, when dramatic portrayals of the "troubled" and "troubling" behaviours of today's youth are especially prevalent. In other words, and as the above quotation by Bernard Schissel suggests, a **moral panic** about youth is sometimes created, a panic that might affect the way most or all youths are viewed and treated within various social institutions and settings, and a panic that might distract politicians, police, teachers, religious leaders, or parents from more pressing and realistic issues where youths are concerned.

It is important to acknowledge, however, that the evidence underlying critical studies of youth portrayals in the news is not without limitations. For example, many of these studies are based on American media coverage of events that occur in the United States, while in Canada the body of work is less developed; it might, therefore, be unwise to generalize about Canada based only on American examples. Also, research on media representations of youth only sometimes accounts for differences between or within media. Hence, the way in which ideologies associated with certain newspapers or television networks (i.e., are they right wing or left wing?) might be related to the nature of their coverage is only sometimes addressed. Finally, it is also worth considering the possibility that media portrayals of youth might actually be more balanced and informed than critics suggest, or that concepts like "moral panic" might be less applicable now than they may once have been.

The primary goal of this chapter is to make some way toward addressing these concerns, while at the same time reconsidering and reflecting on dominant ways of thinking about youth portrayals in the news. In section one, we discuss the theories and studies noted above, with a particular focus on "moral panics." And in section two, we describe some of the key findings from a study we conducted on Canadian newspaper coverage of two high-profile incidents of youth violence: the Columbine High School massacre (Littleton, Colorado), and the shooting that occurred at W.R. Myers Secondary School (Taber, Alberta), both in April 1999. We conclude with a reevaluation of existing theory and research on media coverage of youth-related issues.

THEORETICAL CONSIDERATIONS: YOUTH, MEDIA, AND MORAL PANICS

Attempts to explain and describe media reactions to perceived forms of youth deviance have often led scholars to the concept of "moral panic," a term first introduced by Stanley Cohen (1972) in his classic study, *Folk Devils and Moral Panics: The Creation of Mods and Rockers*. According to Cohen,

> Societies appear to be subject, every now and then, to periods of moral panic. A condition, episode, person or group of persons emerges to become defined as a threat to societal values and interests; its nature is presented in a stylized and stereotypical fashion by the mass media; the moral barricades are manned by editors, bishops, politicians and other right-thinking people; socially accredited experts pronounce their diagnosis and solutions; ways of coping are evolved or (more often) resorted to . . . Sometimes the panic passes over and is forgotten, except in folklore and collective memory; at other times it has more serious and long-lasting repercussions and might produce such changes as those in legal and social policy or even in the way society conceives itself. (p. 9)

A "moral panic" may occur, in other words, when news organizations, in consort with dominant groups such as police, religious authorities, and politicians, come to identify a threat posed by a person, group, or event(s) in a way that is exaggerated and sensational.

Formulating a similar approach, Stuart Hall and his colleagues—writing on the construction of a panic about street crimes by black youths in 1970s Britain—argued that moral panics are constructed when the ruling class wishes to distract the public from deeper problems in the political-economic system (Hall, Critcher, Jefferson, Clarke, and Roberts, 1978). Like Cohen, Hall et al. see the media as playing a crucial role in creating and sustaining moral panics. Journalists invest events and people with cultural significance, which is to say the media "define for the majority of the population what significant events are taking place, but, also . . . how to understand these events" (1978, pp. 56–57). However, insofar as news media play a central role as the main purveyors of representations of the social world, Hall et al. argue that the point of origin for a moral panic is located not in the media *per se*, but rather in the contradictions of capitalism. In times of economic crisis, they argue, the ruling classes steer the media away from examining economic problems and toward threats to social values by "troubled" or "troubling" individuals or groups (such as youths). Instead of being concerned about the "real causes" of unemployment and other problems rooted in broader decisions by governments and corporations, authorities exaggerate the threat posed by, among other things, street crimes committed by already marginalized social groups (e.g., black youth). The result, as Cohen prophesied, was that "more moral panics will be generated . . . because our society as presently structured will continue to generate problems for some of its members . . . and then condemn whatever solution these groups find" (1972, p. 204).

Notwithstanding important differences between these approaches to moral panic, the assumption underpinning both is that a moral panic contributes to *ideological* and *hegemonic* social relations between dominant and subordinate groups. In this context, the term "ideological" refers to the ways that the reality of a situation is somehow distorted or hidden from plain view when various social control agencies (e.g., police, government, the courts) work together to pursue their own interests, whether this entails legitimizing existing laws or advocating new ones, or to expand the power and influence of a particular profession in everyday life. The distortion that underscores ideological relationships is therefore engineered by and beneficial to those with power and influence. For example, a panic about youth crime is less likely the result of objective conditions or a pattern of dramatically increasing violence among youth than it is the result of strategic agenda-setting by powerful groups who are able to influence media reporting, and who have a vested interest in either distracting readers from more pressing societal issues or leading them to problematize others.

In addition to being ideological, moral panics are also "hegemonic." Following Gramsci's (1971) theory of hegemony as entailing the successful persuasion of subordinate groups to the moral, political, and cultural values and beliefs of dominant groups, moral panics become hegemonic when the dominant group's interpretation of an event or a situation (such as youth crime) not only seems like the only or most reasonable interpretation, but also effectively prevents any effort to challenge the logic or substance of that interpretation (and also the dominant group's authority). The media play a crucial role as a field in which hegemonic struggles occur, that is, where different groups with varying levels of political, economic, and cultural authority and resources attempt to win the hearts and minds of the public and to sway the public to see their position as the most obvious. This situation is distinct from societies where power is maintained coercively, and alternative perspectives are suppressed through force. According to many cultural theorists, hegemonic relationships are far more effective because they make social inequalities seem natural, and are thus less likely to be effectively challenged, if they are challenged at all.

There are many instances where media-driven moral panics about youth (and youth crime) can be seen to be both ideological and hegemonic. Acland (1995) offers the example of the youth crime problem sometimes being linked with the breakdown of the traditional family unit. Acland argues that in these cases, the breakdown is sometimes connected to a conservative discourse about the negative societal conse-quences of women's advancements in the workplace (referring to the idea that women are no longer "home with the kids" to the extent they once were, and that this disrupts the moral order and the reproduction of positive social values). Acland suggests that the concern about a "youth crime problem" is part and parcel of a broader backlash against the achievements of the feminist movement, such as daycare, legalized abor-tion, and pay equity (p. 143). Adams (1997) elaborates on this point by describing how, following WWII, pressures exerted by government, business, and civic organizations on women to return to their families ("giving back" factory jobs to men) were framed in relation to problems of juvenile delinquency and the need for women to be at home (p. 41). Finally, according to Springhall (1998), rather than informing us about the true nature of youth crime, media sponsored moral panics "tell us a great deal more about adult anxieties, fear of the future, of technological change and the erosion of moral absolutes" (p. 161; see also Schissel, 1997).

In what is to follow, we explore how Canadian news coverage framed the shoot-ings at Columbine High School and W.R. Myers Secondary School, and discuss the ideological and hegemonic nature of the coverage. In doing so, we are interested primarily in how the events were framed: what was the problem defined; what were its causes; were moral judgements made; and what can the coverage tell us about actual or likely outcomes or remedies?

METHODOLOGICAL CONSIDERATIONS: DATA-GATHERING, NEWS ANALYSIS, AND FRAMING

Our analysis focuses on news coverage of these shootings in three Canadian news-papers: *The Globe and Mail*, *National Post*, and *The Toronto Star*. We located the microfilm reels for each newspaper and collected every article published between

21 April (the day after the Columbine shootings) and 21 May 1999, which yielded a total sample of 218 reports, inclusive of both "hard" news and "opinion" news items.[1] Scholars interested in conducting a critical analysis of media coverage can utilize a variety of approaches and techniques. Researchers normally distinguish between two methods: Content analysis is used to "delineate trends, patterns and absences over large aggregates of texts" (Deacon, Pickering, Golding, and Murdock, 1999, p. 117). content analysis normally relies on the application of simple or advanced statistical techniques to create a "big picture" of how a particular issue or event has been covered. For example, this might entail identifying for each crime-related news article its location within the newspaper (e.g., front page or back page), the age of offender(s) mentioned in the article, the ethnicity and/or gender of the perpetrator(s) and victim(s), or the type of crime (e.g., assault, drug possession, etc.). Discourse analysis, on the other hand is principally concerned with examining the representation of ideologies or "codes" that a given report or larger body of texts may be said to signify. Discourse analysis is less concerned with assembling measurable data to "prove" what has happened than it is with demonstrating how language operates to make some points or perspectives more visible than others (see Fairclough, 1995). For example, what type of language is used to describe youth crime or crime prevention programs and thus codify them with meaning and significance? Metaphors such as "crime waves" and "war on crime" evoke themes that are embedded in popular memory and culture, and thus serve to link current events to other events, which may bear little or no resemblance or are unrelated to them.

Our goal in this paper is to strike a balance between content and discourse analysis. While we present some of our findings with the use of descriptive statistics, we attempt to explain these data in terms of their implications for how social problems like youth violence (and the policy solutions adults devise to deal with them) are represented ideologically. To do so, we treat each paragraph within a single news item as the primary unit of analysis. Because we are interested in knowing how news coverage diagnosed the causes for the shootings and what probable outcomes or remedies would or should arise, we code every paragraph in each of these reports "cause" or "effect." This allows us to assess whether news media attributed responsibility and blame for the killings to "personal troubles" (i.e., individual pathologies) or to the "public issues of social structure" (Mills, 1959). In terms of practice, this entailed our reading each news item numerous times and then discussing whether the paragraph under analysis explained or helped to explain what caused the shootings or what types of effects the shootings obtained.

To analyze the coverage we draw on the tradition of "frame analysis" (e.g. Entman, 1993). Frames refer to the mental constructs or *schemas* people use to place their experiences of a complex world into meaningful terms or categories. According to Robert Entman, framing essentially involves "selecting some aspects of a perceived reality [to] make them more salient in a communicating text, in such a way as to promote a particular problem definition, causal interpretation, moral evaluation, and/or treatment recommendation" (p. 52). Because individuals lack the capacity to fully understand the social world in its complexity, they rely upon media frames for guidance in assigning importance to one topic or interpretation over others. This is what Gaye Tuchman means when she writes that news frames "both produce and limit meaning" (1978, p. 209) and what Todd Gitlin refers to when he writes that frames "organize the world for journalists who report it and, in some important degree, for us who rely upon their reports" (1980, p. 7). Framing, in other words, entails a dual process of "encoding" and "decoding" in which preferred readings are highlighted by drawing upon dominant ideological themes prevalent in the broader culture, and in which news audiences attempt to *make meaning* by drawing on the aspects of the text that resonate with their own lived experience (Hay, 1995, pp. 205–206). Seen in this way, news texts are not ideological in themselves but only become ideological because of the way they are appropriated (p. 203). Hence, while frames exert a powerful influence on the formation and crystallization of opinions and beliefs, they cannot determine what a reader will believe to be true. This is because when individuals construct meaning about the world, they are influenced not only by the mass media, but by other factors, such as their own experiences, and conversations with co-workers, family, and friends. One way of describing the "contingent influence" of mass media is to note that while news media cannot tell readers *what to think*, they can powerfully suggest what to *think about*, and they provide clues about *how* to think (McCombs, 1997).

DATA ANALYSIS: FRAMING CAUSES AND EFFECTS

A key strategy in the framing of an issue or event is "saliency." Saliency means that a piece of information has the quality of being more noticeable, meaningful, or memorable to an audience (Entman, 1993). The decisions about whether to write a story, what the story will be about, and the location or placement it receives in the overall layout of the newspaper are reliable indicators of "issue saliency."

The data shown in Table 6.1 provide a snapshot of the overall level of issue saliency of the Columbine and W.R. Myers school shootings. All the newspapers studied accorded these incidents a high level of importance, publishing 64 (*The Globe*), 75 (*Post*), and 79 (*The Star*) articles during the one-month period of analysis.[2] Additionally, if we examine all the front pages and opinion items from all three papers (84/218 or 39 percent), we also observe that the shootings were treated as incidents demanding moral evaluation and judgment. And although the proportion of opinion items to total news reports in each newspaper (*The Globe* 27 percent; *Post* 24 percent; *The Star* 16 percent) is somewhat lower than we might expect given the contentious nature of the events, the total number of opinion items (*The Globe* 17; *Post* 18; *The Star* 13) is still impressive given the short duration of our sample.

TABLE 6.1   News Coverage of the Columbine and W.R. Myers School Shootings: Frequency Counts by Newspaper, News Type, and Location

	Front Page	All Hard News	Opinion Discourse*	TOTAL
The Globe and Mail	12	47	17	64
National Post	10	57	18	75
The Toronto Star	14	66	13	79
TOTAL (N)	36	170	48	218

*Opinion discourse counts include editorials, opinion columns, guest commentary, and cartoons.

Framing Causality

> Ever since people started talking about teenagers as a separate social and economic class, and ever since the discovery of that class was met with mass marketing of targeted forms of mass culture—comics, movies, magazines, TV shows, music, video games, Web sites—we've wanted to make causative connections between the culture kids consume and the horrors they commit. . . . It's a perpetual loop of incident and cause, cause and effect, effect and outrage. The characters and setting may change, but the script itself never seems to . . . there's a pattern in the way we insist on these relationships, a pattern that may reveal more about our need to find comfort in times of crisis than the reality of those crises themselves. (Pevere, 1999)

Among the many functions of a news frame is that of diagnosing the cause of an incident by identifying who or what is responsible for the problem. The data presented in Table 6.2 show the frequency and types of causal attributions for the shootings that were reported in all three newspapers.

What we find especially noteworthy about these data is that all three papers attributed causality less frequently to *individual* factors than to *social structural* factors (i.e., forces that operate beyond the direct power and control of the individual but that nevertheless affect the individual deeply). In particular, where the coverage attempted to identify the underlying causes for the shootings, the negative influence of mass media received the most attention overall (26 percent). Immediately following the Columbine shootings, the coverage focused squarely on the influence of media violence, linking the massacre to the putative effects of such popular movies as *The Matrix*, which features a scene where two of the lead characters, cloaked in black trench coats and equipped with an arsenal of firepower, open fire in a highly secured building, killing everyone and destroying everything; *Heathers*, a dark comedy depicting cliquish schools and out-of-touch parents and school administrators, which ends with the lead character attempting to blow up the school; and *Basketball Diaries*, in which the lead character experiences a drug-induced fantasy of gunning down his

TABLE 6.2 Attributions of Causality in News Coverage of School Shootings (by Percentage)

	The Globe & Mail	Post	The Star	TOTAL
Mass Media	29	27	23	26
Access to Guns	20	13	22	19
School Environment	16	10	15	14
Revenge/Retribution	9	10	10	9
Nazism	7	9	6	7
Poor Parenting	9	8	5	7
Mental Illness	4	13	3	6
Gothic Subculture	2	6	5	4
Government Cutbacks	3	1	5	3
Other	2	4	5	4
TOTAL (%)[a]	101	101	99	99
(N)	414	357	440	1211

Note: When more than one causal factor was identified in a single paragraph, each was separately counted.
[a]Columns do not add to 100 due to rounding.

classmates and teachers ("Film Parallels," 1999; "Some See Eerie Links," 1999; "Eerily Familiar," 1999). In addition to movies, popular music and the influence of bands like Marilyn Manson and the German techno group Rammstein (ominously linked to the neo-Nazi movement), as well as video games like Wolfenstein 3D, "where players are encouraged to act out their violent fantasies" by "dismembering monsters and gunning down people with an arsenal of weapons" (Gee, 1999) were also causally linked to these murders.

The second most frequent causal category was access to guns (19 percent). The shootings at Columbine served as a "trigger point" for expressions of nationalism that distinguished Canada as a peaceful and safe nation and identified the United States as more dangerous and violent. References to guns most often entailed comparisons between Americans who love their guns and Canadians who control them:

> South of the border, they're saying it again: We never thought it would happen here.... What do you mean, you never thought it would happen? ... Forget the "troubled teens" angle, the two killers' apparent devotion to the Goth subculture.... Forget their supposed racism, their disdain for athletes. You'll find that, or something similar in pretty much every high school in Canada, too.... They don't turn into killers. Because missing from the mix are two essential ingredients: Access to guns and the ingrained instinct to use them. ("Guns Don't Kill People," 1999)

> What could be more American than mom, apple pie, and a sawed-off shotgun? Despite the bloody massacre at Columbine

High School in Littleton, Colo., Americans' romance with their guns goes on. ("Right to Bear Arms," 1999)

Appealing as the Americans-and-their-guns theme may be, it could not explain what happened eight days later in Taber, Alberta. The latter event was, of course, less spectacular as the shooter fired only two rounds from a .22 calibre rifle, killing one and wounding another. The horrific and tragic nature of this incident notwithstanding, it paled in comparison to the bombs, sawed-off shotguns, and handguns used at Columbine. So with Canadian news media attributing the Columbine killings to the "typically American" obsession with guns, the causal frame had to be modified to fit the Alberta incident.

A close reading of the coverage suggests that this lack of fit was dealt with in two ways. First, the Alberta case was explained as a statistical anomaly that simply reinforced the importance of stricter gun control:

> Experts blame the [Columbine] killings on everything from bad parenting to bad music to bad clothes. We in Canada have the same parenting, music and clothes. . . . But, with one or two exceptions, the previous time a Canadian kid opened fire in his high school was nearly a quarter of a century ago. In the United States, there have been eight student shootings in the past two years, an average of one every three months. I like to think we've avoided a bloodbath each semester because Canadian kids have a harder time getting guns. . . . We have seven million guns in Canada. The U.S. has 230 million. (Wong, 1999)

The second way in which news coverage dealt with the apparent contradiction between the access-to-guns theme and the Canadian incident was to point to Alberta as the exception to the Canadian standard. And as the following quotation illustrates, this explanation was linked to the one above:

> No one wants to say it out loud around here, but people have begun fearing an awful truth: If a dreadful shooting like the one this week at the Taber high school had to happen anywhere in Canada, Alberta was a more likely place than most. The reason is the province's spirited gun culture. This is the province with greater gun ownership than any other. ("Gun Ownership in Alberta," 1999)

This was an exceptional explanation, however, as it only surfaced in two reports. And while the report cited above also included claims such as "gun control only serves to increase crime," it assembled the necessary statistics to lend credibility to the central theme of the report: Alberta's gun ownership levels (39 percent of households have at least one gun) far exceed the national average (26 percent), and Alberta has more than twice the number of gun-related deaths in children under 15 (0.9 per 100,000) than the national average (0.4 per 100,000).

Lastly, the coverage also attributed causality to the dynamics of the school environment (14 percent), although this was more frequently the case in the Columbine coverage. An article in *The Star*, for example, profiled one of the Colorado killers (Eric Harris) as "bright and energetic," and, like most boys his age, interested in "playing soccer and taking girls on dates." Harris was described as "a typical product of the American middle-class, ambitious for success and kind to those around him." But as the article then went on to explain, this is what he was like before moving to Littleton and enrolling in the "intensely competitive environment" at Columbine High:

> At Columbine, he was nothing special and the "jock" culture never fully took him into its embrace. . . . Cliquish animosity infected the school at every level. "It's a rat race to see who's more popular," said Alisa Basore, a senior student. "The jocks rule the school and think they own the world," said another. . . . The more ostracized they became, the more inseparable Harris and [Klebold] became. They started visiting neo-Nazi sites on the Internet, used the Hitler salute, and were devotees of German underground bands such (sic) KMFDM, whose full name roughly translates as "No Pity for the Majority."[3]

This picture of *social structural causality* was not uniform across these media, however. In both *The Globe* and *The Star*, the access-to-guns theme appeared in approximately one-fifth of the total paragraphs in each paper, whereas it featured in the *Post* only slightly more than 10 percent of the time. By contrast, the individual factor mental illness received next to no coverage in the *Globe* and the *Star*, while in the *Post* it was tied as the second most frequent (13 percent) causal variable. Noting these differences is important because it shows that these newspapers were not entirely in agreement about the underlying causes of the shootings. This is significant for a couple of reasons: First, it reminds us not to view news media as a monolith—research frequently paints "the media" with a broad brush as if it were a single institution, when in fact in Canada (as elsewhere) mass media can be diverse in both format and content (although oftentimes this is issue-specific). Second, since these three newspapers are among the most widely circulating in the country and have the ability to influence not only public opinion but also the opinions of policymakers, the diversity in how they framed the issue may have generated an equal diversity of remedies and effects in considering the problem of youth crime.

The Hierarchy of Responses

In this second part, we examine how the media framed the potential *responses to* the shootings—in other words, how it framed the ways the shootings would drive us to seek remedies or solutions that could help prevent similar events in the future and restore moral order, and/or how it provided advice to readers about steps for protecting themselves and their loved ones.

Among the most significant observations from Table 6.3 is the considerably lower total frequency count of paragraphs focused on responses (N = 479) as compared to causes (see Table 6.2 where N = 1211). It is also noteworthy that the *The Globe* (N = 72) provided far less coverage of responses (remedies and solutions) than either the *Post* (N = 151) or *The Star* (N = 255). Furthermore, when we look at the proportional values of responses to total paragraphs within each paper, effects/remedies paragraphs accounted for only 15 percent of the total in *The Globe* (72/486)[4], as compared to the *Post*'s 30 percent (151/508), and the *Star*'s 37 percent (255/695). Thirdly, when we look at the aggregate coverage, there does not appear to have been one overwhelmingly preferred response to the problem of youth violence. Indeed, a range of only 21 frequency counts separates the top four categories, which is quite significant given the reasonably large sample of 218 reports. What is revealing, however, are the *types* of responses these media reported, and the implications these have for understanding how social order is reconstructed in the aftermath of incidents that "shock" the society.

Of the total references to responses or remedies (N = 479), the coverage tended to focus mostly on discussions about whether the best way to prevent similar events from reoccurring was to (a) increase surveillance and security (23 percent),[5] (b) implement education reforms such as increased funding for guidance counsellors or after-school and anti-violence programming (21 percent), (c) restore traditional values (19 percent), or (d) introduce or reform gun control policies (17 percent).[6]

Although we noted the somewhat moderate levels of uniformity across these three newspapers in terms of attributing causality, there appears to have been less agreement on which responses or remedies were most desirable or likely to occur. When *The Globe* reported on responses or remedies it tended to place greater priority on calls for education reform (33 percent) and on a lament for the loss of traditional values (31 percent):

TABLE 6.3   **The Hierarchy of Responses in News Coverage of School Shootings (by Percentage)**

	The Globe & Mail	Post	The Star	TOTAL
Surveillance/Security	13	27	23	23
Education Reform	33	11	23	21
Traditional Values	31	25	12	19
Gun Control	6	21	20	17
Media Reform	3	5	16	11
Reform YOA	15	11	5	8
TOTAL (%)[a]	101	100	99	99
(N)	72	151	255	479

Note: When more than one effect was mentioned within the same paragraph, each was counted separately.
[a]Columns do not add to 100 due to rounding.

> We are less attached to more traditional institutions, such as our community or church. "There's a whole lot of confusion about norms and values," says Frank Graves, president of Ekos Research. "People feel things are moving too fast, that they can't cope, can't keep up, and that the core sources of decency and reverence are gone. Loyalty and trust are endangered species. . . . Indeed, this atmosphere of apprehension has had a rather incongruous impact on the family." . . . But how much are TV and technology to blame for this anxiety? Prof. Friedman acknowledge the age-old debate . . . "The media are to blame," he says. "It is the very fact of TV, its ubiquity, its power; its messages of mobility and consumption that erode traditional values." ("Social Distress," 1999)

For the *Post*, which is the most conservative paper in our sample, education reform was a fairly low-priority issue (11 percent) in contrast to more authoritarian themes such as traditional values (25 percent) and surveillance and security (27 percent):

> All we hear in the aftermath of the Littleton, Co., school massacre is that we need to revisit what triggers teen violence and reassess how we raise our children. William Moloney, the commissioner of the Department of Education in Colorado, said on the Fox News Channel, "there are no quick fixes." There are. Those guns and those bombs could not have made it through the front door of that high school if an armed guard with a metal detector had been standing there. (Morris, 1999)

When *The Star's* coverage referred to responses or solutions, these mostly concerned surveillance and security (23 percent), although here the emphasis was placed less on formal policing and more on vigilant social monitoring of troubled students, education reform (23 percent), and gun control (20 percent):

> The Trenchcoat Mafia students seem to fit the same pattern of alienation that some students in Toronto face. . . . The issue in this story is not whether they were Goth or they were this or that, it's that anyone can snap and we have to watch for that. . . . Students who don't seem to be fitting into a school setting have to be watched and treated delicately. ("Warning Signs," 1999)

The Littleton and Taber tragedies also created an "opportunity" for *The Star* to report on (some might say campaign for) the need for reversing recent cuts to public education funding, particularly after-school and anti-violence programs:

> There were three main messages from the group of students, politicians and youth workers gathered in a basement classroom of Jarvis C.I. yesterday: kids can help kids; school

tragedies like the one this week in Littleton, Colo., can happen here; and it's important to provide resources and support to preventative anti-violence programs. Organizations like L.O.V.E. (Leave Out ViolencE) and V.I.P (Violence Intervention Project), and YouCan, among others, all run independent of the Toronto district public and Catholic school boards. Their future is at risk . . . with education cuts most of these programs and after-school groups are also in jeopardy. ("L.O.V.E. Working to Prevent," 1999)

By far the most interesting and significant finding from our data analysis is the low aggregate value of paragraphs indicating that media reform (from censorship to funding media literacy programming) would be a likely response or desirable remedy.[7] This is significant because it illustrates a contradiction at the heart of the coverage: while the putative influences of movies, video games, music and (to a lesser extent) news coverage of violence were seen to be causal factors, this was a problem for which few, if any, solutions were readily available. Why were solutions seemingly available for causal factors such as access to guns and the school environment, and for weaker factors such as the home environment, while violence in the media, which was reported to be the strongest causal factor, yielded very little attention overall?

Our focus on news content to the exclusion of the social relationships underpinning news production precludes us from knowing for certain why some responses or remedies were more visible than others. For example, the minimal coverage of "media reform" might have been due to a strong lobbying effort on the part of the media industry (of which the press is a part) to discourage reporting of policy solutions (e.g., censorship, tighter regulations, etc.) that might limit or restrict media producers from making available programs for which there is strong market demand. It might also be due to the complexities of dealing with "the media problem": mass media are diverse in format and style, and it is indeed a slippery slope to call for regulations or restrictions on some kinds of media (e.g., violent video games and movies) but not others (e.g., news reporting of mass murders). And lastly, the notion that violent programming *causes* violent behaviour is a leap in logic that lacks reliable, systematic evidence. Anecdotally, it is certainly the case that *some* forms of violent media influence *some* adolescents to mimic what they see, read, and hear. Moreover, few would likely argue against the notion that media portrayal of youth violence is increasing in both frequency and intensity. Yet, as other research has shown, media portrayals of increasing youth violence are far out of step with "actual levels" of youth crime (Schissel, 1997). In other words, while more youths are being exposed to more mass-mediated violence, fewer youths are committing violent crimes. As David Buckingham argues, "to seek evidence of 'the effects of media violence' is to persist in asking simplistic questions about complicated social issues" (2000, p. 130).

CONCLUSION

Our primary goal in this chapter has been to illustrate the role news media play in constructing meaning about social problems such as youth violence. In exploring this issue, we took as a case study Canadian newspaper coverage of two high-profile school shootings, the mass murder of 15 students at Columbine High School in Littleton, Colorado, and the murder of 1 student at W.R. Myers Secondary School, in Taber, Alberta, in April of 1999.

News coverage of youth crime tends to follow a moral panic narrative in which events such as school shootings provide a tipping point for articulating collective anxieties about broader changes in the social structure. In the aftermath of incidents that disrupt the social order—and these events were excellent cases in point—moral entrepreneurs, such as police, religious authorities, or newspaper columnists, generally denounce both the troubled and troubling or the dangerous and endangered nature of youth, and call for restrictions on youths' actions and behaviours. Frequently, news coverage of youth-related crime tends to be ideological and hegemonic, distorting the reality of the situation (i.e., that youth crime rates are on the decline) by advancing definitions of the situation that benefit institutional authorities and reproduce their values and interests.[8]

The two most significant findings to emerge from our analysis pertain to the *likely* impact that high levels of issue attention had on public opinion, and the implications of this for framing the causes of youth violence and the likely or reasonable responses to it. First, these shootings achieved a high measure of issue saliency, which likely had the effect of leading readers to overestimate both the amount of youth violence that actually exists and the degree or seriousness of the problem. Despite the aforementioned reduction in official youth crime rates, news headlines such as "Parents may be scared of their kids, but who isn't" (Blatchford, 1999) suggests that youth violence is increasing in both severity and frequency.[9]

Secondly, each of these newspapers attributed causality more frequently to social structural issues than to personal problems or pathologies. By far the most popular causal factor was the dangerous effects of media violence on adolescents; however, the coverage was far less willing to endorse remedies or solutions for dealing with this problem. Instead, the most likely response or preferred remedy for the problem of youth violence was to increase security and expand the surveillance functions of schools to identify troubled youths before they become a problem. Improving education funding and restoring traditional values were also popular as responses/remedies, as were access to guns and the school environment as causal variables. Importantly, however, these categories varied across news formats, illustrating the importance of not speaking of "the media" as if it were a single, monolithic institutional structure.

We return here to our earlier claim that the findings presented in this study offer evidence that news coverage of youth crime is both ideological and hegemonic. The coverage is ideological in the sense that certain messages about youth crime are emphasized (e.g., that youth crime is on the rise), while others are barely detectable (e.g., that media institutions should be targeted in campaigns for change). Importantly, while some interpretations of youth crime are more prominent than others, the *more prominent interpretations are not necessarily "better" or "more reasonable" than other interpretations* (e.g., they are not better supported by research on youth and violence-prevention strategies). In this way, a certain set of ideas is circulated and preferred, while others remain on the margins. By defining issues in these (dominant) ways, certain groups benefit—especially media institutions themselves who (in the newspapers they produce) identify "the media" as contributing to some of the problems with "today's youth," but are not implored to change their ways by journalists—as our findings showed.

These messages are hegemonic because they would potentially mobilize readers to support the dominant perspectives that have been encoded by journalists and editors. The articles appearing in newspapers like *The Globe*, the *Post*, and *The Star* contribute to the shaping of popular opinion about youth crime-related issues (opinions consistent with the dominant messages offered by these news sources) because they are *subtle yet salient*—which is to say, the messages appear, in many cases, as "neutral" representations of reality, and yet, as we have shown, the contents of the articles and the frequency of certain kinds of representations would promote a narrowed selection of viewpoints. In this case, the media have gone some way toward securing consent for the view that youth are "troubled and troubling," and that there is an urgent need to do something to prevent (the continued increase of) youth violence.

As with all studies, there are important limitations in our analysis that the reader should keep in mind, and these are due primarily to the analytical techniques and procedures we used. Firstly, and most obviously, there is a temptation in writing and reading about media constructions of moral panic to attribute "malicious intentions" (Schissel, 1997, p. 99) to newsmakers. Indeed, because we have focused on just the content of news, it is important *not* to make assumptions about intentionality unless we are prepared to speak to reporters and other news professionals about what guides their decision-making when it comes to writing on social issues such as youth crime. News production is a complex and nuanced process where journalists operate with a limited degree of professional autonomy (Ericson, Baranek, and Chan, 1987). Secondly, it is also tempting, when speaking of framing and agenda-setting, to assume that the news audience will adopt a definition of the situation that is in lock step with the manifest or latent content of the coverage. It is important to remember that news reports become ideological only after an audience has appropriated them. This underscores the potential of newsreaders to challenge, transform, or resist dominant interpretations and ideologies. Without speaking to newsreaders, therefore, we can only assume, on the basis of theory, what likely decodings they will obtain. Indeed, as Paul Attallah argues in Chapter 3 of this text, different types of media address us as audiences in quite different ways. And thirdly, it is important to note that empirical analyses are always limited by the choices of news outlets researchers use. In this study, we have focused on three mass-circulating newspapers but did not examine any other newspaper formats, such as tabloids, or lower circulation, regional, or community newspapers, or other types of media, such as television or radio. To enrich our understanding of the complex role news media play in constructing knowledge about the social world, and of important public issues such as youth crime and violence, we must be sensitive to the myriad ways news media engage their audiences, and vice versa.

QUESTIONS

1. Define the concept of "moral panic" and discuss how it is both ideological and hegemonic. Based on the evidence provided in this chapter, do you think that news coverage of the Columbine and W.R. Myers shootings conformed to the moral panic narrative?
2. What are the major differences between "content analysis" and "discourse analysis"? What strengths and drawbacks can we attribute to each approach for the study of media coverage?
3. Why is the analysis of news frames important for understanding the relationship between media, moral panic, and public opinions about youth deviance?
4. Identify the key difference between "hard" news and "opinion" news formats, and explain why it is important to distinguish between them when examining news coverage of social problems such as youth crime.
5. Why do you think the news media attributed causality in this case to issues of the social structure more frequently than individual factors?

NOTES

1. Whereas "hard" news reporting is purportedly based on such professional criteria as *balance* (the point/counterpoint format of representing source claims) and *objectivity* (separating fact from opinion), "opinion" news items (i.e., editorials, op-ed pieces, columns) are intentionally biased accounts that seek to assign responsibility and blame (Greenberg, 2000). Issues that are considered of utmost public importance and that demand normative evaluation and interpretation tend to achieve greater levels of prominence across both types of formats.
2. The Columbine shootings received more attention, accounting for 64 percent of the total.
3. *The Toronto Star*, "Violent Revenge of the Misfits in Trenchcoats," April 25, 1999, pp. A1, A8. See also *National Post*, "Cliques Divide Wealthy Students of Columbine High," April 22, 1999, p. A13. Although the dynamics of W.R. Myers Secondary School were not subject to similar analysis, the shooter

was described as "the sort of teenager others made fun of" (*The Globe and Mail*, "Outcast Boy Had a Rifle and a Score to Settle," April 29, 1999, p. A1).

4. References to surveillance/security included calls for closed-circuit security cameras, increased police presence and use of metal detectors, and more vigilant social monitoring of students (by teachers and other students) who may pose a problem down the road.

5. Seventy-two represents the total number of "response" paragraphs in *The Globe and Mail*. Four hundred and eighty-six represents the total number of paragraphs, whether cause or response, and is calculated by adding the paragraphs in Table 6.3 with those in Table 6.2.

6. Most of the discussion about gun control pertained to the need for "stricter" measures to prevent access to guns. References to liberalizing gun control were much less frequent and occurred primarily in the Columbine case, where the merits of the constitutional right to bear arms was discussed and debated.

7. There was clearly far more coverage of the media reform category in *The Star* ($N = 42$) than in either the *Post* ($N = 8$) or *The Globe* ($N = 2$). Nevertheless, when we take the total frequencies of *The Star* paragraphs addressing "media reform" as a proportion of the overall response paragraphs (16 percent) or total (cause + responses) paragraphs (6 percent), this is still a fairly insignificant measure of issue attention.

8. Given that this chapter draws on empirical data, we should note that while previous studies of youth crime and the media *guide* our research, we must also remember that actual news content might not correspond with what these other studies lead us to expect. In other words, responsible content analysis of news must be able to make arguments based not only on a sophisticated theoretical edifice but also on observable evidence.

9. That "youth crime" is socially constructed is underscored by the somewhat depressing side note that over the first few days following the Columbine shootings, U.S. network executives poured excessive amounts of resources into covering the incident—CNN sent 70 reporters and technical staff to Littleton while NBC and ABC dispatched more than 50 each, far outpacing the number of news staff sent to cover the (then current) war in Yugoslavia or the 1994 genocide in Rwanda. See *The Globe and Mail*, "Rampage leads to ratings bonanza," April 29, 1999, p. C1.

REFERENCES

Acland, C. (1995). *Youth, murder, spectacle: The cultural politics of "youth in crisis."* Boulder, CO: Westview Press.

Adams, M. (1997). *The trouble with normal: Postwar youth and the making of heterosexuality*. Toronto: University of Toronto Press.

Blatchford, C. (1999, April 21). The cold, dark side of our exotic youth: Parents may be scared of their kids, but who isn't? *National Post*, pp. A1, A5.

Buckingham, David. (2000). *After the death of childhood*. Cambridge, England: Polity Press.

Cohen, Stanley. (1972). *Folk devils and moral panics: The creation of mods and rockers*. London: Macgibbon and Kee.

Deacon, David, Michael Pickering, Peter Golding, and Graham Murdock. (1999). *Researching communications: A practical guide to methods in media and cultural analysis*. London: Arnold.

Eerily familiar death spree puts Hollywood on trial. (1999, April 22). *National Post*, p. A13.

Entman, Robert. (1993). Framing: Toward clarification of a fractured paradigm. *Journal of Communication, 43*(4): 51–58.

Ericson, Richard V., Patricia Baranek and Janet Chan. (1987). *Visualizing deviance: A study of news organization*. Toronto: University of Toronto Press.

Fairclough, Norman. (1995). *Media discourse*. London: Arnold.

Film parallels fuel net debate. (1999, April 22). *Toronto Star*, pp. A1, A7.

Gee, Marcus. (1999, April 28). Littleton and the culture of violence. *The Globe and Mail*, p. A13.

Gitlin, Todd. (1980). *The whole world is watching*. Berkeley, CA: University of California Press.

Gramsci, Antoni. (1971). *Selections from the prison notebooks*. New York: International Publishers.

Greenberg, J. (2000). Opinion discourse and Canadian newspapers: The case of the Chinese "boat people." *Canadian Journal of Communication, 25*(4), 517–538.

Gun ownership in Alberta approaches U.S. levels. (1999, April 30). *The Globe and Mail*, p. A1.

Guns don't kill people—people kill people, with guns. (1999, April 22). *The Toronto Star*, p. A1.

Hall, Stuart, C. Critcher, T. Jefferson, J. Clarke, and B. Roberts. (1978). *Policing the crisis*. London: MacMillan.

Hay, C. (1995). Mobilization through interpellation: James Bulger, juvenile crime and the construction of a moral panic. *Social and Legal Studies, 4*, 197–223.

L.O.V.E. working to prevent tragedy. (1999, April 23). *The Toronto Star*, p. A13.

McCombs, Maxwell. (1997). Building consensus: The news media's agenda-setting roles. *Political Communication, 14*, 433–443.

Mills, C.Wright. (1959). *The sociological imagination*. New York: Oxford University Press.

Morris, Dick. (1999, April 27). Metal detectors are the answer. *National Post*, p. A18.

Pevere, Geoff. (1999, April 23). Shooting prompts usual fingerpointing. *The Toronto Star*, p. D1.

Right to bear arms is as American as apple pie. (1999, April 22). *National Post*, p. A14.

Schissel, Bernard. (1997). *Blaming children: Youth crime, moral panics and the politics of hate*. Halifax, NS: Fernwood Publishing.

Social distress, teenage unrest. (1999, April 24). *The Globe and Mail*, pp. D1, D3.

Some see eerie links with Hollywood's *Heathers*. (1999, April 22). *The Globe and Mail*, pp. A1, A16.

Springhall, John. (1998). *Youth, popular culture and moral panics*. New York: St. Martin's Press.

Tuchman, Gaye. (1978). *Making news*. New York: Free Press.

Warning signs are here, experts say. (1999, April 22). *The Toronto Star*, p. A6.

Wong, Jan. (1999, April 29). Why do they have guns? *The Globe and Mail*, p. A13.

7

Women and the Media

Rebecca Sullivan
University of Calgary

The relationship between women and the media is a longstanding concern for feminist scholars and activists. Since Betty Friedan's landmark book *The Feminine Mystique* (1963) highlighted media representations of women as endemic to women's oppression, many others have followed in her footsteps to expose the roots of this oppression and suggest strategies for improvement. Their efforts move from analyzing and critiquing representations, to lobbying government and businesses, to seizing the tools of the media in order to produce work that is explicitly feminist and challenges the status quo. This chapter examines some of the key principles of feminist media studies, in particular the representation of gender as difference, discourse, and ideology. It then moves on to explore the history of feminist media activism in Canada and considers some new directions resulting from the **third wave** movement. While the emphasis will be on Canadian content, it is impossible to sever analysis completely from the United States, which is the origin of much mass-mediated popular culture. Still, there are significant differences worth considering in order to understand how the relationship between women and the media in Canada is shaped by Canada's unique history and national character.

The media play a significant role in shaping public understanding of gender roles and relations. Changes in the political, economic, social, and even technological spheres are made meaningful and given a sense of value in the way we represent them both in the news and in popular culture. Thus when we speak about the media, we are using a general term that encompasses all kinds of forms and technologies—from film and television to advertising, newspapers, and more. While each medium is different and unique, the argument of feminist scholars is that all media still conform to similar conventions in the representation of women. It is not as simple as saying that the media reflect reality; rather, the media refract it. We cannot expect 100 percent accuracy in the way the media depict social events and relationships. To say that they promote "false consciousness" is really to miss the point. The media promote a version of reality by providing a lens through which to view and understand the world.

For example, the turbulent struggle for women's rights in the 1960s and 1970s was mediated on television through sitcoms such as *That Girl*, starring Marlo

Thomas, and *The Mary Tyler Moore Show*, Marlo and Mary in turn paved the way for

While this is a pretty
ange, feminist media
ability to historicize,
men in order to better
tandards while others
women's real lives and
esentations. It means
nowledging that even
respond to the media
to us.

often maligned these
"bra burners" ensure
here is certainly some
ly not about claiming
eminist media studies
gendered. Gendered
als, but to different
cial, sexual, political,
lives.

tions theory. It is based
r gender. Furthermore,
ction with the symbolic
his difference must be
rence" is central, femi-
d conflict. For example,
men? If difference and
women from different
represented and valued
women the only gender
ities like homosexuality
time there must be some
social action aimed at
be successful.

nal gender roles further
of **gender hegemony**,
central to most of femi-
aches to revealing and
ch to understanding the
. Feminism begins from
asis of their sexual status.
women's subordination
lture. Some scholars are

interested in exploring how discourses about gender are shaped. Then there are those who are more interested in ideology and formulating a cultural politics for women. Still others challenge how these critiques still depend on a belief that "women" can be separated out as a category, preferring to use feminist theory as a launch point to create better acceptance of gender difference. This chapter will go over each of these positions in turn. While breaking them down into different sections suggests that they are each completely unique approaches to studying women in the media, they actually share a number of things in common in that they all show how gender is a far more complex and open-ended concept than we are generally led to believe.

GENDER DIFFERENCE

When we look at the representation of women in the media, we are in effect turning real social subjects into signs. What this means is that the person becomes less important than what he or she symbolizes. Understanding gender as a sign separates out sex from gender, where the former is a biological trait and the latter resembles a series of social or cultural traits. The theory of gender difference, therefore, criticizes simplistic attitudes about what counts as appropriate gender behaviour based on a person's biological sex. It also challenges certain gender conventions that assume there are only two sexes, male and female, two genders, masculine and feminine, and maybe only two forms of sexuality, straight and gay. **Queer theory** is a different kind of gender scholarship from feminist or even gay/lesbian studies. It is a term coined by Teresa de Lauretis to challenge the idea that anyone's gender identity is static or necessarily linked to his or her biological or sexual status. Rather, gender is more fluid and can change according to different contexts.

Judith Butler, a feminist scholar who is also known for her work in queer theory, argues in favour of gender troubling—that is, undermining gender relations and breaking down oppositional relationships. She promotes the idea of gender as a performance in which norms that we often take for granted are exaggerated to show how strange and arbitrary they really are. She is particularly interested in transgressive sexualities like transvestites or transsexuals because they crisscross their biological sex and societal expectations for gender in ways that force us to consider how both are taken for granted but are not necessarily straightforward and easy to categorize. In her opinion, these kinds of performances undermine what she calls *hegemonic heterosexuality*, the way that gender norms are reiterated in culture to the point where they become accepted and standardized even though there is no real historical or social justification for them.

What scholars like Judith Butler help to clarify is that difference has often been the reason for gender oppression. People of different sexual orientation than heterosexual, or who look or act more like the opposite sex, are frequently censured and criticized. Feminist scholars believe that difference is a very important idea that can help to break down gender expectations and create a more open, tolerant society. They identify the media as a crucial source for disseminating images that perpetuate conventional gender representations, but also as a place where we can seek out and enjoy gender performances that embrace difference. For example, the reality TV show *Queer Eye for the Straight Guy* uses the standard genre of the women's makeover show, but targets men who are in need of a style update. It does so by having a group of gay experts on subjects ranging from fashion to food teach their subjects how to be less "masculine" and more "queer." In so doing, the show both exploits stereotypes of gay and straight men—the former are all preening peacocks while the latter are a bunch of uncouth slobs—while showing what good can happen if these two opposites collide.

Although "queer" has traditionally been a negative slang term for homosexuals, queer theory isn't only about gay, lesbian, bisexual, or even transsexual persons. It is about encompassing all expressions of gender and sexual identity and not insisting that they be linked directly to one's biological sex. In fact, it even challenges the belief that there are only two sexes, XX and XY, preferring to view biological sex as existing on a continuum of chromosomal and hormonal differences. The benefit of queer theory to feminist media studies is twofold. In the first place, it makes it possible to discuss gender without necessarily or exclusively meaning women. Secondly, and somewhat more complexly, it provides opportunities to think about gender representations as part of a spectrum rather than looking narrowly to see how they conform specifically to either masculine/feminine or gay/straight ideals. Once gender ceases to be a static, fixed category and becomes a sign or a performance, it becomes easier to break down the way that different genders are represented.

THE DISCOURSES OF GENDER

Discourse is a term that can refer to a series of communicational processes that form a pattern in the way we make meaning and try to maintain a sense of order and continuity in society. Scholars interested in gender discourses seek to *deconstruct* these patterns in order to reveal the reasons why gender is organized the way it is and who benefits the most from it. We have frequently mentioned the distinction between masculinity and femininity, but what exactly are the common assumptions behind these two terms? In general, our society tends to define the feminine as nurturing, compassionate, private, or passive. The corollaries for masculinity often include such terms as assertive, public, virile, and active. That is why, for example, some argue that a woman's natural place is in the home, where she can nurture children and take care of her husband. By contrast, it is the man's role to protect the home and to earn the money to maintain it. When we state these stereotypes so bluntly, they seem almost impossible to believe or to accept. Yet, it is generally true that masculine characteristics are valued more highly than feminine characteristics, even more so than the biological categories of male and female. If a woman acts "too masculine," by being ambitious at work or very athletic and competitive, she can be criticized for being "unfeminine." This is known as a *double bind*. In order to gain authority and power, one needs to act in a masculine way, but if a woman does so, she is a threat to gender norms. Similarly, a man who is perceived as effeminate can be at an even greater risk, even though biologically he is the more powerful sex.

Dorothy Smith, a Canadian sociologist, argues that gender is rigidly defined in order to perpetuate a clear boundary between masculinity and femininity, even more so than between male and female or men and women. The reason isn't to make sure that men enjoy higher status. Rather, it is so that masculinity remains the privileged position in gender representations. In this way, gender can be understood as a kind of *doctrine*, or universal moral order. We are expected to conform to these gender standards as if they are immutable truths, not arbitrary categories. However, we don't simply adhere to these doctrines but negotiate our gender identity within their boundaries. The practice of negotiation and articulation of gender doctrine is called *discourse*. Gender is communicated differently in different cultures. Different histories, languages, and images circulate according to the different ways that gender is valued socially, politically, and economically. So while "maternalism" may be a universal doctrine of femininity, for example, the discourse of motherhood varies from culture to culture depending in part on how it is being represented in the media and how audiences interpret it in turn.

Smith's two levels of gender as doctrine and discourse are a helpful way to think about gender difference because they acknowledge certain intransigent attitudes about gender and show how femininity has tended to be seen as a less powerful, subordinate position. At the same time, Smith's emphasis on discourse points to how men and women negotiate their gender identity as it is represented in the media. Thus, gender operates on two distinct levels. On the one hand are the representations of gender in the media that tend to rely on narrowly defined stereotypes so that audiences can readily identify characters and the sorts of values they represent. On the other hand are the ways that audiences accept these representations. Media scholars are interested in examining how audiences pick and choose through a range of stereotypes to find the ones that best suit their own ideas about their gender identity. The array of images available to us in the media can appear endless, bombarding us beyond our ability to absorb them all. Therefore, we adopt strategies for dealing with them, to sort through and select the representations that work best for us. Dorothy Smith calls this the *work of gender*, or the way in which we express our individuality and subjectivity according to how we relate to these representations. The work of gender implies that individuals have a say in how the doctrines and discourses of gender are made meaningful to them.

THE IDEOLOGY OF GENDER

Scholars who are more interested in ideology share many similarities with those who are interested in discourse, but they have a more explicit agenda of cultural politics. While they critique media discourses of gender, they also examine how media industries work to create these discourses and put more emphasis on the role of the audience in creating meaning. Understanding gender as ideology means acknowledging that although certain symbolic systems of gender appear to be unchanging, if we link them to the material conditions of economic and political power we can see how they are strategies to preserve the status quo for those who enjoy more privileges in society because of their gender. *Ideology* in this context can be defined as the unseen forces at work in culture that perpetuate women's subordinate social status. It is not merely norms or common sense, but deliberate systems and structures that create, maintain, and reproduce power relations. However, feminist cultural politics also asserts that individuals have *agency*. This is the belief that we all have some control over our actions and decide for ourselves how we want to be represented. We all have some say in our destiny, although it would be an exaggeration to claim that this destiny is unlimited.

The idea that the ideologies of gender can be changed is best proven by acknowledging moments of social change in the past. *History* is at the centre of feminist cultural politics because gender subordination has been perpetuated over time and across generations. Remembering history also lets us chart changes in attitudes toward gender minorities in the media. For example, the very fact that a show like *Queer Eye for the Straight Guy* is on television is something of a breakthrough, even though the gay men on the show tend to fulfill certain negative assumptions about homosexuality as a form of emasculation. Finally, any form of feminist cultural politics must have a theory for future social change. *Praxis* is the bridge between agency and ideology. It is the theory of how action is taken to increase democratic participation and social equality in the media. While some argue that media studies doesn't really take action, others point out that showing how the media work to perpetuate gender inequality is the first step toward creating more tolerant attitudes toward gender minorities.

Michèle Barrett's work on "gender as ideology" identifies four stages to analyze gender representations. The first, *stereotyping*, is a pervasive element in all communication processes because it is a shorthand to establishing a set of characteristics or a personality type. Feminist cultural politics identify rigid and often negative representations of women that condemn behaviours, traits, or attitudes that fail to conform to societal ideals of femininity. For example, consider the images that are often associated with female pop stars like Avril Lavigne (rebel rocker), Sarah McLachlan (sensitive rocker), or Shania Twain (sexy rocker). We immediately categorize them and assume certain characteristics not only about them but also about their fans. Why is it that "Alanis," the teenybopper singer from the '80s, had almost no credibility while "Alanis Morissette," the angst-ridden singer-songwriter, was hailed by critics—even though they are the same person? Stereotyping has a lot to do with how we assign meaning and value to the portrayal of individuals in the media, allowing audiences to connect with them on many different levels, and pass judgment on them accordingly.

Many scholars question why we accept these stereotypes, but Barrett argues that the media offer their audiences *compensations* in the way that they reward those who stay within the appropriate doctrines of gender and punish those who stray into the territory of difference. Sometimes this happens simultaneously to the same character, another example of the double bind in which the media place women. This is evident in reality TV makeover shows like *The Swan* or *Extreme Makeover*. Women are given a "once-in-a-lifetime" opportunity to completely remodel their looks. The clear implication is that personal happiness and success are just a nose job away. However, to achieve happiness, contestants must first admit their flaws and failure to live up to conventional standards of feminine beauty.

These happy-endings-with-an-edge go a long way toward building audience *collusion*. As Barrett points out, we can't simply reject these makeover shows, for example, as being "bad for women" when many women enjoy them and don't feel oppressed. In other words, what we watch, read, or listen to provides pleasure on multiple levels. Janice Radway and Ien Ang illustrate this very fact in their studies of women audiences for Harlequin romance novels and nighttime soap operas like *Dallas*. Neither actually argue that these cultural forms are feminist, but they do sympathetically portray why women enjoy these fictional tales of cat fights, sexual romps, and high melodrama. Indeed, collusion doesn't mean that women who like makeover shows are dupes and stooges; it means that it is important to allow for the possibility that audiences are knowledgeable about gender stereotypes and can see beyond them.

The final element is *recuperation*. This is the recognition that major social change does occur while preserving the dominant framework of patriarchal power. We need to explore how certain radical ideas are recycled into popular culture in ways that on the surface seem progressive but that obliquely reinforce traditional ideologies of gender. For example, *The Mary Tyler Moore Show* was part of the media response to **second-wave feminism**. This show aired from 1970–1977, at the height of the radical Women's Liberation Movement. It featured a young woman who left her fiancé and family to take a job as an associate producer at a local news show in Minneapolis. While on the one hand it was groundbreaking to see an independent, single, career woman as the star of a television sitcom, on the other hand Mary was virginal, obsequious to her male boss, and conventionally pretty in a feminine way. She wasn't really a feminist, but more an example of acceptably feminine independence. Yet, if we look at what kind of women characters dominate prime time today, Mary may seem more radical than we first thought. It is difficult to think of any current sitcom that stars a woman and is set in a workplace. This lack of representation is even more problematic when we realize how many domestic sitcoms have a male lead: *My Wife and Kids*, *According to Jim*, and *Everybody Loves Raymond*, to name a few. So even when television is set in the home, supposedly the domain of women, their experiences are secondary. However, many contemporary medical and legal dramas, or even Westerns such as *Dr. Quinn, Medicine Woman*, star female characters either principally (*Crossing Jordan*, *Cold Case*) or as part of an ensemble (*ER*, *Grey's Anatomy*) in a clear attempt to locate women within the workplace.

Over the years, media representations of women have relied on a formulaic set of distinctions between appropriately feminine independence, which is portrayed approvingly, and activist feminism, which is portrayed as boorish and ugly. How many times have we heard the phrase, "I'm not a feminist but . . ." followed by a list of explicitly feminist claims such as equal pay for equal work, sexual and reproductive rights, and so on? Why has feminism become a bad word when the aims of feminism have not? What other examples do we see daily that create an artificial divide between an "independent woman" and a "feminist"? The brief survey of feminist media critiques based on difference, discourse, and ideology can help us to identify and change the way that gender is represented by being more engaged and thoughtful as audiences. Yet, some argue that isn't enough. The media are such a powerful force in the construction of gender norms that they have led many to work directly within or against media industries to create alternatives to the status quo. These are the sorts of issues worth considering as we look briefly at the history of feminist media activism in Canada.

WOMEN AND THE MEDIA: FROM *CHATELAINE* TO *BITCH*

Beginning in the 1960s, the second wave of feminism—so-called to distinguish it from the **first wave** of suffragettes at the turn of the 20th century—heralded a new form of politics that was concerned with gender identity and meaning rather than with specific goals such as getting the vote. It can be argued that in Canada, the movement began not in the streets but on the pages of a women's magazine, *Chatelaine*. The magazine is still available on newsstands today, and it hardly looks like it could harbour a radical feminist agenda. In fact, if anything, it seems to be complicit in the "beauty myth," which emphasizes makeup tips, fashion, health and fitness, and decorating. Yet beginning in 1957 when a young journalist named Doris Anderson became its editor, this magazine craftily snuck in stories about women's rights, before reverting in the 1980s to a conventional lifestyle magazine. Valerie Korinek, who wrote *Roughing It in the Suburbs: Reading Chatelaine Magazine in the Fifties and Sixties*, claims that *Chatelaine* was the first women's magazine in all of North America to incorporate explicitly feminist material and to do so without alienating its readers or altering the perception of the magazine as anything other than a mainstream outlet targeted at middle-class housewives.

When *Chatelaine* was first launched in 1928, women in Canada weren't even yet recognized as "persons" under the law. Yet, the founder, H.V. Tyrrell of Maclean Hunter Publishing Company, wanted a magazine that didn't just address women as homemakers but also would introduce readers to exceptional women in the fields of politics, education, and the professions. He also wanted it to be a venue for quality fiction. Thus, the seeds were planted early on for *Chatelaine* to transcend the limits of the average women's magazine and become a conduit for feminist ideas. Doris Anderson, the editor of *Chatelaine* from 1957 to 1977, is largely credited with this change in focus. While continuing to acknowledge the magazine as "a kind of trade magazine for Canadian homemakers," she also included articles on such controversial topics as divorce, abortion, and drug addiction. Not everyone—least of all the publishers and advertisers—was happy with this change in direction, but the magazine clearly touched a nerve. By 1968, 51 percent of the total female population of Canada read *Chatelaine* in some form. While never a radical feminist magazine, *Chatelaine* did provide a liberal feminist approach that believed the system was not necessarily broken beyond repair but just needed some adjustments to better fit women in. Because of its liberal approach, *Chatelaine* and its editorial staff lobbied the federal government heavily to launch a public commission that would identify and address the unique problems of Canadian women.

THE ROYAL COMMISSION ON THE STATUS OF WOMEN (1967–1970)

Begun in 1967 and lasting three years, the Royal Commission on the Status of Women was a unique public event that made women and their demands front-page news. It was chaired by Florence Bird, a CBC journalist, and travelled the country seeking out women's input into everything from childcare to employment equity to the role of the media. Doris Anderson presented the commission with a survey conducted by *Chatelaine* on women's issues. Such topics as "the feminine mystique," "advertising and false consciousness," and "women's news sections" were addressed by groups ranging from the Canadian Women's Press Club to the women students council at Collège Ste-Anne-de-la-Pocatière. This emphasis on the media having a role to play in women's emancipation returns us to the idea that the term "woman" refers as much to a form of discourse or ideology as it does to a legal or social subject.

The Royal Commission took criticisms of the media seriously, especially as its own representation in the news frequently veered toward a more snide than factual tone. Barbara Freeman's book *The Satellite Sex* examines how the media reported on the commission and notes that for the most part, journalists were very suspicious of feminism. Once again we see how the discourses and doctrines of gender framed the representation of women's independence in ways that allowed for some controlled social change while reinforcing feminine ideals of passivity, decorum, gentility, and nurturing. One example that Freeman gives is the image of more aggressively political women as shrill harridans. The media published unflattering images of these women, often with their mouths agape and their bodies distorted. By contrast, other witnesses who conformed to feminine ideals were often described approvingly with special attention to their looks and demeanour.

In the end, Freeman concludes, the media not only created a sense of division between women who were feminine versus those who were feminist but also set the conditions by which women would be identified and valued, where "feminine" was good and feminist was bad. The very fact that the debate was framed in this way shows that feminism has long been treated as a negative in the news. Out of frustration with the status quo, two new associations were launched. The National Action Committee (NAC) on the Status of Women was founded in 1972 to have a permanent lobbying association for women's rights. It has recently fallen on hard times and is in danger of shutting down. Thus, more important is MediaWatch, a feminist organization dedicated to improving media representations of women; it began in 1981 and is still going strong.

THE 1980S: ORGANIZING FOR WOMEN'S RIGHTS IN THE MEDIA

MediaWatch was originally a subcommittee of NAC before branching out on its own. Using research, advocacy, education, and lobbying, its goal is to "transform the media environment from one in which women are either invisible or stereotyped, to one in which women are realistically portrayed and equitably represented in all their physical, economic, racial and cultural diversity" (http://www.mediawatch.ca/herstory.html). To that end, in the 20-plus years of its existence, MediaWatch has funded a number of studies to provide proof of the unequal and hurtful representation of women in news and entertainment and to advocate for more progressive representations instead.

In the 80s, many of its studies focused on pornography and violence against women. For this, it was frequently branded—along with all feminists—as being anti-sex and/or anti-men. MediaWatch encouraged members to send complaints about women's portrayal to its offices where it would coordinate them by industry and forward them en masse. Their efforts to prove that the problem was widespread frequently backfired. Targeted industries ignored complaints that came through MediaWatch because they felt that the organization had orchestrated them, which meant that the complaints were not in their view "legitimate." This double bind in which women are even less powerful as a group helps mute a feminist voice working against huge media conglomerates. It also serves to fuel, among individual women, a sense of dissatisfaction with what have become the traditional forms of feminist organization. In other words, by pitting individual women against feminist collectives, the media in effect change the terms of the debate so that the problem that women must address is no longer "sexism" or "patriarchy" or even "misogyny." It becomes "feminism" itself.

The feminist backlash of the 1980s and 1990s is documented by journalists like Susan Faludi and Naomi Wolf. Simply put, the media put feminism on trial, accused it of a litany of crimes, denied it fair representation, and then sentenced it to death. In 1991, *Newsweek* produced a cover feature on "the failure of feminism" in which such claims as "feminism freed men, not women" and "feminism made women disposable" thrust the burden of failed marriages, inadequate daycare, and the tyranny of youthful beauty on the shoulders of a movement that had fought to alleviate these problems. By 1998, *Time* didn't even give feminism a chance to defend itself when it asked the rhetorical question on its cover, "Is feminism dead?" Featured were pictures of Susan B. Anthony, a leader in the first-wave suffragette movement, Betty Friedan, and Ally McBeal, a fictional television character. The actress who played Ally, Calista Flockhart, was not aware that she was being used as the poster girl for post-feminism and claimed later that she thought she was posing for a feature on her hit show. However, it was critical for *Time* to have someone like her on the cover, to bolster its own claim that "if feminism of the '60s and '70s was steeped in research and obsessed with social change, feminism today is wed to the culture of celebrity and self-obsession." The interesting thing about this charge is that it was the media who openly castigated the image of the grim, dowdy "feminazi" and promoted a version of feminism that was still charming and sexy, as we can see in their coverage of the Royal Commission on the Status of Women. Now confronted with a feminism that did not deny sex (not that feminists ever did, they were just accused of it), these journalists still blamed feminism for failing to represent women, without admitting that it's really they who are representing feminism as a failure. Ironically, the casual denunciation of feminism by *Newsweek* and *Time* didn't result in its dissolution. The feminism that they created and declared dead may well have been, but a new brand of women's empowerment rose from its ashes.

THE NEXT CENTURY: THE BITCH IS BACK

Two young women read the *Newsweek* issue denouncing feminism and, rather than blaming the movement, as the magazine clearly intended, they decided to prove it wrong. In 1992 Tammy Rae Carland and Kathleen Hanna hosted the Riot Grrl Convention in Washington, D.C. Key to this alternative movement was a hard-driving punk rock music scene, edgy subcultural style, and, perhaps most important, a 'zine culture of DIY journals, comics, essays, and fiction. Riot Grrl was not an organized political movement but more a call to arms to young women, summoning them to use their creative force to challenge both the "pretty feminism" favoured in the media and the old-school forms of radical feminist collectives. It touched off what has been called a third wave of feminism, one with a heavy emphasis on identity politics, sexuality, and personal empowerment.

The most significant distinction between the third wave and the second wave is the generation gap. Specifically targeting young women, especially those in their 20s and early 30s, it sometimes seems as if third-wave feminism is not so much rebelling against its mothers as against what the media claimed their mothers said. The fact that it arose out of popular culture—in particular, music and magazines—has helped to place the emphasis on issues like identity and representation and to create the conditions for more open and fluid notions of sexuality. These are cultural goals more so than political ones, but that does not mean that the third wave is a kind of "false consciousness." While the media orientation of third-wave feminism may not lead to a national daycare program, it can nonetheless revitalize the image of women and potentially produce new outlets for creative gender expression.

In *Roughing it in the Suburbs*, Valerie Korinek argues that an explicitly feminist magazine simply cannot exist in the present climate. She claims that any kind of mass market magazine on feminism would be an "anachronism" today. However, such magazines are starting to reappear and to take their place on the newsstands alongside the now-chastened *Chatelaine*. Coming out of the United States but distributed in Canada, magazines like *Bitch* and *Bust* have a distinctly pop-cultural slant to their politics. Dismissed by *Time* in its article on feminism for its "peekaboo view of the world of sex that leaves one feeling not like an empowered adult but more like a 12-year-old sneaking in some sexy reading behind her parents' back," *Bust* certainly has its problems and could be seen as a cooptation of the riot grrl 'zine culture rather than as its full flowering. *Bust*'s emphasis on celebrity covers and sex lifestyles isn't exactly a challenge to the status quo. *Bitch* fares somewhat better. Formed in 1996, three years after *Bust*, it directly addresses the emptiness of the "grrl power" image and the double bind image of feminism.

What is interesting about both *Bitch* and *Bust* is their dual existence as both magazines and on-line blogs. Both their Web sites include a forum for readers to discuss issues and offer their own opinions. This raises the important issue about the Web in creating accessible alternative spaces for women's cultural and political expression. In Canada, we saw the emergence of *Marigold*, a now-defunct e-zine inspired by *Bust*, and *Third Space*, an on-line collective that doubles as a journal and resource centre for new feminist organizing. These examples suggest that the mainstream media were slightly premature in declaring feminism over. If anything, they show how the ongoing question of women's relationship to the media is one of constant evolution, perhaps more so than revolution. Feminist critiques of the media can take many shapes and go in many directions, but that only serves to prove that the media will always play a key role in the construction of women's identity and independence.

QUESTIONS

1. What does Judith Butler mean by "hegemonic heterosexuality"? How does this concept fit within feminist media studies?
2. What are the discourses and doctrines of gender, as defined by Dorothy Smith?
3. Michèle Barrett describes four stages by which the media produces gender as ideology. Describe them.
4. What is the value of feminist media activism in society? Can you see a way in which it has an effect on gender representations?
5. What are the implications of third-wave feminism prioritizing cultural issues like representation and identity instead of social or economic issues such as employment standards, access to education, and reproductive health?

REFERENCES

Ang, Ien. (1985). *Watching Dallas: Soap opera and the melodramatic imagination*. London: Methuen.

Barrett, Michèle. (1988). *Women's oppression today: The marxist-feminist encounter*. London: Verso.

Baumgardner, Jennifer, and Amy Richards. (2000). *Manifesta: Young women, feminism and the future*. New York: Farrara, Strauss and Giroux.

Bellafante, Ginia. (1998, June 29). Feminism: It's all about me! *Time*, *151*(25), 54–61.

Bradley, Patricia. (2003). *Mass media and the shaping of American feminism, 1963–1975*. Jackson, MI: University Press of Mississippi.

Butler, Judith. (1999). *Gender trouble: Feminism and the subversion of identity*. New York: Routledge.

Cleto, Fabio. (1999). *Camp: Queer aesthetics and the performing subject: A reader*. Ann Arbor, MI: University of Michigan Press.

de Lauretis, Teresa. (1991). Queer theory: Lesbian and gay sexualities. *differences*, *3*(2), iii–xiv.

Ebeling, Kay. (1990, November 19). The failure of feminism. *Newsweek*, *116*(21), 9.

Faludi, Susan. (1992). *Backlash: The undeclared war against American women*. New York: Anchor Books.

Freeman, Barbara M. (2001). *The satellite sex: The media and women's issues in English Canada, 1966–71*. Kitchener, ON: WLU Press.

Henderson, Lisa. (2001). Sexuality, feminism, media studies. *Feminist Media Studies*, *1*(1), 17–24.

Heywood, Leslie, and Jennifer Drake (Eds.). (1997). *Third wave agenda: Being feminist, doing feminism*. Minneapolis, MN: University of Minnesota Press.

Korinek, Valerie J. (2000). *Roughing it in the suburbs: Reading* Chatelaine *magazine in the fifties and sixties*. Toronto: University of Toronto Press.

McRobbie, Angela. 1999. *In the culture society: Art, fashion and popular music*. New York: Routledge.

Radway, Janice. (1984). *Reading the romance: Women, patriarchy, and popular literature*. Durham, NC: University of North Carolina Press.

Rakow, Lana (Ed.). (1992). *Women making meaning: New feminist directions in communication*. New York: Routledge.

Smith, Dorothy E. (1990). *Texts, facts, and femininity: Exploring the relations of ruling*. New York: Routledge.

Stacey, Jackie, and Hilary Hinds. (2001). Imaging feminism, imaging femininity: The bra-burner, Diana, and the woman who kills. *Feminist Media Studies*, *1*(1), 153–177.

Van Zoonen, Liesbet. (1994). *Feminist media studies*. London: Sage Publications.

Wolf, Naomi. (1997). *The beauty myth*. Toronto: Vintage Canada.

Part III
Communication Industries

Introduction

Paul Attallah
Carleton University

The chapters in this section examine the social diffusion of six communication media: radio, film, music, television, advertising, and alternative media. Often, they are called communication or cultural industries because they use industrial processes to manufacture and circulate images, representations, and values. This is a fairly recent concept, perhaps no more than 100–150 years old. Indeed, at one time, the very notion of communication as an industry would have seemed shocking and distasteful. Writing in the 1940s, German social philosophers Max Horkheimer and Theodor Adorno even used the concept of cultural industry not merely to describe but to denounce the degradation of culture and of rational thought as a result of media industrialization.

Nowadays, though, we find nothing very surprising in the concepts of a news industry or cultural industry or computer industry. For us, these are just common-sense ways of meeting wants and desires on a large, industrial scale.

Communication industries, however, have always played an ambiguous role. On the one hand, we turn to them for news and entertainment; on the other, we suspect that they may have the power to distort facts and shape opinion. This is because they are media of instantaneous mass address. They can both expand the range of democratic debate and subject us to manipulative pressures. They can amplify free speech and make widely known valuable ideas, but they can also generate vast wealth and power that is then concentrated into the hands of a few.

Understanding the origins and evolution of the modern communication industries—the media or mass media—is, therefore, one of the most important tasks for communication scholars. This is especially true in a country such as ours, which has an unusually high degree of domestic media concentration and is also remarkably open and permeable to media from the entire world.

Traditionally, studies of Canadian media express great torment over the presence and popularity of American media. For example, the fact that Canadians watch more American television than Canadian television, or that sales of U.S. and British music regularly outstrip sales of Canadian music, or that Canadian film remains a minority interest on Canadian screens usually generates paroxysms of anguish and frenetic calls for more or better or more diligent government action.

And yet, most Canadians happily consume whatever media they want, independent of the warnings and imprecations of the anguished few.

How that situation came about—the disconnect of the Canadian media from the very people they are supposed to reach—is one of the outstanding features of the Canadian media system. It is also the main reason why the study of the history and development of media in Canada is a central concern of communication scholarship. The goal here is not to claim that people *should* like Canadian media; it is to ask how the industrial and regulatory structures, forms, and contents of Canadian media have (or have not) achieved their goal of reaching audiences. It may be that the very way in which we ask the question prevents us from supplying a good answer.

The way we tell the story of Canadian media has direct consequences for our policy or regulatory framework, for the types of technological choices we make, and for the types of audiences we expect to address. For example, if we genuinely believe that watching American television is bad, then it is logical to impose restrictions on and barriers to American television, making it difficult or impossible to access. And such barriers have historically been implemented. Likewise, the view that audiences should consume more Canadian music has led to the imposition of other types of incentives (to encourage the production of more Canadian music) and restrictions (to ensure that people are necessarily exposed to what has been produced).

The downside of this approach is that it leaves audiences out of the equation. It does not ask why audiences prefer some types of content over other types; it merely asserts that they should like the approved type of content.

As a result, the Canadian media have long been the targets of cultural protectionism whose outcomes have not always been intended or salutary. Furthermore, new technologies, made possible by digitization, challenge not only old forms of protectionism but also the very business models upon which the protectionism was based. For example, if music can be downloaded in digitized format directly from the Internet, then the historical network of music stores and the promotional strategies associated with them fall into crisis. Likewise, if digital video recorders allow television viewers to skip through commercials, then the entire advertising basis of the traditional television industry needs to be rethought. Additionally, if digitization permits individuals to make accurate high-quality copies of films, then the enormous temptation exists to design future technology that specifically defeats that type of behaviour, even when the behaviour is not illegal.

The communication industries place before us certain intractable questions. Should we be concerned by technological transformation? Do the communication industries really shape culture and politics? In what ways will globalization change the media and our relationship to them? Should we even worry about this?

The first chapter in this section, by Pierre Bélanger, provides a historical overview of the emergence of the radio industry in Canada and of the ways in which various powerful stakeholders—the radio industry itself, the recorded music industry, the federal government—have attempted to ensure that it corresponds to their particular views.

The second chapter, by Bart Beaty, examines the Canadian film industry. He argues that Canada has developed a "cinema of failure" not because Canadian filmmakers lack talent or because Canadian audiences are brutishly ignorant but because of the industrial structures and contradictory cultural mandates we have given ourselves.

The third chapter, by Martin Laba, engages the contemporary music industry from the point of view of a social practice sometimes called "piracy." It poses directly the questions of old business models, new technologies, and shifting audience tastes and attitudes.

The fourth chapter, by Paul Attallah and Derek Foster, describes the Canadian television industry. It argues that while some of the objectives of cultural nationalism— to create a vibrant and popular indigenous television industry, for example—are laudable, Canada has nonetheless managed to encumber itself with counterproductive structures and regulations. As a result, Canada may be the only country in the world— with the notable exception of French-language productions—whose indigenous television is less popular than U.S. imports. The problem lies not in the obtuse or unenlightened nature of television audiences but in the failure to engage creatively with observable audience tastes, technological innovations, ownership structures, and so on.

The fifth chapter, by Russell Johnston, studies the rise and institutionalization of the advertising industry in Canada. Advertising not only piggybacks upon existing mass media—television, radio, newspapers—it also generates its own media—flyers, billboards, jingles, and so on—and its own empirical research (audience and content statistics). It is an extremely vibrant sector of the economy that interfaces directly with the shifting nature of audiences, the emergence of new technologies, the development of new strategies of audience contact, and the crisis of established business models.

The sixth and final chapter, by David Skinner, considers the role and status of alternative media. While not always easy to define, alternative media pose direct challenges not only to the nature and quality of more traditional media forms but also to their concentration of authority and power. It also extends the notion of alternative media to new technologies, such as the Internet, and raises the question of the connection between media and their intended audiences.

The general goals of this section are to familiarize readers with the history of the emergence and social diffusion of various media, the major questions or issues surrounding them, the ways in which we have thought about or have failed to think about media, and the status of their various audiences.

8

Radio in Canada: An Industry in Transition

Pierre C. Bélanger[1]
University of Ottawa

Radio, or *wireless*, was perfected in 1895 by Italian physicist Guglielmo Marconi. However, a name that may merit wider exposure is that of Canadian inventor and Marconi competitor Reginald Fessenden. Indeed, when Marconi could still only transmit Morse code, Fessenden was already able to broadcast music and the sound of the human voice. On Christmas Eve, 1906, startled radio operators on ships at sea heard Fessenden's voice and some musical selections.

In 1912, the sinking of the *Titanic* underlined the value of radio as major newspapers found themselves dependent on wireless reports for news of the tragedy. Following the sinking, all ships at sea were required to maintain continuous wireless operations.

In 1918, the Department of Naval Service granted Marconi the first radio licence ever, for station XWA (later CFCF) in Montreal. XWA only began broadcasting in 1919. By 1923, CKAC Montreal became the first French-language station to go to air.

In 1924, the newly formed Canadian National Railways (CNR) installed *radio cars* on some of its trains so that passengers could enjoy highbrow musical programming consisting of opera, orchestras, and drama. By 1932, the CNR had a national and regional network comprising some 20 radio stations constructed alongside its tracks. That network would eventually become the basis of the CBC.

Events moved rapidly as radio enjoyed unprecedented social diffusion. The 1920s were the era of the "radio craze." Canada's Diamond Jubilee celebration highlighted the growing importance of radio: On July 1, 1927, the telephone and telegraph lines that made up the CNR network were interconnected so that orchestras located in its 23 cities from West to East could simultaneously play the national anthem. As they played, the network switched seamlessly from orchestra to orchestra. An estimated five million Canadians and Americans tuned in that day. Radio was now firmly implanted in the national consciousness of Canadians. The Toronto *Globe* called radio "a democratic science, ready to instruct and entertain all manner and conditions of humankind who prepare to receive its blessings" (Nash, 1995, p. 49).

"CANADIANIZING" THE AIRWAVES

However, a typical pattern emerged with radio, as with film and magazines. Canadian listeners turned in great numbers to American radio. Approximately 80 percent of their listening time was devoted to programs originating from south of the border.

This worried many who feared that exposure to American radio would damage the cultural fabric of Canada. As a result, the federal government struck the first of many royal commissions on broadcasting in 1928. The Aird Commission, named for its chairman Sir John Aird, was mandated to study the state of Canadian broadcasting; to recommend how it should be administered, managed, and monitored; and to provide an informed assessment of its financial needs and its responses to the Canadian audience. The Commission's final report concluded that American networks were, predictably, a threat to our airwaves and our culture.

The Aird Commission, however, also recommended the creation of a public broadcasting network and, after three years of debate, the federal government formally enacted the Canadian Radio Broadcasting Act (1932). The Act stated that Canada would have a *mixed* broadcasting system, consisting of both public and private radio stations. The Act also authorized the creation of the Canadian Radio Broadcasting Commission (CRBC), which went to air in 1933. The CRBC's mandate was twofold: (1) to regulate and control all broadcasting activities in the country; and (2) to provide a national broadcasting service.

One of the most fervent supporters of public broadcasting in Canada was Graham Spry whose slogan was "the State, or the United States!"[2] The CRBC, however, proved to be a failure. It angered some listeners by broadcasting in both French and English on the same channel, and other listeners by airing content deemed to be politically biased and socially insensitive. Consequently, in 1936, the Broadcasting Act was amended and the CRBC was replaced by the Canadian Broadcasting Corporation (CBC).

The CBC took over the CRBC's staff and facilities as well as its regulatory authority. Indeed, it is worth noting that the CBC was not only a broadcaster in competition with private stations but also the regulator of the entire system, able to grant or deny licences to its private competitors. This fact provoked much criticism from the private radio industry. As a result, in 1958, the federal government revised the Broadcasting Act again and transferred regulatory power away from the CBC to an independent regulatory body, the **Board of Broadcast Governors (BBG)**. The BBG would regulate *both* the private broadcasters *and* the CBC. In 1968, the BBG itself was replaced by the Canadian Radio-Television Commission (CRTC).

THE RADIO REGULATORY ENVIRONMENT

The CRTC[3] grants, renews, and denies broadcasting licences, and sets standards and quotas for both radio and television. It is an independent public agency whose members are appointed by the Prime Minister and that reports to Parliament through the Minister of Canadian Heritage. It is governed by the Broadcasting Act of 1991 and the **Telecommunications Act** of 1993. It attempts to balance the cultural, social, and economic goals of broadcasting and **telecommunications** legislation in the public interest. In the case of radio, this is accomplished chiefly by requiring programming to reflect Canada's linguistic duality, its multicultural diversity, and the special place of Aboriginal people in Canadian society.

The most definitive aspect of Canadian broadcasting regulation concerns Canadian content requirements or **CanCon**. Although specific CanCon requirements change over time, they always embody the same basic objectives: to ensure that the Canadian public is exposed to the work of Canadian artists and producers.

As of August 31, 2003, there were some 515 commercial AM and FM radio stations in Canada, of which 80 percent broadcast in English (CRTC, 2003). The CRTC requires that at least 35 percent[4] of popular music selections played by commercial AM and FM radio stations between 6 a.m. and 6 p.m., Monday through Friday, be Canadian. (An exception applies to stations whose playlists consist of at least 35 percent instrumental music, because the music pool from which they draw is more limited.) (CRTC, 2004a)

The CBC must abide by slightly more stringent conditions. On a weekly basis, at least 50 percent of its general popular music and 20 percent of its traditional and special interest selections between 6 a.m. and midnight must be Canadian. Nowhere is the contribution of public broadcasting to the promotion of Canadian talent more apparent than in the number and diversity of music styles played on its regional stations and national networks. For example, CBC Radio One and Radio Two air a weekly average of 4800 different musical selections. Of these, approximately 60 percent (roughly 2900 different musical selections) qualify as CanCon, thereby exceeding the CRTC requirement of 50 percent. Moreover, the CBC doubles the CRTC's 20 percent quota for special interest and classical music, since 40 percent of its average of 2500 weekly musical selections also qualify as CanCon.

The approximately 100 French-language private stations are subjected to even more demanding criteria. They are required to ensure that at least 65 percent of the popular vocal music selections they broadcast each week are in French. If taken literally, however, this requirement could result in a radio station playing only artists from France, Belgium, or another French-speaking country, since the French Canadian market could hardly meet the demand without an annoying degree of redundancy. In order to prevent the exclusion of French-language vocal music produced in Canada, the CRTC further specifies that no less than 35 percent of popular music selections aired weekly by French-language commercial AM and FM stations be Canadian and that at least 55 percent of the popular French vocal music selections be played between 6 a.m. and 6 p.m., weekdays.

Just as the CBC meets stricter criteria than private English-language radio stations, so too must Radio-Canada (the French-language wing of the CBC) meet stricter requirements than private French-language radio stations. Radio-Canada's *Première chaîne* (the equivalent of Radio One) must air 95 percent French-language content, of which 50 percent must be by Canadian artists. No more than 5 percent of its playlist may be devoted to English-Canadian vocal selections. *La chaîne culturelle* (renamed, in September 2004, *Espace musique*—the equivalent of Radio Two) must guarantee a minimum 20 percent airplay to Canadian traditional and special-interest music. Finally, every song must be played in its entirety in order to be counted toward the CanCon quota.

HOW FAR CAN THE CRTC GO IN REGULATING RADIO?

Not only does the CRTC set the licensing conditions by which the various radio broadcasters must abide, it also overlooks the daily operations of the various licensees. Far from being a complacent observer, the CRTC does, occasionally, react negatively. A well-publicized recent instance occurred in the summer of 2004 when the CRTC cancelled the licence of CHOI-FM in Quebec City. A brief outline of the debate and decision follows.

Genex Communications Inc. acquired CHOI-FM in 1997. Between then and 2004, 92 complaints concerning the "conduct of the hosts and the spoken word" were received. Already in 2002, the CRTC had notified Genex that it was running afoul of the Radio Regulations of 1986 and of the Broadcasting Act. At that time, the CRTC renewed the CHOI-FM licence for two years only, whereas licences are usually renewed for seven years. The CRTC also imposed a set of conditions (including an eight-second delay) intended to prevent the broadcasting of material that would lead to further complaints.

The content of CHOI-FM did not change, and in February 2004, the CRTC called Genex to a public hearing in Quebec City. The offending comments cited included statements about African students at Laval University, a rival radio host involved in a juvenile prostitution ring, and the desirability of euthanizing psychiatric patients. Most of the complaints dealt with spoken-word content that seemed to constitute a pattern of behaviour that was not only repeated but even grew worse. Genex denied there was a problem or that it was failing to comply with its conditions of licence.

When a licensee is judged as failing to meet its licence obligations, the CRTC has three options: it can (a) issue a short-term licence renewal; (b) issue a mandatory order; or (c) suspend, revoke, or not renew the licence.

The third option would be applied only exceptionally, but that was the CRTC's decision. As a result, for only the sixth time since 1968, the CRTC did not renew a licence. All previous non-renewals also involved radio stations from Quebec. More significant, though, is the fact that the CHOI-FM decision was the first time that the CRTC refused to renew a licence because of on-air views.

Genex immediately launched an appeal to the Federal Court, and the CRTC's decision generated unprecedented waves of protest in Quebec, including expressions of support from Quebec Premier Jean Charest, NDP Leader Jack Layton, and Conservative Leader Stephen Harper. By August 26, 2004, however, Genex and the CRTC had agreed to ask the Federal Court to allow CHOI-FM to remain on air until its appeal was finally heard.

WHAT QUALIFIES AS CANADIAN CONTENT?

The CRTC (2001) goes to great lengths to define what qualifies as a "Canadian selection." The definition was conceived with two goals in mind: (1) a cultural goal of increasing audience exposure to Canadian performers, lyricists, and composers; and (2) an industrial goal of supporting the Canadian music and recording industry. This definition is critical to the entire radio industry and has given rise to a typically Canadian acronym, **MAPL**.

The letters in MAPL stand for *M*usic (is the selection composed entirely by a Canadian?), *A*rtist (is the selection performed principally by a Canadian?), *P*roduction (does the selection consist of a live performance that is (a) recorded entirely in Canada or (b) performed entirely in Canada and broadcast live in Canada?), and *L*yrics (are the lyrics written entirely by a Canadian?).

Some exceptions apply. If the selection was recorded before 1972 or if it is an instrumental performance of a musical piece written or composed by a Canadian, it need not conform to the MAPL standard.

Despite the fact that the MAPL system appears to be fairly efficient and reasonable, it has attracted very harsh criticism. Critics argue that CanCon is a bad solution to a structural problem inherent in the music industry. The public tends to develop a strong attachment to a limited number of artists. For example, Alanis Morissette, Shania Twain, the Tragically Hip, Céline Dion, Amanda Marshall, Brian Adams, the Barenaked Ladies, and Sarah McLachlan have been able to generate very strong followings over the last few years. But scores of other artists have not. Nonetheless, the successful artists are icons not just of the Canadian music scene, but of the international music scene. That so many Canadian artists have garnered international acclaim may be a cause for celebration. But, the critics ask, should we not be concerned about the impact of so few big names on the entire music industry?

These critics, therefore, argue that CanCon merely magnifies the dominance of a small group of stars to the detriment of promising new artists who simply cannot generate the same kind of bonding with audiences. As Larry LeBlanc, Canadian editor of *Billboard* magazine says: "The negative impact of CanCon regulation is very simple. If you're releasing a record today at the same time as Shania Twain or Nelly Furtado, you're going to have a lot of trouble" (cited in Everett-Green, 2001). Critics do not hesitate to point an accusing finger at radio stations that have become part of a sophisticated marketing system in which only those artists capable of producing and promoting a CD and a video receive airtime. Furthermore, many accuse commercial stations of not giving fair consideration to artists who are not distributed by one of the four major multinational conglomerates that dominate the entire music industry. Should the current regulations be amended, then, in order to force radio stations to increase the diversity of the artists who make up their daily playlists?

CANADIAN PUBLIC RADIO

CBC/Société Radio-Canada is a major architect of the Canadian radio industry, and it maintains a unique connection for most Canadians. Public radio provides a unique style within the industry, and its non-commercial nature allows it to explore unorthodox programming styles and hence reach audiences that are not targeted by other stations. CBC Radio provides a wide range of programming in both French and English that, consistent with the Broadcasting Act, informs, enlightens, and entertains while reflecting Canada and its regions to themselves.

For most listeners, CBC Radio is easily identifiable. It has a distinctive sound and mode of delivery and, above all, is commercial-free. What is less apparent is its deep presence in every province of the country, which makes it unique in the international broadcasting community. According to its 2002–2003 annual report, Radio One consists of 36 owned and operated stations, whereas Radio Two consists of 14 stations. Additionally, several hundred rebroadcasting stations relay their signals. Statistics Canada estimates that more than 50 percent of Canadians use at least one of the four CBC radio services weekly. This translates into an average weekly unduplicated Radio One and Radio Two audience reach of some 3.8 million Canadians for English-language radio, while French-language radio is currently at an all-time record high with over one million listeners each week.

Over the last few years, CBC Radio has explored new delivery platforms, including satellite radio, digital radio, Internet applications, external syndication, and after-market distribution. Already the CBC's news headlines are distributed to wireless telephone users by most major Canadian cellular phone providers. Its digital pay audio service, Galaxie, available through satellite, cable, and microwave distribution systems offers 45 continuous, commercial-free music channels to a subscriber base of some 3.25 million. In addition, through its Rising Stars Program, it contributes about $500,000 annually to young Canadian artists and music organizations.

One of CBC's most technologically innovative ventures for reaching younger audiences is Radio Three, an award-winning service dedicated to the promotion of independent art and culture. Despite its name, Radio Three is available only on the

Internet, at http://www.cbcradio3.com. Created in 2000, Radio Three currently draws a monthly average of about half a million unique visitors in the much sought-after 18-to-34 demographic, although the Web site creators prefer to speak of a common "psychographic" that connects their audience members. The site consists of four interconnected sections catering to different musical and artistic genres. Thus, while the main CBCradio3.com site features articles, essays, and videos on artists and youth culture, for example, 120seconds.com features individual musical contributions, NewMusicCanada.com features bands, JustConcerts.com features recordings of live concerts, and RootsMusicCanada.com showcases country, folk, and world music.

RADIO TYPES, FORMATS, AND LISTENING PREFERENCES

The Canadian radio environment is multi-tiered. There are four main types of licences granted to mainstream stations: (1) AM licences; (2) FM licences; (3) digital licences (spread over Montreal, Toronto, Windsor, and Vancouver); and (4) pay-audio licences (DMX Music and CBC Galaxie, available via satellite, cable, or wireless system). Licences are also granted to community stations, campus stations, Native stations, ethnic stations, and religious content stations (CRTC, 2004a).

The province with the most commercial stations (see Table 8.1) is Ontario (171), followed by British Columbia (104, including the Territories), Quebec (100), Alberta (74), Manitoba (29), New Brunswick (24), and Nova Scotia (22). The station ownership situation remains fluid because of ongoing transactions and a converging marketplace.

The CRTC also uses over two dozen different content categories to describe the various programming styles available. Whereas radio was a unifying force in its early days, the proliferation of niche stations has seen a fragmentation of audiences that cuts radically into the common experience of listeners. The original mass media

TABLE 8.1 Number of Commercial AM and FM Stations in Canada, All Languages, 2004

Province/Territory	AM	FM
Newfoundland & Labrador	11	7
Prince Edward Island	2	2
Nova Scotia	9	13
New Brunswick	5	19
Quebec	23	77
Ontario	51	120
Manitoba	14	15
Saskatchewan	18	21
Alberta	26	48
British Columbia (includes Yukon Territory, Northwest Territories, and Nunavut)	40	64
Networks	19	18
TOTAL	218	404

Source: CRTC 2004b, Broadcasting Policy Monitoring Report 2004.

nature of radio has given way to a form of localized **walled garden** programming that caters to highly specialized tastes and preferences.

The vast majority of Canadian radio listening (see Table 8.2) falls into 13 main formats. According to Statistics Canada (2004c), the most popular format is adult contemporary (AC) music (also known as light or adult rock), which captures 24.2 percent of all listeners. However, AC is not as dominant as it once was, having fallen 3.9 percent since 1999 and 7.3 percent since 1998.

Adult contemporary is followed by golden-oldies/rock at 18.6 percent of listeners. CBC is third with 10.9 percent (up from sixth place five years ago). The sudden growth in the popularity of public broadcasting can be explained by an aging population as well an increasing number of people with a postsecondary education. News/talk radio is fourth with 10.6 percent. Of Canada's 31 news/talk stations, 19 are concentrated in the four largest markets. Country ranks fifth at 9.7 percent, but since 1993, it has lost almost half of its listeners. Nowhere in Canada does country succeed in winning a market, and in the two largest markets, Toronto and Montreal, there are no country music stations at all.

The growth of FM stations over the last dozen years has been spectacular. Indeed, Canadians now spend 74 percent of their total listening time with FM stations. Overall, Canadians listen to radio on average 19.5 hours per week, one hour less than in 1999. Also, radio appears to be losing ground with 12- to 17-year-olds as their listening has fallen from 11.3 hours per week in 1999 to 8.5 hours per week in 2003. A similar pattern is observed with young adults aged 18 to 24, although the reduction in their listening time is not as marked as with teenagers (Statistics Canada, 2003, 2004c).

TABLE 8.2 Percentage Share of Radio Listening by Format, Fall 2003

Format	Canada	NL	PE	NS	NB	QC	ON	MB	SK	AB	BC
Adult contemporary	24.2	8.0	6.5	34.3	32.9	27.2	29.1	9.7	24.0	13.1	14.7
Album-oriented rock	2.5	13.8	0.0	0.0	0.1	3.6	1.2	3.6	1.3	3.6	3.3
CBC	10.9	13.4	20.8	16.0	13.1	11.6	9.3	10.6	10.8	7.7	15.0
Contemporary	7.9	31.8	26.0	3.2	4.0	18.9	1.3	7.8	0.2	7.6	6.7
Country	9.7	14.3	25.9	23.1	13.9	0.9	8.3	15.8	35.3	23.3	7.2
Dance	1.8	0.0	0.0	0.0	0.0	0.4	3.7	0.1	0.0	0.0	2.2
Easy listening	2.9	0.0	0.0	0.0	0.0	3.7	4.2	6.7	0.0	0.9	0.0
Golden-oldies/rock	18.6	12.8	20.0	19.7	13.2	14.6	18.6	23.6	19.3	22.5	23.1
Middle-of-the-road	2.7	0.0	0.0	0.0	0.0	0.9	4.4	1.3	0.0	1.7	4.2
Other	4.4	6.0	0.9	3.4	17.3	4.2	3.1	4.8	2.4	8.5	3.7
Sports	0.9	0.0	0.0	0.0	0.0	0.3	1.6	0.0	0.1	1.1	0.7
Talk	10.6	0.0	0.0	0.0	0.0	12.3	10.5	15.4	6.1	9.8	14.3
U.S. stations	3.0	0.0	0.0	0.2	5.6	1.5	4.7	0.7	0.3	0.2	5.0
Total listening	**100.0**	**100.0**	**100.0**	**100.0**	**100.0**	**100.0**	**100.0**	**100.0**	**100.0**	**100.0**	**100.0**

Source: Statistics Canada. (2004, July). *Radio Listening: data tables, Fall 2003*, catalogue no. 87F0007.

THE CORPORATE STRUCTURE OF CANADIAN RADIO

The role of the CRTC is not limited to allocating broadcasting licences and setting content quotas. From an economic standpoint, recent changes in the CRTC's commercial radio policy have significantly modified the Canadian radio landscape.

The most important change concerns ownership rules. Since the spring of 1998, in markets with eight or more *commercial* stations broadcasting in a given language—this calculation excludes public, community, campus, Native, religious, or ethnic stations—a person or company may own or control as many as two AM and two FM stations in that language. In markets with fewer than eight commercial stations operating in a given language, one can own as many as three stations, with a maximum of two stations in any one frequency band (AM or FM). Those hoping to acquire more than one AM and one FM station in a given language in the same market are asked to assess the likely impact of their ownership on the following issues: (1) the diversity of news voices, (2) the level of competition in the market, (3) the benefit to the local community and the furtherance of the objectives of the Broadcasting Act as a result of the programming they will typically broadcast, and (4) any other issues that may arise in the case of applicants who already own other media or have an interest in other radio stations in the same market.

The CRTC introduced this change as a result of the bleak financial situation faced by many commercial stations in the mid-1990s. Pressures for relaxation of ownership rules also mounted as consolidation (to achieve economies of scale, for example) similar to the American trend became economically sensible. Although never perfect, the CRTC's new regulation was perceived by many as an acceptable compromise.

Essentially, the post-1998 policy encourages consolidation. Radio station owners may solidify their financial situation, attract much-needed new investment, and—particularly important in the era of convergence—compete more effectively with other media.

However, in exchange for softening the ownership rules, the CRTC obtained two concessions: (1) the percentage of CanCon that private radio stations must play rose from 30 to 35 percent; and (2) purchasers of profitable stations must contribute at least 6 percent of the value of the transaction to support Canadian musical talent. The 6 percent contributions are to be distributed as follows:

a) 2 percent to either FACTOR in English Canada or MusicAction in French, at the discretion of the purchaser, to support talent development and the record industry;

b) 3 percent to the newly created Radio Starmaker Fund and its French-language counterpart, Le Fonds RadioStar, for the promotion of new artists and new recordings over the next decade;

c)   1 percent, at the discretion of the purchaser, to either (a) or (b) above or to any other eligible third party directly involved in the development of Canadian musical and artistic talent.

The CRTC wishes to encourage closer collaboration between the radio and music industries. As a result of the changes in ownership, approximately $26 million has been injected into the radio broadcasting system. Le Fonds RadioStar and the Radio Starmaker Fund received 48 percent of the new money, FACTOR and MusicAction received about 33 percent, and various discretionary projects received the remaining 20 percent.

As with most media businesses nowadays, the ownership and total number of Canadian stations vary as key players revisit their strategic priorities, partnerships, and market positions. If we exclude the CBC and its 79 radio stations, then only eight commercial operators dominate the Canadian radio scene. They own 330 of the country's 622 stations and generate 79 percent of the industry's total revenue, up significantly from 1998 when they held 148 stations and collected 61 percent of the revenue. Likewise, their share of tuning or listenership has also risen between 1998 and 2002, from 53 percent to 64 percent of the total radio listening time.

Corus Entertainment, a division of Shaw Communications Inc., is the leading station owner; it holds 50 stations and captures 18 percent of the total national radio revenue (see Table 8.3). Standard Broadcasting Corp. Ltd., with 51 stations, and Rogers Communications, with 43 stations, respectively take in 14 percent and 13 percent of the total radio revenue. Astral, CHUM, and Newcap Broadcasting respectively rank fourth, fifth, and sixth in terms of revenues generated.

TABLE 8.3 Ten Largest Radio Operators, Radio Revenue, and National Share, 2003

Operator	Number of Radio Undertakings	Radio Revenue ($ 000's)	Share of National Revenue (%)
Corus Entertainment Inc.	50	210,529	18
Standard Broadcasting Corp.	51	164,966	14
Rogers Communications Inc.	43	158,264	13
Astral Media Inc.	36	126,627	11
CHUM Limited	30	116,968	10
Newcap Inc.	41	55,509	5
Jim Pattison Industries Ltd.	18	33,365	3
Rawlco Radio Ltd.	12	27,020	2
Elmer Hildebrand (Golden West Broadcasting)	21	25,221	2
Maritime Broadcasting System Ltd.	21	23,593	2
TOTAL	323	942,062	79
TOTAL Canada (Private Radio Revenues)	532	1,189,483	100

Note: *Radio undertakings include networks.*
Source: CRTC. (2004b). Broadcasting Policy Monitoring Report 2004.

THE ECONOMICS OF RADIO

Year after year, experts predict that an aging population, satellite radio, the Internet, and music downloads will eventually bring radio to its knees. And year after year, they are proven wrong. After a period of deep losses in the 1980s and 1990s, caused partly by ownership rules that prevented the development of networks, 2003 brought much needed optimism: advertising reached $1.2 billion, an increase of 8.4 percent over the previous year. This was the best sales level since 1975 and the year-over-year increase was the second largest in the previous 15 years. What explains such an improvement? Why has private radio generated a higher profit margin than private television in the past six years?

Statistics Canada (2004a) reports that radio's profitability is chiefly attributable to cost-containment measures. These include operating efficiencies, a direct consequence of the 1998 decision allowing consolidation, which mean smaller staffs and increased reliance on computers and automated broadcast technologies. A healthier economy also contributed. Indeed, while FM revenues grew by 8.4 percent, their expenses rose by only 3.7 percent. Additionally, airtime sales grew by almost 10 percent in 2003, which translated into a 25.2 percent profit margin before interest and taxes. By comparison, AM advertising revenues grew by 4.5 percent while their profit margin grew by 1.6 percent. As Statistics Canada explains, "modest as they may appear, the 2003 results represent a significant turnaround for AM radio."

With a profit margin slightly over 23 percent, radio stations in Canada's 5 largest metropolitan areas continue to outperform those in smaller markets by 8 percent. The two most profitable markets are Calgary and Ottawa-Gatineau. Finally, the Canadian radio industry employed approximately 9000 people in 2003.

THE DEATH KNELL OF AM RADIO?

In small and mid-sized markets, AM radio is slowly fading. The migration of AM stations to the FM dial continues unabated. There were 19 signal shifts from AM to FM in 2001, and another 9 in 2002. Between 1998 and 2000, some 33 stations moved to the FM band. It may not be long before the same trend occurs in bigger cities.

Naturally, the desertion of the AM dial by young listeners who obtain their music from TV, the Internet, and P2P file sharing has severely affected the financial health of AM radio. Furthermore, pop music is nowadays segmented into so many sub-genres and categories that it is very difficult for AM radio to generate an audience large enough to appeal to potential advertisers. But that is only part of the equation. There is a more concrete, pragmatic, dollars-and-cents issue at stake: the cost of broadcasting an AM signal.

AM transmitters are expensive, with a capital cost of about $100,000. They require tall towers on large plots of land, thereby generating property taxes and high energy costs. It is estimated that the cost of setting up an AM station in a major city runs close to $1 million. An FM station, however, might cost only $250,000 to set up. The economics speak for themselves.

Additionally, AM radio simply cannot compete with the sound quality of FM. CDs and high-fidelity sound systems have accustomed listeners to high-quality sound, and people therefore avoid the tinny, monaural sound of AM radio. This is one reason for the transformation of AM radio into all-talk formats where sound quality is less evident.

In the mid 1990s, Rogers Communications gambled by switching the formats of its main AM stations in Toronto and Vancouver from music to all-news. Not only has the concept successfully spread to other major centres such as Victoria, Winnipeg, Edmonton, and Montreal, but 680 News in Toronto generates more revenue than any other AM station in the city. Corus has jumped on the talk-radio bandwagon by introducing "guy-talk" Mojo sports in Toronto and Vancouver. Others are trying their luck with "memory music" from the 1940s and 1950s, hoping that older audiences won't be so demanding in terms of sound quality.

However, if profits are so hard to generate and with so few viable formats, why are operators keeping their AM licences? The answer can be seen by looking to the future.

THE MORPHING OF RADIO

Technological developments are currently forcing radio into one of the most profound transformations since the arrival of stereo FM signals in the 1960s.

Digital Pay Audio Services

The two main providers of digital pay audio are Galaxie, with over 4 million residential and commercial subscribers, and DMX Music, with some 9000 commercial customers. These services offer approximately 50 commercial-free, uninterrupted, no-talk channels of music covering a range of styles including rock, urban, contemporary, jazz, classical, nostalgia, and various niche genres that receive limited airplay on conventional channels.

Despite this substantial subscriber base, most traditional radio operators believe that digital pay services compete with CDs or audiocassettes, not local radio. Local radio operators might be right for now, but what will happen once people discover the added value of getting their favourite music in a streamlined, seamless fashion? Might they then treat radio as they already treat television and start turning to specialty channels? The main limitation on mass adoption of digital pay audio is the fact that such services still depend on fixed appliances; that is, they plug into a home television or stereo and are therefore stationary devices. Fortunately for traditional radio, mobile listening, whether in the car or on a Walkman, is a strongly ingrained habit that is not about to change.

Digital Audio Broadcasting

It is a well-known fact that the FM band is saturated and that the scarcity of available frequencies makes launching new stations highly problematic. As a result, many see digital audio broadcasting (DAB) as the ideal solution for new services.

Often referred to as "high-definition radio," DAB is a digital radio system that operates in the L-Band. If popularized, DAB would create a level playing field for AM and FM radio by equalizing their sound quality. DAB offers CD-quality sound, interference-free reception, program-associated data, and graphics and text (including lyrics). A display window attached to the receiver provides dynamic labels describing the artist, song title, serial number of the album, and so on. Traffic and news briefs scroll in a text format while listeners enjoy their music. As DAB matures, services such as maps, visual traffic reports, pictures, and real-time stock market information will become available in both free and subscription formats. Furthermore, as they drive across Canada, listeners will be able to stay tuned to the same station with no signal fade and without changing frequency.

To this day, some 36 countries have adopted DAB or introduced legislation to test it. Over 500 DAB services are currently offered, reaching 300 million people around the world. In Canada, DAB reaches over 15 million people in places as diverse as Vancouver, Chilliwack, Calgary, Red Deer, Edmonton, Windsor, Toronto, Hamilton, Kitchener, London, Guelph, Cornwall, Ottawa, Montreal, Quebec, and Trois-Rivières. Some 70 radio stations are broadcasting in DAB and operators such as Astral Radio, CBC/Radio-Canada, Corus, Rogers, CHUM, and Standard Radio are all onboard.

However, DAB is an innovation that has generated more skeptics than supporters. Despite the deployment of DAB services in Canada and abroad, the technology faces a major roadblock: in order to enjoy its benefits, listeners must purchase a special DAB receiver. While the price has fallen from $1000 to about $100, DAB is still a long way from reaching a critical mass of users. Unless DAB enters the car market, its prospects remain uncertain.

Furthermore, the CRTC has decided that Canada will adopt a European DAB standard known as Eureka, which will be incompatible with the US IBOC (in band on channel) standard. Meanwhile, people are becoming more comfortable using MP3 players, CD and DVD burners, iPod, streaming media, and satellite radio. DAB, therefore, seems caught in a vicious circle: while receiver manufacturers claim innovative broadcasting will drive consumer demand for their devices, broadcasters say they are waiting for greater consumer demand before launching DAB services. Hence, digital radio has all the allure of a missed rendezvous.

Subscription Satellite Radio

The year 2004 marked the 75th anniversary of the first car radio, the "Motorola." It was also the year in which the CRTC heard applications from three groups vying to provide satellite radio services to Canadians. Available in the United States since 2001, satellite radio is intended primarily for automobile use, although residential listening is possible, provided one purchases a specialized receiver. Two players control the American satellite radio market: XM Satellite Radio Inc., the current leader with over 2 million monthly subscribers and projections to reach 20 million by 2010; and Sirius Satellite Radio which, in the summer of 2004, reached the half-million subscriber mark. Together, XM Radio and Sirius own 5 satellites beaming a combined total of 200 channels of CD-quality music, information, weather, traffic, sports, and entertainment, as well as original comedy and kids' shows.

In order to establish a sound business model, both American firms struck agreements with auto manufacturers, who now offer $350 (U.S.) satellite receivers as an option in over 100 model lines. XM has partnered with General Motors, and Sirius with BMW, DaimlerChrysler, Ford, Mazda, and Audi. For the moment, the devices are not interoperable, although the companies are working on a solution to this irritant. They also intend to add video signals to cater to families wishing to keep their kids entertained in the back seat with over 500 channels of satellite TV.

Because the service was not licensed in Canada until 2004, Canadians wanting satellite radio would drive to the United States, obtain an American billing address, purchase a $100 (U.S.) receiver and become part of the so-called "grey market" of subscribers. The licensing of this service in Canada may direct some of those subscription fees toward Canadian operators. At the November 2004 hearings, the CRTC examined contiguous questions such as CanCon requirements, how much licensees should contribute to Canadian talent development, the number of providers that should be authorized, and the probable impact of satellite on existing radio broadcasters and congruent digital broadcasting services. In June 2005, the CRTC licensed three subscription radio services, SIRIUS Canada Inc., Canadian Satellite Radio, and CHUM/Astral.

Subscription radio is likely to have a substantial impact on the entire Canadian radio industry. Until now, traditional radio operators have paid little attention to satellite radio because subscription has been low relative to the pool of people who can listen to "free" radio, and because it has been available only on specialized receivers. But that complacency may soon give way to a different attitude when satellite radio providers ramp up their marketing strategies. For example, when people start to realize that their "free" listening is actually a type of payment (they give their time away for exposure to advertising), many listeners might find their time worth more and begin to look favourably on satellite radio.

Internet Radio

Of all the new technologies, none has had a greater impact on conventional radio than the Internet. Today, home Internet connections are closing in on cable television as 55 percent of Canadian homes have at least one member who regularly uses the Internet from home (Statistics Canada, 2004b). Clearly, Internet users develop habits, preferences, and expectations toward on-line content that are significantly different from the ones they express vis-à-vis traditional media. The "my content when I want it" mantra is creating a mindset that many conventional media are scrambling to catch up to. Many people are discovering the pleasures of being their own music and entertainment programmer or webcaster. As a result, media content is increasingly dissociated or disconnected from its traditional mode of distribution. Niche content also acquires a much larger role in the media diet of Internet users. With streaming audio, MP3 players, P2P file transfers, and so on, our former mass-media consumption becomes characterized by a behavioural triad based on (1) asynchronous listening (i.e., I choose the time that best suits me to listen), (2) personalization of content, and (3) mobility (i.e., I choose *where* to listen).

Just a few years ago, on-line radio was the domain of geeks experimenting with choppy, low-quality sound. In the spring of 2004, however, Arbitron estimated that in the United States alone some 19 million people turn to on-line radio at least once a week—a stunning 12 million more people than in 2000 ("The Revolution in Radio," 2004). Fuelled by a significant upswing in **broadband** connections, on-line listenership to the top five Internet broadcasters—AOL's Radio@Network, Yahoo's Launchcast, Live365, Musicmatch, and Virgin Radio—is up 32 percent between June 2003 and February 2004 ("Forget Radio," 2004). For example, Live 365, the self proclaimed largest Internet network with over 5000 stations available, reports that its listeners spend an average of 50 minutes per session and 32 hours a month tuned in.

Many critics contend that AM/FM radio has laid the groundwork for its own demise with its coast-to-coast homogenized, repetitive, ads-and-promo "McRadio" offerings that have become both politically conservative and aseptic. Despite packaging their stations with cool monikers like BOB, JACK, DAVE, and JOE, radio stations are having the hardest time retaining the younger segments of their audiences. Indeed, 13 percent of Americans aged 12 to 24 now declare they listen to on-line radio on a weekly basis, up from 6 percent in 2001 ("The Revolution in Radio," 2004). Many believe that if on-line radio could launch a popular "shock jock" like Howard Stern, the market would explode.

With thousands of stations available worldwide, Internet radio makes AM and FM stations with their limited range and choice look like throwbacks to another era. The great disadvantage of Internet radio is that it mostly requires a sedentary mode of listening. However, recent developments are about to expand the number of options. Replay Radio, a computer program available for under $50, allows the capture of scheduled radio programs as MP3 sound files that can be transferred to a portable MP3 player. In addition, many cellular phone manufacturers are working to provide Internet and traditional radio reception. Nokia's Visual Radio service is designed to help users purchase songs they hear on their phone's radio. In synchrony with a radio broadcast, Visual Radio is capable of displaying pictures during the news, weather, sports, and so on. Nokia estimates that about 75 percent of consumers who have an FM receiver on their handset typically use it about once a week. Other players such as Intel and Sony are forging ahead with innovations of their own.

In Canada, pay-per-content is gaining acceptance. The country's second-largest radio operator, Standard Broadcasting Corp., has launched Puretracks, a pay-for-music site that sells songs on-line from all record labels, much as Apple's iTunes, Roxio's **Napster**, RealNetworks, and Wal-Mart do. In the spring of 2004, Telus Corp. unveiled Pureradio, a customizable on-line music service—with 75 commercial-free stations—that also lets subscribers purchase songs. At $4.99 a month, Pureradio and the like hope to capitalize on a growing demand for on-line services where music **fans** look for legitimate outlets to buy their favourite music.

A CLOUDY FUTURE

Despite all the excitement surrounding novel forms of digital distribution, traditional radio remains a stalwart of the Canadian media landscape. The industry's recent financial results indicate that at least for the time being, the main operators seem to have found ways to stem the tide of losses. As a group they are fully cognizant of the challenges that lie ahead and are sparing no effort to extend the love affair that listeners have had with radio since its inception.

However, the industry cannot afford to turn a blind eye to the fact that non-traditional radio listening behaviour is bound to grow by leaps and bounds in the foreseeable future. The most popular Christmas presents in the United States in 2003 for people under the age of 40 were Apple iPods and satellite radio subscriptions. In 2004 alone, it is estimated that 10.8 million next-generation players will be sold, bringing the total installed base to 21.5 million ("Digital Music Player Market," 2004). A walk around any Canadian university campus should indicate just how pervasive listening to music from non-radio sources has become. The recent epidemic proportions of music downloading and/or pirating illustrates clearly a drastic change in philosophy: people no longer want to "own" entertainment, they merely want to be connected to it wherever they go. As such, Internet radio and other peripheral digital devices are steadily undermining the last great advantage of broadcast radio, portability.

But there is more to consider. Our current rating systems such as **ACNielsen** and **BBM** present a somewhat distorted picture of the radio audience. By measuring listeners who use radio as background, ratings tend to measure the behaviour of people who are not really passionate about music. True music fans have flocked massively to Internet-based radio with its myriad of genres. In the words of Guy Zapoleon (2004), this has created a situation in which "radio studies the listeners that are left; and as it programs to those existing listeners, it becomes a 'self-fulfilling prophesy,' and no longer appeals to the passionate music listeners who no longer consume a lot of radio." Zapoleon fears that the upcoming widespread adoption of Internet radio, digital jukeboxes, and satellite subscription systems might turn broadcast radio into the next media "dinosaur." As emerging broadcasting standards such as WiFi and WiMax take root, they will make it easier for people to connect to the Web and choose their own type of radio. When this happens, the perennial force-fed programming mentality will give way to one of requests. Unquestionably, this type of customization is bound to have a profound impact on the ways traditional radio conducts its business.

QUESTIONS

1. What is CanCon and what are the arguments for and against it?
2. What is MAPL?
3. "CBC Radio plays an important role in solidifying Canadian identity." Discuss.
4. Should the amount of Canadian music played on radio be linked to the sales of Canadian music?
5. Is the success of radio bound up with the intimacy of the human voice, or is it the result of some other factor(s)?
6. How will the delivery and consumption of radio be transformed?
7. Based on the CHOI-FM case in Quebec City, is the CRTC justified in not renewing a licence for an entire station when the vast majority of the complaints concerned only a specific program and one or two hosts? Are there limits to freedom of expression in broadcasting?

NOTES

1. The author wishes to acknowledge the assistance provided by Philippe Andrecheck during the research phases of this chapter.
2. Graham Spry (1900–1983) was a journalist, diplomat, and activist who campaigned tirelessly on behalf of public broadcasting in Canada. In 1930, he cofounded the Canadian Radio League, which was instrumental in orchestrating support for public broadcasting.
3. The CRTC's name was changed in 1975 to the **Canadian Radio-television and Telecommunications Commission**, although its acronym (CRTC) remained unchanged.
4. Prior to the spring of 1998, the requirement stood at 30 percent.

REFERENCES

CRTC (Canadian Radio-television and Telecommunications Commission). (2001). Fact Sheet: The MAPL System. Retrieved from http://www.crtc.gc.ca/eng/INFO_SHT/R1.htm

———. (2003). Broadcasting Policy Monitoring Report 2003: Radio, Television, Broadcasting Distribution, Social Issues, Internet. Retrieved from http://www.crtc.gc.ca/eng/publications/reports/PolicyMonitoring/2003/bpmr2003.htm

———. (2004a). Fact sheet: Canadian content for radio and television. Retrieved from http://www.crtc.gc.ca/eng/INFO_SHT/G11.htm.

———. (2004b). Broadcasting Policy Monitoring Report 2004: Radio, Television, Broadcasting Distribution, Social Issues, Internet. Retrieved from http://www.crtc.gc.ca/eng/publications/reports/PolicyMonitoring/2004/bpmr2004.htm

Digital music player market set to double in 2004. (2004, July 21). *USA Today*. Retrieved from http://www.usatoday.com/tech/news/2004-07-21-digital-music-players_x.htm

Everett-Green, Robert. (2001, March 1). Why Nelly became a radio star. *The Globe and Mail*, p. R1.

Forget radio, tune in to net. (2004, June 28). *Wired*. Retrieved from http://www.wired.com/news/digiwood/0,1412,63982,00.html

Nash, Knowlton. (1995). *Microphone wars: A history of triumph and betrayal at the CBC*. Toronto: McClelland and Stewart.

The Revolution in radio. (2004, April 19). *Time*, 38–39.

Statistics Canada. (2004a, July 5). Private radio broadcasting, 2003. *The Daily*. Retrieved from http://www.statcan.ca/Daily/English/040705/d040705b.htm

———. (2004b, July 8). Household Internet use survey, 2003. *The Daily*. Retrieved from http://www.statcan.ca/Daily/English/040708/d040708a.htm

———. (2004c, July 28). Radio listening, Fall 2003. The Daily. Retrieved from http://www.statcan.ca/Daily/English/040728/d040728b.htm

Zapoleon, Guy. (2004). Online radio will cater to music fans abandoned by AM and FM. Retrieved from http://www.kurthanson.com/archive/news/052504/index.asp

9

The Film Industry in Canada

Bart Beaty
University of Calgary

In April 2004, the government body charged with the development of the Canadian film industry took the unusual step of hiring a Hollywood agent. **Telefilm Canada,** an organization with an annual budget of almost $200 million, signed with Creative Artists Agency (CAA), the American talent agency that represents Steven Spielberg, Tom Cruise, Julia Roberts, Bruce Springsteen, and other mega-celebrities. Telefilm contracted CAA to work in the United States with the goals of developing material for Canadian films and persuading Canadian expatriates, such as CAA client Mike Myers, to return home to make films, at least from time to time. Why would a public agency enter into a deal whereby Canadian tax dollars would be directly funnelled to Hollywood? The answer says a lot about the priorities of the Canadian government today with relation to the film industry.

In 2003, Canadians spent $949 million on movie tickets. Of this, 96.4 percent went to films produced in other countries, the overwhelming majority of which were products of Hollywood (see Appendix 9.1, Canadian Box Office Receipts, for details on recent box office trends in Canada). Because Canada's movie theatres are fully integrated into the American film industry—with American weekend box-office reports including Canadian theatres as if the country were merely a fifty-first state—few Canadians living outside of the country's largest cities even have the opportunity to see Canadian films on the big screen. Despite the fact that dozens of Canadian films are released each year, it is rare to find Canadian films screening at local movie theatres outside of Vancouver, Montreal, and Toronto; many large cities, such as Calgary, Winnipeg, and Ottawa, may have fewer than half a dozen Canadian films screened in any given year, and those usually only at art-house or independent cinemas in the downtown core (see Appendix 9.2, Number of Films by Market and Origin, for recent release figures). Cities and towns without art houses are, for the most part, totally bereft of the opportunity to see Canadian movies, despite the extensive funding provided to Telefilm each year. Commentators on Canadian film often recognize three distinct difficulties that afflict our film industry: first, Canadian films are unpopular with Canadians; second, in the rare instances that they are popular, they are often regarded as inartistic; third, when they are successful, they are regarded as somehow "un-Canadian," and therefore regarded as cultural, if not financial, disappointments. Often, individual films are charged with being all of these things at once. The result is that Canada has developed a cinema of failure; our films are unable to compete with the output of Hollywood, and, according to some, they don't even deserve the opportunity to try.

For owners of movie theatres and distributors of motion pictures, the reason for the lack of exposure of Canadian films is self-evident. Canadian films, they argue, must compete for audiences in a competitive marketplace, and if they fail to find an audience, this is simply proof that the films have not connected with an audience and are therefore unpopular. Proponents of this free-market argument note that the most popular English Canadian films of the past five years have had box office receipts totalling only $3.7 million (*Men With Brooms*), $3.4 million (*The Red Violin*), and $1.6 million (*eXistenZ*). That these numbers seriously trail the revenues of recent Hollywood "bombs" such as *Catwoman* ($39 million) and *Aliens vs. Predator* ($63 million) suggests that Canadian and American filmmakers are barely engaged in the same business. Further, when the production budgets of films like *eXistenZ* ($31 million) are taken into account, the extent of the economic failure seems even more pronounced. Figures such as these indicate that audiences are generally not encountering Canadian films in theatres, or, if they are, that they are not attracted to what they see. At the same time, many in the Canadian film industry observe that since Canadian films are almost completely shut out of both the Canadian and American film markets, it is unfair to make box-office comparisons with well-promoted American blockbusters. Cultural nationalists argue that Canadian films must be judged using a different set of criteria, including their artistic achievements and their ability to present distinctly Canadian stories to Canada and the world.

Typically, two responses have circulated around the box-office failure that has defined the Canadian film industry. The first suggests that Canadians should attempt to produce films that will appeal to a broad, international (i.e., American) audience. These people point to the success of films like *Porky's*, which grossed more than $100 million in 1982, and which remains the top-grossing Canadian film of all time. The box-office-oriented argument suggests that Canadian filmmakers should try harder to be "popular" or "commercial." The second response rejects the financial success of *Porky's*, generally arguing that while the film was successful, it was also terrible. Critics adopting this position argue from an elitist position, suggesting that the financial success or non-success of Canadian films is not an issue. Rather, we should focus as a nation on producing the best quality films possible, forsaking the short-term financial gains that can be made by pandering to a lowest common denominator for the long-term prestige that accrues to award-winning directors. Highbrow cultural commentators suggest that we should give up on the idea of "popularity" altogether. Among the most cited filmmakers for proponents of the idea that Canadian film should be well made, not widely watched, is Atom Egoyan. Egoyan's films are critically acclaimed, generally playing at important international film venues such as the

Cannes Film Festival. He has been nominated for two Academy Awards (for *The Sweet Hereafter*) in the United States, and is a regular winner at the Canadian Genie Awards. Nonetheless, despite these critical accolades, Egoyan's films often fail to earn back their costs. Critics who privilege the unpopular Egoyan over the inartistic *Porky's* regularly fall into a line of argument that suggests that Canada is hard-pressed to create films (due to budgetary shortfalls) that can compete with the biggest Hollywood blockbusters, but that as a nation Canada has more than enough talent to produce serious, artistic, critically-acclaimed, and award-winning films that lose money with style. Proponents of this view make the argument that by focusing on critically acclaimed films, Canada can eventually build a reputation that will expand the entire industry, and, further, that the well-made film is itself its own reward.

The argument that Canadians should continue to finance artistically adventurous filmmaking, even if there is little apparent market for the films, is often shaded by a third discursive factor in Canada, the presumed necessity of producing films that are distinctly Canadian. The nationalist argument tends to be distilled into the hoary axiom about "representing Canadian stories to Canadian audiences." For proponents of this point of view, a film such as *Porky's* (which is set in Florida) is a clear failure, and represents nothing of Canadian values. On the other hand, the equally populist *Men With Brooms*, which is about curling, a sport that is popular in Canada but not widely popular in many other nations, is seen to speak to a distinct sense of Canadian identity. Many people argue that, since Canada produces so few internationally popular films, and since so many Canadians seem perfectly at ease with the Hollywood films that fill Canadian movie theatres, the film industry should be focused on augmenting the productions of Hollywood by creating Canadian-themed films that our American neighbors are unlikely to undertake. From this perspective, the Canadian film industry would play a compensatory role, filling the demand for a presumed need while American cinema would continue to remain the staple of Canadian filmgoers. These three arguments—financial, artistic, and nationalist—are not new; rather, they have structured discussions of the Canadian film industry for more than a century, and can be seen as recurrent themes in the history of Canadian film policy.

THE ORIGINS OF THE CINEMA IN CANADA

The cinema came to Canada very quickly after it was established as a new mode of communication in France, England, and the United States. The first screenings in Canada on June 28, 1896, were a series of short films produced by France's Lumière brothers that were shown to audiences in Montreal. Paying a nickel to see a program of short, non-fiction films showing news and celebrities, or brief comedies and dramas, became the way that the public experienced the new medium. In 1906, Ernest

Ouimet built the Ouimetoscope in Montreal as the country's first movie palace. It seated 1200 people, but the venture could not compete with the better-established nickelodeons. While Canadian audiences flocked to movies in ever growing numbers, the overwhelming majority of films that they were seeing originated beyond the country's borders, as Canadian filmmakers were slow to react to new demand. In 1898, the Canadian Pacific Railway hired James S. Freer to travel the country with a camera, producing a series called *Living Canada* that would sell foreigners on the beauty and vibrancy of the young nation, consequently boosting immigration and, of course, rail travel to Canada's more remote locations. The scenic nature of Canada made it an enticing location for filmmakers, most of whom arrived from the United States. Because Canada had a small population that lacked a strong theatrical and music hall **(vaudeville)** tradition, few Canadian performers clamoured for the opportunity to appear in American films shot in Canada. The stars of the Canadian stage had generally departed for New York already, just as future generations of actors would make their names in Hollywood.

Because of the problems of audience and talent, there were few efforts to create an indigenous Canadian film industry. Given Canada's small population, for a film to be financially successful it would have to be released abroad as well as at home, but Canadian producers had difficulty cracking these foreign markets. However, foreign film companies, particularly those from Britain and the United States, had few difficulties entering Canada. When the Allen brothers opened their Canadian theatre chain, they booked American and British films whose distribution was controlled from abroad. Not only did these foreign companies bring their own films to Canada, they also failed to return the favour by distributing Canadian films in their home country. The process of block-booking, which required theatres to buy an entire season's worth of films sight unseen from a distributor, augmented this problem, leaving few holes in the schedules of Canadian cinemas for non-American films. This process exists in a modified form to this day, obligating cinemas to book films well in advance of their opening weekends, and reducing opportunities for Canadian films to be seen. By the 1920s, as the Hollywood studio system vertically integrated by owning both the studios that made the movies as well as the theatres in which they were seen, Canada had been all but squeezed out of its own film industry. America's Paramount Pictures owned the Allen theatre chain, the largest in the country, and American distributors like First National and Fox were battling for the remainder of the Canadian market.

Despite the odds, there was still a small but passionately dedicated community of amateur and professional filmmakers in Canada. Their legacy can be traced back to the 1920s, just two decades after the first film screenings in Montreal. Ernest Shipman is perhaps the best known of these early filmmakers. He produced films such as *The Man from Glengarry* (Henry MacCrae 1922) and *The Critical Age* (Henry MacCrae 1922), but his best remembered film was *Back to God's Country* (David Hartford 1919), which became notorious for the fact that his wife, Nell, appeared in it nude—although behind a distant waterfall. Nonetheless, for the most part Canadian entrepreneurs rarely produced films, particularly after the substantial losses suffered by *Carry On, Sergeant* (Bruce Bairnsfather 1928), the first big-budget Canadian film failure. In 1923, the federal government created the Canadian Government **Motion Picture Bureau,** the world's first government-sponsored film agency, to produce travelogues that were widely distributed in the United States in an effort to boost trade and investment. In 1927, with the coming of sound to the cinema, the Bureau neglected to keep pace with technological change, and its films disappeared from the international scene. Similar government agencies, such as the Ontario Government Motion Picture Bureau and the National Parks Bureau, continued to produce films for non-professional circuits, such as schools, community centres, and churches, yet few Canadians produced feature-length fiction films at this time.

While many countries, including the United States, Britain, France and Germany, adopted laws in the 1920s to foster and protect their film industries, Canada took little interest in the phenomenon. Indeed, the first piece of important legislation bolstering the Canadian film industry was not passed in this country, but in Britain. In 1927, Britain attempted to staunch the flow of American films into that country by adopting a quota system, requiring theatres to show a sliding percentage, between 5 and 20 percent, of films made in Britain or in the British Commonwealth. One result of the quota was that American filmmakers could shoot films in Canada and have their movies qualify as British under the new law. From 1928 until 1938, American filmmakers produced low-budget films—dubbed "quota quickies"—in Canada for the British market. When the law was renewed in 1938, Canadian-produced films were excluded from the quota in order to close this loophole, and the American companies returned to the United States, bringing filmmaking in Canada to a virtual standstill. At this point in history, the American studio system, with its eight large companies, was well entrenched and had almost total control of the Canadian film market, with Canada existing essentially as a part of the American domestic box-office. This situation persists to this day, although government-sponsored efforts to spur the creation of a Canadian film industry have sought to alter the situation.

THE CREATION OF THE NATIONAL FILM BOARD

The first significant challenge to American domination of Canadian movie screens came about in 1938. John Grierson, the leader of Britain's documentary film training centre, was invited to undertake a study of the government's film programs. Noting that the Canadian Government Motion Picture Bureau was moribund, Grierson recommended the creation of a central coordinating body. In March 1939, the government created the **National Film Board (NFB)**, and Grierson became the Board's first commissioner. With the outbreak of the Second World War in the fall of that year, there was suddenly a pressing need to produce films that represented Canada's unique position in the war effort. By the end of 1939, the NFB had 787 employees dedicated to this task. As patriotic sentiment swept the nation, the major problem facing Canadian filmmakers—where to show the films—was solved when Famous Players Canada agreed to show NFB wartime propaganda films in their 800 cinemas. Despite this access, reaching rural Canadians where no Famous Players cinema existed was more challenging. To bring film to these people, the NFB established 92 circuits, each serving approximately 20 rural communities. Each month, a travelling projectionist would visit these communities with NFB-produced films. Additionally, the NFB set up a series of libraries across the country at which Canadians could see their films.

The primary productions of the NFB in its early years were war-related documentaries or propaganda films. Two well-crafted series, *Canada Carries On* and the *World in Action*, were intended to educate the public about their duty to the nation. Each of these series produced one new film each month, generally with stirring visuals and authoritative voice-over commentaries often supplied by actor Lorne Greene. One of the *World in Action* films, *Churchill's Island*, won an Oscar in 1941, the first such prize for a Canadian film. NFB documentaries were reassuring and upbeat, offering the promise of a better society by the end of the war. Given his own personal history of producing documentary films in Britain, it is not surprising that Grierson actively sought to slow the creation of feature films in Canada. Leaving features for American producers, Grierson hoped to establish Canada as a world-leader in documentary filmmaking. (Indeed, the documentary legacy still remains in Canada, with the NFB and CBC jointly operating a digital television channel dedicated to the promotion of the documentary film.) For Grierson, the fiction film was mere escapism, similar to the dance hall or the sensational newspaper. He envisioned Canadian film production existing on a loftier plane, producing films that were uplifting and educational. Grierson's notion persisted at the NFB long after his departure following the end of the Second World War, at a time when the NFB's films were losing their access to Canadian and American screens.

With the war over, Famous Players cancelled their agreement to show Canadian films, and distribution reverted to its previous dire state. Having abdicated the feature film industry to the United States, and then having lost access to Canadian theatres for documentaries following the end of the war, Canadian film producers were once again largely shut out of their own market. To combat this situation, and to help redress Canada's trade imbalance with the United States, the Canadian Co-operation Project was initiated in 1948. In this deal, the Canadian government promised not to interfere with American domination of the Canadian film industry in return for increased coverage of Canada within American films, more American films shot on location in Canada, and the distribution of NFB shorts in the United States. This policy presented the Canadian film market to American companies on a silver platter. It was not until the 1950s that the American dominance of

Canadian filmgoing became an important domestic issue. In the wake of growing nationalism fuelled by Canadian participation in the two World Wars, a wide-ranging cultural commission was formed to address the question of Canadian identity in relation to the arts. The Massey Commission report of 1951 suggested that America's influence over Canada had inhibited the production of Canadian culture, but the Commission had few recommendations for alleviating American dominance in the film industry. Generally, the Massey Commission pointed the government in the direction of more public funding for the arts in Canada. The NFB, whose mandate was to "interpret Canada to Canadians and to other nations," seemed well positioned to benefit from any increase in government funding. At the same time, however, the NFB had to contend with the newly launched Canadian Broadcasting Corporation (CBC) television network, which did not work closely with the existing film board but sought to produce most of its programming in-house. As television signals increased in Canada, they placed even more pressure on the NFB and film production in general. By the end of the decade, half the NFB's output was produced with the intention of broadcasting the films on television, rather than releasing them in theatres.

As if in protest, filmmakers associated with the NFB stepped up their efforts to produce a distinctly Canadian film culture. Technologically, new lightweight cameras and the ability to record synchronous sound abetted the *Cinéma direct* movement. Socially, the movement was inspired by an increasing awareness of Canadian, particularly Québécois, filmmakers as artists with a unique contribution to make to their country—however they defined it. The Quiet Revolution that shifted Québécois society from rural and church-dominated to urban and state-based in the 1950s and 1960s spurred filmmakers to examine the lives of everyday people as the basis for their art. French-speaking directors in Quebec imagined that the directly observational style of documentary, which eschewed the type of authoritarian voice-over common to the NFB documentaries of the wartime era, could represent the Québécois to themselves. French-language film production greatly expanded at the NFB in the 1960s, and a distinct Francophone unit was created in 1964. The filmmakers associated with this unit, including Jacques Godbout, Gilles Carle, Clement Pérron, Denys Arcand, and Gilles Groulx, chafed at what they perceived as a colonial attitude at the NFB, and they bristled at the refusal of the board to permit feature film productions. Many of the documentary films produced in the Cinéma direct style demonstrate a strong sense of Québécois nationalism. *Les racquetteurs* (Michel Brault and Gilles Groulx 1958) depicts a snowshoe festival in Sherbrooke, Quebec, celebrating the rural traditions of the area. *Pour la suite du monde* (Pierre Perrault 1963), Quebec's first feature-length documentary, similarly focuses on rural traditions in Quebec, addressing the reconstruction of a Beluga whale fishery. *Québec–USA ou l'invasion pacifique* (Michel Brault and Claude Jutra 1962), depicts the influx of American tourists into Montreal as a new form of colonization. Interestingly, as English Canadian directors adopted the Cinéma direct style it was generally stripped of its explicit politics. The *Candid Eye* (1958–1959) series, for example, turned an objective lens on aspects of Canadian life without developing a strong sense of critique. The most famous English Canadian film to come out of the movement was *Lonely Boy* (Wolf Koenig and Roman Kroitor 1961), a look at the life and celebrity of Canadian pop star Paul Anka. *Cinéma direct* began as a documentary movement, in keeping with Canada's historic status of a featureless film policy. However, the artistic strides taken by these filmmakers anticipated even bolder steps into the arena of full-length feature films.

TOWARD THE DEVELOPMENT OF A FEATURE FILM INDUSTRY

The NFB's success in helping to re-define the status and aesthetics of the documentary form in the 1960s did not immediately carry over to an enthusiasm for fiction filmmaking, at least within the bureaucratic machinery that controlled the industry. Despite the success of the NFB's feature-length documentaries, the board still shied away from the possibility of producing feature-length fiction films, and those features that were released were done so reluctantly. *Drylanders* (Don Haldane 1963) dealt with settlers in the dust bowl of Saskatchewan at the turn of the century, a film with strong Canadian content and nationalist appeal that was distributed in the United States by Columbia. Both *Drylanders* and *Pour la suite du monde* were originally intended as television features, but both ran past the one-hour television format, necessitating a theatrical release. As the 1960s progressed, the number of feature films produced continued to grow, with notable films including *Nobody Waved Goodbye* (Don Owen 1964), *Le chat dans le sac* (Gilles Groulx 1964), and *La vie heureuse de Léopold Z* (Gilles Carle 1965). Importantly, none of these films was produced with the knowledge of the board, and the NFB responded to this type of directorial entrepreneurialism by placing tighter restrictions on budgets and discouraging auteurist productions. One result of this clampdown was that a number of notable directors, including Claude Jutra and Pierre Patry, left the NFB to work on their own projects elsewhere, in the hopes of establishing a Canadian feature film industry without the aid of the government. The most significant film stemming from these defections was Jutra's *À tout prendre* (1963), an autobiographical love story.

Based on the limited success of Canadian feature filmmaking in the 1960s, in 1964 the government launched an inquiry into the possibility of creating a full-scale feature film industry in Canada. The report, released in October 1965, concluded that contrary to longstanding politics and general sentiment, there should be a feature film industry after all. Nonetheless, the committee recognized that distribution significantly hampered the possibility that this industry might flourish, and also noted that there seemed to be little evidence of global demand for Canadian films.

Therefore, it was suggested that the industry become "internationally oriented," or more succinctly, that Canada's film industry strive for mass market popularity by mimicking the tried-and-true formulas made popular in Hollywood, although with fewer financial resources and distribution possibilities. Thus, in 1967 the government created the **Canadian Film Development Corporation (CFDC)** to spur private investment in the film industry. The CFDC would be responsible for aiding film production and distribution, although its successes with the latter were severely limited. This $10 million fund, upon which the NFB could not draw, sparked new productions by lending up to half of a film's budget. In the early 1970s, the CFDC supported a number of films that are now recognized as important milestones in the history of Canadian cinema, including Don Shebib's *Goin' Down the Road* (1970), *The Rowdyman* (Peter Carter 1972), *La vraie nature de Bernadette* (Gilles Carle 1972), and *Kamouraska* (Claude Jutra 1973). Additionally, the CFDC was successful in launching the careers of several important Canadian filmmakers. For example, the corporation invested in David Cronenberg's *Crimes of the Future* (1970), and later supported half a dozen of his films through the early 1980s.

At the same time, not all films sponsored by the CFDC were memorable, and more than a dozen were low-budget Québécois porn films. Nonetheless, distribution remained an ongoing problem, and while interesting and distinctive Canadian films were being made for the first time, few were being seen due to the American monopoly on exhibition. In 1972, The Toronto Filmmakers Co-op recommended to the federal government the creation of a 15 percent Canadian content quota on commercial exhibitors that would echo the regulations imposed on radio and television. The CFDC endorsed the idea of a quota in 1974, but cinema-owners and the existing distribution companies who wanted to maintain the flow of American films into their theatres aggressively fought the proposal. A voluntary quota agreed to by Famous Players and Odeon in 1973, which guaranteed Canadian films two weeks' screen time in Vancouver, Toronto, or Montreal, was acknowledged as a failure by 1975, with the theatre companies neither promoting the presence of these Canadian films nor providing them with strong theatre locations. Further suggestions intended to solve the distribution crisis, including a 10 percent tax on distributor's receipts to build a sustainable production fund, were never actualized.

Faced with only limited success in building an artistically viable feature film industry, the Canadian government next turned its attention to efforts to build an industry that was, at least, financially healthy. The late-1970s was a period in Canadian film production known as the tax-shelter boom that focused almost exclusively on attempts to re-create the popular style of Hollywood films north of the border. To spur investment, the government introduced a law whereby investors in a Canadian feature film could write off 100 percent of their investment in the first year, a significant incentive. At the same time, the government continued to emphasize the necessity of making films for an export market by de-stressing specifically

Canadian aspects. The tax-shelter boom was the first effort to re-create Canada as Hollywood North—a space in which American companies would be invited to make films as a job-creation strategy, and Canadian companies would attempt to match their efforts. By stressing foreign sales, the CFDC began to place greater emphasis on English-language films that could be sent to the United States, much to the detriment of filmmakers in Quebec, even though that province had the most successful film industry in the country. At this time, the CFDC completely retreated from nationalist ideologies and championed the idea of market-based success. Among the notable films produced in this era were *Meatballs* (Ivan Reitman 1979), *Murder by Decree* (Bob Clark 1979), *The Changeling* (Peter Medak 1980), and, of course, *Porky's*. Based on the films produced at the time, it is clear that the tax shelter policy had a number of drawbacks. Primary among these was the sense that Canadian film policy had completely abandoned the idea that the country should be producing "high quality" Canadian films. Second, as budgets exploded, the necessity of reducing or eliminating Canadian content rose accordingly. Thus, as the film industry continued to expand, government policy had the perverse effect of reducing the amount of Canadian content being produced. Finally, it had become increasingly clear that unscrupulous film producers were frequently cheating investors out of their tax deductible investments by starting production on films, securing financing, and then paying themselves exorbitant production salaries or walking away from the production altogether, leaving investors with nothing to show for their money. While a few films made during the period were of high quality or did represent Canadian ideas and values, including *Les Plouffe* (Gilles Carle 1981), *Les bons débarras* (Francis Mankiewicz 1980), and *The Grey Fox* (Phillip Borsos 1982), the vast majority of the films are barely recalled by contemporary audiences.

In 1984, government policy on film production underwent a radical shift. Recognizing the increasing role that television played in the dissemination of Canadian feature films, whether on basic, cable, or pay television, film and television funding were merged under a single entity, with the CFDC becoming Telefilm Canada. The new organization had an increased budget of $60 million to support Canadian film production. Nonetheless, the problem of distribution remained unsolved. A proposal to retain 7 percent of the American distribution industry's revenues for Canadian firms was killed by the Conservative government of Brian Mulroney in the lead-up to the free trade election of 1988, and the problem of distribution persisted with no regulation in sight. Thus, despite the critical acclaim of films like *Le déclin de l'empire américain* (Denys Arcand 1986), *Un zoo la nuit* (Jean Claude Lauzon 1987), and *I've Heard the Mermaids Singing* (Patricia Rozema 1987), the Canadian film industry continued to struggle to find audiences in Canada. An attempt to remedy this problem was introduced in 1988 with the creation of the Feature Film Distribution Fund, which extended credit to Canadian film distributors to support marketing and promotion, an increasingly key aspect of the industry.

While attempts to open up the distribution of Canadian films have still not been successful, one effort to think outside the box (office) has met with some good results. Failing to place Canadian films in Canadian theatres, many production companies have increasingly turned to **international co-productions** as a means of opening up new markets to Canadian filmmakers. This tendency dates back as far as 1962, when the NFB explored co-production possibilities with England and France. In the 1990s, international co-productions became the hallmark of Canadian filmmaking, with more than 230 such projects between 1994 and 1999, as Canada signed co-production treaties with more than 40 countries. Among the noteworthy international co-productions produced in recent years are *Black Robe* (Bruce Beresford 1991), *Le confessional* (Robert Lepage 1995), *Margaret's Museum* (Mort Ransen 1995), *The Red Violin* (François Girard 1998), and *Les triplettes de Belleville* (Sylvain Chomet 2003). These films, which have significantly higher average budgets than most Canadian-produced films, are sometimes decried by those who cherish the "Canadian stories" model, but are serving to highlight the inadequacy of strictly nationalist ideologies in an increasingly globalized and multicultural world.

OTHER APPROACHES TO FILMMAKING

The feature film industry in Canada has developed over the past four decades in a series of fits and starts. The current reality is that, for all its many levels of provincial and federal funding, Canada is a country in which it is possible to make a film but not a place where it is easy to have it seen by the public. At the same time, the NFB has struggled to re-define itself in relation to private sector filmmaking. The mid-1960s saw the decentralization of the NFB, as offices were established across the country in an effort to minimize the vision of Ottawa. While nation-building remained one of the key goals of the board, the new emphasis on regional voices stressed the ideal of inclusiveness. Exemplary of this tendency was the *Challenge for Change* series that existed between 1969 and 1980. *Challenge for Change* represented a series of social-action films addressing issues pertaining to minority and disadvantaged groups across the country. At the same time, however, the board was thrown into turmoil in the early-1970s by increasingly radical filmmakers from Quebec. NFB commissioner Sydney Newman suppressed several films, including two by Denys Arcand (*On est au coton* (1970) and *Québec, Duplessis et après* (1972)), because of their political points of view. The censorship at the NFB outraged many in the French-language production side of the board. One of their more successful attempts at diversity was Studio D, the first publicly funded women's film production studio in the world. Directed by Kathleen Shannon, who had emerged through the *Challenge for Change* series, Studio D focused on the production of documentaries that would insert women's voices into the predominantly masculine history of Canadian filmmaking. Studio D emphasized a form of social realist filmmaking that was interested in stirring discussion, and three of the studio's films won Academy Awards: *I'll Find a Way* (Beverly Schaeffer 1977), *If You Love This Planet* (Terri Nash 1982), and *Flamenco at 5:15* (Cynthia Scott 1983).

Despite these successes, the NFB found itself increasingly isolated in the Canadian cultural landscape. Following the cultural bonanza that accompanied the 1967 centennial celebrations, the CBC ended its contract with the NFB, effectively ending their policy to seek out broadcasting options in the face of dismal theatrical options. By the 1980s many were questioning the relevance of the Board. Following the free trade election of 1988, the government turned toward a philosophy of economic **neoliberalism** that stressed smaller government agencies and more latitude for the private sector. As a result, the budget for the NFB, like that of the CBC, was deeply slashed in the 1990s under the Liberal government of Jean Chrétien, and the innovative Studio D was closed down in March 1996. To celebrate the sixtieth anniversary of the NFB in 1998, the Museum of Modern Art in New York staged a retrospective of NFB-produced animation and documentaries, and the Academy of Motion Picture Arts and Sciences in Los Angeles held a retrospective honoring the NFB's 11 Oscar-winning short films and 63 nominated films. Despite this massive critical and industry success, with more than one Academy Award–nominated film produced on average for each year of the board's existence, many in the government and private sector insisted that the NFB increasingly had no role in Canadian film culture, existing only as an outmoded relic of a previous era. For these critics, the logic of financial success clearly trumps questions of artistic merit and nation-building.

SADLY, AS GOOD AS IT GETS

Most Canadians would welcome a film industry that produced films that were popular, well crafted, and in touch with Canadian concerns, but these have been few and far between. In English Canada, while many films are artistically innovative and speak to particularly Canadian issues, these films are rarely popular. The few films in recent years that have met all three criteria have tended to come from Quebec. Clearly, a separate language and culture have given Quebec a different relationship to American popular culture. One clear distinction in the Québécois film industry is the existence of an indigenous star system that provides marquee value through the use of popular film and television stars. In December 1997 and January 1998, for example, James Cameron's *Titanic* was the top-grossing film in every market in the world— except Quebec. In Quebec, more people flocked to see Louis Saïa's *Les Boys*, a light comedy about a benighted Montreal bar-league hockey team that starred well-known Québécois actors and comedians like Rémy Girard, Marc Messier, and Patrick Huard. The success of films like *Les Boys* proved that certain Canadian films could compete with the biggest successes in the world, if they spoke plainly to the interests of Canadian audiences. More recently, Denys Arcand's *Les invasions barbares* (2003) became the first Canadian film to win the Academy Award for Best Foreign Language Film. A critical success that also made money around the world, Arcand's film is a rare example of achieving the triple crown of Canadian film success: economic, artistic, and nationalistic. It stands as a rare success story upon which the industry can hope to build in an effort to overcome a long legacy of missed opportunities, foreign domination, and critical, financial, and nationalistic failures.

QUESTIONS

1. According to the author, what are the priorities of the Canadian government with relation to the film industry?
2. Do you think that Canada has developed a "cinema of failure"? Cite some recent Canadian films and state whether or not they have been, in your opinion, successful or not.
3. What have been some of the historical struggles in developing an indigenous Canadian film industry?
4. Do you feel there is something intrinsically "Canadian" about the documentary tradition and the National Film Board?
5. Why has Quebec's film industry been more successful compared to that of the rest of Canada?

REFERENCES (SELECTED)

Berton, Pierre. (1974). *Hollywood's Canada: The Americanization of our national image.* Toronto: McClelland and Stewart.

Buxton, Bill. (2000). *Canada's film century: Traditions, transitions, transcendence.* Montreal: Lonergan University College.

Clandfield, David. (1987). *Canadian film.* Toronto: Oxford University.

Dorland, Michael. (1998). *So close to the State/s: The emergence of Canadian feature film policy.* Toronto: University of Toronto Press.

Evans, Gary. (1991). *In the national interest: A chronicle of the National Film Board of Canada from 1949 to 1989.* Toronto: University of Toronto Press.

Fetherling, Douglas. (1988). *Documents in Canadian film.* Peterborough, ON: Broadview Press.

Gittings, Chris. (2002). *Canadian national cinema.* London: Routledge.

Marsolais, Gilles. (1968). *Le cinéma canadien.* Montreal: Éditions du jour.

Melnyk, George. (2004). *One hundred years of Canadian cinema*. Toronto: University of Toronto Press.

Monk, Katharine. (2001). *Weird sex and snowshoes: and other Canadian film phenomena*. Vancouver: Raincoast Books.

Morris, Peter. (1978). *Embattled shadows: A history of Canadian cinema, 1895–1939*. Montreal: McGill-Queen's University Press.

Pendakur, Manjunath. (1990). *Canadian dreams and American control: The political economy of the Canadian film industry*. Toronto: Garamond Press.

Pratley, Gerald. (2003). *A century of Canadian cinema: Gerald Pratley's feature film guide, 1900 to the present*. Toronto: Lynx Images.

Verroneau, Pierre, and Piers Handling (Eds.). (1980). *Self-portrait: Essays on the Canadian and Quebec cinemas*. Ottawa: Canadian Film Institute.

APPENDIX 9.1

CANADIAN BOX OFFICE RECEIPTS ($ MILLIONS)

English Market

	2001		2002		2003	
Canadian	$2.1	0.3%	$8.7	1.0%	$7.2	0.9%
USA	$674.9	92.0%	$747.7	90.1%	$756.8	93.8%
Other Foreign	$56.3	7.7%	$73.3	8.8%	$42.6	5.3%
	$733.3		$829.6		$806.7	

French Market

	2001		2002		2003	
Canadian	$12.1	9.9%	$17.5	12.6%	$27.1	19.0%
USA	$94.5	77.3%	$99.7	71.6%	$101.6	71.3%
Other Foreign	$15.5	12.7%	$22.1	15.9%	$13.6	9.6%
	$122.2		$139.3		$142.4	

English and French Markets

	2001		2002		2003	
Canadian	$14.3	1.7%	$26.2	2.7%	$34.4	3.6%
USA	$769.4	89.9%	$847.4	87.5%	$858.4	90.5%
Other Foreign	$71.9	8.4%	$95.4	9.8%	$56.2	5.9%
	$855.6		$969.0		$949.0	

Source: http://www.cftpa.ca/newsroom/pdf_studies/2004.10.IntlProductionInCanada.pdf

APPENDIX 9.2

NUMBER OF FILMS BY MARKET AND ORIGIN

English-language Market

	2001	2002	2003
Canadian	54	60	62
USA	235	257	244
Other Foreign	153	143	114
Total	442	460	420

French-language Market

	2001	2002	2003
Canadian	47	56	73
USA	153	152	170
Other Foreign	119	108	117
Total	319	316	360

Source: http://www.cftpa.ca/newsroom/pdf_studies/2004.10.IntlProductionInCanada.pdf

10

"Pirates," Peers, and Popular Music

Martin Laba
Simon Fraser University

The trade in "pirated" cultural goods, especially music, occurs in both established and emerging marketplaces that are global in reach, and both local and virtual in nature. On the one hand, there exist in cities around the world actual, physical marketplaces that are dense, cluttered, and boisterous places of negotiation, tactic, and barter. These marketplaces are actual locations where street-stall entrepreneurs operate, if not quite underground, then by their own rules and within unsanctioned networks of production, distribution, and profit. On the other hand, there also exist virtual marketplaces created by the speed and facility of digital Internet music, of Internet service providers, and of millions of "swappers," sharing files without border or boundary.

The efforts of the music industry to contain and eradicate both of these marketplaces—the physical locations and the virtual spaces—in which music is plundered have been vigorous but have also produced very uneven results. The fact is that the relationship between the popular music industry and its audiences has always been marked by a certain degree of tension, and new digital technologies have helped to thrust this tension into very high relief. Industry threats, policing strategies and actions, lobbying, and litigation are all, effectively, attempts to constrain cultural practices that are illegal in certain jurisdictions—and the attempt to constrain cultural practices is daunting and problematic at best. The point to emphasize here is that on-line practices such as downloading and uploading of music in a dynamic and volatile digital environment have become, as Eben Moglen (1999) has pointed out, "socially dominant" in contemporary culture. The story of peer-to-peer file sharing is infinitely more than a story of the shift from analog to digital technology; it also details a profound cultural shift, a deep and active engagement with the possibilities—some obviously illegal—of new enabling technologies.

In discussing the importance for any media analysis to include the interplay between technology, marketing, and culture, authors Kline, Dyer-Witheford, and de Peuter (2003) offer some insight into the type of "cultural shifts" described above. Drawing on Innis's notion of "oligopoly of knowledge" (1991), they observe the often paradoxical nature of **new media** that at first might "seem to reinforce the power of an established elite," but might also eventually help to "subvert" the elite by challenging and destabilizing the very relations of power into which the new media are introduced (Kline et al., p. 32). In other words, digitization of the music industries may increase industrial profits and efficiency but may also transfer unanticipated control to individual users. Hence, following Innis, the authors note that the introduction and extension of new media technology can result in cultural changes, shifts, or "disturbances" (Innis, 1991, p. 31). Clearly it can be argued that numerous and varied commodities and applications of digital technology have supported, consolidated, and extended commercial marketplaces, corporate control and concentration, and profitability in the industries of popular music. It can also be argued that these new digital media are techno-cultural innovations that have undermined the very foundations that serve and reinforce marketing, control, and profit. Nowhere are these cultural "disturbances" more profound than in the apparently uncontainable cultural practices of the complex international trade in pirated music, and especially in on-line music file sharing.

PIRACY IN LAHORE

I wrenched my bags from the clutches of the team of touts at the Lahore airport, and, liberated at last, I made my way to the departure zone. I had spent the past month working with NGOs and community-based groups in rural Pakistan on communication/education strategies for capacity-building, and I had taken as much time as possible during the visit to seek out and appreciate the musical practices of Qawwali, the great Sufi devotional music of Pakistan. I spent long hours on the scorched rural roads of Punjab, the jeep bucking over the ruts, squeezing at high speed past and between donkeys, carts, buses, scooters, water buffaloes, and cars, all vying for space on the constricted routes. The soaring voice of Nusrat Fateh Ali Khan somehow processed through the jeep's cassette player and speakers that had been long thrashed by the road, the elements, and old age, and that were held in place by ragged slashes of gaffing tape. Back in the city, I was often piloted by my good friend Mohammad Tahseen through the night streets of Lahore to ancient mosques to hear music, particularly Sufi drumming. Passing though a wall of hashish smoke, we found a place on the ground and settled in for hours of trance, dance, and drumming.

Waiting for my flight back to Bangkok, I noticed a boisterous crush of activity around a small kiosk. I ambled over, and the proprietor immediately took note of my interest and enthusiastically waved me over to the counter. There packed into the smallest space was a pirate's treasure trove—pirated music and movies, in various formats, available for a pittance of market value, the artwork of the covers photocopied and inserted in CD cases and taped on video and DVD covers. Unencumbered by copyright and royalty concerns, customers were in a buying frenzy and the seller was doing a particularly thriving business. At the counter I was asked what kind of music I liked, and when I replied that I was partial to Qawwali, out of a drawer below came dozens of pirated CDs of Qawwali and numerous other musical genres in Pakistan. The solicitous proprietor offered a comprehensive and finely detailed dissertation on the progress and nuances of Pakistani music, popular and traditional, and offered his wares, all pirated, for my perusal and purchase.

PIRACY IN BANGKOK

Navigation through the stalls of the night markets of Sukhumvit was an intense affair. The air was dense with heat, and the toxic emissions of Bangkok's 24-hour traffic jam made breathing an altogether precarious activity. The gauntlet of street vendors shouted their entreaties, special deals, tonight only, discounts only for me. Every knock-off of every designer logo and object was displayed on makeshift tables—watches, jeans, sunglasses, movies, music, and more, all to be had for a fraction of the cost of the authentic object in official markets, even before bartering.

Business was brisk in the early evening as consumers scooped up recent mainstream hits by major pop celebrities from Asia, North America, Europe, Australia, and elsewhere. The heat and pollution were stifling, but consumer tourists were undeterred. They picked through hundreds of titles fanned out on the tables, and pirated music and movies were purchased and carried away by the bag-load.

Copy shops, CD factories, and a host of distribution sites and networks in Thailand, and in many other countries around the world, operate in an environment in which it may be illegal to violate international copyright protection laws and agreements,[1] but the cost of administration and enforcement in many developing countries has made intervention far too costly. Indeed, noncompliance with international copyright agreements has been a troublesome issue for a wide range of industries, from software to music. The music industry in particular has been most aggressive in its litigation efforts against copyright infringement. The **piracy** business is global and thriving, as Lawrence Lessig (2004) has noted: "All across the world, but especially in Asia and Eastern Europe, there are businesses that do nothing but take other people's copyrighted content, copy it, and sell it—all without the permission of a copyright owner" (p. 63).

These profiles offer only one version of the controversy over copyright and "use" in popular music; but "piracy" is both old and new, and an increasingly complicated term in the digital age. The Recording Industry Association of America (RIAA), always vigilant and forceful in its litigation efforts against copyright violations, is pithy in its characterization of contemporary violators: "Old as the Barbary Coast, New as the Internet. . . . Today's pirates operate not on the high seas but on the Internet, in illegal CD factories, distribution centers, and on the street" (Record Industry Association of America, 2003). In Canada, the Canadian Recording Industry Association (CRIA) is equally forceful in its "global response to internet piracy," conducted in concert with the International Federation of the

Phonographic Industry (IFPI) and the RIAA, and in its warning that it maintains an "anti-piracy unit" to carry out surveillance of the Internet against on-line music infringement (http://www.cria.ca).

DEMONS AND VILLAINS

The music industry has demonized peer-to-peer technology, service providers, and the users of Internet music by using such terms as "piracy" and "thievery." As new technologies continue to subvert and transform musical production, distribution, and well-established structures of manufacture and sale (and the very foundations of profitability), the industry has engaged in major legislative and litigious assaults. The terminology has been severe and has helped lend rationale and force to the industry's lobbying campaigns, and to its warnings to on-line music swappers. The RIAA outlines in gruesome detail the penalties for on-line pirates: up to three years in prison, $250,000 in fines, additional liabilities of $150,000 per infringed copyright, and up to six years in prison for repeat offenders (http://www.riaa.com/issues/piracy/penalties.asp). CRIA assures its members that it is involved in the gathering of evidence of copyright infringement against Canadian Web sites, and that "Notification in writing is sent to the website operators, service providers or both, informing them of the infringing copies of sound recordings on the music files of the sites they host and the legal implications if they do not voluntarily cease and desist offering the infringing copies on these sites" (http://www.cria.ca/antipiracy.php).

However, in his critique of the staleness of the music industry's business model and the reluctance of the industry to rethink and re-define copyright control, Reebee Garofalo (2003) suggests that "the music industry has been trying to convince consumers that there is a monster in their computers: the monster of copyright violation" (p. 30). He takes issue with the use of the music industry designation of file sharing as "piracy" and "theft," and argues that the industry would do well to learn from on-line music services and the various communities of users of those services. In particular, he notes, the industry in its current structures cannot equal on-line services that are unencumbered by "categories of artists, songs, and labels," and that offer users the capacity and facility to customize compilations from comprehensive music libraries (p. 41). The argument here is based on the recognition of the "culture" of file sharing; that is, an understanding that in many cases, this activity involves infinitely more than trading/downloading music files and extends to extensive and frequent "chat" between users on music—arguments around musical merits and preferences, information about new artists and sounds, ideas on musical and technological trends and developments. In other words, users "self select into communities of taste, which, without spending a dime, constitute a better promotional vehicle than anything the music industry currently has at its disposal" (Garofalo, 2003, p. 42).

"Piracy" and "theft" are, of course, highly pejorative terms that lack all nuance and fail to capture the nature and qualities of cultural practices at issue while indicting all users as unsavory and potentially morally bankrupt. If we developed a more considered and qualitative description of users, however, we would also gain a critical perspective on the uses and intentions involved in music downloading. For example, even within the strictest terms of copyright violation, different uses obviously carry different levels of harm (if any) to copyright. Lessig demonstrates this fact by categorizing users and the type of content they share. There are those who download music instead of purchasing music; those who use file sharing to hear samples of music before purchasing; those who search for copyrighted music that is no longer available, or for whom the costs of obtaining copyrighted music are prohibitive; and those who download music that is not copyrighted or is provided for free by the copyright owner (2004, pp. 68–69). One can use these categories, as Lessig does, to assess relative "harm." If music is downloaded as a substitute for purchasing, then, as Lessig maintains, it is illegal and harmful to copyright owners. If music is downloaded to listen to music before purchasing—a veritable "listening post"—then it may be a violation but is clearly beneficial to the copyright owner. If music is downloaded because it is no longer available, then no harm is done to the artist. Finally, in the case of downloading music that is not copyrighted, the practice is entirely legal and unproblematic (Lessig, 2004, p. 69).

Unfortunately, the language of "piracy" and "theft" lumps all downloading together and prevents us from understanding the complexity of the activity, some of whose outcomes may be benign or even beneficial. Of course, even a more refined terminology that places the accent on downloading as a cultural practice is not intended to excuse practices that are clearly illegal. Rather, a view to the cultural dimensions of peer-to-peer practices properly takes to task the broad and blunt characterization of all those who engage in downloading as pirates and robbers by actually considering the range of uses and the variable and controversial impacts and "harms" of such uses.

Global marketplaces for popular music are often understood and analyzed as a function of transnational corporate control and of media convergence and concentration. This is a valuable perspective that highlights the deleterious effects of the transnational mainstreaming of popular music (and of fast food, fashion, and other entertainment commodities). The criticism of transnational corporate cultural control rests on the fact that transnational mainstreaming can actually limit cultural expression and herd audiences together because that suits the business model, which seeks maximum audience control in order to achieve maximum profitability. As a result, the business produces and promotes bland, homogenized (but enormously profitable) formulaic musical goods and pop celebrity. That the popular music industry produces, promotes, delivers, and profits enormously from its products as entertainment commodities should hardly come as a revelation. Indeed, music consumers have long suspected a villainous streak in the behaviour of the mainstream entertainment industries; they have long felt that the industries are "in it just for the money." Consequently, consumers have little compunction about file sharing because they have little affection or concern for an industry that pulls in very handsome profits globally and that engages in "demonizing the record buying public and online community" and threatens litigation as its response to peer-to-peer practices (Garofalo, 2003, p. 43).

SWAPPING IN CANADA

On June 3, 2004, Chad Kroeger, front man for the Vancouver-based band Nickelback, addressed the press at Toronto's Eaton Centre. As noted by a McDonald's Restaurants of Canada Limited news release, Mr. Kroeger "joined McDonald's . . . to celebrate the Canadian launch of McDonald's new international restaurant promotion, *Big Mac Meal Tracks*" (http://www.mcdonalds.ca/en/news/canadian_pr.aspx?pr_ID=51). Customers who bought the specified meal items at McDonald's during the promotion were offered an access code redeemable for one free download at Sony's on-line music store, Connect. Mr. Kroeger took the opportunity to pillory those who engage in illegal downloading, to declare, in general terms, the ignorance of "young people," and to ruminate on the state and future of the music industry in almost apocalyptic terms:

> If trends continue the way they are, there isn't going to be any new music for people to download. From a guy who runs a record company, who produces bands and plays in a band, it's a horrifying thought. I love playing my guitar for people and singing for people and I would hate to think that could all be taken away with a couple of clicks on a mouse. Young people don't think. I'd be surprised if young people know what the hell Sam the Record Man or HMV was. Everyone just goes to the computer, downloads whatever the hell they want, they burn it and then just play it in their cars. That's killing the music industry. (Roadrunner Records, 2004)

Mr. Kroeger emphasized that he was not in the business of selling hamburgers, but rather his motivation was purer—that is, he wanted to inspire people to stop stealing music not because of fear of litigation but because they should realize that downloading is simply wrong. McDonald's, on the other hand, emphasized the brilliance of its international marketing campaign. In the official news release, McDonald's Canada Vice President of Marketing Laurie Laykish offered, in the declarative rhetoric of corporate promotion, considerable insight into the strategy of media/marketing tie-ins, which may contain inspiration for the music industry in how they might harness—and profit from—on-line music. Laykish states that the *Big Mac Meal Tracks* promotion "embodies the 'I'm lovin' it' global brand theme and highlights a McDonald's Canada commitment to ongoing innovation in meeting our customers' needs by aligning our business with other leaders in the music, fashion, entertainment and sports industries" (http://www.mcdonalds.ca/en/news/canadian_pr.aspx?pr_ID=51). The "innovation" referred to here is a recognition that young customers' "needs" for popular music can be met (or more accurately, manufactured and directed) by mixing media in the marketplace and creating compelling tie-ins between music, fast food, fashion, sports, celebrity, and many other entertainment commodities.

As I have noted elsewhere, popular music is a cultural expression of numerous and varied commodity forms and media—it must be understood in the context of a wider universe of popular commercial culture, and "cannot be analyzed apart from the interconnected interests, orders, forms, and technologies of commercial media that structure, promote, and disseminate the widest range of commodities and messages" (Laba, 1996, p. 75). In the contemporary marketing realities of media tie-ins—this is the "alignment" that Laykish speaks of between McDonald's and "leaders in music," in this case Chad Kroeger—the well-honed relationship between music and marketing becomes even more precise. These "realities" are now all about new and emerging technological capacities—music downloading and uploading above all—that are forging new terms for old alliances between the popular music industry and other consumer entertainment industries of fast food, fashion, advertising, film, professional sports, television, and many, many others. Yet, while there are delicious prospects it seems for profitability in music–burger tie-ins, for example, all is not calm and contained in the media marketplace of on-line music. The vitality and malleability of **interactivity** in computer-based communication has had cultural consequences, as already emphasized; and to invoke Innis once again, these consequences are "disturbances" in the traditional order, logic, progress, and profit production in the music industry. Canada has been a particularly lively and controversial environment for attempts to inhibit and contain on-line music.

A Supreme Court of Canada ruling on March 4, 2004, with regard to photo-copying legal case material has had substantial repercussions for the issue of copyright in general, including Internet music downloading. In overturning a previous lower court judgment, the Supreme Court ruled that the Law Society of Upper Canada (the self-governing body for lawyers in Ontario) did not violate copyright of three legal publishers when the work of these publishers was sold at the Great Library at Osgoode Hall in Toronto and no licensing fee was paid. In its decision, the Supreme Court was concerned with, and ruled in favour of, users' rights and "fair dealing" (i.e., special privileges afforded to individuals and institutions to use copyrighted materials—students, researchers, teachers, libraries, for example). As reported in *The Globe and Mail* coverage of the issue (Won, 2004), Scott Jolliffe, lawyer for the Law Society, argued that "the judgment has wider implications in that anyone can now make a single copy of any copyrighted material for research purposes—be it for an academic or commercial undertaking—and not pay a licensing fee to its creator under the notion of 'fair dealing'" (http://www.theglobeandmail.com/servlet/ ArticleNews/ TPPrint/LAC/20040308/PFRULING08/TPBusiness/).

Most relevant for Internet music and for providers/sellers of MP3 technology was the ruling that the Law Society did not engage in copyright infringement when it provided self-service photocopiers in the library. It could be argued, then, that providing the technology to copy music or listen to any available copy through the technology is not copyright infringement. At the time of this Supreme Court ruling, CRIA was pursuing the prosecution of 29 alleged "swappers" and "distributors" of music over peer-to-peer networks, and the ruling played a vital role in the outcome of this litigation.

On March 31, 2004, Justice Konrad von Finckenstein of the Federal Court of Canada determined that under Canadian copyright law, individuals who engage in peer-to-peer file sharing are not distributing music in the sense of actively sending out copies of music or promoting the fact that they have files available for sharing; in other words, individuals engaged in peer-to-peer file sharing are not necessarily engaged in copyright infringement activities under Canadian copyright laws. Justice von Finckenstein appeared to invoke the Supreme Court ruling on the Law Society case when he offered the analogy of the provision of photocopiers in a room full of copyrighted materials; that is, offering the means to make illegal copies is not in itself a copyright infringement. Further, Justice von Finckenstein noted that while Canada is a signatory of two **World Intellectual Property Organization (WIPO)** treaties (WIPO Copyright Treaty and WIPO Performances and Phonograms Treaty, 1996) that strictly prohibit the act of making available copyright content without the owner's permission—and there could be a compelling case that Internet service providers were precisely "making available" such content—Canada has not ratified and implemented the treaty and therefore the WIPO is not to be interpreted as a part of Canadian copyright law.

CRIA has appealed the von Finckenstein ruling, an action that may gain greater force with the *Interim Report on Copyright Reform*, tabled by the House of Commons Standing Committee on Canadian Heritage.[2] Among the recommendations of the report, the Committee urges the government to ratify the WIPO treaties, an initiative that it regards as key in the context of peer-to-peer file sharing on on-line networks. "Fair dealing" then, would not extend to users of enabling technologies for file sharing of copyrighted music, and Internet service providers would be liable for copyrighted materials available on their networks.

CRIA and RIAA, as well as the major music production and distribution corporations, were particularly critical of the ruling. Canada's rather independent approach to the issue of copyright has caused some tension with the U.S. music industry, which has the full weight of legislation (such as the Digital Millennium Copyright Act) on its side. President Clinton signed this act in October 1998 and brought the United States into compliance with the WIPO Copyright Treaty and the WIPO Performances and Phonograms Treaty. Contrary to the von

Finckenstein ruling, which offers a broad and liberal approach to fair dealing, the Digital Millennium Copyright Act very much limits "fair use" (fair dealing, in Canadian terms) by ruling illegal any practice that circumvents technological measures developed and implemented to protect the domain of copyrighted materials, such as music. Included in these prohibitions were devices and services that evaded or thwarted those protection measures.

In his report on the decision of the Copyright Board of Canada in December 2003[3] that downloading copyrighted music from peer-to-peer networks was legal (while uploading or distributing such material was illegal), John Borland (2003) suggests that the Canadian approach to downloading has "raised the hackles among copyright holders"—Canada's "reluctance" to ratify agreements and enact legislative measures to expand copyright protection has been a point of contention with the music industry. While the Copyright Board did implement a "tariff of levy" (up to $25) on MP3 players (such fees were already in effect for audiotapes and blank CDs), the Board did not extend a fee to personal computer hard drives and left such a ruling to judicial or legislative bodies in the future. Borland observes that Canada may well become "a model for countries seeking to find a balance between protecting copyright holders and providing consumers with more liberal rights to copyrighted works" (2004).

The latest Canadian ruling (at the time of this writing) is a decision of the Supreme Court of Canada (June 30, 2004) that continues this Canadian articulation of liberal principles around access and rights to copyrighted materials. The Society of Composer, Authors and Music Publishers of Canada (SOCAN) was seeking a court decision that would force Internet service providers to pay royalties, because, according to SOCAN, Internet service providers were "communicating" and "authorizing" the transmission of songs by the terms of the Copyright Act. The unanimous decision of the Supreme Court, however, ruled against SOCAN and determined that Internet service providers are conduits or "intermediaries" in the downloading process, and that they neither authorize nor counsel anyone to engage in the exchange of music files. What people download then, is not the responsibility of the Internet service providers, and accordingly, providers are not in violation of federal copyright legislation.[4] The decision articulates an overarching principle about freedom of information flow and dissemination in new and emerging digital technologies. In keeping with the series of rulings in Canada outlined in this section, the Supreme Court's decision recognizes the significance of the Internet in Canadian society, and favours an unencumbered development and expansion of the Internet in recognition of that significance. In other words, the freedom of information, and its flow and dissemination, is infinitely broader than peer-to-peer music file sharing. To address the specific issue of music, Mr. Justice Ian Binnie noted that in the case of an Internet service provider that has been notified that unauthorized copyright material is posted and available on its system, that provider must have the material removed or be liable for royalties.

NUMBERS GAMES

The music industry has railed against file sharing practices and services by declaring the effects of peer-to-peer practices on sales as disastrous to the health, progress, and well-being of the industry. Simply stated, the industry claim is that file sharing and burning are killing the music sector. But while a number of commissioned survey studies are invoked by the industry to support its claim of market decline and industry crisis, the most authoritative study to date substantially contradicts industry claims. *The Effect of File Sharing on Record Sales: An Empirical Analysis* (Oberholzer and Strumpf, 2004) presents compelling evidence in an exhaustive and meticulous empirical analysis of file sharing effects on sales.

The industry has insisted that decline in sales and a sobering prognosis of the industry's future are direct results of file sharing—that is, music and markets are diminished because of file sharing. CRIA, for example, offers in unambiguous detail an ominous picture of current and future erosion and ultimately the destruction of popular music. In the prominently featured essay "Free Music Myth" on the CRIA Web site, the account of the "problem" with downloading encapsulates prevailing industry views and claims (http://www.cria.ca/freemusicmyth.php). The central assertion of the piece is that "illegal copying and internet distribution means less sales," and less sales, according to the argument, means a host of negative consequences: companies have less capital to invest in artists and music; retail stores are forced to close and employees of those stores find themselves out of work; new artists cannot get deals with record companies; independent entrepreneurs cannot survive; new artists retire from the business because sales cannot be sustained.

In a similar vein, RIAA president Cary Sherman suggests that file sharing "robs songwriters and recording artists of their livelihoods, and ultimately undermines the future of music itself, not to mention threatening the jobs of tens of thousands" (*USA Today*, September 18, 2003, quoted in Oberholzer and Strumpf, 2004, p. 2). IFPI chairman Jay Berman also offers a bleak scenario for a world of unrestrained downloading: "Internet piracy means lost livelihoods and lost jobs, not just in record companies but across the entire music community. . . . Artist rosters have been cut, thousands of jobs have been lost, from retailers to sound engineers, from truck drivers to music journalists" (IFPI Network Newsletter, December 2003, quoted in Oberholzer and Strumpf, 2004, p. 2). CRIA, RIAA, IFPI, and other music industry interests account for the decline in sales—15 percent between 2000 and 2002—in terms of file sharing. Interestingly, between 1999 (the year Napster came into being) and 2000, sales rose steadily.

The Oberholzer and Strumpf study is vitally important in assessing the veracity of industry claims, and its methodology is key to the significance of the study because its empirical evidence offers one of the truest pictures of the precise impacts of peer-to-peer practices on the popular music industry. As the authors note, the study does not rely on surveys (a notoriously unreliable measure, and the predominant method used in commissioned studies cited by the music industry), but rather employs "observations of actual file sharing behavior to assess the impact of downloads on sales":

> We analyze a large file sharing dataset which includes 0.01% of the world's downloads from the last third of 2002. We focus on users located in the U.S. Their audio downloads are matched to the album they were released on, for which we have concurrent U.S. weekly sales data. This allows us to consider the relationship between downloads and sales. To establish causality, we instrument for downloads using technical features related to file sharing (such as network congestion or song length) and international school holidays, both of which are plausibly exogenous to sales. We are able to obtain relatively precise estimates because the data contain over ten thousand album-weeks. (p. 3)

The study employed statistical models to compare songs downloaded from 680 popular albums with the actual sales of those albums as reported through Nielson SoundScan.[5] Data was accessed directly from servers, and in total, the study observed 1.75 million downloads during a 17-week period in the fall of 2002. The authors reached the conclusion that "file sharing has no statistical significance on purchases of the average album" in their sample; and most significantly, they assert that file sharing is responsible for, at most, a "tiny fraction" of sales decline (p. 24). It is important to note that the authors point to a wide range of intentions and predilections in peer-to-peer practices—once again, the cultural foundations of file sharing—and therefore recall the importance of "reading" culture when analyzing and ultimately assessing the nature and impact of downloading popular music. Their description captures precisely what is problematic about music industry assertions with regard to the file sharing causality of sales decline:

> Participants could substitute downloads for legal purchases, thus reducing sales. Alternatively, file sharing allows users to learn about music they would not otherwise be exposed to. In the file sharing community, it is common practice to browse files of other users and to discuss music in file server chat rooms. This learning may promote new sales. . . . Individuals may use file sharing to sample music, which will increase or decrease sales depending on whether they like what they hear. The availability of file sharing could change the willingness to pay for music, either decreasing it (due to the ever present option of downloading) or increasing it because music tracks have gained a new use, sharing with others. Finally, it is possible there is no effect on sales. (p. 2)

In the absence of a conclusive theoretical prediction of the precise effects of file sharing on sales, empirical analysis is the only sound method by which such a prediction can be made; the authors note that in terms of the effect of file sharing on record sales, "the estimated effect is statistically indistinguishable from zero" (p. 3)

Other independent research (as opposed to surveys commissioned by RIAA and IFPI) provides similar and persuasive evidence that the music industry's blame of file sharing as the source of industry decline is misguided at best, and willfully erroneous at worst. Of particular note are two Internet research studies by Ipsos-Reid and Jupiter Research, both done in 2002. These studies conducted surveys—the same method employed by music industry commissioned studies—but reached very different conclusions. The Ipsos-Reid study concluded that "downloaders" generally do not stop purchasing CDs, with 81 percent of the respondents stating that their purchases of prerecorded music stayed the same in number or increased since they began file sharing. The Jupiter Research study—*File Sharing: To Preserve Music Market Value, Look Beyond Easy Scapegoats*—also analyzed data from surveys to conclude that while both positive and negative effects on record sales can be interpreted from the data, purchases of commercially available prerecorded music generally increased with the incidence of file sharing practices; that is, there was a net-positive impact of file sharing on music purchasing. The Jupiter study recognizes that it is one of many independent and authoritative studies that contradict music industry claims, and accordingly, the study articulates a concern with the industry's insistence that file sharing is the sole source of the apparent decline of music sales.

The music industry's obsession with file sharing as the reason for its economic woes is evidence of a persistent blind spot. The best independent research and analyses—many cited here—detail and emphasize the broader and eminently plausible factors that account for declining sales: less than favourable macroeconomic factors, conditions, and trends; the normal and historically patterned cyclical trends of the music industry; the ever increasing competitive environment in which numerous and varied forms of entertainment media and content contend; decreases in consumer spending overall in key years under analysis; an increasing concentration of the music industry in which major mergers—the merger of MCA and PolyGram into the Universal Music Group as a prime example—have meant substantial staff downsizing, a reduction in artist rosters and releases, and an ever greater reliance on celebrity superstardom and limited titles for the majority of sales; the refusal of the music industry to adapt and re-orient to dramatic changes in both the technologies and business of music production and dissemination, while spending its time and resources demonizing the fan base; and other factors.[6]

In the numbers games, if one is to put faith in solid empirical and survey-based independent research on file sharing (as one should), the evidence is irrefutable. The effect of file sharing on sales ranges from statistically negligible to somewhat beneficial. The industry's insistence and expenditure of resources on vilifying file sharing and "downloaders," threatening and carrying out litigation, lobbying government, and generally advocating draconian measures against technology and culture, are off the mark.[7]

CONCLUSIONS ON A SHIFTING GROUND

Among the many problems with the music industry's approach to surveillance, containment, and ultimately, the eradication of piratical Internet file sharing, most glaring is the failure to recognize that the ground upon which the industry traditionally operates is shifting constantly and dramatically. The considerable merit of Lessig's (2004) call for the "liberation" of "locked down" culture is his understanding that our means of access to the Internet are "technologies in transition" (p. 297). Lessig, along with many analysts and critics of contemporary culture, technology, and policy, urges policy development on the basis of where technology is going, rather than where technology is at the moment. It is hardly prophetic, but rather an informed recognition of technological direction and social and market demands to point out that ease of access and ubiquity are objectives that are driving an accelerated research and development of the Internet. As Lessig argues, "When it is *extremely* easy to connect to services that give access to content, it will be *easier* to connect to services that give you access to content than it will be to download and store content *on the many devices you will have for playing content*" (p. 298).

The idea here is that with an inevitable enhancement in the ease of Internet connection and its ever-increasing position and prominence in our social and cultural lives—the ubiquity of the Internet, in other words—there will be far greater facility in subscribing to content services at reasonable costs than downloading and managing one's own database. In open on-line conversations with RIAA President Cary Sherman, one contributor, Mark Mavroudis, summed up the peer-to-peer user position succinctly and argued for the industry to re-orient its business practices to file sharing rather than litigating against it:

> I have blank CDs and a CD burner. You, the record company, have content. Sell me the content and let's skip the plastic box, the pre-printed CDs, and the little flaps of paper with writing too small to read. I will burn my own CD or MD, or place the content on my file server for safekeeping. If you make the price reasonable, I'll buy all my music this way and you can eliminate ALL the middle men. The majority of people are honest and would pay a reasonable amount for the convenience and quality you could offer. (http://www.blogcritics. org/archives/2002/08/13/082132.php)

The music industry however, remains tenacious in its efforts to maintain its centralized control despite the fact that its business model is not particularly well suited to or viable in new and emerging technologies and cultural practices of the 21st century. While the mergers and expansions of global entertainment empires speak of continued concentration and control of popular music and other commodities, cultural life on the edges is creating enormous problems for the business of popular music. The substantial resources of the industry have been spent on containment and eradication strategies—surveillance, policing, litigation, lobbying, and threats, general and specific—all intended to win the hearts and minds, or failing that objective, to strike fear into "pirates." The big five of the music industry (an ever shrinking number)—Universal Music, Warner Music, Sony Music, EMI, and BMG—have recognized that downloading holds extraordinary market potential, and they have started to develop deals with pay-for-service file sharing companies. Universal has even dropped its CD prices. Whether the industry is capable of a new business model, complete with subscription services and licensing arrangements that benefit artists, consumers, and companies, remains to be seen. At the moment, the industry still appears more hell-bent on litigation than renovation of its practices.

In Canadian courts, the industry has been stymied in its relentless efforts to cast emergent and malleable technological and cultural environments according to established methods and principles of its business model. The courts have recognized that the rights and access of individuals to new information technologies and content are social imperatives, and that, in the highly contested and transitory domains of digital technology, the protection of rights and access must be balanced with legitimate proprietary claims and interests, and particularly copyright.

As detailed here, piratical practices around popular music are multitudinous and varied, localized and international, and they are organized and carried out in both cluttered marketplaces and borderless electronic environments. No matter what the context, the industry has set for itself a project to eliminate the technological and other means of exchange of popular music it deems as violating copyright, and more broadly, to contain those practices occurring in the techno-cultural shifts that are disturbing the industry's control of products and profits. Such a project is not merely daunting, but impossible in the face of real conditions of technological and cultural change. The industry has yet to properly imagine alternatives.

QUESTIONS

1. What criticisms can be made of terms such as "piracy" and "theft" in the music industry?
2. How does the transnational mainstreaming of music limit music choices?
3. What are the differences between Canadian and American legislation concerning the downloading of copyrighted music?

4. What do the studies of music downloading conducted by Oberholzer and Strumpf, Ipsos-Reid, and Jupiter Research conclude?
5. Under what conditions might subscription to on-line music services replace the downloading of copyrighted music?

NOTES

1. For example, the Agreement on Trade-Related Aspects of Intellectual Property Rights (TRIPS), 1994, and the UN's World Intellectual Property Organization (WIPO) treaties, WIPO Copyright Treaty and WIPO Performance and Phonograms Treaty, Geneva, 1996.
2. For the full text of the report, see http://www.parl.gc.ca/InfocomDoc/Documents/ 37/3/parlbus/commbus/house/reports/herirp01-e.htm.
3. See the Copyright Board of Canada, Tariff of levies to be collected by CPCC in 2003 and 2004 on the sale of blank audio recording media in Canada, December 12, 2003, http://www.cb-cda.gc.ca/new-e.html.
4. For detailed reports on this Supreme Court decision see *CBC News Online* (July 1, 2004) (http://www.cbc.ca/news/background/internet/downloading_music.html); and "Music industry takes a hit in court," *The Globe and Mail* (July 1, 2004), pp. A1–A2.
5. Nielson SoundScan is an information data collection system that tracks music product sales in Canada and the United States.
6. Garofalo (2003), Oberholzer and Strumpf (2004), and the Jupiter Research study (2002) all refer to the need to consider broad factors in the analysis of music sales decline, and all are critical of the music industry's insistence that file sharing is the sole source of the industry's economic problems.
7. Without doubt, the most draconian proposal to date has been the legislation introduced to the House of Representatives in the United States by Rep. Howard L. Berman in 2002. The stated intention of the bill was to promote technology solutions to peer-to-peer piracy, and it would effectively rewrite U.S. federal law by removing legal constraints and giving immunity to groups such as RIAA to carry out surveillance, block, impair, or disable peer-to-peer file sharing networks. The RIAA endorsed the bill, while experts in intellectual property law and civil libertarians condemned the initiative.

REFERENCES

Borland, John. (2003). Canada deems P2P downloading legal. *CNET News.Com.* Retrieved from http://news.zdnet.com/2100-3513_22-5121479.html

Garofalo, Reebee. (2003). I want my MP3: Who owns Internet music? In Martin Cloonan and Reebee Garofalo (Eds.), *Policing pop* (pp. 30–45). Philadelphia, PA: Temple University Press.

Innis, Harold. (1991; 1951). *The bias of communication*. Toronto: University of Toronto Press.

Ipsos-Reid. (2002, June 12). File-sharing and CD burners proliferate. Tempo: Researching the digital environment. Retrieved from http://www.ipsos-na.com/dsp_tempo.cfm

Jupiter Research. (2002). File sharing: To preserve music market value, look beyond easy scapegoats. Retrieved from http://www.jupiterresearch.com

Kline, Stephen, Nick Dyer-Witheford, and Greig de Peuter. (2003). *Digital play: The interaction of technology, culture and marketing*. Montreal and Kingston: McGill-Queen's University Press.

Laba, Martin. (1996). No borders, no problems: Mixed media, culture of youth, and music in the marketplace. In Helen Holmes and David Taras (Eds.), *Seeing ourselves: Media power and policy in Canada* (pp. 73–83). Toronto: Harcourt Brace Jovanovich.

Lessig, Lawrence. (2004). *Free culture*. New York: Penguin.

Moglen, Eben. (1999). Anarchism triumphant: Free software and the death of copyright. *First Monday*. Retrieved from http://www.firstmonday.org/issues/issue4_8/moglen/index.html

Oberholzer, Felix, and Koleman Strumpf. (2004). The effect of file sharing on record sales: An empirical analysis. Retrieved from http://www.unc.edu/~cigar/papers/FileSharing_March2004.pdf

Record Industry Association of America. (2003). Anti-Piracy. Retrieved from http://www.riaa.com/issues/piracy

Roadrunner Records. (2004). Nickelback Singer Gets a Job at McDonald's. Blabbermouth.net News Archive. Retrieved from http://www.roadrunnerrecords.com/blabbermouth.net/news.aspx?mode=Article&news item ID=23339

Won, Shirley. (2004, March 8). Court's copyright ruling in spotlight. *The Globe and Mail*, p. B15.

11

Television in Canada

Paul Attallah, Carleton University, and Derek Foster,
Wilfrid Laurier University

INTRODUCTION

Studying television in Canada can be a lonely pursuit.

First, Canadian television is unloved. Roughly 70 percent of all English-language viewing—90 percent during prime time—is devoted to *American* television. The big exceptions are news, sports, and children's programming.

Second, Canadian television is bureaucratic. We experience American television as a stream of shows, stars, events, and so on. But we experience Canadian television as a series of government regulations, funding formulas, and pressure groups. American television offers itself as the background of everyday lived culture. Canadian television offers itself as good for us rather than good in itself.

Third, Canadian television is understudied. Any library or on-line check will reveal thousands of books on American, British, or Australian television, dealing with the medium's history, its economic structure, stars, best-loved shows, and formal evolution. But Canadian television is largely untouched. References to it lie dormant in royal commission reports, regulatory statements, and official policy documents. There are obviously a few books—some very good—but the number is comparatively small.

The television we love is American and the television we live with is Canadian. Our notion of good or normal television is American, not Canadian. Our television is, therefore, much less watched than its American counterpart. It seems driven by regulatory imperatives disconnected from popular taste, such that few attend to it.

Some decry this situation as a threat to our culture. They look with anguish upon the popularity of American television and seek to wean Canadians from it and induce them to watch their own television.

This *cultural nationalist* perspective has powerfully shaped the development of Canadian television from its origins to the present. It is most frequently associated with proposals to strengthen and protect Canadian television by (a) creating a public broadcaster (the CBC) sheltered from market pressures and the blandishments of American broadcasting; (b) investing funds in Canadian productions via direct grants, indirect subsidies, tax exemptions, and so on; (c) establishing Canadian content regulations; (d) forming activist citizens groups to lobby for Canadian broadcasting (the Canadian Radio League of the 1930s or the Friends of Canadian Broadcasting in the 1990s); and (e) creating a strong regulatory structure to correct perceived market imbalances, exclude foreign ownership, and limit competition.

The goals of cultural nationalism are enshrined in the Broadcasting Act, which governs all broadcasting in Canada and is interpreted and applied by the Canadian Radio-television and Telecommunications Committee (CRTC).

The cultural nationalist perspective, however, has increasingly been challenged by a contrary *free-market* or *neoliberal* orientation. This contrary view believes that it is unwise to make all of culture depend on the sole experience of television. It adds that if Canadians prefer American television, then there is something wrong with Canadian television. A television system which fails to attract its own audience—despite subsidies, regulatory protections, tax exemptions, and governmental intervention—must be flawed. This view is most frequently associated with proposals to (a) deregulate broadcasting, including foreign ownership; (b) abandon content requirements; (c) encourage market- or audience-driven private-sector production; and (d) open the airwaves to all competitors. As audiences become less tolerant of government intervention, the tide may be turning to this perspective.

Clearly, these orientations disagree over the organization, funding, regulation, and audiences of television. The cultural nationalists accuse neoliberalism of destroying Canadian television, and hence Canadian culture, through blind adherence to market forces and ignorance of genuine culture. They view neoliberalism as an expression of American cultural imperialism.

Neoliberalism condemns cultural nationalism for failing to respect the freedom and intelligence of the public by rejecting popular taste in favour of elite judgments, and thereby creating a broadcasting system that serves elite interests. They see cultural nationalism as the expression of a moribund view of culture, one that has been overtaken by technology and democratization.

This chapter occupies the improbable space between these two views.

A BRIEF HISTORY OF CANADIAN TELEVISION

Canadian television was launched on September 6, 1952, when station CBMT went on the air in Montreal, in both English and French. Two nights later, on September 8, station CBT went to air in Toronto. Its opening image consisted of a map of Canada over which were superimposed the words *Canadian Broadcasting Corporation, Société Radio-Canada*. Unfortunately, the map appeared upside down.

A year earlier, however, there were *already* some 150,000 television sets in Canada. People were watching American TV. The tension between audience preferences, the availability of American TV, and the existence of Canadian TV virtually defines the story of television in Canada.

In 1949, the government had struck a Royal Commission on National Development in the Arts, Letters and Sciences—the Massey Commission. Its findings were published in 1951 and became official Canadian television policy.

The Commission distrusted television, especially American television. Consequently, if American television was commercial and devoted to fun and entertainment, Canadian television would be public and "a valuable instrument of national unity, of education, and of entertainment" (Canada, 1951, p. 301). It characterized opposition to its recommendations as "barbarism."

The Massey Commission represents one of the clearest expressions of Canadian cultural nationalism. As a result, Canadian television was born into a patrician atmosphere that distrusted popular taste and presumed to instruct the population in what it should and should not enjoy. Canadian television, therefore, has not achieved sustained popularity, has not established itself as a permanent source of entertainment, and has not bred the habit of regular tuning.

1952–1960: Dominance of the CBC

In 1952, television fell under the exclusive authority of the CBC. There were no private television stations (though there were private *radio* stations), and the context of Canadian television was very different from that of American television. To begin with, there were no powerful radio networks in Canada—besides the CBC itself—to lend financial support to the nascent television industry. Furthermore, whereas American television could turn to the huge technical, managerial, and financial resources of Hollywood, there was no Canadian equivalent to Hollywood. Television began, therefore, without a film centre comparable to Hollywood, without a backlog of filmed stories to draw upon, without a star system, without a promotional infrastructure, without huge teams of writers, producers, technicians, and directors.

CBC television therefore drew upon its internal radio expertise. The CBC radio network had reached maturity during World War II and addressed an audience eager for information about the Canadian war effort. CBC television soon also developed an expertise in news, documentaries, and public affairs. It likewise developed an early expertise in sports programming and in children's programming (*The Friendly Giant, Chez Hélène, Razzle Dazzle*). Indeed, news, sports, and children have remained strengths of the CBC, and of all Canadian television, up to the very present.

In the 1950s and 1960s, the CBC also developed some variety programming— *Wayne and Shuster, Don Messer's Jubilee, Cross-Canada Hit Parade, Juliette*—and some drama—*Seaway, Quentin Durgen, M.P., Wojeck, Adventures in Cariboo Country*, for example.

In June 1953, Queen Elizabeth II was crowned, and many Canadians bought their first set to watch that event. However, given the country's enormous landmass, television proved to be colossally expensive, and private stations were soon authorized to rebroadcast the CBC signal. The "rebroadcasters" showed that a private network might someday be sustainable.

Significantly, though, unlike U.S. television, there were almost no independent production houses in Canada. In the United States, the Hollywood studios became major television suppliers, and numerous independent companies also manufactured television content.

The lack of independent production in Canada meant that virtually all television was produced "in-house," mostly by the CBC's own staff, crew, producers, and writers. As the same crews worked on all genres—from variety shows to hockey broadcasts—the CBC rapidly developed a recognizable network style: clear, expository, deliberate, with an emphasis on the didactic and the documentary. This was consistent with its mandate to be a public broadcaster devoted to *national unity* and *education* rather than to entertainment, and capitalized on the CBC's own accumulated expertise in news and public affairs.

In this period, the CBC was *also* the regulatory authority, granting licences to private broadcasters and overseeing the entire system. The private broadcasters felt this to be grossly unfair and lobbied the government for change. In 1958, the newly elected Conservative government of John Diefenbaker gave the private broadcasters what they wanted. It transferred the CBC's regulatory authority to a new body, the Board of Broadcast Governors (BBG). The BBG's major act, in 1961, was to authorize the first private television network, CTV, whose directors were perceived as friendly to the Conservative party.

1961–1968: From the BBG to the CRTC

CTV expanded television choice but also confirmed the laws of television economics. Canadian content was expensive to produce and its natural market was small. Hence, Canadian content was often produced at a loss.

Nowadays, a U.S. network drama typically costs about $2 million per hour to produce. The size of the U.S. market allows the network to sell $10–15 million per hour of advertising time. The $2 million show can therefore yield a profit in excess of $10 million.

In order to have similar appeal, a *Canadian* show would likewise have to cost close to $2 million per hour. However, no Canadian network could sell more than $2 million per hour of commercial time. That level of expenditure would result in permanent losses and the eventual bankruptcy of the network.

What do Canadian networks do? Their most important strategy is to avoid producing their own content. Instead, they buy content from the United States. Indeed, since the U.S. network has already recouped its costs on its home market, the show costing $2 million can be sold abroad for as little as 10 percent of its value. Hence, Canadian networks buy U.S. content for as little as $200,000 per hour and then sell more than $200,000 per hour of advertising time.

Buying U.S. content can translate into profits; producing Canadian content often translates into losses. This is because the Canadian market is small and because English-speaking audiences appear to prefer American content.

However, since the Broadcasting Act requires Canadian networks to air 50 percent Canadian content, they have also developed other strategies. They tend to produce the least expensive content—talk shows, morning news shows, talent shows—and to schedule it in the least valuable time slots (when the fewest people are watching).

Indeed, as television costs spiral out of control across North America, even U.S. networks are turning to the least expensive type of television possible: reality shows. Not only do these shows attract huge audiences, they also have minuscule per-episode costs, their talent is free or extremely cheap, and their stars have no clout to use against the network.

CTV eventually surpassed the CBC in popularity but similarly developed expertise in the traditional Canadian genres of news and public affairs (*CTV News, Canada AM, W5*), sports (*Wide World of Sports*, Olympic coverage), and children's programming (*Romper Room*). Mainstays of the network have long included *The Littlest Hobo* and, more recently, *Canadian Idol*, both textbook examples of low-cost production.

The main difference between CTV and CBC was that CBC was highly centralized and CTV highly decentralized. Indeed, CTV affiliates participated equally in network management, lending it a weak and chaotic structure.

In 1968, the BBG was replaced by the Canadian Radio-Television Commission (CRTC) under the chairmanship of Pierre Juneau. It proved much more activist than the BBG. Three characteristic and noteworthy CRTC decisions are (a) the imposition of Canadian content quotas, (b) the framework for cable (satellite) TV, and (c) the simultaneous substitution rule.

The content quotas, introduced in 1970, required all private television broadcasters to air at least 50 percent Canadian content per day and for the CBC to air at least 60 percent per day. From the very beginning, the quotas became a bone of contention as private broadcasters were accused of failing to meet or of systematically evading them. The CBC, however, has traditionally met and exceeded its quotas. While imposing production costs on all broadcasters, these rules also effectively bar international competition on the ground that it can never meet the 50 percent quota. International channels seeking entry to the Canadian market therefore often partner with a Canadian channel.

Cable television underwent a huge expansion after 1968, and satellite TV followed in the 1990s. Under CRTC rules, cable and satellite must ensure a preponderance of Canadian over American channels, locate the Canadian channels in the least expensive tiers, and ensure that no American channels duplicate Canadian services. These rules protect market incumbents by guaranteeing them the widest exposure to the widest audience, eliminating potential competitors, and channelling viewers to specific choices.

Simultaneous substitution occurs when a Canadian network airs a U.S. show at the same time a U.S. network does. Cable and satellite operators are required to substitute the Canadian signal onto any U.S. channel carrying the same show. As a result, even viewers watching the American channel are exposed to the Canadian version with its embedded Canadian advertising. Many find this frustrating, especially during the Super Bowl, but this rule, again, protects market incumbents by giving them privileged access to the audience and eliminating potential competitors.

OUR REGULATORY STRUCTURE: SOLUTION OR PROBLEM?

The question of broadcasting regulation deserves serious consideration. No country would willingly abandon its own broadcasting to another. But is our regulatory structure the best way to encourage Canadian television?

Audience measurements consistently show that English-speaking Canadians prefer U.S. prime-time drama. Content quotas, however, restrict the supply of U.S. programming that Canadians most enjoy and increase the supply of programs they least enjoy. By making the most enjoyable programming harder to watch, quotas may actually heighten its desirability and provide incentives to seek it out.

More significantly, quotas set aside time which *must* be filled with Canadian content. Since that content *must* be shown, it hardly matters whether it is good or popular. Indeed, if something *must* be shown, it is often more logical to make it quickly and cheaply than to lavish time and effort on it.

Additionally, simultaneous substitution actually *encourages* Canadian broadcasters to replicate U.S. schedules as closely as possible, precisely in order to benefit from the signal substitution. Its essential function is not to encourage Canadian production but to protect the profits of private broadcasters.

The CRTC's ban on international satellite signals has driven many Canadians into the "grey" and "black" markets. Yet in our wired world, when virtually anything is available on the Internet, there is no strong reason to ban television signals. Indeed, the elimination of international competition merely means that Canadian broadcasters need never measure themselves against the best and most popular in the world, thereby allowing themselves to slide into the merely acceptable or mediocre.

If our regulatory structure is problematic, might there be a better way? Some of the factors that have made American television successful include a massive promotional infrastructure and a star system, both of which are underdeveloped in Canada. The promotional infrastructure—the talk shows and game shows on which celebrities make guest appearances, the magazines and books which celebrate them and their programs, the fan clubs, the gossip columns, the specialty publications— tends not to have a strong presence. Likewise, the Canadian star system is still embryonic. There tend not to be very many "bankable" Canadian stars, and those who are, along with many writers, directors, designers, and producers, have gone to the United States. Hence, while there is a lot of very good Canadian television, it is made in Hollywood.

The rationale governing CRTC decisions is that our cultural survival depends upon exposure to Canadian television. In order to achieve maximum exposure, policies were enacted to eliminate international competition, protect and strengthen Canadian market incumbents, substitute Canadian signals of U.S. shows for American signals of the same shows, develop Canadian alternatives to American content, and so on. Ultimately, the CRTC represents a high culturalist, or elitist, attitude toward what Canadians may watch and hear.

The goal of building a viable Canadian television industry is laudable, but the chosen means may be counterproductive. Exposure to international television signals is not a threat but a strength. First, it reflects the demographic composition of Canada. Second, it allows Canadians to measure their television against the best—and the worst—that the world has to offer. We would never protect Canadian writers by banning non-Canadian books. Nor would we protect Canadian film by banning films from other countries. We may, therefore, be doing more harm than good by restricting access to outside television, because it narrows the range of knowledge and impoverishes culture, it grants to a minority the right to decide for the majority, and it allows the protected industry to become complacent.

1968–1983: Consolidation

The 1970s in both Canada and the United States witnessed an explosion of cable and specialty channels. Indeed, cable became the medium of choice for an overwhelming majority of Canadians, with the result that Canada is one of the world's most heavily cabled countries. The expansion of cable was matched by the rise of large-scale operators, notably Shaw, Rogers, and Vidéotron. In 1975, the CRTC was re-named the Canadian Radio-television *and Telecommunications* Commission as it acquired responsibility for telecommunications.

The expansion of cable replaced the channel scarcity of the 1950s and 1960s with channel abundance, and Canadians began to demand more American channels. Additionally, cable operators needed new channels to maintain their rates of profit. Cable had become a mature industry in which revenue growth could only come from new services.

Cable's desire for increased profits and consumer demand for increased choice placed the CRTC in a quandary. The most requested new services were American; however, the CRTC was reluctant to license American channels. Instead, it licensed Canadian specialty channels that could serve as functional equivalents to the U.S. channels (TSN for ESPN, TMN for HBO, MuchMusic for MTV, Discovery Canada for the Discovery Channel, etc.). Essentially, the CRTC introduced *managed choice*, in which the services it deemed appropriate were licensed in an attempt to satisfy both (a) cable's desire for new services and (b) consumer demand.

The CRTC's first foray into specialty channels occurred in the early 1980s when it mandated a raft of movie channels (First Choice, Alberta Superchannel, Ontario

Superchannel, Star Channel, TVEC) and a lively arts channel (C-Channel). In short order, they all collapsed or altered their business plans. Also in the 1970s, CanWest Global was licensed and the number of independent stations multiplied.

1983–1993: The Rise of Independent Production

Canadian television was historically characterized by an absence of independent producers. That changed in 1983 when the federal government created Telefilm Canada and altered the CBC's mandate. Telefilm funds both film and television productions. However, only independent producers are eligible to receive assistance (CBC and CTV, as broadcasters, are not eligible). The funding assists production, distribution, and exports and encourages international co-productions.

The shift in the CBC's mandate required it to obtain 50 percent of its entertainment programming from independent producers. In this manner, the government transferred funds from the CBC to Telefilm (because CBC was reducing its in-house production), and from Telefilm to independent producers (from which CBC would buy). It turned the CBC from an in-house producer to a purchaser of outside content. The Telefilm strategy, therefore, brought into existence an independent television production sector.

By the end of the 1990s, Canadian television had begun to resemble American television. It was dominated by three major broadcasters (CBC, CTV, CanWest Global) who produced in-house but also acquired product internationally and from the nascent production industry.

Unlike their U.S. counterparts, however, who could recoup their costs from their domestic market, Canadian producers could not usually recover their costs in Canada alone. Telefilm funding, therefore, made up for the absent market. But besides calling upon Telefilm, independent producers also devised two other strategies. They could (a) seek out international partners for a co-production and (b) obtain assistance in the form of tax credits by conforming to the point system. Often, producers would use all three strategies (Telefilm, co-production, and tax credits) in tandem.

In the television point system, points are awarded for observable "Canadian" features: two points if the lead performer is Canadian, one point if the director, writer, or camera operator is Canadian, and so on. If a production achieves six points, it becomes eligible for tax credits.

As a result, many shows are now produced in Canada but target the international or U.S. markets. Examples include *Stargate Atlantis, Monk, Andromeda,* and *Psi Factor*. But they also include the top-rated show in the United States, *CSI: Crime Scene Investigation*. Of course, including international markets can result in programs that many do not consider Canadian. For example, *The Outer Limits* and *The X-Files* have been dismissed as *inauthentic* or *industrial Canadian* and therefore unworthy of public support. Others have countered that they are valuable precisely to the extent that they connect with a popular audience and help strengthen the industry.

During the 1980s and 1990s, the CRTC licensed rafts of new channels in 1984, 1988, 1995, and 2000. These waves introduced such mainstays as Newsworld, YTV, Bravo!, TSN, Drive-in Classics, and Lonestar. The new specialty channels all helped consolidate the position of the major cable companies but did not fully satisfy viewer demand for American channels.

More significant was the introduction of satellite TV and the Internet which, by their very nature, do not respect political boundaries. And, by using digital compression, they make the 500 or 5000 channel universe both achievable and affordable.

But the new delivery systems also challenge existing broadcasters and signal providers who fear being left behind. We should not overlook the possibility that, when faced with 5000 channels, consumers will actually be drawn to recognizably Canadian content as something distinctive and desirable. Nonetheless, the existing players have launched a frenzy of mergers and calls for increased regulatory protection in order to guarantee their own survival.

1993–2001: The Impact of Digital Technology

The period since 1993 has seen new digital technologies and media mergers. Digitization provides more signals of higher quality, but it also allows viewers to watch what they want, when they want. This puts viewers in charge of the television experience and disrupts traditional delivery strategies and habits.

Direct broadcast satellites (DBS) in particular struck fear into the heart of the Canadian television industry. Cable even dubbed satellites "Deathstars" and claimed that they threatened "Canadian culture" (Hoskins, MacFadyen, and Finn, 1994).

The CRTC agreed and fashioned a direct-to-home (DTH) policy intended to block U.S. providers. The CRTC also determined that *Canadian* satellites would be required to observe the rules that governed cable, thereby diminishing the value of their digital capacity. However, this move protected market incumbents by limiting competition and constraining the effectiveness of competitive technologies.

Nonetheless, U.S.-based DirecTV went to air in 1994, fully three years before any Canadian satellite service, and, just as at the dawn of television, many Canadians turned to it in order to watch U.S. television. This is the so-called grey market of Canadians who want satellite television but who are not waiting for the government to act. It reactivated the most atavistic fears of American cultural threat.

However, DBS actually represented the first real competition to cable's monopoly. It threatened, therefore, not culture but cable TV, and with it, the CRTC. Indeed, if viewers can unplug from the regulated universe of cable TV and choose instead the relatively unregulated and international universe of satellite TV, then the very role and credibility of the CRTC are thrown into question.

By 1997, two Canadian satellite providers, Bell ExpressVu (a division of BCE) and StarChoice (a division of Shaw Communications), had begun operation. Significantly, BCE and Shaw are both market incumbents who only branched out into the satellite business. They were not new market entrants and represented little competition or innovation. The CRTC helped consolidate the power of existing giants.

Beyond DBS and digitization, however, lie other forces. Most important is convergence. Convergence describes the integration not only of technologies (broadcast, cable, satellite, computer) but also of corporations hoping to use the technologies.

Additionally, as technologies and corporations converge, they also tend to produce **audience fragmentation.** Indeed, given all of the TV options that digitization makes available, almost every conceivable interest can be targeted with specific programming. This allows media owners, producers, and advertisers to splinter audiences into ever narrower segments and niches.

CONVERGENCE IN CANADIAN TELEVISION

In 1995, the CRTC published its *Convergence Report*, whose goal was to open the media playing field by allowing content *carriers*—cable, telephone, and satellite—to acquire financial interest in content *production*. They could do so by obtaining digital and broadcast licences.

However, rather than opening the market to new players, the policy merely allowed existing giants to seize control of the new field. In 2000, Canada's two largest private broadcasters both engaged in mergers. In a $3.5 billion deal, CanWest Global acquired Western International Communications and the Southam newspaper chain. Likewise, for $3.2 billion, Bell Canada Enterprises (BCE) acquired the CTV television network and *The Globe and Mail*. Rogers Communications, the largest cable distributor, aligned itself with American giants Microsoft and AT&T. And Quebecor Inc. (owner of the Sun Media newspaper group, the Quebec-based TQS television network, and the Internet portal Canoe.ca) acquired Groupe Vidéotron, Quebec's largest cable company, for $4.9 billion.

In all these mergers, those who control the means of delivery are acquiring content and content providers. The case of BCE is eloquent. Not only does BCE own the largest and richest wired network in Canada (telephone lines), it also owns Bell ExpressVu and the Sympatico Web portal. With the acquisition of CTV and *The Globe and Mail*, it created Bell Globemedia, a monolith that produces content in-house (*The Globe and Mail*, CTV) and distributes it via satellite (ExpressVu) and Internet (Sympatico), while using its telecommunications business (telephone lines) to generate continuous capital for further investments.

Shaw Communications, the second largest cable operator, used its subsidiary Corus Entertainment to acquire Nelvana, the leading creator of animated programs in Canada (*Babar*). Likewise, independent production companies Alliance Communication and Atlantis Television merged in 1998 to form Alliance Atlantis, a company with stakes in numerous specialty channels (History Television,

Showcase, the Life Network, Home & Garden Television, Headline Sports—The Score, Food Network Canada).

Some say that "new" media (Internet, DBS) will cannibalize "old" media (TV). However, in Canada, with regulatory help, old media and those who control them have seized new media in order to (a) reach diverse audiences, which they themselves had fragmented and (b) block new market entrants who might generate competition. Old media do not disappear in the wake of the new; they survive within the corporate structure as part of a new conglomerate.

The trend for content providers (manufacturers) and content suppliers (delivery mechanisms) to merge is clear. Whether the providers are independent production houses or television networks, and whether the suppliers are satellite undertakings or cable channels, the goal is always to control both the pipeline as well as the content that fills the pipeline.

FRAGMENTATION

Large corporations try to position themselves across multiple media platforms (newspapers, television, the Internet). In so doing, they implicitly recognize that the audience is *already* fragmented. Different people have different media habits and it is increasingly difficult to assemble truly large audiences around a single medium or event.

Indeed, the new media environment is defined by the abundance of content and of delivery channels. As a result, Canadians are not just watching more content but also more specialty services. For example, the percentage of viewing time devoted to specialty channels rose from 14 percent in 1990, to 19 percent in 1995, to 22 percent in 1998 (Taras, 1999, p. 97). These figures indicate not just an increase in channel availability but also a demand for products that speak to increasingly specialized and sophisticated viewer interests.

Fragmentation is also promoted by the increasing *personalization* of media. For instance, MP3s plug users into a private world of music enjoyment but also unplug them from the broader world of shared musical experience. Likewise, in the mid-1990s, Rogers Communications advertised a new tier of cable services as "Me TV"; and in 2004, satellite providers promised to let subscribers build personalized menus. This was also the reason for the success of **VCR**s, which, like video-on-demand (VOD), let people watch what they want, when they want.

This has merely been amplified in recent innovations such as personal video recorders (PVRs), the digital ability to timeshift, integrated programming guides (IPGs), and pay-per-view movies with VCR stop/start capability.

Increasingly, watching TV means giving viewers personalized control over the experience. Traditionally, viewers watched only what the networks provided in time slots and in an order controlled by centralized programmers. Now, digital technology lets viewers store content from multiple sources for viewing in time periods and in sequences unpredicted and uncontrolled by networks.

Digital technology encouraged audience fragmentation. It also encourages audiences to reconstruct the experience of television.

Some will claim that this is bad, a threat to our culture. Others may observe that digitization is neither self-evidently good nor bad. Indeed, some events (such as the civic ritual of elections, the Olympic Games, sensational trials, war coverage, etc.) seem to defy fragmentation and to assemble old-fashioned mass audiences. But then, is the mass audience good in and of itself?

A NEW TELEVISION DISPOSITION

Our current experience of television may be called a **new television disposition.** It is characterized not only by new technologies and the possibilities they open up but also by new industrial alignments, new audiences, new types of content, and new strategies of contact.

One of the most outstanding features of the new television disposition is the sudden prevalence of digital and high-definition television (HDTV). All the major networks now produce most of their programming in HD. The single glaring exception is reality TV. HD cameras are still too expensive and delicate for shooting in remote locations (*Survivor, The Great Race*) or withstanding the hurly-burly of the domestic environment (*Trading Spouses, Wife Swap*). But most "traditional" programs now trumpet their HD status and the renewed "cinematic" experience of larger, wider, high-definition screens.

Indeed, when equipped with surround sound, HDTV aspires to the status of the movie theatre. This has implications for both producers and viewers. HD programming is more expensive to produce, requiring investment in new hardware. It also requires a rethinking of makeup, lighting, set design, and so on, for the digital eye can be unforgiving. But it also implies an increased investment on the part of the viewer, and a higher degree of attention to, and involvement in, the TV show.

The logical extension is the promise of greater interactivity. More and more, television is marketed as an enhanced, less passive experience. For example, broadcasters increasingly offer "interactive" versions of sporting events, which use multiple cameras, including "AltCam" (alternative views of the action) and "PlayerCam" (to follow a star player). "Second Look" lets viewers roll their own instant replays whenever they want.

Indeed, in the new television disposition, television is increasingly offering itself as "an information hub"—not just a provider of entertainment whose content could be followed up later on-line, but an actual real-time multimedia experience. For example, Bell ExpressVu now offers an "interactive" CBC News Plus service, which it advertises as "Fast access to the latest CBC News from Canada and around the world. It's all on your TV. You choose what stories to read—scroll through news with your remote. You're in control."

However, even as it fragments audiences and enhances viewer control, digitization also provides television producers and distributors some unexpected means of re-asserting control. For example, approximately 12 million homes in Canada are equipped with a television set, and, of these, roughly 3.9 million subscribe to a digital service (both cable and satellite) (Summerfield, 2004, p. 26). This number will likely only rise. Digital subscribers have access to interactive content, PVRs, and VOD. Yet each use of a digital service also generates a data trail which gives providers enhanced access to audience habits and interests. In short, digitization allows for data mining at the individual level. For example, PVRs collect information about the shows one records and allow the tailoring of commercials; VOD provides especially rapid details about who selects which programs. In the United States, the TiVo PVR actually keeps a record of viewer preferences and records programs based on past choices *in anticipation* of the owner's likely viewing patterns without the owner having to program the machine.

NEW TYPES OF PROGRAMMING

The challenges of digitization are obvious enough. Timeshifting, for example, lets viewers set their own viewing times *and* skip commercials. One U.S. survey of PVR users found that 92 percent of commercials were not viewed and 3 in 10 users said they watched no commercials at all ("Built-in ads," 2004, D01). As a result, advertising is increasingly built directly into programming, which is then strategically aligned with other media. Reality TV illustrates the process. *Canadian Idol* incessantly promotes products from its sponsors as contestants on the show participate in segments intended to heighten brand awareness.

A similar phenomenon defined *Making the Cut* (which depicted hockey hopefuls wanting to play in the NHL). The show's major sponsor was Bell Canada, and its brand was unavoidable. It appeared on rink boards, on players' sweaters, and on cell phones when players called home. Furthermore, Bell ExpressVu offered its subscribers interactive features and programming during each episode. The Sympatico Internet portal publicized the show before it went on air, provided updates as the show progressed, and promoted on-line information exclusive to Bell Sympatico/MSN subscribers. Each episode ended by directing viewers to the show's Web site.

The Quebec television hit, *Star Académie*, was an even more striking example of programming strategies in the new television disposition. Similar in concept to *American Idol*, *Star Académie* featured copious product placements and regularly delivered up to 3 million viewers to the TVA television network. Significantly, both the show and the network are owned by Quebecor, which used the show to launch its VOD service on Videotron (which it also owns) and to market Quebecor-produced CDs, DVDs, books, magazines, and tabloids that were sold in Quebecor's music, book, and video-rental shops. It also drew thousands of new subscribers to Videotron's highspeed Internet service by incorporating Web voting for contestants. Audience members could also vote via their remote control if they subscribed to Videotron's digital interactive TV service.

As the popularity of the show grew—at one point garnering a 70 percent audience share—customer base and brand awareness also grew. Products were cross-promoted and offered via print, cable, the Internet, and the music industry. Yet the show was not a success because of the web of convergence. On the contrary, the web of convergence proved successful because of the show. Popular content can drive convergence as well as audience conglomeration.

All of these examples illustrate an unexpected feature of the new television disposition, *overflow*, which is the phenomenon of viewers spending more time with their TV shows than the shows' time slots alone might indicate. People's interest in and engagement with television personalities is facilitated by new technologies and new media partnerships that allow the personalities' stories to be told over and over again. Paradoxically, digital delivery and audience fragmentation may have *intensified* viewers' relationships to television.

Even more paradoxically, they may have created the conditions for the achievement of one of the most ancient of Canadian cultural objectives, "telling Canadian stories to Canadians." Indeed, we should remember that *Canadian Idol*, *Star Académie*, and *American Idol* are all knockoffs of a British original, *Pop Idol*. This original, highly formulaic concept was endlessly copied around the world because it was inexpensive and hugely popular. However, in the process, it was also inserted into local cultures, thereby providing the opportunity for "Canadian voices." A projected Quebec version of *The Apprentice* is about to illustrate the phenomenon once again.

CULTURAL NATIONALISM AND THE CRISIS IN CANADIAN TELEVISION

The *Idol* formula encourages a youthful fantasy of stardom and is a global success because it creates local celebrities and a sense of community. During the second season of *Canadian Idol*, 32 million votes were cast, literally one for every Canadian! As Wente wrote, both "audience and contestants were a feast of multicultural faces. . . . That's who we are. . . . It's the new Canada" (2003, p. A27).

However, reality TV has a bad reputation, and many link it to a "crisis" in Canadian English-language television. Reality TV is often accused of "dumbing down" television generally (Allossery, 2004), but cultural nationalists, in particular, also accuse it of driving out other, worthier types of content. In particular, they lament the decline in production of original Canadian television drama.

Consequently, the fact that *Canadian Idol* is a huge hit is less important than the fact that dramatic productions are fewer in number and less watched now than ever before. Indeed, the number of hour-long Canadian TV dramatic series has dropped from 12 in 1999 to just 3 in 2003. For cultural nationalists, reality TV is not merely the basest expression of American vulgarity, but also a threat to Canadian values and programming.

However, the impact of reality TV is hardly confined to Canada alone. The same lament about the exclusion of dramatic or scripted television is heard in Hollywood, where actors, writers, and directors greatly fear being supplanted by a more popular alternative form of programming. Nonetheless, after years of lamenting the "unpopularity" of Canadian television, is it useful now to condemn a suddenly popular genre because it does not conform to the parameters of dramatic television?

Some believe the "crisis" is rooted in a 1999 CRTC rule change that "allowed broadcasters to substitute Canadian drama with less expensive reality television and news magazine shows" (Dixon, 2004). But the distinction between "dramatic" programming and "reality" programming is not absolute. *Making the Cut* was arguably constructed around a distinctive Canadian obsession, and its "story lines" were as compelling—and rendered dramatic through the conventions of fictionalized drama—as its more traditional competition. It was also more expensive to make than some traditional Canadian drama and featured high production values. Is *Making the Cut*—a "hockeymentary" according to its producers—a reality show or a dramatic 13-part miniseries?

Is the objection to reality TV perhaps that it portends a shift in the television industry and its production practices? Or is it that reality TV attracts the wrong audience, one whose celebration of co-presence and shared values is simply incompatible with the values held by cultural nationalism?

Perhaps we should even celebrate reality shows that don't focus on obviously Canadian traditions. *Canadian Idol* is a good example. First, it is a Canadian show that appeals to *youth*, a truly remarkable feat for Canadian television. Second, it espouses the values and audience aspirations of *Idol* fans around the world. In other words, it locates Canadian culture within a global youth phenomenon such that its interchangeability with other *Idol* shows is precisely the marker of a shared international youth culture. *Canadian Idol* is "Canadian" not in the folkloric sense of having been designed by committee with the specific intent of inculcating appropriate themes and attitudes but in the sense of connecting successfully with its audience. Finally, it embodies impulses toward **modernity** in its celebration of youth and popular culture, its production values that obviously take Hollywood as their norm, and its democratic structure that invites an audition from anyone.

Some Difficulties of Canadian Content

What, then, counts as a Canadian story? Is *CSI: Crime Scene Investigation*, co-produced by Alliance Atlantis for CBS, a Canadian show?

We face a conundrum. We regularly denounce television shows produced in Canada as inauthentically Canadian because they contain American input; that is, they seem to espouse or express values which many do not spontaneously recognize as Canadian. That appears to be the source of the condemnation of *Canadian Idol*.

But what are Canadian values? Are they values enshrined in a document to which behaviour must conform in order to count as Canadian, or are they simply the values espoused by Canadians, whatever those turn out to be and however they may evolve over time?

If *CSI* is not Canadian because it's *too American*, are there American shows that can be accused of being *too Canadian?* For example, should we not count as *partly Canadian content* American shows with Canadian stars, such as *Will and Grace* (Eric McCormack), *JAG* (David James Elliott), *Friends* (Matthew Perry), *24* (Kiefer Sutherland and others), *The Daily Show* (Samantha Bee)? Are these examples of Canadian cultural imperialism or of Americans being Canadianized?

Furthermore, how can we ever separate out the Canadian components from the American components in a show such as *Saturday Night Live*, which is produced by a Canadian (Lorne Michaels) and which has launched the careers of numerous Canadian performers (Mike Myers, Dan Aykroyd, etc.)?

Oddly enough, if we applied the Canadian point system to U.S. television, we might discover many American shows qualifying as Canadian!

CONCLUSION

Regardless of whether or not one partakes of the newest technologies, recent developments in the television industry have re-ignited the perennial debate over Canadian culture. It is certainly reasonable to expect Canadian media to represent Canada. But it may be equally reasonable to revisit what we mean by "Canadian stories" and the regulatory structures that define the enterprise.

Consumer desire, layers of policy, and industry strategizing ensure that television in Canada will remain a complicated terrain. Perhaps rather than make *Canadian* television, we should focus on making *successful* television in Canada. The demographic composition of the country alone speaks against narrow and traditional definitions of culture.

New technologies and convergence are both a challenge and an opportunity to television in Canada. They have brought bigger corporations but also increasingly sophisticated, cosmopolitan audiences for whom traditional content and distribution are increasingly irrelevant. In the 500 or 5000 channel universe, Canadian programming will almost certainly be distinctive by definition. But the truly successful programming will also likely be the one that is as sophisticated as its intended audience.

QUESTIONS

1. Is there a specific feel or sensibility to Canadian television?
2. Is the Canadian television audience really any different from the American television audience?
3. Are content quotas the best way to ensure a Canadian television industry?
4. Would it matter if there were no public broadcasting in Canada?
5. What is the impact of digital technologies on Canadian television?
6. Is reality TV good or bad for television and its audiences?

REFERENCES

Allossery, Patrick. (2004, June 14). TV is getting worse, say majority of Canadians. *Strategy*, 1.

Built-in ads will be hard to zap. (2004, September 13). *The Toronto Star*, p. D1.

Canada. Royal Commission on National Development in the Arts, Letters and Sciences [Massey Commission]. (1951). *Report of the Royal Commission on National Development in the Arts, Letters and Sciences, 1949-1951*. Ottawa: King's Printer.

Dixon, Guy. (2004, May 7). CRTC responds to domestic drama crisis. *The Globe and Mail*. Retrieved from http://www.friends.ca/News/Friends_News/archives/articles05070401.asp

Hoskins, Colin, Stuart McFadyen, and Adam Finn. (1994). The environment in which cultural industries operate and some implications. *Canadian Journal of Communication, 19*(3/4).

Summerfield, Patti. (2004, September 17). Beyond the 30-second spot. *Strategy*, 26.

Taras, David. (1999). *Power and betrayal in the Canadian media*. Peterborough, ON: Broadview Press.

Wente, Margaret. (2003, September 18). In praise of the banal. *The Globe and Mail*, p. A27.

12

Advertising in Canada

Russell Johnston
Brock University

Advertising is a term with many meanings. It is commonly used as a collective noun to refer to all advertisements. In communications and cultural studies, it refers to a system of communication through which goods and services are brought to the attention of the general public.

Raymond Williams (1987) argues that advertising has two phases. First, the content of advertising has insinuated itself into every medium of communication. Advertisements may be understood as one-way, mediated communication intended for mass persuasion. They manipulate the shared words, images, and symbols of a society to create a favourable impression for a product, service, or cause. For this reason advertising has been referred to rather poetically as "salesmanship in print." Nonetheless, the barriers to communication that separate advertiser and audience clearly distinguish it from the interpersonal communication that is necessary between a sales clerk and customer.

Second, the business of advertising structures media operations in a capitalist economy. It is a common perception that the media serve the public by providing ready access to news and entertainment. In fact, the media serve advertisers first and the public second. Most media outlets face enormous production and distribution costs. The modest fees paid by the public do not cover these costs. Indeed, much radio, television, and Internet content is available free of charge. To finance their operations, then, media outlets must rely on advertising revenue.

The public is still important. A media outlet will become financially self-sufficient or profitable only if it attracts an audience desired by advertisers (Smythe, 1981). When an advertiser selects a media outlet to carry its ads, the outlet's value is determined by the size and quality of its audience. "Quality" here is determined by demographic considerations that have an impact on purchasing decisions—things such as age, gender, ethnicity, family pattern, occupation, and lifestyle choices. Ultimately, advertisers want to reach the highest number of potential consumers at the lowest possible cost.

Advertisers do not need the mass media. They can publicize themselves through event sponsorship, telemarketing, direct mail, flyers, catalogues, billboards, or their own Web sites. This puts pressure on the mass media to increase their value to advertisers. Some media try to produce the largest audiences possible by appealing to all demographic categories. This is the mass market, and this is the strategy of mainstream outlets like family newspapers and national television networks. By contrast, specialty media outlets try to produce closely-defined audiences similar to the target markets of specific advertisers. For example, *Modern Dog* magazine appeals to dog owners and attracts advertisements from the manufacturers of pet products. Either way, every media outlet tries to produce an audience sought by advertisers. Again, this means that advertising structures media operations. The character and quality of media outlets and their content is driven by the kinds of audiences and advertisers they want to attract.

HISTORICAL BACKGROUND

No one person invented advertising. Unlike film, radio, or television, there is no one person or date to mark its origins. If one accepts that town criers and shop signs are forms of advertising, then advertising is as old as civilization. Modern advertising, however, is integrated with the mass media. Its functions and practices emerged piecemeal over the last 250 years in step with new media technologies.

The first newspaper published in Canada, the Halifax *Gazette* (1752), contained ads for a grocer, a job printer, and a tutor located in Halifax itself. Over the next century, newspapers across British North America were filled with ads from similar merchants, craftsmen, and professionals who used local papers to reach local audiences. The text of these ads—known as "copy"—was drafted in a polite style common to business cards. They were set in the paper's typeface and were almost indistinguishable from news stories.

A second style appeared in the early 1800s. Some companies wanted their ads to trumpet their goods and services from the printed page. Salesmanship replaced the polite invitation as copy was infused with boastfulness and persuasion. These ads also looked different. They arrested attention with a single, unique font or a jarring variety of fonts. Copy might be enclosed in borders or accompanied by simple iconographic images (for example, the silhouette of a locomotive might illustrate a train schedule.) This style of advertisement grew in popularity as local economies grew and business rivalries intensified.

1880–1920

Advertising underwent significant changes during the Industrial Revolution. In Canada, these developments led to the organization of advertising as a system of communication. The process took decades, but by 1920 there was a common set of practices and institutions, ones which shape the industry to the present day.

New manufacturing technologies introduced after 1830 increased the productivity of Canadian industry. As capacity grew, companies expanded their sales territories beyond local markets into distant regions. Many achieved national distribution by the 1890s. Producing and shipping, however, were quite different from selling. Advertising bridged the gap between manufacturers and the public by opening a channel of communication between them. It helped that the printing trades had also industrialized. Steam-powered cylinder presses, introduced to Canada in the 1840s, produced thousands of pages of text per hour. The simultaneous development of lithography allowed detailed images—such as product designs or trademarks—to be reproduced also. Advertisers took advantage of both developments.

A new kind of business emerged at this time, the advertising agency. National advertising campaigns are challenging work. Media outlets must be identified and assessed, their rates negotiated, and contracts signed wherever a company does business. This is called "media buying." When agencies first appeared it was their only function. They completed these tasks on the manufacturer's behalf. In essence, they were and remain consultants with expertise in media, brokering deals between advertisers and outlets to place ads before the most suitable audiences at the lowest possible rates. Newspapers remained the most important advertising medium until the 1950s, but magazines, catalogues, flyers, posters, transit cards, and billboards were used as early as the 1860s.

Agencies did not flourish in Canada until the national economy expanded in the 1880s. The first, Robert Moore's British American Advertising, opened in Montreal in 1860 but closed soon after. More successful was The Mail Advertising Agency of Montreal, founded in 1878. Anson McKim, its manager, persuaded several manufacturers to advertise, and his astute counsel developed confidence in the entire business. McKim capitalized on his reputation by opening his own agency in 1889.

Agencies added a second function in 1900: creative service. By that time ads already cluttered the visual landscape of cities, and modest ads were not always noticeable. The most effective ads featured memorable copy and imagery. Agencies supplied these flourishes by hiring professional copywriters and artists. J.J. Gibbons Ltd. (founded 1900, Toronto) was the first agency in Canada to offer both media buying and creative work. Its innovative approach prompted rival agencies to follow suit by establishing their own creative departments (Johnston, 2001).

Agencies added a third function after 1910: market research. As manufacturers expanded into new markets, their customers grew more remote. Consumer demand in a national market was more difficult to understand than in a local market. Manufacturers understandably became anxious since their business decisions relied on timely, accurate information. Market research addresses these concerns by investigating consumer behaviour. Such information provides reassurance; the plans for new products, services, or sales territories are informed by hard data rather than hunches. Agencies also use this information to inform media buying and creative services.

There are two strands to market research. First, demographic analysis offers an empirical, quantitative picture of consumers. Every media outlet knows the size of its audience. Media buyers, however, want to know how that audience is composed. Are they male or female, young or old? Where do they live? What is their disposable income? To answer such questions, periodical publishers of the 1910s adapted research techniques from the social sciences. Their findings helped media buyers to select the most appropriate outlets to reach their target markets. Second, psychological research offers a theoretical, qualitative picture of consumers. American psychologists like W.D. Scott sought to create more potent ads by investigating the links between advertising and human cognition. In 1910, some believed ads should alter the public's purchasing habits without their knowledge, as if under hypnosis. Today, psychological research makes less sinister claims, but the intent remains: to tailor copy and art to the cognitive patterns of consumers. W.A. Lydiatt established the trade magazine *Marketing* in 1918 to champion these new techniques. By 1920, all the leading agencies in Canada relied on market research (Johnston, 2001).

Taken together, media buying, creative services, and market research provided agencies with a unique set of job skills. They also provided agencies with two significant legacies. First and most important, the research methods adapted from the social sciences appeared to have mathematical precision, which bolstered the agents' professional credibility. This credibility, however, was not entirely secure until George Gallup developed reliable public opinion polls in the 1930s (Robinson, 2000). Second, when combined with client relations, these skills gave shape to agency structures. Most major agencies organized their operations by function and divided their core staff into four departments: account management, media research and buying, creative work, and market research. This traditional structure has been challenged recently as agencies experiment with client-specific teams and flexible workspaces.

1920–1960

After 1920, the advertising industry adapted to broadcasting. Radio became popular in 1922, and Canadian television began in 1952. Both were quickly integrated into the existing structures of advertising.

Guglielmo Marconi did not invent radio for advertising. He wanted to improve the safety of ships at sea. The public, however, was fascinated with the technology and began building its own sets. In 1919, electronics companies in Canada and the United States realized these "amateurs" had become a market unto themselves. By airing free programs, electronics companies attracted amateurs, publicized their products, and thereby invented commercial broadcasting. The initial response was critical. Marine radio operators believed it interfered with their work, and some amateurs believed it sullied their hobby. Nonetheless, by 1922 commercial broadcasting had drawn a massive audience to the medium.

The federal government wanted to outlaw broadcast advertising. Events in the United States stayed its hand. There, two major radio networks began soliciting ad contracts in 1926 to finance their programming. Some Americans complained, but most did not. An hour of entertainment was worth a few minutes of sales talk. Most Canadian listeners could receive American signals and grudgingly agreed. Subsequently, Canadian broadcasters wanted to finance their programming with advertising to prevent the domestic audience from switching to American stations. The federal government acquiesced. Advertising has remained a component of broadcast financing ever since (Johnston, 1997).

Advertising agencies adapted their media buying and creative services to radio. In the periodical press, media buyers pay for space; in broadcasting, they pay for time. There are two ways to handle time. First, "sponsorship" associates an advertiser's name with an entire program. Sponsored programs generally reflect the character and status that the sponsor wants to cultivate in the public mind. For example, Imperial Oil sponsored broadcasts of the Toronto Maple Leafs in the 1930s. Announcer Foster Hewitt created a family-friendly atmosphere for Leaf fans and portrayed Imperial as a neighbourhood retailer that families trusted with their home-heating. Second, "spots" or "commercials" use a brief segment of on-air time for sales talks (usually 15 seconds to 2 minutes long). Spots are now the predominant form of radio advertising, but sponsorship was common until the 1950s.

Television continued these practices. Many believed it improved on radio, and would replace the older medium entirely. This appeared inevitable when many radio programs and their sponsors shifted to television, including Imperial Oil's *Hockey Night in Canada*. The only major adaptation was the development of stage and film techniques to produce effective visuals in televised ads. Otherwise, media buyers continued to buy time as they had in radio, creative staff continued to write persuasive appeals, and market researchers continued to investigate consumer habits.

1960 to the Present

The functions of the industry have not changed significantly since 1960. That said, Canadians' gradual acceptance of the country's multicultural heritage altered both media buying and creative services. This change started in Quebec.

Montreal was the country's commercial centre through much of the 20th century. During that time francophones composed roughly 20 to 30 percent of the Canadian market and 80 percent of the Quebec market. Surprisingly, francophones owned and operated few agencies and had little influence within anglophone agencies. This neglect of a massive segment of Canadian society reflected poorly on the entire industry. The situation changed abruptly after 1960 when Quebec francophones began to fight for greater authority in all aspects of public life. Advertisers responded with French-language campaigns distinct from their English-language campaigns, which created opportunities for francophone agencies. Jacques Bouchard and his agency BCP (founded 1963, Montreal) led the way with a groundbreaking campaign for Labatt's (Elkin, 1973; Côté and Daigle, 1999). Today, agencies embrace multiculturalism and tailor ads to any ethnic group that forms a substantial market.

These changes led to an ironic twist of historical fate. Cossette Communication-Marketing was a graphic design studio founded in 1962 to serve Quebec-based clients. Ten years later, Claude Lessard transformed the studio into an agency. It found early success doing French-language creative work for

TABLE 12.1   Top Marketing Communications Companies in Canada, Ranked by Billings, 2002

Company	Agency Group	2002 Billings
1. Cossette Communication-Marketing, Quebec City	independent	$128,860,000
2. MacLaren McCann Canada, Toronto	Interpublic	92,993,000
3. Young & Rubicam, Toronto	WPP	71,674,000
4. BBDO Canada, Toronto	Omnicom	70,523,297
5. MDC Partners, Toronto	independent	69,128,112
6. DDB Group Canada, Toronto	Omnicom	59,816,240
7. Publicis Canada, Montreal	Publicis	53,435,665
8. Draft Worldwide Canada, Toronto	Interpublic	47,676,766
9. Maritz Canada, Mississauga	independent	45,093,864
10. Ogilvy & Mather Canada, Toronto	WPP	44,257,010

Note: *After 2002, reliable billing data cannot be obtained from foreign-owned agencies.*
Source: The Rankings. (2002, June 24). *Marketing*, pp. 12–14.

anglophone agencies and Automobiles Renault. It also caught the attention of McDonald's, which gave the agency its work for one francophone region of Quebec in 1977. Cossette produced several effective campaigns for the restaurant chain and subsequently won the entire national account, in English and French, in 1991. The same strategy won several other blue-chip clients. It is now the largest agency in Canada and among the top 30 in the world (see Table 12.1).

While Quebec nationalists focused on advertising content, English Canadian nationalists were concerned with media buying. As previously noted, advertisers seek to reach the greatest number of potential consumers at the lowest possible cost. Certain American media outlets are attractive because they reach more Canadians than their Canadian rivals. For example, Detroit radio stations can outdraw those in Windsor. If advertisers only use American outlets, however, their Canadian counterparts lose revenue and face closure. Nationalists argue that this undermines Canadian culture. To prevent this, the federal government regulates media buying through the Income Tax Act and Foreign Publishers Advertising Services Act. Canadian companies may claim the cost of advertising in Canadian media outlets as legitimate business expenses against income, but they may not claim the same cost in foreign outlets.

INSTITUTIONS

The advertising industry is complex. There are many players, they are highly competitive, and they operate across all media. Institutional structures bring order to this complexity. They were developed as people in advertising responded to pressures both inside and outside the industry. That these institutions are necessary and permanent suggests an important point: the issues they address are crucial to the industry's day-to-day operations (see Table 12.2).

TABLE 12.2 Major Trade Associations Related to Advertising in Canada

Canadian Newspaper Association (CNA): founded 1858; reorganized 1919; reorganized 1996
- represents daily newspapers

Canadian Community Newspaper Association (CCNA): founded 1919
- represents weekly newspapers

Canadian Magazine Publishers Association (CMPA): founded 1919
- represents consumer magazines

Canadian Association of Broadcasters (CAB): founded 1926
- represents radio, television, cable, and satellite providers

Institute of Communication and Advertising (ICA): founded 1905; reorganized 1925
- represents advertising agencies

Canadian Public Relations Society (CPRS): founded 1948
- represents PR firms

Association of Canadian Advertisers (ACA): founded 1916
- represents national advertisers

Canadian Marketing Association (CMA): founded 1967
- represents all sectors of the industry

Every sector of the industry has its own association. In each case, rival companies came together to promote their common interests. The CNA is an apt example.[1] It formed in 1858 when several Ontario newspapers lobbied the federal government for lower postal rates. Over time, other issues were raised and resolved cooperatively. The appearance of agencies after 1880, for example, posed several problems. The association's handling of these issues attracted new members, and by 1920 it represented daily newspapers across Canada. Today, its mandate is to "represent the needs of its members and the public in the areas of public policy, marketing, and member services," and to "raise awareness of the benefits of newspapers to advertisers and readers" (Canadian Newspaper Association, n.d.). In other words, it lobbies the government for policies favourable to newspapers and promotes newspapers as an advertising medium.

The CCNA and CMPA have similar mandates. Both originated as sections of the CNA but broke away in 1919 over their competition for advertising dollars. Dailies and magazines competed for the same national advertising contracts; dailies and community papers competed for retail advertising. After commercial broadcasting took root in Canada, the CAB formed to establish labour and copyright standards for broadcasting. However, it too was concerned with advertising, and it became an advocate for private-sector commercial broadcasting. Today, its membership embraces radio and television stations, and cable, satellite, digital, and pay-per-view channels, in the private sector.

The ICA was founded by Anson McKim and J.J. Gibbons in 1905. Newspapers and advertisers both questioned the value of agencies until 1907 when an agreement between the CNA and ICA confirmed their role as media buyers. Newspapers would accept media buying contracts from them, but in exchange agencies had to undergo credit checks to demonstrate their fiscal responsibility. Agency accreditation remains a key service of the CNA, and the CAB has since established its own accreditation process. This means all agencies that handle newspaper or broadcast advertising in Canada must be recognized by the media associations.

Advertisers formed the ACA in 1916. They wanted proof that advertising actually generated sales. This put pressure on media outlets and agencies to produce demonstrable results from their campaigns. This remains the mandate of the association today, to "maximize the value" of its members' "marketing communications investments." It "demands an advertising marketplace that is accountable for the value provided to the advertiser" (Association of Canadian Advertisers, n.d.). The association also lobbies the government on advertising-related issues, particularly to safeguard "commercial free speech."

The members of these sector-specific associations also belong to the broad-based CMA. It is the largest association linked to advertising in Canada and provides a forum for all sectors to advance their common interests. It promotes effective marketing practices and represents the industry before government and government agencies like the CRTC and Industry Canada.

Over the last century, these associations have met with each other to establish common standards for their industry. Their negotiations have usually focused on one of two areas: media buying or creative services. The 1907 agreement between the CNA and ICA was the first of many to regulate media buying; credit checks were designed to ensure the reliability of agencies as buyers. The development of audience measurement ensured the reliability of media outlets as sellers (see Table 12.3). Agencies and advertisers are reluctant to take media outlets at their word. They expect audience research to be verified by an independent auditor. The first such organization, the Audit Bureau of Circulations (ABC), was founded in the United States in 1914 through the cooperation of the press, advertisers, and

---

TABLE 12.3 Audience Research Agencies Operating in Canada

Audit Bureau of Circulations, founded 1914
- audits the circulation of newspapers and magazines

NADbank, founded 1984
- audits the circulation of daily newspapers

Print Measurement Bureau, founded 1973
- audits the circulation of magazines

Canadian Outdoor Measurement Bureau, founded 1965
- audits the visibility of posters, transit ads, and billboards

Bureau of Broadcast Measurement, founded 1942
- audits the audience size of radio and television outlets

ACNeilson Canada, founded 1944
- audits the audience size of television outlets and the use of Internet sites

agencies. Many Canadian companies participated in its establishment, including *The Toronto Star*, Canadian Pacific Railway, and J.J. Gibbons Ltd. The ABC's audit procedures were designed by representatives from all three sectors to ensure their acceptability. A similar mechanism to measure audience size was developed for each new mass medium. Some, like the ABC, were created through industry cooperation; examples include the Print Measurement Bureau, the Canadian Outdoor Measurement Bureau, and the Bureau of Broadcast Measurement. Others were created by independent entrepreneurs; these include Canadian Facts Ltd., which developed the first radio ratings in Canada during the 1930s, and **ACNielsen Inc.**, which developed television ratings in the 1940s and Internet ratings in the 1990s (Eaman, 1994).

On the creative side, the most prominent organization is Advertising Standards Canada (ASC). This nonprofit organization functions as a watchdog monitoring the content of advertisements. Over the last 40 years, several codes have been developed to govern what advertisers may claim or depict in their ads. In each case, the code was developed voluntarily by the industry in response to public complaints or government pressure (see Table 12.4).

Voluntary participation is key. The Canadian constitution protects freedom of speech. The government and courts, however, insist that protected freedoms not be abused. For example, federal hate crime legislation places restrictions on speech. Similarly, the government has placed restrictions on commercial speech

---

TABLE 12.4 Selected Laws, Regulations, and Codes for Advertising in Canada

Government of Canada
- Broadcasting Act, 1992, c. 11
- Canada Corporations Act, R.S. 1970, c. C–32
- Canada Elections Act, 2000, c. 9
- Consumer Packaging & Labelling Act, R.S. 1985, c. C–38
- Copyright Act, R.S. 1985, c. C–42
- Food & Drugs Act, R.S. 1985, c. F–27
- Foreign Publishers Advertising Services Act, 1999, c. 23
- Income Tax Act, R.S. 1985, c. 1, Suppl. 5
- Personal Information Protection and Electronic Documents Act, 2000, c. 5
- Trade-marks Act, R.S. 1985, c. T–13

Government of Quebec
- Charter of the French Language, 1977, c. 5
- Children's advertising provisions, s. 248–249 of Consumer Protection Act, 1978, c. 9

Advertising Standards Canada
- *Canadian Code of Advertising Standards* (2004)

Ad Standards and Concerned Children's Advertisers
- *Broadcast Code for Advertising to Children* (2004)

Canadian Marketing Association
- *Code of Ethics and Standards of Practice* (2004)

with regulations governing false advertising and standards of decency. For example, until the 1940s it was illegal to discuss birth control in public; condom manufacturers could not advertise. Today, alcohol ads may not portray people drinking alcohol. Watch closely—actors may hold open bottles, raise toasts, and clink glasses, but they will never actually drink. The government argues that such regulations protect community standards, but they are inspired as much by profits as morals. If any one ad is tainted by falsehoods or associated with controversial behaviours, then it may affect the public's confidence in all advertising. The government tries to reinforce consumer confidence in all advertising by discouraging those who abuse the system.

The federal government has several pieces of legislation that govern the content of ads. Some, like the Food & Drugs Act and Consumer Packaging & Labelling Act, hold companies liable for misleading claims made about their products. Others, like the Trade-marks Act and Copyright Act, protect companies from rivals with unfair marketing practices. Two important laws are designed to uphold community standards. The Broadcasting Act empowers the CRTC to regulate the character and quantity of all advertising aired by radio, television, cable, and satellite, while the Canada Elections Act monitors political advertising by all groups during federal election campaigns.

Under Canada's constitution, the provinces have jurisdiction over trade and commerce. This has created 10 separate legal frameworks that affect advertising. Apart from laws governing general trade practices, there are specific laws that regulate the advertising of pharmaceuticals, alcohol, tobacco, firearms, lotteries, and consumer credit. Several provinces have regulations to prevent billboards from appearing next to major highways. Quebec also has two unique pieces of legislation: guidelines governing advertising to children and the Charter of the French Language. The provincial government created the charter to protect and promote the French language in Quebec. Its original provisions banned the use of any language other than French on signs posted in public space, thereby affecting the content of billboards, posters, shop signs, and window displays. This provision was struck down by the Supreme Court of Canada in 1988, which held that it violated the Canadian Charter of Rights and Freedoms, but the Quebec government invoked the "notwithstanding" clause of the constitution to override this decision and maintain the intent of the provision. Now, a second language is permitted on signs only if French appears more prominently.

Advertisers and agents resent state intervention. ASC provides a mechanism for the industry to regulate itself. Its key function is to maintain and administer the *Canadian Code of Advertising Standards*. This document, first drafted in 1963, was most recently revised in 2004. It articulates 14 principles that all advertisers should respect. Its chief concerns are the accuracy and clarity of ad copy; the handling of prices, guarantees, and testimonials; the portrayal of women and visible minorities; and the character of advertising to children. Anyone who objects to an ad in a Canadian media outlet may lodge a complaint with ASC. In 2003, 1133 complaints were received regarding 716 ads, most of which appeared on television. ASC investigated 860 of these complaints (76 percent) and found that 57 ads (8 percent) violated the code (Advertising Standards Canada, 2004). When this happens, the advertiser is asked to stop the ad or alter it. However, the ASC has no recourse to the justice system because it is a private-sector organization. Its sanctions depend on the voluntary cooperation of media outlets, advertisers, and agencies. Still, the industry hopes that the ASC demonstrates its willingness to monitor its own practices and thus renders aggressive government intervention unnecessary. Two recent ads with sexist overtones reveal the difficulty of this position. In 1999, a television spot for Labatt Ice depicted a young woman changing in the back seat of a taxi on her way to a nightclub. The driver watches in his mirror, then declines her fare. When ASC upheld complaints, Labatt simply changed the ending so the driver did not decline the fare (Heinzl, 1999). In 2004, Schering Canada televised a spot for Claritin that depicted a young couple on their first date. As he turns to sneeze, she checks her dentures unseen. The Canadian Dental Association immediately objected, arguing that this vignette implied that anyone with dentures was "not a suitable romantic candidate." In this case, the ASC rejected the complaint (McArthur, 2004).

CURRENT ISSUES

Globalization

Advertising has long been an international industry. Consumer goods manufacturers like Unilever and Lipton's sold their wares throughout the British Empire in the 1800s and advertised accordingly. J. Walter Thompson Advertising, one of the largest American agencies throughout the 20th century, established branch offices wherever its clients sold their goods. By 1930 it was on three continents, including offices in Montreal (established 1929) and Toronto (1930). Clients appreciated that a single agency handled their campaigns worldwide. Other agencies readily emulated Thompson's model.

In the 1970s, the pace of international expansion intensified when a major American agency, McCann-Erickson, united with a major English agency, Lintas (Mattelart, 1991). Together they formed the Interpublic Group of Companies. The "agency group" model is significantly different from the "international agency" model. Groups recognize that every country has its own marketing challenges created by differences in language, customs, laws, and media use. When agencies from different countries form a group, they offer both convenience and cultural credibility. Through a single company they offer international marketing support that can be implemented anywhere by a local office. In 2003, the six dominant groups were Omnicom and Interpublic, both of New York, WPP of London, Dentsu of Tokyo, Publicis of Paris, and Havas of Suresnes, France ("60th annual agency report," 2004).

As agency groups extend their reach, they affect smaller, regional agencies. This is particularly true in Canada. The country composes only one small region in the global marketplace, and its manufacturing sector is dominated by foreign-owned companies that produce processed foods, consumer durables, and automobiles—all high-volume advertisers. When the parent companies of Canadian branch plants integrate their Canadian campaigns with their global marketing plans, accounts shift from Canadian agencies to agency groups. For example, McDonald's transferred its media-buying account from independent Cossette to OMD Canada, a division of Omnicom, in 2004.

Few Canadian agencies compete directly with agency groups. Most either join a group or find a modest niche for themselves within Canada. Some of Canada's oldest agencies took the first path. McKim joined Omnicom, Vickers & Benson (founded 1924, Montreal) joined Havas, and MacLaren Advertising (founded 1935, Toronto) joined Interpublic. Agencies that take the second path generally provide high-quality creative services geared to Canadian audiences—something, they claim, that groups cannot provide. Taxi Advertising, Toronto, and Rethink Vancouver have gone this route. Two notable exceptions follow a third path: Cossette and MDC Partners (founded 1980, Toronto) are Canadian-owned and expanding internationally themselves.

The Death of Advertising?

Industry observers such as Sergio Zyman (2003) suggest big-budget ad campaigns may become a casualty of the media-savvy 21st century. Two lines of thought inform this idea. First, the proliferation of new media outlets and audience fragmentation has advantages and disadvantages for advertisers. To remain competitive, media outlets dependent on ad revenue must increase audience share or reduce ad rates. This is good for advertisers. However, new media outlets typically focus on narrow target markets that may be unresponsive to traditional mass market campaigns. Advertisers and their agencies are then pressured to create unique ads for each outlet. At the same time, new technologies have allowed advertisers to create their own catalogues, Web sites, and magazines and therefore abandon the mass media altogether. Shopper's Drug Mart, for example, produces the magazine *Glow*.

Second, commentators like Doug Saunders (1997) suggest the public has grown cynical of advertising messages and tunes them out. Radio listeners change stations, while television viewers leave the room or fast-forward recordings when ads appear. Agencies and their clients have responded by making ads more entertaining or controversial. Beer ads crafted for the Stanley Cup playoffs and Super Bowl illustrate this trend. Another response is to modify the technology itself. Pre-recorded DVDs can be encoded to prevent fast-forwarding.

What is the alternative to traditional advertising? Some companies look to public relations and "guerrilla marketing." Public relations as an industry has existed since the 1920s and has its own practitioners and institutions. The Canadian Public Relations Society, founded in 1948, serves PR firms just as the ICA serves advertising agencies. Despite their professional separation, however, the function of public relations is the same as that of advertising: to enhance the public's appreciation for companies, their brands, and their products and services. It does this by delivering messages through channels the public generally trusts (Johansen, 2001). One such channel is news organizations. Many people may question a company's advertising but accept news stories covering its affairs. PR firms can generate positive coverage by staging press conferences and spectacles in conjunction with corporate events. PR firms can also win public acclaim for their clients by arranging sponsorship opportunities with worthy charitable, cultural, or sports organizations. In times of crisis, it is also the PR firm's responsibility to safeguard a client's reputation (Ries and Ries, 2002).

"Guerrilla marketing" was inspired by the term "advertising campaign." If the traditional ad campaign is a formal, planned strategy for brand promotion, guerrilla marketing is a catch phrase that describes several alternative strategies. Rather than using mass media to reach national audiences, guerrilla marketers seek unconventional channels of communication to reach local audiences. This includes posters on telephone poles in busy urban areas, packages of coupons delivered door-to-door, or "personal" telephone calls known as telemarketing (Levinson, 1985). National magazines *Chatelaine*, *Homemakers*, and *Style at Home* produce coupons similar to—and distributed with—those of small businesses such as dry cleaners, diners, and window washers. Newspapers now use telemarketing and display booths at local festivals and fairs.

"Viral marketing" is an extreme form of guerrilla marketing. Viral marketing circumvents traditional advertising by using personal relationships to promote a product or service on a company's behalf . This is accomplished by sparking word-of-mouth excitement in surreptitious ways. For example, marketers have exploited the fact that digital content is easily copied and shared. Images, jokes, and Web addresses can spread nationwide in a matter of days. Hence, Web sites are created with entertaining free content and e-mail links to facilitate sharing. Family, friends, and colleagues are thereby co-opted into promoting what is, essentially, a promotion. Such strategies are not limited to the Internet. In June 2002, Nike opened a nightclub in Toronto's Kensington Market district. This neighbourhood, a magnet for artists and students, has street credibility among those who appreciate alternative lifestyles and cultural events. The club's exterior was not branded, but the interior design and employee uniforms were. It was hoped that unsuspecting hipsters would learn to love Nike apparel (Rumack, 2002).

Taken together, audience fragmentation, public relations, and guerrilla and viral marketing have diminished the authority of traditional mass market advertising.

Indeed, this trend has affected Canada's largest agencies. Many have stopped describing their work as advertising, and prefer "marketing" or "communication" (Zyman, 2003). The public, however, simply sees more advertising delivered through more channels than ever before.

Privacy

As noted above, advertising was not welcome on radio when commercial broadcasting began. Similar concerns have dogged the recent development of new marketing practices. Particularly troublesome is the practice of collecting and selling databases of personal information. For decades, periodical publishers have maintained the names and addresses of everyone who subscribes to their magazines. These mailings list are valuable. In effect, they are databases of individuals who have self-identified their lifestyles and spending habits through their choice of reading material. If a magazine reaches a well-defined target market, certain advertisers will want to buy space in it. Direct marketers, however, would rather send their own materials (sometimes called "junk mail") to each subscriber rather than use the magazine itself. Publishers sell their mailing lists to direct marketers for this purpose.

Many other organizations generate similar databases. Digital technologies allow data to be collected across vast networks of businesses. Most prominent is the Air Miles program operated by Loyalty Group. The program encourages consumers to favour certain retailers, products, and services by rewarding them with points for every purchase, and the points can be used toward air travel. The Air Miles database starts with each person's name, address, and telephone number. In its day-to-day operations, it records that person's purchases, and where, when, and how much was spent. After collating this data, Loyalty Group can generate highly specialized databases of individuals sorted by their buying habits. For example, it could generate a list of everyone who purchases dog food. With this list, a dog food manufacturer could send a brochure and coupons to everyone on it. Alternatively, the same manufacturer could send the same information by e-mail (sometimes called "spam"). Either way, the manufacturer can be confident that all of the recipients are potential customers because it already knows they buy dog food. This is far more efficient than advertising through any media outlet where 50 to 75 percent of the audience may not even own a dog. Similar databases can be generated by every other loyalty program and credit card offered in Canada.

These practices have fostered anxiety among Canadians. Although consumers provide certain data to companies they trust, they are not willing to have those data shared with a third party. This is apparent in the disdain for junk mail, spam, and telemarketing. Data sharing is unlikely to stop, however, since the success of these marketing methods relies on accurate lists. More troubling is the idea that corporate data systems may not be secure. Information contained on electronic databases may be divulged by insiders or hacked into by outsiders. In 1997, the Province of Ontario Savings Bank accidentally placed its electronic records for 50,000 customers in the public domain—including their names, addresses, phone numbers, account numbers, account balances, and social insurance numbers (Information and Privacy Commissioner, 2000). Such leaks can undermine confidence in all electronic transactions.

The federal government cooperated with the CMA to develop legislation governing the use of personal data for advertising and marketing. This is the Personal Information Protection and Electronic Documents Act (2000, c. 5), commonly known as PIPEDA. It requires all organizations to have the consent of individuals before they collect, store, or distribute personal information. Organizations must also ensure their databases are secure from unauthorized use, and that individuals have access to their own files. Most subscription cards for Canadian magazines now state whether the publisher sells its list to other organizations. If it does, the publisher must let subscribers opt out under the terms of PIPEDA. The CMA wants the law extended to telemarketing. The association maintains its own registry of people who do not want to be called and its members must observe it. However, companies outside the CMA do not observe it, so public complaints against all telemarketers continue. The CMA has asked the federal government to amend PIPEDA and create a national registry that binds all companies. It has called for similar controls on the growth of spam (Canadian Marketing Association, n.d.).

SUMMARY

Advertising in Canada has come a long way from the first newspaper ads in 1752. The creative content of advertising today is colourful and slickly produced, the tone is aggressive, and the technology more highly advanced. Still, its purpose remains the same: to persuade the public to buy. Less obvious is the effect that advertising has upon our public debates and culture. The influence of industry lobbies such as the ICA, ACA, and CMA affects the shape of federal and provincial law. Just as importantly, the logic of media buying affects the nature of Canadian culture as it is produced and distributed through the mass media.

QUESTIONS

1. What is advertising?
2. Who has prompted reforms in the advertising industry, and why?
3. Is self-regulation a sound and principled way to regulate the advertising industry?

4. How does media buying affect the content of Canadian radio and television?
5. Why might some observers claim that advertising is either dead or dying? Are they correct?

NOTE

1. Many of the industry associations discussed in this chapter have changed their names since they were founded. Only their current names are used here.

REFERENCES

Advertising Standards Canada. (2004). *2003 Ad complaints report.* Toronto: Author.

Association of Canadian Advertisers. (n.d.). About ACA. Retrieved from http://www.aca-online.com/about/Default.asp?language=English

Canadian Marketing Association. (n.d.). Dealing with spam. Retrieved from http://www.cmaconsumersense.org/dealing_spam.cfm

Canadian Newspaper Association. (n.d.). Profile of the Canadian Newspaper Association. Retrieved from http://cna-acj.ca/client/cna/cna.nsf/web/TheCna

Côté, Luc, and Jean-Guy Daigle. (1999). *Publicité de masse et masse publicitaire.* Ottawa: Presses de l'Université d'Ottawa.

Eaman, Ross. (1994). *Channels of influence.* Toronto: University of Toronto Press.

Elkin, Frederick. (1973). *Rebels and colleagues.* Montreal: McGill-Queen's University Press.

Heinzl, John. (1999, 10 April). Labatt forced to yield. *The Globe and Mail,* p. B9.

Information and Privacy Commissioner/Ontario. (2000). *A special report to the legislative assembly of Ontario on the disclosure of personal information by the province of Ontario savings office, ministry of finance.* Toronto: Province of Ontario.

Johansen, Peter. (1997). The emergence of broadcast advertising in Canada, 1919–1932. *Historical Journal of Film, Radio, and Television, 17*(1), 29–47.

———. (2001). Professionalism, building respectability, and the birth of the Canadian Public Relations Society. *Journalism Studies, 2*(1), 55–71.

Johnston, Russell. (2001). *Selling themselves.* Toronto: University of Toronto Press.

Levinson, Jay C. (1985). *Guerilla marketing.* Boston: Houghton Mifflin.

Mattelart, Armand. (1991). *Advertising international* (M. Chanan, Trans.). London: Routledge.

McArthur, Keith. (2004, 18 September). Schering television commercial criticized. *The Globe and Mail,* p. B6.

The rankings. (2004, 21 June). *Marketing,* 13–20.

Ries, Al, and Laura Ries. (2002). *The fall of advertising and the rise of PR.* New York: Harper Business.

Robinson, Daniel. (2000). *The measure of democracy*. Toronto: University of Toronto Press.

Rumack, Leah. (2002, 11 July). Presto! You're cool. *Now Magazine*. Retrieved from http://www.nowtoronto.com/issues/2002-07-11/news_story6.php

Saunders, Doug. (1997, 7 June). Adacity. *The Globe and Mail*, pp. C1, C11.

60th annual agency report. (2004, 19 April). *Advertising Age*, 75(16), S1–2.

Smythe, Dallas. (1981). *Dependency road*. Norwood, NJ: Ablex.

Williams, Raymond. (1987). Advertising—The Magic System. In *Problems in Materialism and Culture* (pp. 327–335). London: Verso.

Zyman, Sergio. (with Brott, A.). (2003). *The end of advertising as we know it*. Hoboken, NJ: John Wiley & Sons.

13

Alternative Media

David Skinner[1]
York University

Alternative media provide a range of perspectives and modes of communication that are not readily available through the profit-driven media that dominate the Canadian mediascape. They include both traditional media forms—newspapers, magazines, television, radio, film—and Web-based media. Some people also include street theatre, murals, postering, music, 'zines, newsletters, and culture jamming. However, because the term "alternative media" poses the question "alternative to what?" the field is notoriously difficult to define. Should it be confined to only radical or underground media? Should it include media that operate in languages other than English or French? Should it encompass media directed toward specific ethnic and cultural groups? Should only non-profit media be considered? There are no easy answers to these questions. To define the term too broadly means including the growing number of industry, trade, and specialty media that focus on everything from the professional concerns of accountants to radio stations that play nothing but Elvis records. Defining the term too narrowly runs the risk of leaving out media that address issues and concerns that are not accommodated by their mainstream cousins.

This chapter considers some definitions of alternative media, compares and contrasts some of the features of alternative media with those of their corporate cousins, and goes on to look at the history and structure of several different types of alternative media in Canada.

Communication researchers have approached the problem of defining the field of alternative media from several directions. For instance, John Downing (2000, pp. v–xi), one of the research pioneers in this area, limits his focus to what he calls "**radical alternative media,**" that is, media which explicitly challenge dominant institutions, ideas, or values. As he points out, these media "expand the range of information, reflection, and exchange from the often narrow hegemonic limits of mainstream media discourse" (p. 44). They "often have a close relationship with an ongoing social movement" (p. 44), and, if these "media have one thing in common, it is that they break somebody's rules, although rarely all of them in every respect" (p. xi).

Building on Downing's work, Clemencia Rodriguez (2001) casts her net a little more widely. For Rodriguez, the term "alternative media" traps us in a binary way of thinking whereby it appears that there are only two types of media: "mainstream (or corporate) media and their alternative, that is, alternative media" (p. 20). Rather than divide media into these two camps, she argues that we should instead focus on media that are actively involved in "intervening and transforming the established mediascape" and thereby working to empower the communities with which they are involved. She calls these "citizen's media" and uses that term to describe a broad range of media that are all, to some degree, involved in cultural politics and that work to transform both explicitly and implicitly established ways of seeing and operating in the world.

While echoing both Downing's and Rodriguez's concerns with the socially transformative elements of media, Chris Atton (2002) retains the term "alternative media" but elaborates on another dimension: organizational structure. As he states, alternative media "typically go beyond simply providing a platform for radical or alternative points of view [to] emphasize the organization of media to enable wider social participation in their creation, production and dissemination than is possible with mass media" (p. 25). He sees this restructuring as enabling alternative media both to provide news and information that are more directly relevant to the communities they serve and to play a communicative role that is more directly responsive to the needs and interests of those communities.

Finally, in an effort to offer a frame of reference that "involves no judgments about the empowering effects of the media practices analyzed," Nick Couldry and James Curran (2003, p. 7) define alternative media as "media production that challenges, at least implicitly, actual concentrations of media power." From this point of view, the key feature of **media power** is the "power to represent the reality of others." They argue that the way in which the media portray social groups and events "is an increasingly significant theme of social conflict" and, consequently, the role of alternative media in providing alternative ways of seeing these groups and events is of increasing importance (p. 7). An example of what they mean can be found by comparing the way most corporate media portrayed WTO protesters in Seattle in 1999 and the way Independent Media Centres portrayed them. The former often characterized demonstrators as a violent mob, while the latter showed them to be largely peaceful and motivated by a range of clear and coherent concerns (Galatas, 2001).

So what are we to glean from these different definitions?

First, they provide important insight into the role alternative media play in the promotion of public dialogue, the exchange of ideas, and the promotion of social action. They share the concern that media are a key means for how we come to understand the world and our place within it and that, in particular, alternative media are key means of both building community and animating social change. As Downing (2000, pp. 43–45) puts it, alternative media are agents of "developmental power."

Second, and perhaps more importantly, these definitions are all based on a concern that the dominant corporate media do not adequately represent the interests of all members of society. This is not to say that corporate media do not sometimes contain radical perspectives or opinions and, on occasion, even support or promote radical ideas on both the right and left. However the concern is that, in many ways, they tend to support dominant ideas and patterns of social behaviour over others. Consequently, before more closely considering examples of alternative media, it may be useful to review some of the shortcomings of corporate media.

WHY ALTERNATIVE MEDIA?

While, as Michael Schudson (2000, p. 283) argues, it would be a mistake to adhere too rigidly to a model of the news media that sees "large corporations and the media working hand in glove to stifle dissent or promote a lethargic public acceptance of the existing distribution of power," there is ample evidence of gaps and omissions in the news offered by large, profit-driven media corporations. For instance, NewsWatch Canada has documented the media's "apparent unwillingness or inability to adequately cover" issues in the areas of labour, social inequality, and corporate power, as well as gaps in coverage around issues such as "environmental degradation as a systemic and ongoing problem," "human rights abuses by Canada's 'friends,'" and "gender-related stereotypes" (Hackett and Gruneau, 2000, p. 166). Other studies illustrate problems in the way the media cover issues and events concerning poverty, race, ethnicity, and Aboriginal peoples (Alia, 1999; Keung, 2004; Swanson, 2001).

These problems stem from a number of complex factors. For instance, over the last several decades, the push to wring increasing profits from Canada's major media outlets has driven their ownership into fewer and fewer hands. Such concentration of ownership can lead to a narrowing of perspectives in at least two ways: (a) owners may try to use news, columnists, and other information products in as many of their media outlets as possible; and (b) owners may impose common editorial policies on the increasing number of media outlets under their control (Hackett and Gruneau, 2000).[2] Thus, media consolidation can affect both the structure of media organizations and the content of media products.

Other problems with corporate media can be traced to the fact that "news and commentary . . . are shaped by a consumerist orientation" and the drive to capture audiences with particular demographic qualities (Hackett, Pinet, and Ruggles, 1992, p. 14). In newspapers, for instance, large portions of the paper—such as the "Home," Lifestyles," and "Automotive" sections—are devoted to showcasing and reviewing consumer products, and throughout the paper, most of the pages are laid out so that the eye lands first on the advertising and not the news. Even the narrative form of news stories is shaped by economic concerns. Most hard news is written in the "inverted pyramid style," where the story has no particular conclusion and the facts are laid out in what the author perceives is a descending order of importance (Hackett et al., 1992, p. 14). This way the story can be easily cut to fit the "news hole"—the space allotted to the news after the ads have been placed on the page. Moreover, stories often take the perspective of the consumer, analyzing conflicts and events such as labor strife, tax increases, and rising oil prices in terms of their impact on the wallets of readers and audience members, rather than their larger impact on social justice, equality, and the environment. Meanwhile, news and opinions that are not of direct import to the target audience, or information and ideas that might prove too controversial or offensive to that group, may be left out (cf. Hackett and Gruneau, 2000, pp. 63–64). Similar forces structure the news and information presented on commercial television and radio, and in other media.

The codes and practices of professional journalism can also often lead to the marginalization of particular voices and perspectives. Source selection, news values (that is, the kinds of people and events that qualify as news), and story form—all of these professional choices affect the diversity of perspectives and ideas found in the news. For instance, when developing their stories, journalists seek the opinions and perspectives of official sources—that is, politicians, business people, and community leaders (Hackett and Zhao, 1996, p. 50, 1998). Consequently, within news narratives the significance of events is often judged and framed by "those in charge," and news stories tend to reinforce dominant ideas and existing relations of social power. By the same token, stories are often written from an "objective" point of view, seemingly taking no particular side but in fact representing only a narrow range of perspectives. News that doesn't meet with professional and institutional standards often isn't published (White Eye, 1996). While journalists may be aware of the constraints professional values impose upon the products they produce, pressures on time and resources often make such choices difficult to avoid.

Alternative media generally follow a different logic.

Alternative media are guided by a purpose or mandate other than profit, such as providing a range of ideas and opinions that are not readily available in the corporate press or serving the needs of a particular group or community that is poorly served by commercial media outlets. They are generally independently owned, and usually operated on a not-for-profit or cooperative basis. In some instances, they do not accept advertising, and, when they do, the income it provides is seen as secondary to serving specific community or social purposes.

While corporate media are structured to promote consumption of the products they advertise, alternative media are more about "mobilizing" their audiences to other than economic ends (Atton, 2001, p. 25). It is because alternative media often act to forward and champion the interests of the communities they serve that writers like Rodriguez argue that alternative media are socially "empowering." Moreover, to the extent that these media are part of a cultural milieu that offers a place in which "experiences, critiques, and alternatives" to dominant social patterns and relationships might be developed, they can also be seen as helping animate autonomous or alternative "public spheres"—that is, communities in which traditions, ideas, and values that differ from the dominant culture might develop and flourish (Downing, 2000, pp. 29–30). This points to a possible distinction between "radical alternative media," which look to be active agents of social change, and alternative "community media," which either explicitly or implicitly challenge dominant ideas and values but do not necessarily advocate for change. Because both these types of media work to challenge concentrations of media power, for our purposes they will both be considered alternative media.

In terms of structure, alternative media sometimes replicate the hierarchy of "the mainstream press, with an owner and editor overseeing reporters, staff writers and technical production staff" (Atton, 2003, p. 42). However, in an effort to decentralize organizational power and create an inclusive production process, they also often reject "hierarchical methods of doing business" and instead operate collectively, sharing tasks and roles among the people working there (Atton, 2003, p. 43).

Out of a concern for the ways in which some of the values of "professional" journalism tend to marginalize and silence particular perspectives, some outlets put on workshops to educate people in how to craft their own stories. The point here is to try and establish a "horizontal" relationship between writers and readers, that is, a situation where there is as little filtering of news and information as possible.

Based upon this short discussion, we can see that alternative media work to challenge concentrations of media power, and particularly corporate media, in several ways. Rather than tailor content, organizational structure, and production practices to maximize return on investment, alternative media foreground specific social issues and values. In terms of organizational structure, they often purposefully shun traditional hierarchical models of organization to facilitate as much input into production as possible. And in terms of production, in order to countermand the tendency to have professional values dictate the subjects, structure, and sources of content, they often seek participation and contributions from members of the communities they serve rather than rely on professional journalists.

ALTERNATIVE MEDIA THEN AND NOW

Publishing

While the term "underground newspaper" may now seem like an anachronism, it had real currency in the heat of the protests and social upheaval that characterized the 1960s and early 1970s. In 1969, 22 charges were laid against Vancouver's *Georgia Straight* and its employees. They ranged from libel, to publishing obscene material, to "counseling another person to commit an indictable offense," which stemmed from publication of an article on how to grow marijuana (Sullivan, 1970, pp. 280–283). In Montreal, the paper *Logos* suffered similar treatment, and across the country both producers and vendors of underground papers were often harassed by police.

Content of these papers varied, but recalling Downing's dictum, they all had "one thing in common" in that they broke "somebody's rules." Journalists and publishers were active in the social movements and the "antiestablishment" culture of the time. And while sex, drugs, and rock and roll were often key themes in their content, the papers were also on the edge of shifting cultural politics and carried news and opinion pieces on the antiwar movement, native rights, the women's movement, justice for workers, and environmental and anti-nuclear issues (Verzuh, 1986). Some, like Toronto's *Body Politic*, which addressed the concerns of the gay movement, were more focused in their concerns. Nationalism was a key issue for papers in Quebec.

While for the most part these papers accepted advertising, commercial imperatives did not rule the production process, and they generally flaunted accepted commercial production standards in terms of layout and design, story form, and advertising placement. As for organizational form, some operated as collectives, while others had more traditional hierarchical structures (Lipton, 1980; Ladner, 1986). Financing was a problem for almost all of them.

By the mid-1980s, shifting social currents sank most of these papers, and a new genre of glossy, business-savvy "news and entertainment" weeklies such as Toronto's *Now*, the Montreal *Mirror*, and a revamped *Georgia Straight* had taken their place. While, at times, these papers still engage with radical politics, their focus is generally on the bottom line. As Dan McLeod, editor of the *Georgia Straight* puts it, "We haven't survived with our ideals and principles intact" (Verzuh, 1986, p. 3).

However, set between the principles of community service and the imperatives of the marketplace, a broad range of alternative newspapers and magazines continue to be published across the country. Although too numerous to enumerate here, they range from papers focused on local or regional politics, to gay and lesbian papers, to publications focused on feminist and environmental concerns. There are also a small number of magazines such as *This Magazine*, *Canadian Dimension*, and *Briar Patch* that carry on the progressive political tradition of alternative newspapers, while the *Western Standard* provides a conservative perspective. Financial difficulties continue to haunt alternative publications, however, particularly in anglophone Canada.

In Quebec, the alternative press has historically been better funded and organized than in the rest of the country. For over 20 years the Quebec government has offered varying degrees of support to l'Association des médias écrits communautaires (AMECQ), an association representing not-for-profit newspapers and magazines. To be a member of AMECQ, publications must be collectively owned and democratically managed. Government support for AMECQ ranges from grants through the Programme d'aide aux médias écrits communautaires (PAMEC) and the Programme de soutien au développement des communications (PADEQ) to a 1995 guarantee that the government of Quebec would spend 4 percent of its advertising budget with its members. While only a few of AMECQ's members actively advocate for social change, in so far as they provide perspectives on community and community relationships not available in the corporate press, they are to a degree "alternative" publications.

The Student Press

The 1960s were a key turning point for the student press in Canada as students across the country became engaged with the social activism that characterized that time. Out of a concern for the biases inherent in corporate journalism, many papers began to shun both the idea of objectivity in news reporting and the use of the inverted pyramid style of news writing (Sullivan, 1970, p. 244). Over the years, however, experiments with alternative story forms and writing styles met with mixed results, and the activist politics of the student press have themselves been the subject of debate.

An important organization in the historical development of the student press is the Canadian University Press (CUP). Established in 1938, CUP is a non-profit cooperative news-gathering organization with over 60 member papers. Since the 1960s, the organization has played a key role in encouraging an activist philosophy among student papers. Its 1977 Statement of Principles declares that "the major role of the student press is to act as an agent of social change," that it should "support (other) groups serving as agents of social change," and that "the student press must use its freedom from commercial and other controls to ensure that all it does is consistent with its major role and to examine issues which other media avoid" (Canadian University Press, 1977). To encourage diversity in perspective in news, CUP has also encouraged its member to seek "alternative" rather than "official" news sources, and until recently their constitution required that member papers be "democratically run," meaning that all members of a newspaper's staff could share in business and editorial decisions.

Broadcasting

The Canadian Radio-television and Telecommunications Commission (CRTC) maintains a range of policies in the areas of community, student, ethnic, and Aboriginal broadcasting that provide the framework for many small radio and television operations. To varying degrees, these outlets can be seen as alternatives to commercial broadcasters.

Television

Inspired by the social movements of the time, the National Film Board launched *Challenge for Change* in the late 1960s. The program was designed to create film and videos that would help animate positive social change, particularly for disadvantaged social groups. One of the objects of the program was to allow people who were subjects of film and video documentaries to speak for themselves by taking an active hand in production. While controversial, the program provided an example of how ordinary people might use film and television to develop and strengthen their communities, and it inspired people across North America to get involved in video production (Halleck, 2002, pp. 146–147).

Responding to people who wanted to take up video as a means of community development, the CRTC encouraged cable companies to provide a community channel where these types of productions might be aired and, in 1975, the CRTC made the provision of a community channel—complete with a small studio and equipment—a condition of license for most cable operators. By the year 2000, there were 851 community channels operating in Canada (Canada, 2003, p. 332).

While many of these outlets provide training and public access to the community channel, these numbers do not speak to the quality of services they offer. As Goldberg (1990, p. 18) points out, outside of Quebec "(c)ontrol over programming decisions, productions, and equipment use was gradually shift(ed) out of the hands of community members and into the hands of the cable licensee and its employees hired to 'run' the community station." This ownership structure made it particularly difficult for community groups to gain access to the channel and "programming and the types of users . . . [became] more conventional." This situation was exacerbated in 1997 when the CRTC ruled that cable companies would no longer be required to provide a community channel. Since that time, there have been numerous complaints that large cable companies have cut back on community programming and moved to create program formats that mimic those of commercial broadcasters (ICTV, n.d.; Canada, 2003, pp. 337–341).

Recognizing that ongoing concentration of ownership has resulted in "reduced representation of local voices," the CRTC announced a new community media policy in 2002 (CRTC 2002-61). The policy is designed to increase public involvement with the community channel and reinvigorate it as a means of public expression, but given that control over the channel remains in the hands of cable operators, exactly what effect these changes will have remains to be seen.

In Quebec, community television broadcasting is structured differently than in the rest of the country. While in some instances the community channel is operated and managed by cable companies, in others, programming the channel is the responsibility of non-profit, community-based associations. There are 46 such associations in Quebec, all represented by the Fédération des télévisions communautaires autonomes du Québec (FEDETVC). The cable operator provides the association with access to the channel as well as some financial support, but has little control over programming. Each association is administered by a council that is elected annually by the association's members, and membership is made up of people and groups who use the channel as well as members of the local community (Goldberg, 1990, pp. 52–53). The associations provide training, and production is undertaken by a combination of employees and several thousand volunteers.

Programming varies but is generally focused locally and is generally structured to cast light on local events and issues of local concern. While for the most part it is not "radical," it does help build and strengthen local community ties. It puts the power of representation in local hands and, in that way, challenges the power of nationally and regionally focused corporate media (FEDETVC, n.d.). Since the CRTC's 1997 decision, some associations have complained that cable companies have cut back on their access to the community channel; some have had their access to the channel cut off altogether (Canada, 2003, pp. 339–341). What effect the CRTC's 2002 community media policy will have on this situation remains to be seen.

Community Radio

The goal of community radio is to be a "participatory" mode of communication that works to "respond to the priorities set by the community, to facilitate their discussion, to reinforce them, and to challenge them" (Girard, 1992, p. 3). Toward this end, the CRTC defines a "community radio station" as a station that is "owned and controlled by a not-for-profit organization, the structure of which provides for membership, management and programming primarily by members of the community at large" (CRTC, 2000). Licensees are expected to help promote community access by informing the public of opportunities for participation and providing training to those who wish to participate. Stations raise funds through a variety of means, including membership fees, fundraising drives, and advertising.

All community radio stations do not operate in the same manner, however. Delivering programming in seven languages to the neighbourhood of Quartier St-Louis in downtown Montreal, Radio Centre-Ville's statement of principles declares that its "programming will, first and foremost, be oriented towards promoting the interests of low income residents of our area" (Radio Centre-Ville, n.d.). Vancouver's CFRO tends to be more radical in focus. As its mandate states, "We provide news and perspectives that are not otherwise accessible—information that is not covered by the conventional media or perspectives that challenge mainstream media coverage" (Vancouver Co-operative Radio, n.d.). More rural stations, like CHMM in Mackenzie—a town of about 5000 people in the interior of British Columbia—take a more centrist approach in an effort to build community by providing opportunities for high-school students, promoting tourism, and helping local businesses reach potential customers via reasonably priced radio advertising.[3]

Like community television, community radio has traditionally played a much bigger role in Quebec than in the rest of the country and has enjoyed support from the Quebec government. The Association des radiodiffuseurs communautaires du Québec (ARCQ) has 25 member stations in 16 regions of the province. These stations have 230 employees, 1500 volunteers, and 18,000 members, and they attract 410,000 listeners 18 years and older each week. Fifty-one percent of the revenue of these stations comes from advertising, 21 percent from government, and 28 percent from community contributions (ARCQ, 2003).

Community-Based Campus Radio

The CRTC defines a community-based campus station as "a station owned or controlled by a not-for-profit organization associated with a post-secondary educational institution . . . with programming produced primarily by volunteers who are either students or members of the community at large" (CRTC 2000-12). In 2003, there were 40 of these stations operating in Canada.

Like their community station cousins, campus community stations carry a range of programming and their political affiliations can vary. Some community and campus stations are members the National Campus and Community Radio Association/Association nationale des radios étudiantes et communautaires (NCRA/ANREC). Founded in 1981, the NCRA represents campus and community stations across the country and works with government and related industry groups on issues such as licensing, regulatory fairness, and copyright. The association has 40 members and holds an annual conference that includes workshops on topics such as station management, programming, fundraising, and working with music labels. The NCRA has a Statement of Principles that recognizes "that mainstream media fails to recognize or in many instances reinforces social and economic inequities that oppress women and minority groups of our society" and commits members to "providing alternative radio to an audience that is recognized as being diverse in ethnicity, culture, gender, sexual orientation, age, and physical and mental ability" (NCRA, 1987).

Ethnic Media

A wide range of studies illustrates severe problems in the ways in which Canada's large corporate media represent ethnic and cultural minorities. From framing minorities as dangerous or deviant, to simply ignoring issues and concerns of ethnic and immigrant communities, the mass media have a poor track record in dealing with diversity (Miller, 1997; Keung, 2004). However, a large collection of media has grown up to serve these communities. The "ethnic" or multicultural press has a history that stretches back to the mid-19th century. Today, there are over 1100 ethnic newspapers and magazines published in more than 105 languages across the country.[4] Although the federal government has been criticized for not adequately accommodating ethnic minorities in broadcasting policy, there are now a number of ethnic radio and television stations in cities across the country, as well as a growing number of pay and specialty television services.

Despite the fact that these media fill in gaps in the corporate press, many of these outlets cannot be considered "alternative" in the ways we have defined the term here. The larger newspapers and broadcast outlets are part of national and transnational media corporations, and many of these publications are decidedly commercial in focus.[5] But not all ethnic media outlets put profit ahead of community service. Some are subsidized by the communities they serve ("All the World's a Page," 2003). And, generally, ethnic media also operate with a different set of news values than corporate media. As Shagorika Easwer, editor of *Desi News*, a Toronto-based English-language magazine serving the South Asian and Caribbean communities, notes, "They don't cover issues that matter the way we do. Issues which are crucial for a particular community often are non-issues for mainstream media" (Jacob, 2001).

While to a large degree ethnic media outlets may not meet a number of the defining characteristics of alternative media, to the extent that they provide culturally relevant information and perspectives not available in the dominant corporate media they, at least implicitly, challenge what Couldry and Curran call "concentrations of media power" and, in that regard, might be considered "alternative" media.

Aboriginal Media

For years the corporate media's representation of Aboriginal peoples has been riddled with difficulty. From the use of negative stereotypes to being simply ignored by the press, Canada's First Peoples have long existed on the margins of the media system (Raudsepp, 1997; Alia, 1999). But poor treatment by the established press has not been the only media-related problem. Particularly in the North, many Aboriginal people live in small, remote settlements, making communication within their communities difficult. In the 1970s and 1980s a number of efforts were made to address these problems.

Starting in 1970, federal support through the Secretary of State's Native Communication Program helped fuel the development of Aboriginal newspapers. These papers offered a wide range of news and information particularly relevant to the communities they served, such as debates over constitutional and self-government issues, and education and health concerns (Demay, 1993). But budget cuts in 1990 hit these publications hard, and by 2000, only 5 of the 12 newspapers that had been funded by the program survived (Molnar and Meadows, 2001, pp. 154–157). The cuts were particularly hard for these publications to absorb as they came with little warning and totally removed existing funding (White, 1990). Moreover, a number of the papers were based in communities with few businesses, making a transition to advertising support particularly difficult (Demay, 1993). Today there are over 30 Aboriginal publications serving national, regional, and local audiences (AMMSA, 2002).

In 1983 the federal government announced the Northern Native Broadcast Access Program (NNBAP) to help fund the production and distribution of Aboriginal television and radio programming in the north. Under the NNBAP, radio was a particularly welcome addition to isolated communities. As Mohr (1992, p. 36) points out, "Programmes focus on international, national, and regional news, culture and traditions, children and youth, and important issues such as native self government, the education system and the extremely high suicide rate among their young. Weather, birthdays, and sports (Hockey is played with a passion in the North) are not forgotten." Programming in Aboriginal languages encourages their use and survival.

To receive funding for broadcasting, organizations must "be legally incorporated non-profit aboriginal communications societies, which are democratically controlled by people in the region to be served, and which have no political or religious affiliation" (Canada, 2003, p. 374). Since 1990 cuts have forced broadcasters to rely increasingly on commercial revenue, but the NNBAP has continued to operate, and in 2003 it was accessed by 13 non-profit communication societies that produced and distributed both radio and television programming (Alia, 1999, pp. 112–113; Canada, 2003).

While the wide range of Aboriginal media outlets operating in Canada today is generally not overtly political, through serving and developing the interests of Aboriginal peoples they operate as agents of cultural power and, in that way, can be seen as operating in the realm of cultural politics. Moreover, insofar as these media provide First Peoples' communities "a forum where they can define their identities . . . legitimize their values and goals . . . (and) work towards their own construction of reality," these media challenge the power of dominant corporate media and provide both Aboriginal people and the public at large alternative perspectives on Aboriginal communities (Raudsepp, 1997, p. 188).

The Web

The Internet has changed the face of media, but its promise of myriad sources of news and information has not been fulfilled. Producing Web content is costly and time consuming, and access to the Web is still a problem for many people, particularly those in lower income categories (Statistics Canada, 2004). Still, it is a growing source of innovative alternative media. For instance, Rabble.ca combines news with activist tools and resources, while Réseau des médias alternatifs du Québec provides a range of alternative media from Quebec with both a Web presence and a means for sharing resources. However, one of the most innovative forms of alternative media on the Web are Independent Media Centres (IMCs).

Independent Media Centres

The first IMC was established in Seattle in 1999, "just before the encounter between the World Trade Organization and the social movements opposed to its policies" (Kidd, 2003, p. 49). Set up to offer a counterpoint to corporate media reports on the meetings and protests, the centre provided the means for over 400 "independent print, radio, photo, video and Internet journalists," to document the protest and the events and circumstances surrounding it. Utilizing the latest streaming technologies, the IMC's Web site provided real-time distribution of reports from the frontlines of the protest, reports that sometimes contradicted those issued by corporate media (Galatas, 2001). During the protest, the IMC's Web site received an estimated 1.5 million hits, and, by the time the WTO meetings drew to a close, the anticorporate globalization movement had established a new media voice.

The success of the IMC in providing a counterpoint to corporate media quickly led to a network of centres being established around the world. For the most part the centres operate as autonomous units, but they often share experience, expertise, software, and personnel. In July 2004 there were 12 centres listed as operating in Canada.

Some of these were established explicitly to provide coverage and support for protests against corporate globalization, others are the product of more local concerns.

Perhaps the key feature of the Indymedia project is the principle of open publishing (OP), which allows anyone with access to the Web to instantly publish work on a globally accessible Web site using open-source software. IMC Web sites are treated as a kind of information commons and encourage people "to become the media" by posting their articles, videos, audio clips, and other work directly to the Web site. The point is to have as few editorial decisions as possible between the content creator and the readers or viewers and thereby create a "horizontal" relationship between them. To increase circulation, IMCs sometimes also publish small newspapers.

IMCs are generally operated by volunteers and run as collectives, with all volunteers or members having the ability to take part in decision-making processes. Most IMC sites also offer listservs for sharing information on news and events, and links to activist resources. In this way they act as organizational nodes for social activism, as well as sources of alternative media.

CONCLUSION

To a large extent, alternative media function in a different manner than conventional corporate media. They are guided by a purpose or mandate other than the profit motive, and they are often organized to facilitate a broader range of input into production than their corporate cousins. They generally operate under a different set of news values than the dominant media, and they provide ways of seeing and understanding events that are marginalized or not available there. In some cases, as with some forms of community radio and media that are tied to activist groups, they also work to facilitate modes of social organization and social action that are generally beyond the purview of corporate media. In all these ways, alternative media work to challenge concentrations of media power.

However it would be a mistake to see media as divided into two camps: "corporate" or "mainstream" vs. "alternative." The range of media available in Canada should be viewed as a continuum rather than as a dichotomy, with alternative media working to engender modes of communication that are framed out of dominant, market-driven media forms. But much needs to be done to support the development of alternative media if they are to continue to increase the range of perspectives and modes of communication that comprise Canada's mediascape. More information is needed on the range of alternative media that are currently operating in the country, and the kinds of programs and policies that would help them become more economically viable. Only through understanding and strengthening the mechanisms that support these media can we create the infrastructure needed to maintain vibrant and diverse avenues of public expression.

QUESTIONS

1. Is media content simply a mirror image of society, or is the relationship more complex than that metaphor allows? What are some of the factors that influence the way in which media represent the world?
2. How would you define the term "alternative media"? What are some of the problems you encounter in trying to come up with a definition?
3. Some definitions of alternative media include 'zines, culture jamming, and street theatre. Do you think these should be included?
4. What are some of the differences in the ways in which community radio and commercial radio envision their audiences?
5. Despite the fact that they are often commercial in focus, ethnic media are sometimes considered to be alternative media. Do you think they should be included in the definition? Why or why not?
6. What does it mean to say that a media outlet has a "horizontal" rather than a "vertical" relationship with its audience?

NOTES

1. The author would like to thank Megan Humphrey, Frédéric Dubois, Kathe Lemon, Scott Uzelman, and Kristiana Clemens for their help in researching this article. This work was made possible by a York University Faculty of Arts Research Award.
2. The Montreal Newspaper Guild has an archive of press clippings that detail struggles over editorial policy at Southam newspapers. See http://www.montrealnewspaperguild.com. (Accessed July 4, 2004.) Compare with the Canadian Journalists for Free Expression article "NOT IN THE NEWS-ROOM! CanWest Global, Chain Editorials and Freedom of Expression in Canada" (April, 2002) at http://www.cjfe.org/specials/canwest/canwintro.html.
3. For more information about CHMM, see their Web site at http://www.chmm.ca.
4. Statistics supplied by Thomas Saras of the Ethnic Press and Media Council of Canada in e-mail correspondence with the author on July 9, 2004.
5. For instance, Canada's largest Chinese-language newspaper, *Sing Tao*, with editions in Toronto, Vancouver, and Calgary, is approximately 50 percent owned by Torstar Corporation. Omni Television, a multilingual/multicultural broadcaster that is available across Canada, is owned by Rogers Communications; as well as hosting a range of multicultural programming, it also airs programs such as *The Simpsons* and *The Late Show with David Letterman*.

REFERENCES

Alia, Valerie. (1999). *Un/Covering the north: News, media and Aboriginal people.* Vancouver: UBC Press.

All the world's a page. (2003, November 2). *The Toronto Star*, p. B7.

AMMSA (Aboriginal Multi-Media Society). (2002). *AMS list of Canada's Aboriginal publications.* Retrieved July 30, 2004, from http://www.ammsa.com/ams/amscanadapubs.html

ARCQ (Association des radiodiffuseurs communautaires du Québec). (2003). Portrait du secteur. Retrieved July 30, 2004, from http://www.arcq.qc.ca/html/vue.htm

Atton, Chris. (2001). *Alternative media.* Thousand Oaks, CA: Sage Publications.

———. (2003). Organization and production in alternative media. In Simon Cottle (Ed.), *Media organization and production* (pp. 41–56). Thousand Oaks, CA: Sage Publications.

Avison, S., and M. Meadows. (2000). Speaking and hearing: Aboriginal newspapers and the public sphere in Canada and Australia. *Canadian Journal of Communication, 25*(3). Retrieved July 4, 2004, from http://www.cjc-online.ca/viewarticle.php?id=586

Canada. (1986). *Report of the task force on broadcasting policy.* Ottawa: Minister of Supply and Services.

Canada. House of Commons. (2003). *Our cultural sovereignty: The second century of Canadian broadcasting: Report of the standing committee on Canadian heritage.* Ottawa: Canadian Government Publishing.

Canadian University Press. (1977). *CUP editor's manual* (2nd ed.). Ottawa: Canadian University Press.

Couldry, Nick, and James Curran. (2003). *Contesting media power: Alternative media in a networked world.* New York: Rowman and Littlefield.

CRTC (Canadian Radio-television and Telecommunications Commission). (2000, January 28). Community radio policy, Public Notice CRTC 2000-13. Retrieved from http://www.crtc.gc.ca/archive/ENG/Notices/2000/PB2000-13.HTM

Demay, Joël. (1993). The persistence and creativity of Canadian Aboriginal newspapers. *Canadian Journal of Commmunication, 18*(1), 89–100.

Downing, John D.H. (with Ford, Tamara Villarreal, Genève Gil, and Laura Stein). (2000). *Radical media: Rebellious communication and social movements.* Thousand Oaks, CA: Sage Publications.

FEDETVC (Fédération des télévisions communautaires autonomes du Québec). (n.d.). Présentation. Retrieved July 30, 2004, from http://www.fedetvc.qc.ca/accueil.html

Galatas, Eric. (2001). Building Indymedia. In Peter Phillips (Ed.), *Censored 2001.* New York: Seven Stories Press.

Girard, Bruce (Ed.). (1992). *A passion for radio: Radio waves and community.* Montreal: Black Rose Books.

Goldberg, Kim. (1990). *The barefoot channel: Community television as a tool for social change*. Vancouver: New Star Books.

Hackett, Robert A., and Richard Gruneau. (2000). *The missing news: Filters and blind spots in Canada's press*. Ottawa: Canadian Centre for Policy Alternatives and Garamond Press.

Hackett, Robert A., Richard Pinet, and Myles Ruggles. (1992). From audience commodity to audience community: Mass media in B.C. In Helen Holmes and David Taras (Eds.), *Seeing ourselves: Media power and policy in Canada* (pp. 10–20). Toronto: Harcourt, Brace, Jovanovich.

Hackett, Robert A., and Yuezhi Zhao. (1996). Are ethics enough? Objective journalism versus sustainable democracy. In Valerie Alia, Brian Brennan, and Barry Hoffmaster (Eds.), *Deadlines and diversity: Journalism ethics in a changing world* (pp. 44–58). Halifax, NS: Fernwood Publishing.

———. (1998). *Sustaining democracy: Journalism and the politics of objectivity*. Toronto: Garamond Press.

Halleck, Dee Dee. (2002). *Hand held visions: The impossible possibilities of community media*. New York: Fordham University Press.

ICTV (Independent Community Television). (n.d.) Deregulation of community television in Canada. Retrieved July 24, 2004, from http://www.vcn.bc.ca/ictv/1pages/dereg.htm.

Jacob, Kokila. (2001). Canada's ethnic newspapers provide crucial multicultural perspective. *CJFE Reporter*, Issue 1. Retrieved from http://www.cjfe.org/reporter/reporter_01_1.pdf

Keung, Nicholas. (2004, July 16). Minorities fare poorly on TV. *The Toronto Star*, p. A2.

Kidd, Dorothy. (2003). Indymedia.org: A new communications common. In Martha McCaughey and Michael D. Ayers (Eds.), *Cyberactivism: Online activism in theory and practice* (pp. 47–70). New York: Routledge.

Ladner, Peter. (1986, March–April). A case study in alternates. *Content*, 7–8.

Lipton, Barry. (1980, May). Prairie fire history illustrates struggles of the alternate press. *Briarpatch*, *9*(4), pp. 31–35.

Miller, John. (1997). How Canada's daily newspapers shut out minorities. In Steven E. Nancoo and Robert S. Nancoo (Eds.), *The mass media and Canadian diversity* (pp. 134–139). Mississauga, ON: Canadian Educators' Press.

Mohr, Lavinia. (1992). To tell the people. In Bruce Girard (Ed.), *A passion for radio: Radio waves and community* (pp. 23–38). Montreal: Black Rose Books.

Molnar, Helen, and Michael Meadows. (2001). *Songlines to satellites: Indigenous communication in Australia, the South Pacific, and Canada*. Sydney, Australia: Pluto Press.

NCRA (The National Campus and Community Radio Association). (1987). The NCRA statement of principles. Retrieved July 29, 2004, from http://www.ncra.ca/business/NCRAStatement.html

Raboy, Marc. (1984). *Movements and messages: Media and radical politics in Québec*. Toronto: Between the Lines Press.

Radio Centre-Ville. (n.d.). Who are we? Retrieved July 30 2004, from http://www.radiocentreville.com.

———. (1992). Inventing and experimenting. In Bruce Girard (Ed.), *A passion for radio: Radio waves and community* (pp. 49–58). Montreal: Black Rose Books.

Raudsepp, Enn. (1997). Emergent media: The Native press in Canada. In Steven E. Nancoo and Robert S. Nancoo (Eds.), *The mass media and Canadian diversity* (pp. 187–206). Mississauga, ON: Canadian Educators' Press.

Rodriguez, Clemencia. (2001). *Fissures in the mediascape: An international study of citizens' media.* Cresskill, NJ: Hampton Press Inc.

Schudson, Michael. (2000). The sociology of news production revisited (again). In James Curran and Michael Gurevtich (Eds.), *Mass media and society* (pp. 175–200). New York: Oxford University Press.

Statistics Canada. (2004). Household Internet use survey, 2003. Retrieved July 26, 2004, from http://www.statcan.ca/Daily/English/040708/d040708a.htm.

Sullivan, Barbara. (1970). The student press in Canada. In *Report of the special senate committee on the mass media, vol. 3* (pp. 241–269). Ottawa: Queens Printer.

Swanson, Jean. (2001). *Poor bashing: The politics of exclusion.* Toronto: Between the Lines Press.

Vancouver Co-operative Radio. (n.d.). About Co-op. Retrieved July 13, 2004, from http://www.coopradio.org/about/index.html

Verzuh, Ron. (1986, March–April). Alternates: Moving uptown? *Content*, 2–6.

———. (1989). *Underground times: Canada's flower child revolutionaries.* Toronto: Deneau Publishers.

White, Geoff. (1990, March 2). Cuts showed little concern for Natives. *Calgary Herald*, p. A4.

White Eye, Bud. (1996). Journalism and First Nations. In Valerie Alia, Brian Brennan, and Barry Hoffmaster (Eds.), *Deadlines and diversity: Journalism ethics in a changing world* (pp. 92–97). Halifax, NS: Fernwood Publishing.

Woodsworth, A. (1972). *The "alternative" press in Canada.* Toronto: University of Toronto Press.

Part IV
New Media

Introduction

Leslie Regan Shade
Concordia University

This section of *Mediascapes* concentrates on new media—its tangible attributes, some of its emerging social issues, and the specific policy issues of privacy and intellectual property. As the authors in these three chapters remark, researching and writing about the dynamic and ever changing technological and cultural landscape engendered by new media is fraught with challenges.

The term *new media* is perhaps a misnomer. When do "new" media cease to be "new" and become "old" media? Don't "new" media contain attributes of the "old"? With digitization, convergence, and cross-media ownership, new media certainly embody technical attributes of their older predecessors, yet it is in their social appropriation that we find both similarities and unintended consequences. Challenges are in creating new policy frameworks that maintain the public interest and account for new stakeholders who want to have an input into policy.

In studying new media, one must be wary of lapsing into technologically determinist generalizations. Technological determinism views the development and diffusion of technology as developing independently of society but somehow producing societal effects or impacts solely because of technological artifacts. Subscribing to a semblance of technological determinism can lead us unwittingly to assume that "technical change is in some sense autonomous, 'outside' of society, literally or metaphorically," and that "technical change causes social change" (MacKenzie and Wajcman, 1985, pp. 4–5). Technological determinists see technology as being the prime motivator for social and cultural change. This viewpoint does not consider the influence of diverse factors that can actively shape technological design, development, and diffusion, such as assorted social groups, institutions and policies.

Determinism assumes that technical progress follows a unified and unilinear path, and that the end result is technological "progress." It also assumes that societies (individuals and organizations) must adapt themselves to technology, and that other societal and organizational outcomes will necessarily follow. The difficulty with assigning "effects" to technology, as determinists would have us do, is that not all of the "effects" are the same for everyone and every situation. Different social actors exhibit varying levels of interpretation in how they design, conceive, or expropriate technologies.

Futuristic scenarios on communication technologies provide a good example of technologically determinist discourse. Many of our current technologies were heralded as signaling a "revolution" in social applications that would lead to widespread social change. For instance, early pronouncements of the telegraph assumed global peace would transpire, as everyone would be "linked up" (Marvin, 1990). Another example of technological determinist theorizing can be found in early "information highway" discourse (in both media and governmental policy statements) which positioned the Internet as a necessary technology for economic competitiveness, social edification, and job creation. This was also extended to proclamations that the Internet could connect and revive dispersed communities in a sympathetic, McLuhanesque "global village."

In contrast to these deterministic proclamations, University of Toronto Professor Emeritus Ursula Franklin describes technology as both practice and a system. Technology, Franklin says, "involves organization, procedures, symbols, new words, equations, and most of all, a mindset" (1999, p. 3). Franklin reminds us that we need to look at the social class of experts and at the changing nature of community and constituency that is implicated in technology. She asks: How have traditional institutions (such as the church and military) influenced technological design and development? With technology, whose power, and whose control, are we talking about? She also reminds us that we must consider the historical trajectory and pattern surrounding technology.

In their chapter here, Valerie Scatamburlo-D'Annibale and Paul Boin also remind us that we need to look at new media in light of more established broadcasting media that were developed via business development trajectories. However, new media can be described through some of its common attributes: convergence, digitization, and interactivity. All three are characterized by synergistic possibilities in technological design and practice.

How new media are integrated into our everyday lives has been the focus of a burgeoning research literature (Haddon, 2004). Scatamburlo-D'Annibale and Boin consider recent Internet access statistics in Canada. *Access* needs to be considered in terms of not only the technical infrastructure—the hardware and software—but also the social infrastructure, which encompasses literacy, diverse content, vibrant communities, and the ability of Internet users to create and communicate rather than simply act as passive recipients of streaming video, flashy graphics, and branded content. Access also includes geographic availability in rural, remote, and Northern communities; the establishment of public access sites for Canadians who don't have residential Internet access (or even a residence); and universal usability—innovative designs that can accommodate a diverse citizenry.

As Herring (2004) points out, increased bandwidth and Web browser interfaces have facilitated emerging social uses of new media; as we discuss here, these include social networking, blogs (Web logs) and the practices of blogging, and use of the Internet for social activism. Indymedia has been especially active in creating collaborative and cooperative global digital media spaces for citizens and is an excellent example of citizen-based media.

Herring also remarks that after 30 years, the various social practices comprising computer-mediated communication (CMC) have become, for many of us, increasingly domesticated (home-based) and part of our everyday lives. Rather than "an object of fascination and fetish," she writes, "CMC has become more of a practical necessity" (p. 33). And it is to be expected that emerging wireless and mobile technologies will become even more embedded in our everyday work and social lives.

Two divisive yet salient policy issues related to new media are those of privacy and intellectual property. Both issues have been the focus of heated debate, pitting diverse stakeholders and ideologies against each other. In the case of privacy, we see human rights in conflict with national security concerns, while for intellectual property, the struggle is between the public domain and privatized enclosures.

As Valerie Steeves relates in her chapter, privacy is an inalienable human right which is continuously challenged by technological forces—digitization—and by post–September 11th political and economic realities. New security regimes in the era of Homeland Security conflict with citizens' rights to personal privacy. Other definitions of privacy include privacy as intrinsic to democracy, privacy as a social value, and privacy as data protection. As Steeves clearly demonstrates, the privacy balance is continuously being tested by a confluence of forces: legal, technological, cultural, and social. And, as new technologies become more ubiquitous, challenges to privacy rights in the public sphere will become more prevalent.

Intellectual property regimes, as Dan Downes argues in his chapter, are also buffeted by conflicting stakeholders with different objectives. The rights of corporations to protect their media properties, and the rights of the public to make fair use of these properties, have been progressively more tested by digitization and normalized social practices—particularly by youth, in the peer-to-peer downloading culture. As with privacy, reconciling these ideological differences involves discussion and debate among industry groups, users, and the legal regime.

One of the main themes that emerges from this section is the issue of control: who controls the current mediascape, whether via actual ownership holdings of new media properties, via new social uses and practices that often go against the tide of established regulation and legal decorum, or via a political landscape that is preoccupied with security protection. Who stands to gain the most: corporations or citizens?

REFERENCES

Franklin, Ursula. (1999). *The real world of technology.* Toronto: Anansi.

Haddon, Leslie. (2004). *Information and communication technologies in everyday life: A concise introduction and research guide.* Oxford, NY: Berg.

Herring, Susan. (2004). Slouching toward the ordinary: Current trends in computer-mediated communication. *New Media & Society, 6*(1), 26–36.

MacKenzie, Donald, and Judy Wajcman (Eds.). (1985). *The social shaping of technology: How the refrigerator got its hum.* Philadelphia: Milton Keynes.

Marvin, Carolyn. (1990). *When old technologies were new.* Oxford, England: Oxford University Press.

Shade, Leslie Regan. (2002). Technological determinism. In Steve Jones (Ed.), *Encyclopedia of new media* (pp. 433–434). Thousand Oaks, CA: Sage Publications.

14

New Media

Valerie Scatamburlo-D'Annibale and Paul Boin
University of Windsor

According to the conventional wisdom of the past two decades or so, we have entered a period of particularly dramatic, rapid, and intensive change. During his tenure as CEO for General Electric Jack Welch stated that, "The Internet changes everything." Welch was echoing the sentiments of many, perhaps over-the-top, media watchers who hold that the scale, scope, and speed of historical transformation is without precedent and that few will be able to escape its impact in their daily interactions and everyday routines. Most often, the changes and transformations are attributed to a revolution in information and communication technologies (ICTs) which have advanced a set of processes that change everything from the ways in which people work to the ways that they communicate and interact with each other and how they spend their leisure time. In many ways, talk of a "technological revolution" has become commonplace, and we are constantly encouraged to be on the lookout for the latest, most innovative developments lest we be relegated to the margins of the high-tech society of the 21st century.

Some of the prognostications about the technological revolution, the "networked society," and the informational bounty of the Internet have been vastly overblown. Yet, it is difficult to deny that profound changes have been ushered in by the emergence, growth, and spread of new communications technologies. Not surprisingly, such changes have spawned furious debates about how best to describe them—as positive developments that lend themselves to democratization, greater communicative potential, and citizen participation, or as negative developments that merely exacerbate existing inequalities and reinforce the interests of dominant economic and political powers. It is important to note, however, that current debates about the promises and pitfalls of technological innovations aren't necessarily new in any major sense. Scholars such as McChesney (2000) and Mosco (2004) have pointed to earlier developments, including the telephone, radio, and television, that were originally introduced with much fanfare and "democratic" promise. And, as history clearly demonstrates, such developments tended to be dominated by business interests that maximized their potential as media of industry, commerce, and economic accumulation and exploitation. Therefore, optimistic claims about **new media** and new communication technologies must be tempered with a healthy dose of scepticism.

Moreover, the larger context in which they have emerged and in which they continue to evolve must be carefully considered.

WHAT ARE "NEW MEDIA"?

Chances are that even the beginning student of communications has heard the phrase "new media." While the concept has been around since at least the 1970s, it has really only gained widespread currency in the last decade. It is now quite common to hear everyone from journalists to CEOs to popular culture observers employ the term. In academic circles, new media have recently become a major focus of research, theorizing, and, not surprisingly, debate. And yet, there is still a great deal of confusion about what the term "new media" really means or what it encompasses. In surveying the burgeoning literature on this topic, one finds that some current definitions often amount to little more than laundry lists of particular technologies or devices. On the other hand, earlier formulations that equated new media with cable and interactive television now seem woefully outdated. More recently some have suggested that the concept of new media has become synonymous with the Internet. In fact, this sentiment was reflected in a CRTC document that essentially defined new media as the "underlying facilities as well as the communications and interactive services offered on the Internet."

We recognize that scholars continue to define new media in differing ways, and we readily acknowledge that no single definition could capture or crystallize the complexities of the new terrain and/or the contested field of new media studies. Nonetheless, following Lister, Dovey, Grant, Giddens, and Kelly (2003, p. 2), we take new media to include "those methods and social practices of communication, representation, and expressions that have developed using the digital, multimedia, networked computer and the ways that this machine is held to have transformed work in other media." Hence, we are most concerned with those communicative forms that are interactive, digital, Internet-related, and that are marked by the convergence of "old" and "new" media.

We believe that the "new" in new media must be understood in a historical sense. To a certain degree, the concept of new media hides from view the fact that even the "old" media were once considered new. Undoubtedly, Gutenberg's invention of printing with movable metal type was new and considered revolutionary in its day. Similarly, we should also acknowledge the ideological dimensions of the "new" and the glamorous connotations it carries with it. "New" is frequently used to mean something better, improved, or even magical. When linked with technology, the "new" often implies, both implicitly and explicitly, a notion of progress and promise. Such positive connotations of the "new" have a lengthy historical lineage, in discourses dating back *at least* to the Enlightenment and the 18th century. Enthusiasm for technological "progress" and faith in the promise of technology are, arguably, hallmarks of modern thought and persist to this day (DeVaney, 2000).

Mosco (2004) argues that almost every wave of new technology is accompanied by a corresponding mythology about its "uniqueness" and revolutionary potential. This mythology often engenders a sense of historical amnesia about what came before. It therefore comes as no surprise to find that *our* "new media" have arrived on the scene with much hype and fanfare. They have been heralded as tools with the potential to usher in unprecedented levels of productivity; some have enthusiastically embraced them as beacons of revolutionary change in education; and others have suggested that democracy itself would be reinvigorated through the increased capacity to educate, motivate, and mobilize citizens. Given this context, it is essential to approach any discussion of new media cautiously and in a historically informed manner, for it is far too simple to be seduced by the term's superficial simplicity which implies that there were once "old" media which have now been replaced by "new" media. Of course, that is not the case at all.

We also believe that the new media are best understood in the plural (as opposed to the singular—i.e., what "is" new media?) given the range of practices, formations, and processes that can be, and have been, included under this rubric. We also prefer to use the term *new media* since it tends to be more inclusive when contrasted with other terms that also circulate widely. For example, using more exclusive phrases like "computer-mediated communication" (CMC) or "information and communication technologies" (ICTs) tends to place too much emphasis on the more technical dimensions and often limits discussion to a particular set of machines (Lister et al., 2003). In focusing on the technical, such formulations tend to displace the social, political, economic, and historical context in which new media have emerged and evolved. New media are, after all, as much the products of social, political, and economic forces as they are of technological endeavour. Additionally, "technocentric" phrases also tend to marginalize the social and cultural implications of new communication technologies and the changes in social rhythms and behaviours that they tend to foster. Indeed, changes in communications can often have profound consequences—challenging (or sometimes merely reinforcing) established values as well as economic and political structures and power arrangements, and sometimes altering the very ways in which people experience themselves and others. In short, new media point to a wide array of changes in production, distribution, and use—changes that go well beyond the merely technical.

CHARACTERISTICS OF NEW MEDIA AND THE NEW MEDIA ENVIRONMENT

The ultimate shape of the new media landscape is anything but certain. Yet, it is possible to delineate some of the key characteristics that are often associated with new media and the new media environment. These include, but are not limited to, three interrelated processes: digitization, convergence, and interactivity. We have, undeniably, moved away from an era of discrete media and into an era of communication networks. Where it was once possible to speak meaningfully about the various media of communication, including books, newspapers, radio, film, and television, as though they were separate forms and entities, it is increasingly difficult to do so in a "digital" world. Essentially, the shift to digital communication coupled with other technological developments has broken the barriers between traditional or "old" media industries as well as those between the broader media and communication sectors, as we explain further on.

Digitization

The transition to digital format of virtually all media is well on its way to being completed in the very near future and marks a distinct break from previous formats and practices.[1] Digital media allow for greater storage capacity and speed of transmission. They also facilitate infinite reproductive capacities; that is, material is much more easily copied without the degradation in quality characteristic of previous formats (e.g., audiotape and videotape). Moreover, digital media are also much more malleable and flexible—users (or "consumers as producers") are better able to directly intervene, alter, and integrate images, texts, and sounds that they may access. In this sense, **digitization** has opened up a communicative realm of participation that is virtually unprecedented.

At the same time, it has also opened up the proverbial Pandora's box, since the digital explosion has essentially re-defined the relationship between content (such as music and movies), programming, and delivery mechanisms and media that carry the content to consumers. This has become especially evident with respect to "conventional" entertainment industries—movie studios, music publishers, and record companies. These industries have essentially declared war on the new digital media and have made courtrooms the battlefield as the borders between "legitimate" and "illegal" behaviour are increasingly the subject of bitter dispute. Controversies such as those surrounding the advent of MP3 technology and the mid-1999 emergence of Napster, which enabled consumers to share and exchange digital music files, highlighted the problems with copyright regulations and laws that were formulated in relation to older media forms and practices. Currently, copyright law and intellectual property rights are under intense scrutiny. While this issue is explored in Chapter 16, it is worth noting here that, thus far, the companies that control intellectual property seem to have enjoyed the upper hand. This has led some observers to suggest that Canadian copyright legislation is ripe for a "Charter" challenge (Potter, 2003)—that is, for the accusation that it limits individual rights and freedom of expression, in light of what some have called "massive, U.S.-style, copyright-term extensions" (Crysler, 2003, p. 17).

Convergence

The process, described above, wherein previously separate and discrete media forms are drawn together and combined through digital technologies, has often been dubbed **convergence**. In its initial incarnation, the term was simply used to describe the unification of content and media forms. However, within the present deregulatory environment, convergence has exceeded its original meaning and is no longer exclusively associated with the aforementioned unification of content. Increasingly, we see the processes of convergence at play at the level of infrastructures (cable, wireless networks, satellite transmissions), and even among previously differentiated industries (electronics, telecommunications, computer hardware and software, entertainment, publishing, broadcasting). This phenomenon has led to the creation of a new type of "hyper-company" that is known as a Media Telecommunications and Electronic company **(MTE)**. MTEs are horizontally and vertically integrated companies that control information (content), the channels within which information passes (carriage), and the electronic devices (platforms) from which content is viewed. Not only have these new multi-industry companies (to call them simply *multimedia* would be an enormous understatement) horizontally integrated their related industries, they have vertically integrated themselves into new industries (Boin, 2002, p. 351). In this regard, convergence also implies a coming together of the traditionally separate medium and message provision of our communications system.[2]

Convergence also refers to the ways in which control over the fields and flow of communication and information is increasingly concentrated through the merging of media empires. One case which is often cited as the definitive example of this type of "media convergence" was America Online's **(AOL)** acquisition of Time Warner in 2000. In this case, AOL (a new media company) merged with the world's largest "old media" corporation, Time Warner, in order to gain access to Time Warner's vast resources, including film studios, cable networks, specialty channels, magazines, and music catalogues. In essence, the merger brought together a media content provider and an Internet Service Provider to create a global media behemoth with the potential to exploit synergies between the content and AOL's Web-based subscription service.

The AOL–Time Warner union seemed to embolden several Canadian communication companies (including CanWest Global and Rogers Communications), which, shortly thereafter and in rapid succession, jumped on the convergence bandwagon. Mergers have proceeded apace and are generally praised by industry executives who welcome the trend toward vertical integration and corporate synergy. Media critics, however, have pointed to the potential perils of such convergence and the narrowing range of perspectives and voices that mega-media mergers tend to bring about. Here we are reminded of the controversy that engulfed CanWest Global (which owns 11 English-language daily newspapers in major metropolitan hubs) when the company established a national editorial policy. The policy's intent was to institute a standardized editorial, emanating from corporate headquarters in Winnipeg and dutifully reprinted in each of its media outlets. Many journalists and citizens were outraged by what they perceived to be the centralizing and undemocratic nature of the edict. As a result, the issue of media ownership was once again thrust to the forefront of public debate. In poll after poll and in various public forms, Canadians repeatedly expressed concern about the increasing levels of media concentration and convergence (Moll and Shade, 2004), for most understand that a highly concentrated system in the hands of a fistful of private companies endangers one of the major precepts of a free press, which is deemed to be central to the maintenance of democracy.[3] Not surprisingly, such concerns are often dismissed by proponents of media convergence, who suggest that the information cornucopia that supposedly characterizes our era essentially means that no single media entity can exert an inordinate influence over citizens' access to news and information. They further claim that the interactive, decentralized nature of the new media environment actually provides greater, if not limitless, choice for consumers.

Interactivity

The concept of "interactivity" has been addressed and explored from a variety of perspectives (cf. Jensen, 1998), but one of the more common ways is to contrast new media with "old" or established media (such as television, print, or radio) that operate with a communications model which is one-way and top-down. That model, often referred to as the "broadcasting model," is defined as one in which a single media institution or a centrally-controlled entity sends its message out to as large an audience as possible. The audience, in turn, passively consumes the messages with little or no interaction. As Lister et al. state:

> Traditional mass media were the products of the communicative needs of the first half of the twentieth century in the industrialized world. As such they had certain characteristics. They were centralized, content was produced in highly capitalised industrial locations. . . . Consumption is here characterized by uniformity. . . . Twentieth-century mass media can be characterized by standardization of content, distribution and production process. These tendencies toward centralization and standardization in turn reflect and create the possibility for control and regulation of media systems, for professionalisation of communicative and creative processes, and for very clear distinctions between consumers and producers. (2003, pp. 30–31)

By contrast, new media supposedly enable greater user engagement and more control over how media artifacts are consumed. For example, on-line forums for users' comments on or reactions to news items, venues like chat rooms, and more recently, blogs (see below) are commonly cited as developments that provide greater interactivity and user input and that illustrate the "democratic" character of new media. In addition to being more flexible and less subject to centralized control, new media are said to offer a much greater degree of audience differentiation and discrimination. It is also generally held that new media offer greater informational and entertainment/leisure choices to consumers—but as we suggest below, this is largely a myth.

The Myth of "Consumer Choice"

In the new media environment, it is argued, consumers are increasingly able to personalize or customize their own media use—picking and choosing that which interests them and filtering out that which does not. To a certain degree, this is true, but heralding this selective capacity as something entirely new and as something made possible by the Internet is somewhat misleading. People have always had the capacity to be selective about how they consume media. It is also necessary to point out that the selections that are available on a variety of Web sites are predetermined—in short, consumers actually have little control over the menu from which they make their selections. Hence, far from being interactive in any substantive sense, "many websites are designed to preserve the one-sided advantages of the broadcast model, with promotion, persuasion and propaganda as the goals" (Meikle, 2002, p. 30). It is equally important to attend to the ideological dimensions of discourses that champion "choice" and the "interactivity" of the new media, for they draw quite extensively from the larger narrative of neoliberalism that fuels the agenda of corporate globalization and treats the user, above all else, as a consumer (as opposed to a citizen). As Lister et al. argue:

> Neo-liberal societies aim to commodify all kinds of experience and offer more and more finely tuned degrees of choice to the consumer. People are seen as being able to make individualised lifestyle choices from a never-ending array of possibilities offered by the market. This ideological context then feeds into the way we think about the idea of interactivity in digital media. It is seen as a method for maximizing consumer choice in relation to media texts. (2003, p. 20)

What is both interesting and telling is that, while the talk of vast consumer choice with respect to media fare is widespread and largely believed, in fact a few global media powerhouses are further consolidating their control over what the majority of people see, hear, and read the world over (McChesney, 2000). In other words, while it may *appear* that we inhabit dazzling, custom-designed, interactive media environments, it turns out "that they are all owned by the same small number of financial interests" (Lister et al., 2003, p. 212).

In this regard, and despite the endless claims of boundless consumer choice provided by the decentralized and interactive nature of new media, old media conglomerates are staking their claim and are systematically going about colonizing the new media environment. Contrary to early predictions that Internet-based media would pose a substantive "competitive" threat to traditional outlets, it is now apparent that the relationship is one of complementariness rather than competition. Furthermore, the victors of the old media world still have enormous control over what is made available—particularly when it comes to "news." Danny Schechter argues that the "concentration in ownership" that restructured old media also led to "conglomeration in news transmission and, a narrowing of sourcing in new media. It is cheaper for Web sites to buy someone else's news than generate their own" (Schechter, 2000). Research done by Chris Paterson corroborates this view. In 1999, Paterson examined the sources of the dominant news sites on the Web (i.e., Yahoo, AOL, MSN, etc.) and found that, far from providing original journalism (or an extra news choice), they simply play the role of "cyber mediator." Paterson states that "through monopolistic control of international news production, effective brand marketing, efficient use of economies of scale in news production and useful alliances in both news gathering and online distribution, news agencies play a dominant and generally unacknowledged role in determining the vast majority of international news in cyberspace." He adds that, as with old media, a few "global multimedia information conglomerates" dominate Internet news and that the "diversity of information" presumably offered in the new media environment is "largely a mythical aspect of information globalization" (Paterson, 1999). Given this situation, the concerns about even greater media concentration and convergence are well founded, since the enhanced communication capabilities of the new media revolution have made it far easier for large corporations to further homogenize news and commercialize culture.

NEW MEDIA AND EVERYDAY LIFE

Who's On-line?

Discussions of new media often suggest that they are increasingly becoming a part of the fabric of everyday life and that they permeate the space, time, and dynamics of day-to-day interactions. Some of the most recently available statistics seem to corroborate such assumptions. Canadians, it appears, have taken to new media in large numbers. By the end of 2005, Canada is projected to have 20.45 million people on-line out of a projected total population of 32.20 million ("Worldwide Internet Users," 2004; "Population Explosion!," 2004). This would mean that 63.5 percent of Canadians would be on-line; such projections would maintain Canada's position as one of the most "wired" nations in the world, alongside Sweden, Norway, the United States, and Japan.

A recent study conducted by Statistics Canada indicates that 64 percent of all Canadian households (7.9 of 12.3 million) had at least one member who regularly used the Internet in 2003, whether it was accessed from home, work, school, a public library, or another source/location. While this represented a 5 percent increase over 2002, it was significantly down from the gains of 19 percent and 24 percent observed in 2000 and 2001. As in previous years, households reporting higher incomes were more likely to have access to, and utilize, the Internet. And, although lower income households (those with income between $24,001 and

$43,999) made some strides, with 45 percent logging on from home in 2003 (up 13 percent from 2002), the proportion of households engaged in regular use of the Internet remained virtually unchanged for those occupying the lowest income quartile (Statistics Canada, 2004). This points to the persistence of the "digital divide," which continues to define not only Canadian society but the globe as a whole, and which, in turn, makes it virtually impossible to talk about the experience of "new media" in any broad, overarching, or universal sense. Various studies conducted by Statistics Canada and other organizations on the "digital divide" and differentials in access to the Internet have, for the most part, come to similar conclusions—namely that socioeconomic factors including income and educational levels, geographical location, gender, and age influence participation in the new media environment (Crowley, 2002).

The 2003 survey reveals that most people accessing the Internet from home used it for e-mail (52.1 percent).[4] This is hardly startling since e-mail has been called the "killer app" of the Internet (Crowley, 2002, p. 473); while concerns about privacy, spam, and viruses are ever-present, there is no doubt that e-mail has transformed the lives of users. This is particularly true for young people, who are the most voracious everyday users and for whom the Internet is primarily a social medium. Increasing numbers of Canadian youth are plugged in and regularly participate in e-mail, chat rooms, the creation of Web sites, and instant messaging—an activity which has grown exponentially in recent years (Crowley, 2002). This is consistent with findings from other countries. For example, in the United States, more than two million children aged 6 to 17 have their own Web site, and 29 percent of kids in kindergarten through grade 3 have their *own* e-mail addresses (Sifry, 2004, p. 20).

Although the survey indicated that more Canadian households are using the Internet to search for health/medical and government-related information, there can be no doubt that Canadians' engagement in the new media environment revolves significantly around leisure, entertainment, and commerce. Besides e-mail, some of the most common activities by purpose of use include general browsing (an unfortunately vague category), making travel arrangements and seeking out travel-related information, playing games, finding sports-related data, shopping, and obtaining music. Canadian households spent over $3 billion shopping on the Internet in 2003—a statistic that represents a 25 percent increase from the $2.4 billion spent in 2002. Downloading music files dropped 10 percent with 38 percent of regular users reporting participation in this activity. While it is somewhat difficult to discern the precise reasons for this drop-off, some have speculated that it may be the result of highly-publicized campaigns initiated by the music industry to curtail the downloading of free music (Statistics Canada, 2004). This would be in keeping with a trend in the United States, reported by the Pew Internet and American Life Project ("Music Downloading," 2003), which revealed that fewer Americans were downloading music for fear of being prosecuted.

Social Networking

In the general on-line community, a contemporary phenomenon that has become wildly popular revolves around social networking sites that are becoming more and more pervasive as they draw millions of participants and foster new kinds of social conversations. Although explicit social networking sites have been in existence for years (e.g., SixDegrees.com), recent commercial interest and increased venture funding have spawned multiple new sites dedicated to helping people capitalize on their social networks for jobs (LinkedIn.com, ryze.com), dating and friend-ship (Friendster.com), and recommendations and listings (Tribe.net). These new dot-coms skillfully assimilate real-life social groups into a large virtual network by enabling individuals to create an electronic web of friends, families, and business con-tacts who are, in turn, connected to other families, friends, and business contacts. Social networks, it is said, offer a way to create far more sophisticated and nuanced human interactions than those provided by a personal Web page or its more interac-tive kin, the blog. For example, Friendster (http://www.friendster.com), voted as one of the "coolest" Web sites of 2004 by *Time* magazine, helps users find dates and new friends by referring people to friends, or friends of friends, and so on. Once users sign up for the service, they post pictures of themselves and a list of their favourite interests. They are then asked to provide a list of their friends and their e-mail addresses. Kahney (2003) notes that once these social links are established, users are capable of traversing the entire web of contacts, finding people they'd like to meet and sending them messages. Friendster is presumably having an "unbelievable impact" and has been heralded as "the new Google." Danah Boyd, a researcher of on-line social networks, suggests that just as "googling" has become virtually synonymous with Internet searching, "friendster" is now used to describe a person that someone meets or knows through the network (cited in Kahney). Friendster and other applications in the so-called "social software" realm have, not surprisingly, raised significant concerns about privacy, the potential for identity theft, and how to protect the connections forged on such sites from the prying eyes of unsavory participants *and* savvy marketers. Indeed, e-marketers have already exploited the possibilities enabled by the interactive capability of new media to collect information about consumers in real time, and social networks merely provide more opportuni-ties for the excesses of on-line targeted advertising.

Blogs

Another development that has been characterized by some as "the next big thing" on the Internet is the Web log or "blog." In the strictest sense, a blog is essentially someone's on-line record of the Web sites he or she visits. In this form, blogs have been around since the earliest days of the Internet. In a more general and con-temporary sense, the term is used to describe an on-line journal, which usually comprises links and postings that appear in reverse chronological order. In 1999, there were a few dozen blogs; today various estimates suggest that there may be as many as 4.3 million blogs on the **World Wide Web,** with a new blog being created every 5.3 seconds (Sifry, 2004, p. 16). The explosion of the blog phenomenon is at least partly attributable to the relative ease associated with establishing one. Even the least Internet-savvy person can create and maintain a blog—all that is really required is a name, a password, an e-mail address, and a visit to a site like blogger.com. Blogs run the gamut of topics—from those about pets, diets, food, and sports (to name just a few) to blogs that are dedicated to politics, contemporary social issues, and activism.[5] Similarly, the audiences for blogs vary widely. The vast majority of blog producers tend to labour in relative obscurity with small "audiences" consisting largely of friends and relatives. There are, however, some blogs (particularly those related to politics and news) that boast audiences in the tens and hundreds of thousands.

Blogs have created a great deal of buzz about their potential to revolutionize journalism, to make it more democratic, and to help more people become involved in shaping public opinion, since blog authors "can respond in real time to news events, articles, and opinions, acting at once as sites to contest the meaning of texts, as well as challenge the veracity and integrity of news and opinion writing" (Gallo, 2004). Such sentiments are reminiscent of the utopian claims made in the early 1990s about the Internet's democratic potential to transform the political landscape. Consider the bold pronouncements of Howard Rheingold (1994, p. 14), who wrote about the possibility of revitalizing a "citizen-based democracy" where each and every citizen would have the potential to "broadcast to every other citizen." From the outset, such optimists envisioned an intensification of participation in the democratic process that would enable the inclusion of voices historically marginalized by the limitations of more centrally controlled "old media."

Independent Media

Undoubtedly, important strides in these directions have been made, since digital technologies have enabled more people to "become the media." An illustrative example of this would be Indymedia, also known as the Independent Media Center (see www.indymedia.org), which was established in 1999 during the **World Trade Organization (WTO)** protests that took place in Seattle. Inspired by the communicative and political philosophies of the Zapatistas, suspicious of the corporate-owned mainstream media, and utilizing an "open publishing" format, activists created an unprecedented participatory, multimedia, multi-point network which put the means of message production and dissemination in more hands and made it possible to experiment with a paradigm-shattering communications model. Indymedia, often referred to as a media resource for the international movement against corporate globalization, has become the fastest growing alternative media network, with well over 100 sites around the world and on every continent (see Scatamburlo-D'Annibale and Chehade, 2004). And while Indymedia remains a guiding beacon for global social justice movements, its role in posing a threat to the journalistic status quo, concentrated media, and corporate power was wildly overestimated by its more ardent supporters.

In a similar vein, it appears as though blogging aficionados may have overstated its potential. While blogs undoubtedly have some democratic potential, and while they have altered the field of journalism insofar as they have created a real-time virtual feedback loop that challenges traditional barriers between journalists and the public, they have already become integrated components of the mainstream media landscape and blended into the "ever-evolving palate of complementary media available to journalists and the public" (Gallo, 2004). Moreover, blogs are already beginning to be colonized by commercial imperatives, as marketers explore the potential of this form as a venue for even more Web advertising.

CONCLUSION

One of the most frequent metaphors invoked in discussions of new media is that of the *commons* versus the *enclosure*, where the former suggests "the attempt to keep the communications open, accessible and usable for all who share the resource" and the latter, "the striving by corporations to enclose both information and communication" (Kidd, 2001, p. 325). The early days of new media were characterized by exhilarating claims about the re-emerging commons, the rebirth of the public sphere in cyber-space, the potential to challenge centralized power and concentrated "old" media, and the rejuvenation of democracy itself. So far, such claims remain unfulfilled and are likely to remain so, given the increasing corporate colonization of this realm and the likelihood that it will be at the mercy of "digital robber barons" who will exploit it for purely commercial purposes. And, we have already witnessed attempts at enclo-sure—a hemming-in that has been initiated by corporations and by governments (mainly in the form of legislation) working at the behest of corporate interests. When the CRTC conducted a public hearing about new media and asked Canadians whether the CRTC should play a role in regulating the Internet, the overwhelming response was an emphatic "No." However, at no time during the consultation, which occurred between July 1998 and February 1999, was the public informed that the new media environment was already undergoing a process of hidden regulation—regulation designed to benefit corporate interests at the public expense. In its report on new media, the CRTC essentially decided that competition between private inter-ests in the larger market would best serve the public interest. But this corporate dominance threatens to reduce the diversity of content available and to further exac-erbate the antidemocratic tendencies of the broader political economy.

So, as we forge further into the 21st century with the knowledge that the new media environment will continue to play a prominent role in re-configuring the way we lead our lives and how our society is structured, some crucial questions will need to be asked: Who should have access to new media? What will this access cost? What about privacy concerns and surveillance tactics? How will disadvantaged populations be included? How much advertising and commercialization will be allowed? How will governments communicate with citizens? How can the "public interest" be re-defined in democratic, as opposed to corporate, terms? How can the "common good" be preserved in a market-driven digital communications system that seems just as likely as earlier systems to widen the chasm between the haves and the have-nots?

These and other questions will need to be asked and answered. And answered not exclusively by corporate CEOs who believe that the "free market" is the panacea for all that ails us or by government officials who act as their servants. The users of new media—the people themselves, the public—must have some say in the design and development of new media. Indeed, perhaps the most vitally important "social use" of new media is for members to participate in their design and development in order to transcend the "democratic deficit" that we currently face.

QUESTIONS

1. What claims are traditionally made for new media?
2. Why are these claims frequently dismissed by scholars of new media?
3. In what ways does interactivity promote individual intervention or corporate control?
4. What is meant by the metaphors "the commons" and "the enclosure" with respect to new media?

NOTES

1. Whereas analog technology conveyed data as electronic signals or pulses of varying frequency or amplitude, a digital system uses numbers to represent a concrete object. Digitization generally refers to the process by which the physical properties of sounds, pictures, text, graphics, and so on, can be converted into computer-readable formats by changing them into a series of electronic digits, or numbers. The baseline of digital technology is a coding system with only two numbers—1 and 0—(often referred to as ons and offs) that carry information in encoded form.

2. Some contemporary examples include AT&T, Microsoft, Rogers Communications, Disney, Bertelsmann, BCE, and Sony. Beyond the emergence of MTEs is the desire of industrial, manufacturing, or financial companies to enter the MTE sector. Examples include General Electric (nuclear power, appliances, weapons industries), which owns the NBC network, and Irving Industries (oil), which owns a stable of newspapers in Eastern Canada. More

recently, France's multinational utility company Vivendi (electricity and water) purchased Seagram to become one of the world's largest media companies. In short, a vast array of companies—from Hollywood studios to nuclear weapons manufacturers—now consider themselves to be in the media game.

3. Of course, media convergence and concentration are not "new" phenomena that have emerged as a result of currently changing technology; they have been part and parcel of modern media systems for decades (McChesney, 2000).

4. After e-mail, the most common activities by purpose of use were general browsing (48.5 percent), retrieving medical and health information (35.6 percent), locating travel information and making travel arrangements (33.6 percent), and accessing government information (32.2 percent). Other uses included electronic banking (30.8 percent), viewing news (30.2 percent), playing games (27.9 percent), accessing financial information (25 percent), formal education/training (24.9 percent), finding sports-related information (24.6 percent), obtaining and saving music (20.6 percent), searching for employment (19.6 percent), purchasing goods and services (18.6 percent), participating in chat rooms/groups (14.4 percent) and listening to radio (13.1 percent).

5. Blogs Canada's directory contains more than 9000 Canadian blog listings. See http://www.blogscanada.ca.

REFERENCES

Boin, Paul. (2002). *Towards a democratic news media and society: Creating and navigating our information society for a sustainable future.* Unpublished doctoral dissertation, Ontario Institute for Studies in Education, University of Toronto.

Crowley, David. (2002). Where are we now? Contours of the Internet in Canada. *Canadian Journal of Communication 27,* 469–507.

Crysler, Julie. (2003, September/October). Take my poetry . . . please. *This Magazine,* 17.

DeVaney, Ann. (2000). Technology in old democratic discourses and current resistance narratives: What is borrowed? What is abandoned? What is new? In Ann DeVaney, Stephen Gance, and Yan Ma (Eds.), *Technology and resistance: Digital communications and new coalitions around the world* (pp. 9–50). New York: Peter Lang.

Gallo, Jason. (2004). Weblog journalism: Between infiltration and integration. *Into the blogosphere: Rhetoric, community, and culture of weblogs.* Retrieved November 18, 2004, from http://blog.lib.umn.edu/blogosphere/weblog_journalism_pf.html

Jensen, Jens. (1998). Interactivity: Tracking a new concept in media and communication studies. *Nordicom Review, 19*(1), 185–204. Retrieved May 19, 2005, from http://www.nordicom.gu.se/common/publ_pdf/38_jensen.pdf

Kahney, Leander. (2003, July 17). Making friendsters in high places. *Wired News.* Retrieved May 19, 2005, from http://www.wired.com/news/culture/0,1284, 59650,00.html

Kidd, Dorothy (Ed.). (2001). Introduction. *Peace review 13, special issue on social justice movements and the Internet*, 325–329.

Lister, Martin, Jon Dovey, Iain Grant, Seth Giddens, and Kieran Kelly. (2003). *New media: A critical introduction*. London & New York: Routledge.

McChesney, Robert. (2000). So much for the magic of technology and the free market: The World Wide Web and the corporate media system. In Andrew Herman and Thomas Swiss (Eds.), *The World Wide Web and contemporary cultural theory* (pp. 5–35). New York and London: Routledge.

Meikle, Graham. (2002). *Future active: Media activism and the Internet*. New York: Routledge.

Moll, Marita, and Leslie Regan Shade (Eds.). (2004). Preface. In *Seeking convergence in policy and practice: Communications in the public interest*, vol. 2 (pp. 7–12). Ottawa: Canadian Centre for Policy Alternatives.

Mosco, Vincent. (2004). From here to banality: Myths about new media and communication policy. In Marita Moll and Leslie Regan Shade (Eds.), *Seeking convergence in policy and practice: Communications in the public interest*, vol. 2 (pp. 23–41). Ottawa: Canadian Centre for Policy Alternatives, 2004.

Music downloading, file-sharing and copyright: A Pew Internet Project data memo. (2003, July 31). Pew Internet and American Life Project. Retrieved November 18, 2004, from http://www.pewinternet.org/report_display.asp?r=96

Paterson, Chris. (1999, December). *News cybermediation and source concentration: Why the Internet is bad for democracy*. Paper presented at the News in a Global Culture conference, Skodsburg, Denmark.

Population explosion! (2004, September 10). *ClickZNews*. Retrieved May 19, 2005, from http://www.clickz.com/stats.old/big_picture/geographics/article.php/ 151151

Potter, Andrew. (2003, September/October). Is copyright unconstitutional? *This Magazine*, 22–25.

Rheingold, Howard. (1994). *The virtual community*. London: Minerva.

Scatamburlo-D'Annibale, Valerie, and Ghada Chehade. (2004). The revolution will not be televised, but it might be uploaded: The Indymedia phenomenon. In Marita Moll and Leslie Regan Shade (Eds.), *Seeking convergence in policy and practice: Communications in the public interest*, vol. 2 (pp. 363–379). Ottawa: Canadian Centre for Policy Alternatives.

Schechter, Danny. (2000, March 29). Why the latest news about online news ain't so good. *The Media Channel*. Retrieved May 19, 2005, from http://www.mediachannel.org/views/dissector/lessnews.shtml

Sifry, Micah. (2004, November 22). The rise of open-source politics. *The Nation, 14*, 16–20.

Statistics Canada. (2004, July 8). Household Internet use survey, 2003. *The Daily*. Retrieved November 18, 2004, from http://www.statcan.ca/Daily/English/ 040708/d040708a.htm

Worldwide Internet users will top 1 billion in 2005. (2004, September 3). *Computer Industry Almanac*. Retrieved November 18, 2004, from http://www.c-i-a.com

15

Privacy and New Media

Valerie Steeves
University of Ottawa

Conceal your life.

—attributed to Neocles, father of Epicure, 3rd century B.C.

In her novel *The Fountainhead*, author Ayn Rand wrote:

> Civilization is the progress toward a society of privacy. The savage's whole existence is public, ruled by the laws of his tribe. Civilization is the process of setting man free from man. (1943)

A short 56 years later, a much-read article in *The Economist* argued that privacy is dead. New communication technologies, and the surveillance society that flows from them, mean that individuals' commercial transactions, travel arrangements, academic grades, health information, financial records, and personal preferences will all be recorded and accessed by a growing legion of bureaucrats, employers, spouses, insurance companies, marketers, and researchers. *The Economist's* best advice? "Get used to it" ("End of Privacy," 1999, p. 15).

And yet we have a long history of rejecting surveillance. In 1763, after Englishman John Wilkes criticized a speech given by King George III, the king ordered his agents to break into Wilkes' home and seize his private diaries from his desk drawer. Professor Jeffrey Rosen points out that the king's actions directly influenced the leaders of the American Revolution: "The writers of the US constitution drafted the Fourth Amendment banning unreasonable searches and seizures of persons, houses, papers and effects, with Wilkes' house and Wilkes' papers in mind" (cited in McDougall, 1999, p. 9).

The balance between the individual's right to a private life and the ability of others to invade that privacy is an old and established one. Why is our privacy so beset, therefore, at the beginning of the new millennium? Part of the answer lies in the enabling effects of new technologies. When Oregon police wanted to investigate whether or not Danny Kyllo was growing marijuana in his triplex apartment, for example, they didn't have to break down Kyllo's door. Instead, they sat in a car and pointed a thermal radiation imager at the Kyllo residence. The scanner, which detects heat radiation, was able to "see" grow lights located in the apartment. Unfortunately, the same scanner could also "see" people sitting at the kitchen table, sleeping in bed, or taking a shower in any of the three apartments in the triplex.

Ordinarily, police are required to obtain a warrant before they enter and search private property. A search warrant is given only if a justice is convinced that the officers have reasonable and probable grounds to support their suspicions that a crime has occurred. In the Kyllo case, the Ninth Circuit Court of Appeals decided that no warrant was necessary because the emissions were "waste heat" and, as with any garbage Kyllo may have left at the side of the curb, others were free to sift through it if they wanted *(USA v. Kyllo)*. When the case reached the United States Supreme Court, the decision was overturned with one important caveat: the police only need a warrant to use a technology that is not in "general public use" *(Kyllo v. US)*.[1]

Unfortunately, the privacy balance has changed precisely because of new technologies like thermal imaging that watch us without physically intruding into our lives. Stories about Web tracking are legion. In the off-line world, advertisers scan passing cars to see which radio station drivers are listening to, and people walking through a growing number of cities have their faces scanned, digitized, and matched against a database of "criminals" by cameras that can see around corners and hear conversations up to a mile away.[2]

Proponents of surveillance argue that the loss of privacy is justified because surveillance increases security, reduces crime, cuts costs, and fuels the information economy. For example, when former Minister of Immigration Denis Coderre first argued that every Canadian should be required to carry a biometrically encoded national identity card, he claimed the loss of privacy was a small price to pay to protect Canadians from terrorist attacks like 9/11—despite the fact that almost all the terrorists in question entered the United States using authentic identity papers, such that biometric identity cards would have done nothing to deter them. After all, the argument goes, people do not have to worry if they have nothing to hide.

This argument merits close examination. Many of us, for example, agree to trade away our privacy for the convenience of preferred-shopper cards. Companies collect detailed records of our purchase preferences and, in exchange, offer discounts or special offers. How could a list of what we buy at the grocery store harm us?

The *Montreal Gazette* reports that a shopper in California sued a grocery store after slipping on spilled yogurt and shattering his kneecap. The store responded by threatening to paint him as a "falling-down drunk" because his records showed he purchased alcohol on a regular basis. Another American grocery store was required to hand over its customer records to the Drug Enforcement Agency, which wanted to check out who was buying lots of plastic bags (Moore, 2004).

Technologies like preferred-shopper cards seem benign, but the information they amass can be used for secondary purposes that may lead to embarrassment, humiliation, manipulation, and discrimination. *The right to privacy is not about secrecy; it's about autonomy.* The right to a private life enables us to enter into relationships of trust and to enjoy a sense of freedom. In the words of Justice La Forest of the Supreme Court of Canada, "[privacy] is at the heart of liberty in a modern state. Grounded in man's physical and moral autonomy, privacy is essential for the well-being of the individual" (*R. v. Dyment*, 1988).

This chapter will examine different definitions of the right to privacy and explore ways in which Canada and other countries are regulating invasive practices. Throughout, we will examine how the digital environment has changed our experience of privacy and identify the major stakeholders in the emerging privacy debate.

DEFINITIONS OF PRIVACY

The most oft-quoted definition of privacy was popularized in 1890 by Samuel Warren and Louis Brandeis. They were concerned about the ways in which new technologies and business practices were changing the modern experience of a private life and were specifically concerned that journalists were using recently invented photographic equipment to take and publish pictures of private persons:

> Recent inventions and business methods call attention to the next step which must be taken for the protection of the person, and for securing to the individual what Judge Cooley calls the right "to be let alone." Instantaneous photographs and newspaper enterprise have invaded the sacred precincts of private and domestic life, and numerous mechanical devices threaten to make good the prediction that "what is whispered in the closet shall be proclaimed from the housetops." For years, there has been a feeling that the law must afford some remedy for the unauthorized circulation of portraits of private persons; and the evil of the invasion of privacy by the newspapers, long keenly felt, has been but recently discussed. (Warren and Brandeis, 1890)

Warren and Brandeis's definition of privacy as the "right to be let alone" was not a legalistic one. Their concerns grew from their own experience of personal and social relationships. Like many today, they worried that new technologies were invading established social boundaries and were being fuelled by the commercial value of the information obtained. Underpinning their argument that commerce should not be allowed to overrun the right to privacy was their strong belief in the "inviolate personality" of the individual.

As new communication technologies continued to develop, others built on Warren and Brandeis's vision. During its seminal public consultation on privacy rights and new technologies, the House of Commons Standing Committee on Human Rights and the Status of Persons with Disabilities concluded:

> Classically understood as "the right to be let alone," privacy in today's high-tech world has taken on a multitude of dimensions. According to certain privacy experts, it is the right to enjoy private space, to conduct private communications, to be free from surveillance, and to respect the sanctity of one's body. To the ordinary Canadian, it is about control—the right to control one's personal information and the right to choose to remain anonymous. (Canada, 1997, appendix I, p. 1)

Choosing between these definitions is not a neutral process. As the Standing Committee noted, "experience has shown us that the way you ask the question will often determine the type of response you get" (Canada, 1997, p. 33). The current ways to "ask the question" reflect four different ways of looking at privacy:

- privacy as a human right;
- privacy as an essential part of the democratic process;
- privacy as a social value; and
- privacy as data protection.

1. Privacy as a Human Right

The dangers inherent in the modern nation-state's ability to seize information about citizens and use it to invade their private lives were exemplified by the Nazi government. When German forces took towns during World War II, the first buildings they seized were often the town halls; Gestapo officers would then search through records to identify the whereabouts of Jewish residents so they could be deported to extermination camps.

The postwar international community responded in 1948 by adopting the Universal Declaration of Human Rights whose Article 12 proclaims that no one "shall be subjected to arbitrary interference with his privacy, family, home or correspondence." This right to privacy, and the other human rights proclaimed in the Declaration, reflected the United Nations' belief that "the inherent dignity . . . of all members of the human family is the foundation of freedom, justice and peace in the world" (United Nations, 1948).

In the international arena, Canada was a leader in establishing privacy as a fundamental human right. Canadian John Humphrey was one of the authors of the 1948 Declaration; in 1976, Canada ratified the International Covenant on Civil and Political Rights (United Nations, 1966), which contains the same guarantee of privacy as the Declaration. However, within Canada, the protection of privacy as a human right is patchy. The Canadian Charter of Rights and Freedoms does not include an express right to privacy, despite the fact that the federal government suggested its inclusion as early as 1979. The Supreme Court of Canada has written a limited right to privacy into the Charter,[3] but the tests it has developed make it unlikely that this limited right will be able to deal with new invasive technologies.

For example, the Supreme Court has ruled that section 8 of the Charter, which protects everyone from unreasonable search and seizure, includes the right to be secure from such a search when the individual has a "reasonable expectation of privacy" (*Hunter v. Southam*, 1984). Under this test, it is unreasonable to videotape what happens in a private hotel room (*R. v. Wong*, 1990), but the police are free to videotape acts of gross indecency in a public washroom because there is no reasonable expectation of privacy in that location (*R. v. LeBeau*, 1988).

"Reasonable expectation" has been defined as follows:

> A person's privacy is intruded on in an unreasonable manner whenever the state, without a prior showing of just cause before a neutral judicial officer, arrogates to itself the right surreptitiously to record communications *that the originator expects will not be intercepted* by anyone other than the person intended by its originator to receive them. (*R. v. Duarte*, 1990)

Unfortunately, in a wired environment, new technologies make it extremely easy for others to intercept our communications. Open communications networks are just that—open. Any user can use the technology to capture and read the unencrypted communications of any other user. It is difficult to argue that we have a reasonable expectation of privacy when we send e-mail, participate in an on-line discussion, or visit a Web site that collects cookies, because the technology itself gives us *no* expectation of privacy.

The law has been slow to understand the extent to which new technologies are changing our experience of privacy. When the police received a "crime stoppers" tip that Mr. Plant was growing marijuana in the basement of his house, they had no evidence to justify a search warrant. However, they reasoned that growing plants indoors must consume a large amount of electricity. They then used their own computer system to log on to the local utility's computer and pull up Mr. Plant's electricity bills. The Supreme Court of Canada applied the reasonable expectation test, and concluded that

> Section 8 of the Charter should seek to protect a *biographical core of personal information* which individuals in a free and democratic society would wish to maintain and control from dissemination to the state. This would include *information which tends to reveal intimate details of the lifestyle and personal choices of the individual.* (*R. v. Plant*, 1993)

Mr. Plant's electricity bills, they argued, did not reveal intimate details of his personal life; they just showed how much electricity he consumed. This may not be an accurate conclusion in a wired environment. As Justice McLachlin, who disagreed with her fellow judges, argued:

> The records are capable of telling much about one's personal lifestyle, such as how many people lived in the house and what sort of activities were probably taking place there. The records tell a story about what is happening inside a private dwelling, the most private of places. I think that a reasonable person looking at these facts would conclude that the records should be used only for the purpose for which they were made—the delivery and billing of electricity—and not divulged to strangers without proper legal authorization. (*R. v. Plant*, 1993, p. 213)

Furthermore, in our wired world no single detail, such as a utility bill, exists in isolation. Data-matching software can locate and connect a multitude of personal details: the amount of realty taxes we pay; the kinds of books we buy on-line; the comments we post in newsgroups on baking or politics. When all these details are linked together, they create an accurate picture of our private lives.

Marketers can use this information to manipulate our purchase choices. For example, in 1999, a Canadian candy manufacturer obtained a membership list from a weight-loss organization. It used the list to mail candy samples to the dieters at Christmas and Easter because they thought that was when the people on the list were most likely to go off their diets.

But marketers are not the only ones interested in the detailed minutiae of our private lives. Governments increasingly rely on private-sector records to obtain profiles of potential suspects. CNN reports that American police officers carry hand-held wireless computers that can search through commercial databases for information on anyone they encounter during a shift (Weinberg, 2004). The war on terrorism has also led to unprecedented levels of information sharing between governments. In 2002, Canadian citizen Maher Arar was arrested in New York as a suspected terrorist. Allegedly based on information provided to American authorities by the Royal Canadian Mounted Police, Arar was deported to his native-born Syria, where he was tortured for a year before being allowed to return to Canada.[4]

Privacy, the right to be free from being watched, spied upon, and tested, is a human right because it is an essential part of human dignity and autonomy. World War I prisoners of war felt that the worst part of their internment was the lack of privacy in POW camps. Observers concluded that the POWs' irritable and resentful behaviour, "revealed in excessive fault-finding and boasting about themselves[,] . . . was an attempt to maintain personal identity in the face of a complete lack of privacy in their day-to-day existence" (McDougall, 1999, p. 4). Life without privacy makes it impossible to enjoy the dignity and freedom that human rights seek to protect.

2. Privacy as a Democratic Value

Because it is so connected to individual freedom, privacy is also an important element of a healthy democracy. As Justice La Forest notes, "[privacy] has profound significance for the public order. The restraints imposed on government to pry into the lives of the citizen go to the essence of a democratic state" (*R. v. Dyment*, 1988). In many ways, privacy is a "preconditional right" that enables us to enjoy all our democratic freedoms.

Western governments readily accept that privacy is an important democratic value when authoritarian states such as North Korea or China use invasive practices to suppress political dissidents. They admit that placing video cameras on street corners to scan, record, and identify individuals makes it much less likely that people will participate in a political demonstration (exercising their right to assemble) or even say what they think (exercising their right to free expression). However, when those same practices are used to watch Canadians, officials often justify them because they are efficient and help to reduce risks.

Communication technologies enable the state to collect and process vast amounts of information about citizens; by looking for "patterns" in the "data stream," officials seek to identify those people who pose some "risk." For example, research indicates that certain "types" of people are more likely to commit acts of violence. People filling out a firearms registration form are therefore required to reveal whether or not, in the past five years, they have been treated for depression, substance abuse, or emotional problems; considered suicide; been through a divorce or the dissolution of a significant relationship; lost their jobs; or gone bankrupt. Any of these "factors" indicates the person is "at risk" because they match the profile of a person more likely to commit acts of violence. The trouble is, the profile also catches a much larger number of people who do *not* pose a risk, but there is no way of distinguishing them from potential criminals.

Following the logic of "risk reduction," all persons who check off one of the boxes must be investigated because they pose a potential "risk." Applicants are asked for full written details—highly personal details of their depressed mental state, divorce, or drug problem—and a regional firearms officer then begins an investigation. The officer may speak to anyone associated with the applicant, including neighbours, bosses, and ex-spouses, to decide whether or not that person is a risk to herself or others. If the officer is not satisfied, he can ask the local police to act as the firearms centre's agent and conduct a full investigation into whether or not the person is dangerous.

Public interest groups and privacy advocates argue that this foray into the private lives of applicants puts the innocent citizen in a position in which she is forced to defend her actions to the state or face the consequences. This process may or may not catch a potentially violent offender, but it will easily catch a bankrupt, depressed, or divorced farmer who, in need of a gun for his livelihood, is forced to reveal intimate details of his life to the state and, even worse, have the state call and discuss his life with his neighbours, boss, and ex-spouse. This willingness to invade privacy in the name of risk reduction means that the state is dealing with individuals not as citizens, but as suspects, safety risks, or threats to "secure," "efficient," and "cost-effective" government. In such a situation, the relationships that are essential to our understanding of democracy are undermined.

Risk reduction is also not a neutral exercise. Many have accused governments of using racial profiling to target Arab Muslims and other minorities in the war against terror. When Canadian imam Ahamad Kutty flew to Miami on September 11, 2003, he spent 16 hours in jail. After being interrogated by more than 10 officials, he and fellow Canadian Abdool Hamid were declared risks to national security and sent back to Canada. Ironically, Kutty is well known for his strong stand against extremist violence. Nonetheless, American border officials saw him as a security risk because of his religion and ethnic origin (Hall, Shephard, and Harper, 2003).

As former privacy commissioner Bruce Phillips notes, the danger—and allure—of the emerging model of risk reduction is that

> we participate voluntarily, only seeing the obvious advantages—convenience, speed and personal safety—not the less tangible and more complex disadvantages. The most chilling of these is that we will conform because we assume that we are all being watched at all times. Put more starkly: freedom is diminished and, in some cases, disappears. (Privacy Commissioner of Canada, 1999)

3. Privacy as a Social Value

Privacy has a strong effect on our social behaviour and organization. Historians suggest that Elizabethan homes, with their kitchens, parlours, and bedrooms, replaced the single medieval common hall because people wanted to enjoy a level of privacy that had previously been available only to the rich. Likewise, in a landmark 1956 study of the Canadian suburb, Crestwood Heights, researchers concluded that

> increased space, a reason why people buy houses in Crestwood, means increased privacy. . . . Privacy for each member of the family is the ideal—but not the isolation of anonymous shelter as offered by a hotel. The essence of the desired privacy is its very presence within the family unit. (McDougall, 1999, p. 8)

Privacy, then, is not the same as withdrawal from social relationships. Rather, it is the power to control and define those relationships.

Contemporary discussions of privacy often focus on this aspect of individual control. We establish social relationships based on different degrees of intimacy; the closer the relationship, the more we share with the other person. When entry into our private lives occurs without our knowledge or consent, this sense of control is lost and we feel violated. Indeed, the very act of surveillance changes the behaviour of the people being watched. And the first casualty of surveillance is trust.

Privacy, as such, encompasses our social understanding of intimacy. The argument that technology determines the level of privacy we enjoy is dissatisfying because it fails to account for the fact that technological developments themselves are also the result of social choices. Emerging forms of invasion redistribute social power. In the proverbial small town, everyone knows what everyone else is up to. However, this also means that everyone is also called upon to account for socially harmful actions. Hence, a small-town banker in the 1940s would face social censure if he refused to give someone a loan because the borrower had a family history of cancer. In the modern information society, however, the watchers are invisible. When banks, marketers, drug companies, and insurance companies invade our private lives, we are not even aware of it, and cannot see what they are doing with their information about us. This lack of reciprocity means that it will become increasingly difficult to hold others accountable for decisions that harm us or discriminate against us. And those who have access to the information gain a significant amount of control over us.

Ironically, new technologies are often the justification for increasing social control. Individual privacy, the argument goes, must accommodate new technologies and give way to society's desire to stop cyberterrorists, on-line pedophiles, and high-tech criminals. However, while the U.S. Patriot Act and Canada's Anti-Terrorism Act have increased the state's ability to invade privacy in the name of security, the trend to place citizens under greater surveillance in the name of risk reduction was firmly in place before 2001 (Canada, Anti-Terrorism Act, 2001; U.S. PATRIOT Act, 2001).

As early as 1993, the Federal Bureau of Investigation hosted the first meeting of the International Law Enforcement Telecommunications Seminar, where police officers from the European Union, Canada, Sweden, Norway, Finland, Hong Kong, Australia, New Zealand, and the United States began to talk about honing their ability to intercept communications. Enfopol 19 established a set of legal and technical requirements designed to ensure that police forces throughout Europe could eavesdrop on electronic communications at will. Similarly, the *Council of Europe Convention on Cybercrime* sidesteps many of the freedoms normally enjoyed in an open society by giving states broad powers to seize and share data in order to facilitate investigations of "new" cybercrimes, such as data interference, on-line copyright infringements, cyberfraud, and on-line child pornography (Council of Europe, 2001).

4. Privacy as Data Protection

Although murder, destruction of property, fraud, and pornography are old and established crimes, the fact that they now occur on-line or in the furtherance of terrorism is being used to justify more invasive forms of social control. Concerns about technology and freedom are not new. However, the advent of the computing age has brought its own unique set of problems. Information technologies enable organizations to collect, manipulate, and use vast amounts of information about individuals. The need to place some limits on the electronic manipulation of personal information was recognized by the Council of Europe in the 1970s. Europeans, remembering the lessons of World War II, were sensitive to the fact that large organizations like governments and banks were using mainframe computers to collect and process information about citizens.

Recognizing that this data made individuals vulnerable to human-rights abuses, the Council of Europe passed the *Convention for the Protection of Individuals with Regard to Automatic Processing of Personal Data* in 1980 that set out a framework for the collection, use, access, accuracy, and disposal of personal information. Concerned that national legislation based on the *Convention* might block the international flow of data, the Organisation for Economic Co-operation and Development (OECD) released its *Guidelines Governing the Protection of Privacy and Transborder Flows of Personal Data* in the same year (OECD, 1980). The *Guidelines* contained a set of fair information practices to ensure that personal information is collected openly and that data records are accurate and kept confidential. This approach, which concentrates on protecting the integrity of the data itself rather than the individual who is the subject of the data, is called "data protection."

Data protection made a certain amount of sense in the 1980s, when computing was dominated by mainframe computers. In the mainframe environment, data processing was centralized, so all the data about a particular individual could be easily located and its use regulated. In addition, mainframes were extremely expensive and required constant technical supervision. Accordingly, only large organizations, such as governments, banks, and universities, were able to afford them. This meant that regulation had to apply only to a few, large, easily located organizations. However, as the nature of computing changed in the late 1980s and mainframes were replaced by distributed networks, data storage and processing became highly decentralized. By 1990, the power to collect and manipulate personal information was no longer in the hands of the few. Because of this, the data itself became an extremely valuable commodity.

That personal information is now worth a great deal of money in the electronic marketplace is one of the most complicating features of the new privacy landscape. The sale of personal information is indeed big business. For example, *The New York Times* reports that the American Medical Association alone generates $20 million (U.S.) per year by selling doctors' biographies to drug companies. The biographies are matched to electronic records of pharmaceuticals sales so that drug companies can better identify which doctors are selling which drugs. The drug companies then spend $12 billion (U.S.) a year encouraging the doctors to sell more of their drugs by treating them to dinner, theatre, and expensive conferences (Gay Stolberg and Gerth, 2000).

PRIVACY LEGISLATION

To date, Canadian privacy legislation has been firmly rooted in the language of the marketplace. When Canada drafted its Privacy Act in 1982, it applied the OECD guidelines to the ways in which the federal government collects, uses, and discloses personal information about citizens and federal employees. The Privacy Act was limited in a number of ways. For example, the "exceptions" to the rules were extremely broad, and although the privacy commissioner was given the power to investigate complaints, he or she lacks any real enforcement powers. The Privacy

Act's greatest limitation was that it focused solely on the public sector, leaving private-sector data collection completely unregulated.

However, as the commercial imperatives of the information economy grew and consumer confidence in the electronic marketplace wavered, the private sector began to lobby for legislation that would encourage consumers to take part in e-commerce by assuaging concerns about privacy. These commercial imperatives were made even more pressing by the European Union in October, 1995. Under a European Parliament directive designed to harmonize data protection standards within Europe, member states are required to pass legislation blocking the transfer of information to non-member states that do not provide an adequate level of data protection (Council of Europe, 1995).

In January 1998, Industry Canada and the Department of Justice released a discussion paper suggesting that data protection legislation should be extended to the private sector but defining privacy solely as a trade issue.

The legislation that grew out of this discussion paper was named the Personal Information Protection and Electronic Documents Act (PIPEDA). Its purpose is to establish, "in an era in which technology increasingly facilitates the circulation and exchange of information," rules that recognize the individual's right of privacy and "the need of organizations to collect, use or disclose personal information for purposes that a reasonable person would consider appropriate in the circumstances" (PIPEDA, 2000). PIPEDA adopts the fair information practices first set out by the Council of Europe, and adds a requirement that personal information should only be collected, used, and disclosed with the individual's consent. However, like the Privacy Act, PIPEDA sets out a long list of exceptions to the general rule requiring consent, including investigations into a contravention of the law.

PIPEDA represents an uneasy compromise on the parts of industry, government, and privacy advocates, the latter of whom hoped some protection would be better than none. That compromise began to unravel even before the act was passed on April 13, 2000. Drug companies, pharmacists, and the Ontario Ministry of Health argued before the Senate Committee on Social Affairs that PIPEDA should not apply to personal health information, because it would unduly hamper the efficiency of health-care delivery and research. In spite of the fact that opinion polls and public consultations have consistently indicated Canadians want more, not less, protection for their health information, a number of provinces have passed health information legislation that makes it easier for the state and "trusted parties" to share medical records without the patient's consent.

Similar problems occurred when U.S. President Bill Clinton passed health privacy legislation near the end of his term. One of President George W. Bush's first actions was to delay implementation of the law, thereby affording health companies time to lobby for lower standards of protection. Although American legislators have been unwilling to interfere with the private sector in general, relying instead on voluntary standards and privacy policies, there has been a great deal of interest in health privacy and the protection of children.

Early attempts to regulate electronic data in the United States were draconian. The Communications Decency Act, for example, made it a criminal offence to use a telecommunications device to "knowingly make, create, or solicit . . . any comment, request, proposal, image, or other communication which is obscene, lewd, lascivious, filthy, or indecent." In June 1996, a three-judge panel in a Philadelphia court struck down the Communications Decency Act for contravening constitutional guarantees of freedom of speech (*Reno v. ACLU*, 1996); a year later, the United States Supreme Court affirmed the lower court decision (*Reno v. ACLU*, 1997). More narrowly drafted was the subsequent Children's Online Protection Act (COPA), which made it unlawful to communicate, on the World Wide Web and for commercial purposes, material that is "harmful to minors" unless good faith efforts are made to prevent children from obtaining access to such materials. On June 22, 2000, COPA was also struck down for unduly restricting freedom of speech *(ACLU v. Reno II)*.[5]

The United States continues to follow the privacy debate, although the major concern appears to be the need to avoid trade sanctions because of noncompliance with the 1995 European Union directive. Now that most of the members of the European Union have passed data protection legislation, pressure is mounting for the Americans to act as well. The Federal Trade Commission has set out voluntary standards for on-line commercial privacy, and the Department of Commerce has developed a "safe harbour" framework under which American firms can "certify" that they comply with a minimum set of fair information standards acceptable to the European Union. In Canada, there is still pressure to move beyond the data protection framework and entrench a quasi-constitutional right to privacy. On March 13, 2001, Senator Sheila Finestone introduced a Privacy Rights Charter (Bill S-21) that (1) seeks to make it clear that every individual in Canada has a right to privacy in the broad sense, and (2) expressly acknowledges the importance of privacy as a human right, an essential element of democracy, and a social value.

TENSIONS IN THE PRIVACY DEBATE

Many experts argue that fair information practices will ensure that privacy is protected in the new millennium. For example, former British Columbia privacy commissioner David Flaherty writes, "I have never met a privacy issue that could not be satisfactorily addressed by the application of fair information practices" (Bennett and Grant, 1999, p. 35). There is, however, a fundamental tension between privacy as a human right and access to information as a tool to enhance competitiveness and control. Fair information practices do not capture the "rights" side of the equation because they were designed by stakeholders to ensure that data will continue to flow into the information marketplace. They create a form of "consensual invasion" whereby the consent process is designed to protect the interests of everyone except the individual who is revealing the information.

In effect, consent is an agreement between the individual disclosing the information and the organization collecting the information. In order for consent to adequately protect the individual's autonomy and freedom of choice, there has to be an equality of bargaining power between the parties to the transaction. But that equality of bargaining power is often absent. If my employer, bank, or insurance company asks me to consent to the release of my personal information, what happens if I refuse? I may find I will lose access to employment, financial services, or insurance coverage.

Consent is also easily sidestepped by legislation and government practices. The United Kingdom has passed a law giving insurance companies the "right" to demand a genetic sample from prospective clients. Iceland sold the genetic records of its entire population to a drug company without first asking its citizens. It is estimated that our images will be captured by 300 surveillance cameras on the way to work in the morning, all of which have been installed and operated without our consent and often without our knowledge. Statistics Canada releases our tax records to epidemiologists conducting medical research because they have decided "it's good for us."

Proponents justify these practices on the grounds that they are efficient and reduce risk. National security, marketplace efficiency, public safety, and the development of new medical treatments are important goals, but not if they are accomplished in ways that sacrifice our individual rights. We have learned this lesson before. During World War II, the United States Census Bureau released statistical data to the state to assist in the arrest and detainment of Japanese Americans. In 2004, the U.S. Census Bureau released information detailing the number of Arab Americans living in specific ZIP code areas to the Department of Homeland Security.

The dynamics of national security and the marketplace could not help Japanese Americans and Japanese Canadians or many other Canadians. To do that, we had to develop a language of human rights. Our choice of language is equally important in the context of the privacy debate. As Franklin (1996) has said: "Ultimately, the level of openness and privacy we enjoy is a social choice. Privacy is not a function of our technological environment or need for security."

In the words of privacy advocate Darrell Evans:

> I think the vanishing of privacy would be a victory of materialism over the human spirit. I find it very hard to picture what kind of room there would be for creativity on the part of human beings in such a world. . . . We are constantly told it is a more secure world, of course, a more efficient world, a world that catches fraud much better, but to me, that is the victory of bureaucracy over human creativity. . . . We want to put individuals in a place of causation rather than being a complete effect of technologies and of a gradual erosion of our privacy. If we are to maintain human freedom, I think that's what we have to do. (cited in Canada, 1997, p. 21)

QUESTIONS

1. Is privacy a fundamental human right? Give reasons for your answer.
2. According to the author, what are the four different ways of understanding privacy?
3. Which do you feel poses the greater threat to privacy—the public sector or the private sector? Give reasons for your answer.
4. In what sense do privacy codes adopt the point of view of business and neglect the rights of citizens?
5. What is a reasonable expectation of privacy in a digital age?

NOTES

1. In 2004, the Supreme Court of Canada held that the police can use infrared technology to take pictures of the heat that escapes from a private home, so long as the scanner cannot see into the house (*R. v. Tessling*, 2004).
2. For example, it is estimated that there are 2.5 million cameras focused on public spaces throughout the United Kingdom. London alone has an estimated 150,000 CCTV cameras monitoring its streets; in 1997 London cameras began to automatically read, recognize, and track automobiles by their licence plates. One year later, the London borough of Newham added face recognition software that scans crowds and matches digitized pictures of the faces of passers-by against a database of "known criminals."
3. The major constitutional protection is afforded under section 8, as discussed below. Recent case law suggests that the Court is also willing to interpret section 7 ("the right to life, liberty and security of the person") in ways that will protect privacy (see *Blencoe v. British Columbia*, 2000; *Godbout v. Longueuil*, 1997). However, section 7 rights have also been limited to reasonable expectations of privacy.
4. An Inquiry pursuant to Part I of the Inquiries Act was established in February 2004 to investigate the actions of Canadian officials, including members of the RCMP, in regard to Mr. Arar's arrest and deportation.
5. Further information can be accessed through the Electronic Privacy Information Center Web site (http://www.epic.org/).

REFERENCES

ACLU v. Reno II (1999), United States Court of Appeal for the Third Circuit, No. 99-1324.

Bennett, Colin J., and Rebecca Grant. (1999). *Visions of privacy: Policy choices for the digital age*. Toronto: University of Toronto Press.

Blencoe v. British Columbia (Human Rights Commission), [2000] S.C.J. No. 43.

Canada. Anti-Terrorism Act, S.C. 2001, c. 41.

Canada. House of Commons Standing Committee on Human Rights and the Status of Persons with Disabilities. 35th Parliament, 2nd Session. (1997). *Privacy: Where do we draw the line?* Ottawa: Public Works and Government Services Canada.

Council of Europe. (1980). *Convention for the protection of individuals with regard to automatic processing of personal data.* ETS No. 108.

———. (1995, October 24). *Directive on the protection of the individual with respect to the processing of personal data and on the free movement of such data.* 95/46/EC.

———. (2001, November 23). *Convention on cybercrime.* CETS No. 185.

End of privacy. (1999, April 29). *The Economist,* 15.

European Union. The Council. (1999, March 15). Enfopol 19. 6715/99.

Franklin, Ursula. (1996, September 19). *Stormy weather: Conflicting forces in the information society.* Closing address at the 18th International Privacy and Data Protection Conference, Ottawa.

Gay Stolberg, Sheryl, and Jeff Gerth. (2000, November 16). Medicine merchants: Tracking the doctors. *New York Times.*

Godbout v. Longueuil (Ville) (1997), 152 D.L.R. (4th) 577 (S.C.C.).

Hall, Joseph, Michelle Shephard, and Tim Harper. (2003, September 13). Revered Muslim cleric held in U.S. *The Toronto Star.*

Hunter v. Southam (1984), 11 D.L.R. (4th) 641.

Industry Canada and Department of Justice Canada. Task Force on Electronic Commerce. (1998). *Building Canada's information economy and society: The protection of personal information.* Ottawa: Public Works and Government Services Canada.

Kyllo v. US (2001), 121 S. Ct. 2038.

McDougall, Bruce (Ed.). (1999). *Perspectives on privacy.* Toronto: Zaxis Publishing.

Moore, L. (2004, July 22). They've got your number: Cutting-edge technologies work as tattle-tales for a surveillance-minded state, Canadian privacy advocates. *The Montreal Gazette.*

OECD (Organisation for Economic Co-operation and Development). (1980, October 1). *OECD recommendation concerning and guidelines governing the protection of privacy and transborder flows of personal data,* OECD Doc. C(80)58 (Final).

PIPEDA (Personal Information Protection and Electronic Documents Act), S.C. 2000, c. 5. Retrieved from http://www.privcom.gc.ca/legislation/02_06_01_e.asp

Privacy Commissioner of Canada. (1999). *Annual report, 1998–1999.* Ottawa: Public Works and Government Services Canada.

Privacy International. (2001). *The 2001 US big brother awards.* Retrieved from http://www.privacyinternational.org/bigbrother/us2001/

Privacy Rights Charter, Bill S-21. (2000). 36th Parliament, 2nd session.

R. v. Duarte (1990), 1 S.C.R. 30 at 46.

R. v. Dyment (1988), 45 C.C.C. (3d) 244.

R. v. LeBeau (1988), 41 C.C.C. (3d) 163 (Ont. C.A.).

R. v. Plant (1993), 84 C.C.C. (3d) 203 at 213.

R. v. Tessling (2004), 3 S.C.R. 432, 2004 SCC 67.

R. v. Wong (1990), 3 S.C.R. 36 (S.C.C.).

Rand, Ayn. (1943). *The fountainhead.* Indianapolis, IN: Bobbs-Merrill.

Reno v. ACLU (1996, June 11), United States District Court for the Eastern District of Pennsylvania, No. 96-963. Retrieved from http://www2.epic.org/cda/cda_dc_opinion.html

Reno v. ACLU (1997, June 26), United States Supreme Court, No. 96–511. Retrieved from http://www2.epic.org/cda/cda_decision.html

United Nations. (1948, December 10). *Universal declaration of human rights.* Resolution 217 A (III).

United Nations. (1966). *International covenant on civil and political rights.* U.N. Doc. A/6316, 999 U.N.T.S. 302.

U.S. Congressional Privacy Caucus. (2001, March 2). Briefing.

U.S. PATRIOT Act, (2001) HR 3162 RDS.

USA v. Kyllo, 96–3033 (CA9 1999).

Warren, Samuel, and Louis Brandeis. (1890). The right to privacy. *Harvard Law Review, 4*, 193–220.

Weinberg, Paul. (2004, July 16). Big brother comes to Canada. *Inter Press Service.*

16

Intellectual Property and Copyright Issues in the Global Economy

Daniel Downes
University of New Brunswick, Saint John

INTRODUCTION

The global media scene raises a number of questions about the operation of the media in the new economy. Who owns the creative works we see, hear, or read? How are the rights of authors and other creators protected such that they will continue to inform, enlighten, and entertain us? Conversely, how do we guarantee that everyone has reasonable access to new information and new ideas? To what extent can we ensure that innovations will not be controlled by a few at the expense of the rest of society? These questions address the concept of intellectual property.

INTELLECTUAL PROPERTY AND COPYRIGHT

Intellectual property is the result of intellectual or creative work. A variety of creative products, including works of art, film, written texts, or even computer software can be created and owned by individuals or companies. One of the ways intellectual property is protected is through **copyright**.

Copyrights determine what is protected, by giving their owners the right to reproduce, to create derivative works, to distribute copies of, to perform publicly, or to display the original work of authorship. They also determine how long a creative work is protected—the duration of the author's life plus 50 years (70 years in the European Union and 75 in the United States). These rights have some important exceptions. In Canada and the United States, government works are not copyrightable, which means that anyone can use them. This is not the case in Great Britain, where government documents are copyrighted. The fair use concept in the United States, like the Canadian fair dealing concept, gives researchers, educators, and libraries special privileges to use copyrighted material. The goal of copyright law is to encourage authors to invest effort in creating new works of art and literature, not to deny others legitimate access to them.

One cannot copyright ideas, concepts, facts, or knowledge. Ideas are not copyrightable. Only the *expression* of ideas, such as the particular words on a page, can be protected by copyright. To qualify for copyright protection, a work must be both fixed and original. There are many ways to fix a work in permanent form. It can be written down on paper or stored in a computer file; it can be recorded on audiotape or videotape; it can be cast in bronze, built from cement, steel, and glass, or carved in wood. A professor's comments to a student or a colleague are not subject to copyright, but the same professor's written lectures are. In effect, all one need do is write something on a piece of paper and it is protected by copyright.

The originality of a work is something more difficult to determine. The work must display a certain amount of creativity (a vague requirement difficult to determine) and the work must be more than a copy of previously existing material.

For media students, copyright is an important concept. Copyright is the primary method for protecting ownership rights in a number of communication and information industries, such as publishing, radio, television and film production, advertising, the music industry and, since the 1970s, the computer software and video game industries. Today, copyright is a key issue as it becomes ever more difficult to control who copies and circulates images, texts, sound, and visual information over the Internet. The control and monitoring of legitimate and illegal copies of copyrighted material is important to those who create information and media content that might be redistributed in digital form. It is also an important issue for people who design and maintain Web pages whose content is often adapted or digitized from existing sources. Further, copyright is important to traditional copyright holders (such as publishers, record companies, or film studios) who want to protect their ability to exploit their copyrights when faced with new distribution systems such as the Internet. Such issues are not unique to the digital era. With the introduction of new technologies such as radio, the VCR, and the personal computer, tensions between the rights of copyright owners and creators have often been weighed against the rights of users to have fair access to information.

HISTORICAL CONTEXT OF COPYRIGHT

Copyright is linked to the rise of a particular development in the history of media—the printing press. Before the invention of the printing press, books were difficult—and expensive—to produce. Further, literacy was not sufficiently widespread to support more than a limited market for books. As printing presses were established throughout 15th century Europe, books became cheaper and more widely available. Consequently there was a need to protect the rights of authors and printers to profit from their written works.

Copyright was a reaction to the fact that the new print technology allowed the fixing of literary works in a tangible medium—books—that could be mass-produced on an unprecedented scale and then sold in the marketplace. Through copyright, intellectual works (the products of human creativity) were turned into commodities quite as tangible as real property. Copyright turns creative acts into exchangeable property or commodities.

The first modern copyright act was the British Statute of Anne in 1710. It granted authors the exclusive right to authorize the printing or reprinting of books for a limited number of years. This act established the main aspects of copyright protection we recognize to this day. Publishers benefit from their published works by retaining the exclusive right to print and reprint books for a limited number of years, after which the works pass into public domain where all can benefit from them.

Changes in copyright law have dealt with the duration of protection and with the variety of creative works that are protected. Indeed, as new technologies emerge, older copyright laws are often outmoded. Today this raises questions about the suitability of print as a model for the Internet and digital media.

CANADIAN COPYRIGHT

Canada's copyright legislation was enacted in 1924. While the original act was not sufficiently broad to deal with subsequent technological advances in the media industries—advances that, throughout the century, affected all aspects of media production, distribution, storage, and exhibition—the act was not revised until 1988, when it was amended in a first phase of copyright reform.

When the Free Trade Agreement (FTA) came into effect in 1989, copyright in Canada was extended to works communicated to the public by means of telecommunication. Prior to this, the re-transmission of television and radio signals by cable systems to private subscribers did not require copyright licensing or royalty payments. By extending copyright to transmission via telecommunication, the nature of cable distribution changed to accommodate payment of royalty fees to copyright holders. In particular, Canadian cable operators became liable for the re-transmission of U.S. broadcast, satellite, and cable signals and were incorporated into a compulsory licence system similar to that established in the United States a decade earlier.

A second phase of copyright reform was completed in 1997 when Bill C-32, an act to amend the Copyright Act, received royal assent and was proclaimed law. A third and still uncompleted phase of copyright review will deal with issues relating to new media and digital technology. This phase of copyright reform began in the fall of 2001 and deals with such questions as whether compulsory licensing should apply to Internet-based transmissions—an idea that has faced opposition from the American entertainment industry (which does not wish to be required to license its material whenever new technologies become available).

Copyright is a form of regulation that increasingly depends upon international cooperation and coordination. Canadian copyright is influenced by our trading relationships with other countries, such as the United States.

AMERICAN COPYRIGHT

The United States Constitution recognized the importance of copyright and included authorization for a national copyright system. Thus, in 1790 the United States passed its first copyright act. Similarly, the French Republic passed a copyright act in 1793.

U.S. copyright law has been amended frequently, often in reaction to new inventions, such as photography and motion pictures. A major revision was the Copyright Act of 1909, which remained in effect until the Copyright Act of 1976 replaced it. The 1976 statute continues to be the legal basis for copyright protection in the United States.

The 1976 Copyright Act extended copyright protection to a wide range of creative expression. Specifically, the 1976 act extended copyright protection to computer programs, literature, music, drama, pantomimes, choreography, pictures, graphics, sculpture, motion pictures, audiovisual productions, and sound recordings. According to the 1976 act, copyright extends to all "works of authorship fixed in a tangible medium of expression."

The 1976 act reflected a new way of thinking about intellectual property because, by including software, it made the basic unit of copyright the temporary "copy" of a file in a computer's RAM memory (not a tangible object). This subsequently made it possible to argue that all computer-mediated communication should conform to copyright rules (Litman, 2001, p. 28). Further, copyright now governed individual consumption as well as commercial reproduction and distribution of information, and individuals were subject to copyright rules as well as companies and institutions. The argument was that copyright had always been intended to offer content producers extensive controls. And now, the computer age had provided the means to enforce laws against all copyright infringement.

The Digital Millennium Copyright Act or DMCA (1998) addresses Internet issues. The Act gives legal support to copy-protection systems (making it a crime to disable or circumvent antipiracy measures built into commercial software). It reduces the liability of Internet service providers (ISPs) for copyright infringement in cases where they are simply transmitting other peoples' information over the Internet. The Act also limits some aspects of fair use by raising the possibility that providing links from one Web site to another without prior permission may violate copyright, and by requiring ISPs to monitor user Web sites for compliance with copyright laws. Finally, webcasters are required to pay licensing fees to record companies for disseminating recorded music on the Internet. The DMCA has spurred a number of legal challenges.

INTERNATIONAL ASPECTS OF COPYRIGHT

There are two international copyright conventions—the **Universal Copyright Convention** signed by more than 50 countries that protects works for the life of the author plus 25 years and the **Berne Convention** that protects works for life plus 50 years. These conventions provide minimum standards for protection and guidelines for enforcement because, in the end, copyright practices are the responsibility of each member state. They depend on national laws and enforcement (Bettig, 1996, p. 204).

The Berne Convention was the first and perhaps the most important international treaty concerning copyright law. First adopted in 1886, it has been revised several times since. Most countries of the world are members of the Berne Convention, including the United States (which refused to join until the 1990s) and Canada (which joined in 1928). The Berne Convention states that countries will extend to each other national treatment of their copyright holders. For example, a book published by an Italian author would enjoy in Canada the same protection as in Italy. The same holds true for protection of Canadian works in other countries.

In 1994 many countries of the world signed an important treaty dealing with copyright law. The Agreement on Trade Related Aspects of Intellectual Property Rights (TRIPS) clarified several aspects of copyright law and strengthened copyright protections internationally. However, through its protection of intellectual property rights, TRIPS has been critically evaluated as strengthening the dominance of transnational corporations and dominant economies (such as that of the United States) in the international trade of services—particularly business services (Castells, 2000, pp. 114–120). Further, in 1994 the World Intellectual Property Organization (the governance forum of the Berne Convention) extended copyright protection to digital formats including the Internet and digital storage of music and film. The Digital Millennium Copyright Act was, in part, the U.S. compliance with the WIPO Copyright Treaty of 1996.

Canada's current phase of copyright reform is, to a great degree, a response to the commitments made in signing the WIPO Treaty. Canada is considering how to incorporate several WIPO provisions, including the establishment of exclusive rights to copyright owners who provide their works on-line and the prosecution of people who circumvent software protection. As well, Canada is considering whether to extend the duration of copyright protection to life plus 75 years, after the examples of the United States and the European Union.

Compliance with international agreements has been a source of particular tension between the United States and countries such as China and others where copyright violation continues to be a serious problem (even after the Chinese government has signed agreements to combat copyright piracy). International agreements like TRIPS and international organizations like WIPO and the WTO provide places where countries can lobby other governments to fight piracy more vigorously.

The justification for copyright protection is that some form of protection is needed to encourage the creation of new creative works. If there is no guarantee that creators will benefit financially from their labour, there is little incentive to create. On the other hand, copyright legislation is designed to place reasonable limits so outdated works can be incorporated into new works.

HOW DOES COPYRIGHT WORK?

In Canada, when an individual creates an original work, it is automatically protected by copyright. The creator has neither to pay a fee nor formally register the work for copyright protection. Copyright owners generally mark their works with their name, the year in which the work was first published, and the copyright symbol, ©. Although this symbol is not obligatory in Canada, or in the United States for works published after 1989, the copyright symbol signals that the work is copyright protected.

If the work is created by an employee or by a contractor, the copyright generally belongs to the employer who commissioned the work (a magazine, for example), unless a written agreement states otherwise. However, even when a creator gives or sells copyright to someone else, the creator still retains moral rights to the work unless the creator waives these rights. Moral rights refer to a creator's right to have the integrity of a work respected. Consequently, while a creator may sell or transfer the copyright (the right to benefit materially) to another person, the author still maintains the moral right to prevent anyone, even the new copyright holder, from changing the work without permission. In addition, the copyright owner cannot use the work in ways that might damage the creator's reputation. Canadian artist Michael Snow prevented the Eaton Centre in Toronto from decorating one of his works with Christmas wreaths, even though the Centre owned the work.

A creator cannot transfer his or her moral rights to another individual, but can waive these rights when he or she transfers copyright. Moral rights exist for the lifetime of the creator, plus 50 years, and pass on to a creator's heirs even if they do not inherit the copyright itself.

EXTENT OF COPYRIGHT PROTECTION

Copyright owners may not want or be able to manage all aspects of copyright. So, copyright law permits a copyright owner to enter into agreements that allow others to use some or all of the owner's rights in return for payment. These transactions are called copyright licences. Licensing greatly increases the ability of the copyright owner to make money from the work. An author or creator can license different aspects of the work—one publisher can hold the hardcover rights to a book, another publisher the softcover rights, and a production company the film rights. Licensing also binds the copyright owner to the licensee for a period of time after which the copyright owner can terminate the licence.

The copyright owner can also sell the copyright entirely. This is called an assignment. Writer Edward Lear sold the rights to his works for £125 and lived to see his publisher profit from 19 editions of his work without receiving another cent in royalties. Similarly, Paul McCartney tried to buy the publishing rights to the early Beatles song catalogue but was outbid by Michael Jackson, who now enjoys the material benefit whenever the songs are reproduced. Recently, recording artists such as David Bowie and Rod Stewart sold the rights to their song catalogues as public offerings, creating the opportunity for people to buy shares in the artists' royalties.

As indicated, a copyright owner may not be able to manage all aspects of licensing. There are times when people can use copyrighted works without having to negotiate a licence with the copyright owner, provided they pay a set fee, called a royalty, determined by the government. This is known as a compulsory licence. The U.S. Copyright Act of 1976 gives cable television systems and satellite television systems this type of compulsory licence. It also grants a compulsory licence to record companies to collect royalties once the copyright owner has authorized someone to make a recording of his or her music. The determination of fair royalty rates is one of the functions of the Copyright Board of Canada. In the United States, royalty amounts are set by Copyright Arbitration Royalty Panels established by the U.S. Copyright Office.

In general, anyone who wants to make a copy of written or visual work must still ask the permission of the copyright owner and pay royalties as requested. Since 1988, the Canadian Copyright Act has recognized collectives such as SOCAN and CANCOPY, which collect royalties and licensing fees that are then distributed among copyright holders.

DURATION OF COPYRIGHT PROTECTION

Copyright generally exists for the life of a creator plus 50 years after the end of the calendar year of the creator's death. In the United States, the Sonny Bono Copyright Term Extension Act of 1998 extended the duration of copyright protection to 75 years from the previous 50-year limit established in the 1976 Copyright Act. The Bono Act was the result of intense lobbying from film companies—including Disney, which was about to lose its copyright on the first Mickey Mouse cartoons. The case went to the U.S. Supreme Court, where Eric Eldred, a publisher who distributed public domain works over the Internet, argued that copyright extension would effectively destroy the public domain by granting perpetual protection to works that were already close to a hundred years old. He lost, but the case polarized opinion about whether copyright is a bargain between creators and society or a property right.

INFRINGEMENT OF COPYRIGHT

An infringement of a copyright is the reproduction, distribution, performance, or display of any copyrighted work without permission of the copyright owner or without a compulsory licence. Infringement includes plagiarism (unauthorized reproduction), although the test for this form of infringement is subjective—whether an ordinary observer would consider the second version "substantially similar" to the copyrighted work. Copyright violation cases more often involve the unauthorized distribution of copyrighted material.

Fair Use and Fair Dealing as Exceptions to Infringement

While it is necessary to protect the rights of creators, it is also necessary to establish principles of use so that people have reasonable access to copyrighted materials. In some cases, copying does not damage the interests of a copyright owner. For example, a passage of a novel quoted in a book review can benefit the copyright holder.

This important exception to the rule of copyright infringement is known as **fair dealing** in Canada and the U.K., and as fair use in the United States. It is through these concepts that broader social interests are protected against unfair or unreasonable control of creative works. Remember, one of the purposes of copyright is to encourage continued production of creative works for the benefit of society. An overly stringent application of copyright protection would deny society the benefit of the creative works.

Fair dealing allows copying of portions of copyrighted material for such purposes as private study, research, criticism, comment, and teaching, even without permission of the copyright owner. The U.S. Supreme Court has ruled that it is also fair use to use a home videocassette recorder to make copies of television programs and movies for later viewing.

Here is another example of fair use that is of particular relevance to university students. A student who copies a limited amount of published materials is not in violation of copyright, whereas a copy shop violates the law if it copies a textbook without paying royalties. In the United States, this principle was established in 1991 when Kinko's lost a challenge launched by the publishing industry. The result was that it now costs more for a university course pack because the copy shop must obtain the rights to copy.

The Supreme Court of Canada ruled March 1, 2004, that individuals could make a single copy of material for research purposes without paying a licensing fee to the creator. The ruling resolved a case launched by legal publishers seeking compensation for more than 100,000 pages copied annually at the library of the Law Society of Upper Canada. Similarly, on March 30, 2004, a federal court judge ruled that downloading music for personal use does not constitute infringement.

MASS MEDIA AND COPYRIGHT PROTECTION

The main issue concerning media and copyright involves the question of who owns a creative work so that they can control its production, reproduction, sale, and use. One of the main arguments for copyright is that such protection provides an incentive for the promotion of creative work. As works are adapted from one medium to another (a filmed version of a stage play or a novel) two issues arise: unlawful copying of a work (plagiarism) and unlawful distribution of a work (piracy). These issues are played out in the distinction between the creator's right to profit from his or her creations and the public's right to have access to creative works.

Throughout the history of copyright, protection has been extended to new forms of authorship. In the United States after 1976, it became possible for computer companies to sue each other on the basis of copyright infringement, since protection was extended to computer applications as expressions of authorship in tangible form. A watershed case is *Sony Corp. of America v. Universal Studios Inc.* (otherwise known as the Betamax case). This case was based on whether viewers infringed on copyright by videotaping programs for later viewing. While representatives of Universal Studios argued that home taping would open the doors for further loss of control of copyright (a situation that would arise through continued technological development), the U.S. Supreme Court judged that home taping fell within the conditions of fair use. Author Ronald Bettig argues that it is an inevitable consequence of the copyright system that copyright owners will seek to impede innovation. According to Bettig, "The general logic of the copyright system drives copyright owners to seek compensation from all new forms of use" (Bettig, 1996, p. 160). In the next section we will look at some recent examples of how copyright holders use their power to forestall or to gain compensation from new forms of media use.

DIGITAL MEDIA AND COPYRIGHT PROTECTION

As we have seen, the traditional media industries have been quick to challenge technological innovations on the grounds that new methods of copying and distributing information pose a threat to revenues earned through the exercise of copyright privileges. Computers have added some recent complications, such as the temporary copies in packet buffers or on screens, and copies left on backup tape. It is often assumed that transfer of information via e-mail or the Internet is another form of the kind of fair use described in the Betamax case. Many copyright holders would have it another way—making each of us potential pirates every time we surf, download, or exchange files over the Internet.

As technological developments such as tape recorders, VCRs, photocopiers, and computers make it easier for people to copy information without paying for it, policymakers have tried different policy and legal solutions to protect intellectual property. These solutions include making unauthorized copying a crime; making copying more difficult; and appealing to people not to take advantage of creators by denying the artists money or recognition for their creative work.

The illegal copying and distribution of works is called piracy. In the United States, commercial copyright violation involving more than ten copies and a value of over $2500 is a crime. In one case, an operator of a pirate **bulletin board system (BBS)** that didn't charge users was acquitted because he didn't charge, but Congress amended the law to tighten restrictions applying to Internet service providers (the Digital Millennium Copyright Act). The DMCA also makes it an offence to break the protection of software even if the purpose is to do something that is allowed by copyright law.

Industry players and copyright holders have also lobbied to protect their rights to exploit the creative works under their control. The Motion Picture Association of America (MPAA) fought the manufacture and sale of VCRs for commercial use as well as the practice of home taping of music. However, its attempts to block the technology were unsuccessful. Home copying of television broadcasts is allowed under the Copyright Acts of Canada and the United States. Copying from one VCR to another is not.

American media companies are particularly concerned about countries that do not acknowledge international copyright agreements. Unauthorized recordings of music on compact discs, copies of computer software, and videocassettes of movies are often available at very low prices in these countries, which creates a black market where American copyright owners lose billions of dollars annually in sales and royalties. Because copyright holders only receive royalty payments from authorized copies, the film industry in the United States has pressured law enforcement agencies to enforce copyright infringements by commercial pirates. They also target individuals.

For example, a Norwegian teenager wrote a program called DeCSS to circumvent the Content Scramble System (CSS) used by the entertainment industry to protect films distributed on DVD. The teen, Jon Johansen, wrote DeCSS so he could view DVDs on his computer. He owned the DVDs and there was no preexisting program to allow him to view DVDs on his machine, which ran the Linux operating system. The courts agreed it was fair use of his property to view the DVDs on his computer using the DeCSS code.

In the past few years the American entertainment industry has been aggressive in its attempts to promote the rights of copyright holders. In 2002, the Recording Industry Association of America (RIAA) sent letters to 2000 university presidents urging tough responses to copyright infringement. The U.S. Naval Academy complied by confiscating student computers in pursuit of pirated software and music files. In 2003, a judge ordered telecommunications company Verizon to provide the RIAA with the name of a subscriber who had hosted files for peer-to-peer sharing. Verizon argued that such a victory would have a chilling effect on e-mail, surfing, and file exchange. The issue for the Internet service providers was customer privacy not piracy. The U.S. Court of Appeal overturned the ruling. Since then, the RIAA has filed almost 400 civil lawsuits against individuals accused of illegal file sharing. Later in 2003, the RIAA sent copies of a six-page memo to Fortune 1000 companies outlining a model for company policies for dealing with employees who downloaded files at work.

As in the U.S. cases, new media in Canada must confront copyright issues. The CRTC has refrained from regulating the Internet as a broadcasting technology on the grounds that new media complement rather than replace traditional media services. According to the CRTC, the Internet gives Canadians access to more information about the things they find interesting and to programming expanded from that available through their televisions.

While the Internet may not be considered a threat to traditional broadcasting within Canada, the global nature of the Internet creates jurisdictional issues. The Copyright Act applies to copyright protection in Canada, but it does not have power to deal with infringements that occur outside Canadian territory. However, where broadcasting regulation fails to protect the interests of the traditional copyright holders in the new media economy, copyright steps in. Some recent examples illustrate this point.

Some of the difficulties that arise with convergence are illustrated by iCraveTV.com, which streamed (i.e., broadcast over a Web site) 17 television signals without paying royalties or licensing fees to the copyright holders of the programs. iCraveTV.com collected over-the-air signals with an antenna and broadcast them over the Internet. Not only is the practice of re-transmission legal in Canada, it is the very basis of the Canadian cable industry. Signals that are piped to private subscribers are not considered public broadcasts. Although cable operators are subject to compulsory licensing, iCraveTV.com argued that it was exempt under the CRTC's 1999 order on Internet broadcasting. Even so, it offered to pay a tariff to be administered by a copyright collective. The offer was rejected.

The problem was that users outside Canada could access iCraveTV.com's Web site even though the Web site had a sign-in mechanism that was supposed to limit access to Canadian users. U.S. copyright holders including Twentieth Century Fox Film Corporation, the Disney Corporation, ABC, CBS, NBC, the CBC in Canada, and the National Football League sued iCraveTV.com. The basis of the suits was that iCraveTV.com violated copyright infringement and the content owners saw the Internet company as posing a real threat to their ability to exploit their copyrights (Stern, 2000).

The company's lawful activities in Canada could offer no protection against copyright infringement in the United States. The case was settled when iCraveTV.com agreed to shut down operations should the plaintiffs drop their suits. Since then, the Canadian Association of Broadcasters has lobbied for amendments to the Copyright Act to specifically ban Internet streaming of television signals.

On another front, the Recording Industry Association of America, representing Sony, Universal, BMG, Warner, and EMI, launched a $6.8 billion lawsuit against MP3.com—an AOL subsidiary—for alleged copyright violations. Specifically, MP3.com was sued for selling digitized music over the Internet without paying royalties to the record companies (Anderson, 2000).

In another lawsuit, the same assembly of dominant players used the courts to shut down Napster—a company that facilitated trading music files across the Internet. Napster.com provided users with free software for exchanging MP3 files. The site also acted as a hub for users to connect with each other in a point-to-point transfer of music files. To use the example of home taping, Napster would be the digital equivalent of two friends meeting somewhere to trade audiocassette tapes of their favourite music. Because there was no sale involved, Napster hoped to invoke the fair use concept in its defence.

According to the Copyright Board of Canada, however, Napster does not offend Canadian copyright law because its server is located outside Canada. Further, because Canadian copyright legislation has a provision whereby copyright collectives (e.g., the Canadian Private Copying Collective) collect fees on audio recording material on behalf of Canadian copyright holders, there is no problem of compensation for Napster's activity. In other words, the administration of copyright means that in Canada, with its tradition of collective copyright collection, a technology such as Napster does not pose a problem. In the U.S. case, Napster agreed to charge for downloads even though the basis of its case was that the site simply facilitated the trading of music files between individuals—no copyright violation. Charging for downloads meant that Napster now had something it could give to the big record companies, a percentage of the download fee. Napster has resurfaced in 2004 as a commercial source of downloadable music.

Cases such as Napster polarize opinion. For example, heavy-metal rock group Metallica sued Napster for copyright violation. By contrast, Canadian recording star Alanis Morissette was a major shareholder in MP3.com.

COPYRIGHT—GOOD OR BAD?

In the past 30 years, the 300-year-old idea of copyright as a bargain between creators and society has been replaced by an economic model that argues that the incentive to create and exploit new works requires longer, broader, and stronger copyright protection. But what are the benefits and dangers associated with copyright protection in the global economy? To answer this question, we must evaluate the main arguments invoked to justify strong copyright legislation and enforcement. First, it is claimed that copyright protects the rights of individual creators—it ensures some compensation for them and their heirs. Second, copyright provides the necessary incentives for creators to continue to produce works of art—copyright ensures innovation. Third, by ensuring the continued creation of creative works, copyright benefits all of society.

Let's deal with each of these claims separately. First, does copyright actually protect the rights of individual creators? It can, but the fact of the matter is that, ever since the first copyright act became law, protection has been more likely to benefit those who publish and distribute creative works than those who create them, because individual creators frequently turn to large enterprises to make their work widely available. As a result, the most powerful copyright owners are large corporations whose employees are paid to produce works whose copyrights the corporations own. Such companies lobby for strong protections. So, while copyright could protect starving artists and their families, it frequently protects corporate profits.

If copyright protects business interests, does it actually promote new creative work? Again, the answer is, not really. Indeed, because copyright protection is so extensive and broad, it can actually impede new work. Copyright vests its holders, often large corporations, with the right to be protected against infringement by others. This means that the disposition of ideas contained within commercial activities is afforded the same protection as the disposition of ideas contained in an individual creative work. For example, the VISA symbol is not only a trademark; it is also a copyrighted work of art. As a result, the company using it is not merely protected against the use of its name by other companies operating in the same field, it is also protected against any company—even one not competing with it—from using the same disposition of ideas in any way. Similarly, when Donald Trump copyrights the phrase "You're Fired!" it is hard to argue that he is helping to promote knowledge and the useful arts! The corporate interest in the form of expression allows the largest rights holders to police the activities of others and limit creativity. In that way, copyright becomes a powerful barrier to the sharing of knowledge.

This leads us to the third argument for strong copyright—such protection benefits society. As already mentioned, those who argue for strong copyright protections talk about protecting starving artists from plagiarists and pirates. However, once we realize that copyright actually protects the interests of copyright owners (who are as likely to be big businesses as individual artists or authors), we can think of the debate over copyright as a tension between private interests (copyright owners) and society (the public domain). The problem is that the concept of protection for life plus 50 years provides almost perpetual protection to commercial rather than artistic work. Further, since such work is frequently produced by employees, copyright belongs to the employer and no benefit goes to the creator's heirs. In the end, copyright protection does not provide incentive to produce.

CONCLUSION

It can be argued that copyright is not about creativity. In fact, it restricts the public sphere, which is the true source of innovation. Intellectual property jeopardizes the public domain as well as the principle of an "intellectual commons" or sphere of exchange of ideas in which we all share equally (Lessig, 2001). Of course, the situation is not entirely bleak. It can and frequently does happen that when too many similar works appear (as in the cases of narrative elements in films), the courts can assign the raw materials of authorship to the "commons" of the public domain, thereby leaving them for all to use (Litman, 1990, pp. 1022–1023). Perhaps the solution is to re-establish the principle that copyright is a bargain between creators, rights holders, and the public rather than the absolute property right asserted by the media giants. Some artists, such as David Bowie, have actually encouraged fans to re-mix their music.

As industries, technologies, and regulation converge, it might seem that information and creative work will inevitably be controlled by a few private interests at the expense of the rest of society. However, in the Canadian and British traditions at least, copyright has always tried to balance the rights of creators and owners with the broader needs of society.

QUESTIONS

1. In what way do new technologies of communication challenge existing intellectual property protection?
2. To what extent is it possible to protect against copyright violations on the Internet?
3. What interests are served by the extension of copyright protection to new forms of creative expression?
4. What are the copyright implications of trade liberalization and globalization?
5. Is copyright a good thing? Give reasons for your answer.

REFERENCES

Anderson, Lessley. (2000, January 31). To beam or not to beam: MP3.com is being sued by the major record labels—does the digital download site stand a chance? *Industry Standard*.

Bettig, Ronald. (1996). *Copyrighting culture: The political economy of intellectual property*. Boulder, CO: Westview Press.

Castells, Manuel. (2000). *The rise of the networked society* (2nd ed.). Oxford, England: Blackwell.

Lessig, Lawrence. (2001). *The future of ideas: The fate of the commons in a connected world*. New York: Random House.

Litman, Jessica. (1990, Fall). The public domain. *Emory Law Journal*, *39*(4), 965–1023.

———. (2001). *Digital copyright*. Amherst, NY: Prometheus Books.

Stern, Christopher. (2000, March 6). Court ruling shuts down iCraveTV.com. *Variety*.

Part V
Social and Policy Issues

Introduction

Leslie Regan Shade
Concordia University

The chapters in this final section deal with various social and policy issues surrounding information and communication technologies. These issues—those of media ownership and concentration, cultural sovereignty, cultural imperialism, indigenous media rights, democratic uses of the media, and communication rights—involve a variety of stakeholders, from governments to civil society groups, and most are contested and ongoing.

Many of our contemporary media issues are reiterations of previous media debates. The technologies have of course evolved, their social uses become perhaps more fulsome, the policy issues more vexatious. Policy no longer takes place on the national stage; media governance is now conducted with a plethora of global actors, and as the World Summit on the Information Society (WSIS) demonstrates, governments, industry groups, and civil society all want a spot at the table (Moll and Shade, 2004).

The section begins with an introduction to globalization, a concept that has been widely used since the end of the Cold War. Karim Karim's chapter examines the various dimensions of globalization (with an emphasis on cultural globalization), international right-to-communicate movements, and the development of transnational ethnic media and communication among diasporic communities. He charts the emergence of transnational communication through both technological developments and iterations of global communication governance policies. From the New World Information and Communication Order (NWICO) debates in the late 1970s to the current debates over the World Summit on the Information Society, Karim emphasizes the important and dynamic role of civil society groups in actively contesting current communication regimes and in promoting an information society for all.

Canada's multiculturalism and diversity is reflected positively and negatively in our mediascape. Karim's case study of Canadian ethnic media highlights the salient role diasporic communities have had in shaping such media, while Yasmin Jiwani's chapter interrogates how racial minorities have been represented in the Canadian media. Her analytical entry points focus on various discursive strategies in the media: the discourse of immigration (the inflamed media commentary surrounding Sunera Tobani's remarks after September 11; how Chinese migrants were described), the discourse of difference (Montreal's *Gazette* newspaper coverage of Muslim women post–September 11), the discourse of culturalization (media reports on crime and immigrants), and the discourse of erasure (the Reena Virk case in British Columbia).

Lorna Roth looks at the development of the Aboriginal Peoples Television Network, a pioneering attempt to establish legislatively based, nationwide television services that reflect the cultural perspectives and languages of Canadian Aboriginal peoples. Tracing the permutations of policy and programs geared toward the development of Northern television, Roth argues that it has served as a vital enabler of indigenous messages to be heard by all Canadians; however, APTN's sustainability is dependent on budgetary constraints.

Media and politics is the subject of Jonathan Rose and Simon Kiss's chapter. The morphing of entertainment and politics has been accelerating with the Internet and various digitized forms of communication—the ability to culture jam via PhotoShop techniques, the creation of flash parody pieces, and blogging sites (from journalists and interested Internet aficionados) devoted to serious or outrageous discussion of current events. As Rose and Kiss discuss in their chapter, such proliferation and speed—hyper-media—has created various forms of blurring: between journalists and governments, between partisan and "objective" political journalism, and between entertainment and news. What then, is the fate of democratic debate? Are these blurred boundaries creating more open avenues for citizens, or are they contributing to a decline in and diminution of the public sphere?

The concluding chapter by Leslie Shade integrates many of the themes in *Mediascapes*, particularly those having to do with Canadian identity and culture. Characteristics of Canada's mediascape are summarized; these include the technological and policy environments—convergence, globalization, conglomeration and consolidation, and deregulation. We see that despite the enthusiasm for synergistic content creation and cross-media acquisitions, the downturn in the telecom and Internet industries in the late 1990s created uncertainty and failed projects.

Shade also examines culture and trade debates under international trade regimes and powerful institutions such as the World Trade Organization (WTO)—and how Canada is situated vis à vis their media policies. In particular, trade policies under the Free Trade Agreement of the Americas (FTAA) and General Agreement on Trade in Services (GATS) have created enormous pressures to preserve and maintain Canadian content and culture amid a proliferation of American media fare. Canada's mediascape is also characterized by one of the most consolidated media systems in the world, with a high degree of cross-media ownership. As she points out, these issues aren't new; they were the subject of debate and policy recommendations in the 1970s and 1980s. The current Canadian media ownership is thus mapped out, in a configuration that will likely not remain stable for long, as new players enter the scene while others are dissolved or integrated into other corporations.

Given the structural realities of Canada's mediascape, questions about the public interest need to be raised. How does such intense media concentration effect and influence the types of news that citizens receive? Are new opportunities for Canadian media diversity created or diminished because of globalization and trade regimes? And how can public service media—such as the Canadian Broadcasting Corporation (CBC)—flourish in a competitive and commercialized mediascape?

The issues are difficult to reconcile amid a rapidly changing technological and cultural environment, where governments, policymakers, corporations, civil society, and the general public are all interested in shaping Canada's mediascape.

REFERENCES

Moll, Marita, and Leslie Regan Shade. (2004). Vision impossible? The world summit on the information society. In Marita Moll and Leslie Regan Shade (Eds.), *Seeking convergence in policy and practice: Communications in the public interest*, vol. 2 (pp. 45–80). Ottawa: Canadian Centre for Policy Alternatives.

17

Globalization, Transnational Communication, and Diaspora

Karim H. Karim
Carleton University

GLOBALIZATION

Globalization has several dimensions, including the economic, political, migratory, and communicative. The economic dimension is generally reflected in the increased flow of goods and services. Treaties such as the North American Free Trade Agreement (NAFTA) facilitate the growth of trade. The **World Trade Organization (WTO)** plays a major role in lowering tariffs and duties while simultaneously reducing the control of governments over their own economies and the environment. Economic globalization also includes changes in regulations for many industries, especially telecommunications, and the increased pace of corporate mergers. Politically, globalization has been closely intertwined with the various initiatives for trade liberalization, changes in industry regulations, privatization of state-owned corporations, and the transfer of some powers to international organizations such as the WTO. The European Union has gone the furthest among regional and international organizations in politically integrating its member states. However, it is a mistake to assume that the power of national governments has been completely eroded or that borders have become insignificant. In fact, the legitimation of the supranational organizations like the WTO occurs *through* national governments.

The transnational migration of people has also grown exponentially in recent decades. The increasing ease and speed of transportation have facilitated migration over large distances. Business travellers, migrant workers, students, tourists, and immigrants regularly cross continents. This has led to the growth of various ethnic diasporas dispersed around the world. Globalization depends on the growth of communicative capacity. The ease with which people can be in touch with other parts of the world has promoted economic, political, and migratory activities. Indeed, Hamid Mowlana (1996) includes all of the following within the larger scope of the transnational flow of information: mail; print materials (newspapers, magazines, books, technical and scientific journals); news agency content; film, and sound and video products; advertising; telecommunications (telephone, telegraph, telex, fax, etc.); broadcasting (radio, television, digital broadcasting); and satellite and computer-mediated data flows (Internet, World Wide Web, chat lines) as well as the physical movement of people in tourism, travel, and migration and government, educational, artistic, and cultural exchanges (conferences, exhibitions, and sports events).

Richard Falk has distinguished between "globalization-from-above" and "globalization-from-below." The first reflects "the collaboration between leading states and the main agents of capital formation" (1993, p. 39). This is the intergovernmental level, where international policy and legislation governing communication are shaped and policed. The WTO, the International Telecommunications Union (ITU), the **World Intellectual Property Organization (WIPO)**, the **United Nations Educational, Scientific, and Cultural Organization (UNESCO)**, and the **International Telecommunications Satellite Organization (Intelsat)** operate at this level. Transnational corporations are also major players in the globalization of communication. They include (a) content providers such as global news agencies, giant advertising firms, Time Warner, NewsCorp, CNN, Disney, MTV, Sony, and Bertelsmann; (b) telecommunications corporations such as AT&T, Microsoft, Nortel, and Cisco; and (c) non-communications global corporations that are nonetheless engaged in massive transnational information flows (e.g., Coca Cola, Nike, Exxon). They carry out massive global advertising campaigns and transfer significant amounts of data through computers and other means.

"Globalization-from-below" is carried out mainly by organizations that do not have strong links to governments or large corporations. Organizations such as Amnesty International and Greenpeace are transnational civil-society groups that monitor the performance of governments on human rights and environmental protection. Others like the International Committee for the Red Cross and Médecins Sans Frontières act as global relief agencies. Academic and professional associations, religious organizations, diasporic groups, and so on, also participate in "globalization-from-below" by developing lateral communication links between members in various parts of the world. They do not necessarily challenge international governmental activities or transnational corporations, but they are distinct from them.

THE EVOLUTION OF TRANSNATIONAL COMMUNICATION

The origins of contemporary globalization reach back in history. People have been trading and communicating with distant lands for thousands of years. The current form of globalization represents the intensification and acceleration of transnational contacts. Ancient and medieval civilizations developed relatively sophisticated systems of transportation and communication. In medieval times, the Silk Road efficiently connected the lands of China, Central Asia, Iran, and eastern Europe and even served as the route for a rudimentary postal system. The Chinese, Indians, Persians, Arabs, and their neighbours in the Asian continent regularly communicated with each other, sharing knowledge and innovations. Trading contacts across the Indian Ocean linked South Asia, Iran, Arab lands, and Africa. Middle Eastern civilizations passed on the scientific discoveries of Eastern civilizations to Europe, enabling it to emerge from its Dark Ages into the Renaissance. European colonization of other continents represented a significant step on the road to contemporary globalization. The eventual result of colonization has been to bring all countries of the world into a political system of nation-states. Systems of transportation and communication linked colonies with "mother countries" in Europe, laying the groundwork for the telecommunications infrastructures and communications patterns that exist today.

The invention of the telegraph in the 1830s ushered in a new era of telecommunications, in which a message could travel long distances without being delivered *physically*. For the first time in human history, people separated by barriers such as mountains, deserts, and oceans could communicate almost instantly. By 1862, 150,000 miles of telegraph lines had been built around the world. This new form of communication produced contradictory results. On the one hand, it diminished the power of some political centres in the 19th century. For example, it helped southern American states to fight the Civil War. It also accelerated the disintegration of the Hapsburg empire, precipitating the growth of nationalism and eventually the First World War in the early 20th century. On the other hand, it strengthened the control of European powers over their colonies.

The telegraph also enabled the growth of "wire services." In 1835, Charles-Louis Havas created the Havas news agency in Paris, which, using the newly invented telegraph, provided information from the regions of France and translations of foreign newspapers. Paul Julius Reuter, a German immigrant living in London, expanded his telegraph company, which served business with stock quotations, into a news agency. It grew to have correspondents on various continents. In 1869, Havas, Reuters, and Wolff (the German news agency), signed a Treaty of Alliance to carve up the world into news zones: Reuters received the British Empire and east Asia; Havas the French, Spanish, Italian, and Portuguese empires; and Wolff the territories controlled by Germany, Austria, the Netherlands, Scandinavia, and Russia. These first transnational companies thus created a global cartel to control their product (news) by operating within their respective governments' spheres of influence.

The invention of the telephone in 1876 also helped to overcome the limitations of distance. People separated by great distances could now communicate without using the telegraphic Morse code, and even without knowing how to write. Companies such as AT&T, which realized the enormous benefits of the telephone, amassed huge fortunes. As a result, telecommunications corporations emerged and became key players in the process of globalization. Guglielmo Marconi developed wireless telegraphy, which eventually became radio. This technology was widely used in World War I. In the 1920s, radio broadcasting saw the birth of mass audiences. It became a medium both for the consolidation of nation-states and for cross-border propaganda. There emerged a number of government-run transnational broadcasters that disseminated information in many languages, in the attempt to influence other countries' populations.

Television was launched in Britain and Germany in the 1930s. By allying the properties of both film and radio, television was destined to achieve great success. However, it was also capital-intensive and traditionally required centralized transmission facilities. Its over-the-air transmission range was quite limited. Cable initially extended television's transmission range, but it was satellite broadcasting that hugely expanded its reach. Television pictures were first broadcast via satellite in the early 1960s. This innovation was especially important for large countries such as Canada, the United States, and Russia, where it has enabled the formation of national markets and audiences. Satellite broadcasts also make possible live intercontinental coverage of events such as international summits, the Olympic Games, royal weddings, wars, and so on. This has led to the growth of mass intercontinental audiences, which are integral to globalization. Ku-band satellites and digital compression have also vastly increased the amount of information that can be beamed over large distances directly to sites equipped with small satellite dishes (70–150 cm). Previously, only the largest networks could afford to use satellites, but now individuals can also take advantage of them, with a resulting explosion in specialty channels. It is now possible to *narrowcast* to specific audiences separated by vast distances but sharing similar interests. But this has also accelerated the fragmentation of mass national audiences, which formerly had been limited to watching national networks only. Will such developments bring about the collapse of national public spheres, or will they cause the democratization of media that have traditionally been controlled by dominant groups? New satellite technologies have also spurred transnational broadcasting conducted not only by media giants but by networks serving diasporic audiences.

On-line media have also affected globalization. Developed by the U.S. military around Arpanet, distributed on-line communication systems were used in the 1980s to link researchers and academics, first in the United States, and then around the world. In the 1990s, the Internet became widely available and has become one of the major symbols of globalization. Based on the decentralized or distributed design of Arpanet, the Internet has generally proved resistant to government control. It allows information to flow easily across borders, enabling closer communicative links between individuals and groups in various parts of the world. To date, the Internet remains largely unregulated in most countries. However, major corporations have been attempting to extend commercial control over it.

THE EMERGENCE OF INTERNATIONAL REGULATION

International organizations did not exist 150 years ago because nation-states generally dealt with each other bilaterally (i.e., government to government) rather than multilaterally. The 19th century saw several important developments in international relations. National governments began to initiate the process of multilateral policy-making, specifically in the area of communications. Some of the earliest European conferences, held in the second half of 19th century, dealt with postal and telegraph services and **intellectual property**. The International Telegraph Convention, the first treaty to address international communication, was signed in 1865; it established the International Telegraph Union, headquartered in Switzerland. A number of basic norms, including the universal right to use international telegraphy and a state's right to stop transmissions considered dangerous to its security or in violation of its laws, public order, or morals were stipulated. This underlined the dilemma that contemporary telecommunications still pose for governments—increased individual use versus ongoing state control. The 1883 Paris Convention for the Protection of Industrial Property and the 1886 Berne Convention for the Protection of Literary and Artistic Works marked international collaboration in the area of intellectual property and copyright.

As newer media were developed, their regulation was incorporated into the ITU as of 1903. For example, the Berlin Radio Convention of 1906 aimed at managing the radio frequency spectrum. In 1927, the World Administrative Radio Conference sought to regulate international radio frequencies. Europeans countries tended to favour state authority, while the United States argued mainly for private-sector control. Private communications companies were prominent at the 1927 conference and "practically wrote the Radio Convention" (Hamelink, 1994, p. 20). Corporations lobbied against public control and promoted the "first come, first served" approach. In 1932, the Radio Union and the International Telegraph Union were merged into the International Telecommunications Union (ITU).

THE NWICO DEBATE

Following World War II, American cultural industries gained a strong position globally because most European countries were preoccupied with rebuilding their infrastructures. The United States also became a key player in the newly established United Nations Organization. In 1946 it gained the agreement of European powers for the Declaration on Freedom of Information that promoted the free flow of information "within countries and across frontiers" (Gunter, 1978, p. 143). The United Nations Educational, Scientific, and Cultural Organization (UNESCO) began studying the role of communication in development in 1960s. It identified certain minimum levels of communication capacity necessary for development, and concluded that this minimum was unavailable to 70 percent of the world's population. Consequently, the UN shifted some of its development activities to address communication needs more directly.

In the early 1970s, several developing countries began to question Western, especially American, dominance over global communication. They argued that although they received technical assistance, they nonetheless remained dependent upon the North, and claimed that **cultural imperialism** had become the successor to territorial colonialism. They said that continued Northern **hegemony** impeded their cultural and economic development. Developing countries pointed to the

North's overwhelming influence on the South in terms of news flow, largely controlled by agencies such as Reuters, Associated Press, United Press International, Agence France-Presse, and TASS. They also saw the ability of the satellite-owning countries to scan their territories and beam in messages for commercial, political, and military purposes as a threat to their sovereignty.

Furthermore, most African and Asian states had not held seats at the UN when the Declaration on Freedom of Information had been adopted in 1946. But by the 1960s, with newly acquired independence and representation at the UN, developing countries were gaining the ability to voice their concerns over matters such as the lack of equal access to telecommunications. Twenty European states had established the ITU in 1865; by 1970, 100 of its 154 members were developing countries. They complained vigorously that the ITU's "first come, first served" principle favoured the more technologically advanced Northern countries in areas such as radio spectrum and geosynchronous satellite orbits. Developing nations also proposed that states that owned satellites should obtain "prior consent" before scanning their territories or beaming in broadcasts. These concerns and demands became part of the celebrated debate for a **New World Information and Communication Order (NWICO)**.

This long, drawn-out international discussion took place in the context of the Cold War between NATO, led by the United States, and the Warsaw Pact, led by the former Soviet Union. Many African, Asian, and Latin American states wished not to align themselves with either side and so formed the Non-Aligned Movement (NAM). It was the early forum for NWICO issues that were later taken into other organizations such as UNESCO and the ITU. These issues were the imbalance in transnational news flows; the overwhelming influence of Western culture; the lack of technology transfer to developing countries; the threat posed to national sovereignty by satellites; and the identification of human communication as a basic right.

Following intense debate at UNESCO, the developing countries were able to obtain the adoption in 1978 of a Mass Media Declaration, which advocated a "free flow and wider and better balanced dissemination of information," thereby re-formulating the earlier notion of the "freedom of information" (Hamelink, 1994, p. 156). "Freedom of information" was criticized for favouring countries with more advanced means of communication. UNESCO also established the International Commission for the Study of Communication Problems to explore four issues: (a) the current state of world communication, (b) the problems surrounding a free and balanced flow of information, (c) how NWICO could be implemented, and (d) how the media could become vehicles for educating public opinion about global problems (MacBride, 1980). Chaired by Sean MacBride, the commission proposed the democratization of communications, while acknowledging that democracy was impeded in many countries by existing systems, by corruption, and by the lack of access to means of communication. The report adhered to UNESCO's Mass Media Declaration and re-contextualized freedom of the press in terms of everyone's right to communicate.

It criticized the censorship of media, as well as the self-censorship carried out by journalists. The commission also assailed one-way flows of information and the constraints placed on communication by commercialism, advertisers, and media concentration.

Western countries, particularly the United States, were not pleased with the report. The American government and media were especially critical, tending to cast NWICO-related issues, such as the social responsibility of the press and the right to communicate, within the framework of government control of the media. Opponents of NWICO argued that the disparity in communications development could be resolved by technical support from the West. However, UNESCO eventually passed a resolution for the attainment of NWICO. Attacks emanating from the United States and the U.K. became more intense, and both governments withdrew from UNESCO—taking with them a significant proportion of its budget.

GLOBALIZATION FROM ABOVE AND BELOW

The New World Information and Communication Order, as envisioned by NAM and UNESCO, did not materialise because Northern countries (including the Soviet Union) did not support it and because of the rapid evolution of technology, shifting political trends and alliances, and increasing international deregulation. NWICO ceased to appear on the UNESCO agenda and in the 1990s lost its profile in international discussions on communications. UNESCO's communication and information section now focuses on research; information flows and exchange; the development of communications systems; and communications means and infrastructures. It seeks to promote freedom of information by promoting international agreements to remove customs duties on educational, cultural, and scientific materials; reduce postal charges for publications; and reduce rates for certain telecommunications services. It sponsors the training of journalists and communications specialists; helps to set up press or information agencies in developing countries; and organizes regional news exchanges.

Communication capacities around the world changed remarkably in the last two decades of the 20th century, with somewhat paradoxical results. From 1980 to 1997, the number of radios in developing countries grew by 42 percent. However, industrialized countries with less than half the world's population continued to own four-fifths of all radios. Likewise, between 1980 and 1997, the average annual rate of growth in television-set ownership in developing countries was a phenomenal 92 percent; but more than three-quarters of all television sets were still found in industrialized countries.

Following the Second World War, the ITU became a specialized UN agency responsible for harmonizing and coordinating the use of telecommunications among countries. It is the key institution for international standard-setting for most new communication technologies. By 2001, 189 member countries had signed the International Telecommunication Convention. However, the power of the ITU was much diminished by the establishment in 1995 of the World Trade Organization, which has become a key player in determining the parameters of the telecommunications policies that individual states can adopt.

There were also major developments on the intellectual property front in the late 20th century. As the importance of intellectual property grew, the World Intellectual Property Organization (WIPO) was created. In 1974, WIPO became a specialized agency of the United Nations, with a mandate to administer intellectual property matters. It expanded its role in the 1990s by incorporating intellectual property rights in the management of global trade. This new focus was solidified in the 1996 WIPO cooperation agreement with the WTO. WIPO also addresses the problems posed for intellectual property by new media.

Unlike telecommunications and intellectual property, the transnational administration of satellites has *not* come under the United Nations system. The United States launched the first communication satellite (Project SCORE) in 1958 and was soon followed by the Soviet Union. Canada became the third country in space with Alouette, launched in 1962. In 1964 the International Satellite Organization (Intelsat) was created, with the United States playing the dominant role. Membership was open to all ITU members. Intelsat's guiding principle was to provide access to all countries on an equal basis; therefore, members and non-members were charged the same rates. The early Intelsat satellites and ground stations were concentrated in the Northern Hemisphere, but they soon spread to cover the entire planet. The rapidly increasing demand for international satellite services by financial networks, transnational corporations, and international news organizations has caused Intelsat services to grow remarkably since the 1980s. The organization carries a large proportion of transnational television broadcasts and telephone calls. Its importance continues to grow as an increasing amount of Internet traffic is routed through satellites.

The liberalization of telecommunications regulations in the 1980s had a large impact on Intelsat. Due to its commitment to ensure that services are provided around the world on a non-discriminatory basis, the organization had previously instituted a policy of cross-subsidization whereby revenues from dense routes (such as North America and Europe) subsidized rates in the thin routes (such as developing countries). This system of price averaging by Intelsat ensured affordable communication on a worldwide basis. However, the technological merging of telecommunications with computer technology, optical fibre cable, and fax machines, and the erosion of distinctions between voice and data, led to pressures from the largest users in the West for a reduction in tariffs, thereby threatening the cross-subsidization scheme. There has therefore been a shift away from cross-subsidization toward market principles.

The ITU's (1998) research shows that, whereas the profits of the top 50 telecommunications operators in the world grew from under $40 billion in 1990 to almost $60 billion in 1996, large numbers of people around the world have very little access to basic telephone services. Around a quarter of the world's countries have a teledensity of less than one telephone line per 100 households, compared to 71 per 100 in the Americas. Likewise, the average cost of making an international telephone call is at least twice as much in developing countries as in industrialized countries. Despite the vision of a "global information society," the primarily North American and European countries of the Organization for Economic Co-operation and Development, with only 19 percent of the world's population, accounted for 91 percent of Internet use in 1998 (UNDP, 1999, back cover).

However, the global **digital divide** does not run exclusively between North and South: Dwayne Winseck (2002) indicates that the world's communications grid is marked by certain nodal points that include Sao Paulo, Hong Kong, Shanghai, Singapore, and Johannesburg. The more affluent residents of certain urban areas in developing countries are better connected with Western cities than with most of their own compatriots.

Nevertheless, there have been a number of success stories in the South that contribute to "globalization-from-below." The commercial success of Bollywood, the popular film industry located in Mumbai (formerly known as Bombay), India, is comparable to that of Hollywood (Mishra, 2002). Although Indian cinema lacks the budgets and special effects of Hollywood blockbusters, it regularly produces the largest number of films in the world. And since the vast majority of these are musicals, there has grown over the last nine decades a massive recording industry centred around Mumbai. Indian television also uses Bollywood films, reviews, retrospectives, music, and gossip as fodder for its programming. Furthermore, although Indian film enjoys less transnational distribution than Hollywood, it nonetheless has significant penetration in South Asia, Southeast Asia, the Middle East, Africa, and the Caribbean (UNESCO, 2000, pp. 304–307). The Indian diaspora remains the mainstay of audiences and of distribution networks in some of these areas, as well as in the West, where cinemas exclusively showing popular Indian films flourish in cities with significant populations of South Asian origins.

Similarly, the Cairo film and television industry exports to Arabic-speaking countries and to the larger Arab diaspora. Hong Kong action movies have also had some success among non-Chinese audiences around the world. However, it is the Mexican and Brazil television networks, Televisa and TV Globo, respectively, that have been able to capture major cross-cultural markets beyond their borders. They have capitalized on the advantages of their own large domestic audiences and their "geolinguistic regions" (Sinclair, 1997)—Spanish-speaking Latin America in the case of Televisa and the string of former Portuguese colonies for TV Globo. Of increasing importance for Televisa is the Spanish-speaking market of the United States, which is growing rapidly and is relatively affluent. Televisa and TV Globo also export products to former colonial powers such as Spain, Portugal, and Italy, and even dubbed versions to Russia and developing countries. Contrary to arguments advanced by cultural imperialism theorists, these networks, which are the largest in the non-English-speaking world, have used both the technological and organizational—as well as the artistic and programming—models of American television to produce their own success stories. The Latin American *telenovela* has provided a workable formula for worldwide cross-cultural exports. The cultural imperialism perspective failed to realize the ability of media entrepreneurs in Southern countries to use and adapt new technologies for their own innovations.

WHAT ARE DIASPORAS?

Diasporas comprise members of ethnic groups who reside in a number of other countries to which they or their ancestors immigrated. Whereas the term originally referred to the existence of Jewish communities around the world, it is increasingly used to designate all dispersed communities (Cohen, 1997). The identities of individuals and groups within specific diasporas are formed by complex historical, social, and cultural dynamics within the group and with other groups. Retention of ancestral customs, language, religion, and marriage patterns, and the ease of communication between various parts of the dispersed community, help determine its characteristics.

The mass migrations of the 1700s and 1800s led to new economic growth in the New World while displacing indigenous economies and communities. These included movements of slaves from Africa, indentured labourers from Asia, and settlers from Europe. Following the lifting of restrictions on race-based immigration in the 1950s and 1960s, Asians and Africans began to migrate in larger numbers to North America, Australasia, and Europe. There has also been substantial migration from Latin America into the United States. These movements of people to different parts of the world have created diasporas that are layered by period of migration, the extent of integration into receiving societies, and the maintenance of links with the land of origin as well as with other parts of the transnational group. As a result of this layering, there exist wide variations in connections and attachments within worldwide communities.

In many instances, diasporas themselves participate in transnational economic activity. From the banking network of the Rothschilds, in 18th century Europe, to more recent global businesses such as the Hinduja Group and Cheung Kong Holdings, diasporic families have been leading players in global transactions. At 450 billion dollars, the annual economic output of the 55 million overseas Chinese was estimated in the 1990s to be roughly equal to that of the 1.2 billion people in China itself (Seagrave, 1995).

However, some commentators writing from cultural studies and post-colonial perspectives tend to view diasporas as standing in opposition to global and national structures of dominance—in effect, as "the empire striking back." The diasporic site becomes a "third space" between the country of origin and the country of residence (Bhabha, 1994). This is the zone of intense, cutting-edge creativity born out of the existential angst of the immigrant who is neither completely attached to the homeland nor fully accepted in his adopted country.

While global Eurocentric cultural structures, particularly media conglomerates, continue to enjoy dominance (Thussu, 2000), a variety of voices from the South and from diasporas have nonetheless emerged over the last few decades to try to present other worldviews. Ella Shohat and Robert Stam (1994) point to the aesthetics of resistance in the New Cinemas of Cuba, Brazil, Senegal, and India as well as to diasporic films made in Canada, the United States, and the United Kingdom. Just within the South Asian diaspora, one can cite numerous authors including Michael Ondaatje, Anita Rau Badami, Rohinton Mistry, M.G. Vassanji, Bharati Mukerjee, Salman Rushdie, and V.S. Naipaul. Bhabha, Shohat, and Stam consider diasporic authors to be at the cutting edge of modernity.

ETHNIC MEDIA AS TRANSNATIONAL MEDIA

The role of ethnic media in global communication flows is steadily growing (Karim, 2003). The transnational ethnic-based commercial broadcasting infrastructure is integral to the increasingly global ethnic economy. Niche marketers look upon advertising in ethnic radio and television as a way to reach growing minority populations in a time of fragmenting audiences. The largest Spanish-language U.S. network, Univisión, which "owns 11 stations and has 19 affiliates, is also carried on 740 cable systems and is seen by 92 percent of Hispanic households in 162 markets across the United States" (Collins, 1996, p. C6). According to sociologists and communication scholars, ethnic media serve two primary purposes—they contribute to ethnic cohesion and cultural maintenance, and they help members of minorities integrate into the larger society (Riggins, 1992, p. 4). However, obtaining space for ethnic broadcasters in the electromagnetic spectrum has involved a continual struggle with national regulators. For example, in the early 1990s, France's centre-right government actively encouraged the exclusion of Arabic stations from cable networks. In response, many Maghrebi immigrant families subscribed to satellite television for programming from Arab countries (Hargreaves and Mahdjoub, 1997).

With the availability of new communication technologies, diasporas are able to obtain cultural materials from other parts of the world with growing ease. A number of ethnic television broadcasters export their programming to other parts of the diaspora; for example, the weekly Vision TV program "West Indians United," produced by a group of South Asian diasporics in Toronto, is regularly rebroadcast in Guyana and the United States. On a much larger scale, one of the two Spanish-language U.S. networks (Univisión and Telemundo) is available on almost every cable system in Latin America. "And in smaller, poorer countries, local television stations often simply tape stories from Univisión or Telemundo's nightly newscasts for their own use, which gives these American networks a degree of credibility and visibility unusual in the region" (Rohter, 1996, p. 4/6). The picture that Latin Americans see of American society in these North-South news flows is very different from that presented by U.S. networks such as CNN or by global TV news agencies such as

Reuters Television. Univisión and Telemundo adhere to Latin American news values that favour more analysis than that found on most American television. The Spanish-language networks also seek out Hispanic perspectives on national news stories.

The relatively small and scattered nature of the communities they serve has encouraged diasporic media to seek out the most efficient and cost-effective means of communication. Technologies that allow for *narrowcasting* to target audiences rather than those that provide for mass communication have generally been favoured. As a result, ethnic media have often been at the leading edge of technology adoption. As Marie Gillespie notes of the Indian community in Southhall, England, many families obtained VCRs as early as 1978 "well before most households in Britain" (1995, p. 79). In Mexico, videotape became the means to increase television program exports. Later, satellite technology was used to interconnect the various Spanish-language TV stations throughout the United States, thereby creating a national network for Mexican-originated programs as well as a national audience of "Hispanics" (see Dàvila, 2001).

Whereas governments in developing and developed countries have expressed fears that direct broadcast satellites **(DBS)** would erode their sovereignty by transmitting foreign programming to their populations in unregulated manners, this technology provides remarkable opportunities for diasporic communities. Ethnic broadcasters, previously having limited access to the electromagnetic spectrum, find far greater options opening up due to DBS. Diasporic programming using this technology has grown exponentially, well ahead of many mainstream broadcasters. Even as mainstream networks in Europe were making plans to introduce digital broadcasting, the Arab-owned and -operated Orbit TV in Rome had begun by 1994 to provide extensive programming via DBS to Arab communities both in Europe and the Middle East. Arab Radio and Television (ART) has several channels that are broadcast to Arab countries, and one each to Europe and North America. Al-Jazeera, based in Qatar, has become the most popular news network among Arabic-speaking viewers in the Middle East and around the world (El-Nawawy and Iskandar, 2002). One of the most fascinating uses of DBS technology in the Middle Eastern context is MED-TV, a Kurdish satellite television station (Hassanpour, 2003). This is a case of a diaspora within and without the divided homeland attempting to counter forceful suppression and to sustain itself through the use of communication technology. MED-TV has faced resistance not only from governments of the various states straddling Kurdistan, but also from antiterrorist police forces in the U.K., Belgium, and Germany.

Quite apart from the DBS television offered by global conglomerates such as Rupert Murdoch's Star TV, which beams programming to several Asian countries, there have emerged several diasporic DBS-based networks serving Asian diasporas. The Chinese Television Network, headquartered in Hong Kong, has been broadcasting to East Asia, Australia, the Pacific Islands, and the United States since 1994. Hong Kong's Television Broadcasts International "reaches into several Asian markets and to Chinese communities just about everywhere" (Berfield, 1997, p. 31;

also see Sun, 2002). The London-based Chinese Channel's programs are received in the U.K. and in continental Europe. Among various transnational satellite services from India, Zee TV has emerged as a very popular global Indian network in recent years (Thussu, 2000, pp. 197–199). Satellite TV service providers in the United States have realized the viability of ethnic channels and are making them an integral part of their services. WMNB (Russian), Network Asia (India-oriented), Ukrainian Broadcasting Network, CiaoTV, Egyptian Satellite Channel, Nile TV, and several other ethnic offerings appear on U.S.-based DirectTV.

Diasporic groups are also making extensive use of on-line services like the Internet, Usenet, Listserv, and the World Wide Web. These global networks allow communities residing in several countries to interconnect relatively easily. On-line media allow easier access, are nonlinear, largely non-hierarchical, and relatively cheap, as opposed to broadcast media which (apart from offering little access to minority groups) are linear, hierarchical, and capital intensive. The ability to exchange messages with individuals on the other side of the planet and to have access to community information almost instantaneously changes the dynamics of diasporas by allowing for qualitatively and quantitatively enhanced linkages. As the number of language scripts and translation capabilities of on-line software grows, an increasing number of non-English speakers are drawn to the medium.

Diasporic Web sites already contain global directories of individuals, community institutions, and businesses owned by members of diasporas. Some sites have **hypertext** links to sites of alumni associations. Listings of forthcoming festivals and cultural events are provided for those travelling to other parts of the diaspora. The availability of on-line versions of newspapers from countries of origin further enhances intercontinental connections. Global on-line technologies also offer other uses. For example, a worldwide registry would be extremely useful for the medical purposes of locating matches for human bone-marrow donors—who are often limited to one's own ethnic group. Similar databanks would facilitate global genealogical research and searches for the biological families of adopted children. Members of endogamous groups are already using the medium to register themselves in matrimonial sections of diasporic Web sites.

Many Web sites catering to transnational communities have chat rooms for users. Usenet also allows for ongoing discussions among individuals with common origins. Discussions range over topics that include culture, literature, entertainment, politics, and current events in the countries of origin and settlement. Indeed, the electronic chat room becomes the "place" where some members of global communities come together to reconstitute the relationships that existed before migration.

The opportunity that Usenet creates for users to participate in creating content appears to allow them to circumvent the hierarchical mass media as well as to counter material from dominant government and commercial sources. However, even though the use of on-line media and DBS is increasing around the world, there remain wide differences in how various ethnic groups use them. As we move beyond North America, Europe, and Australia, the ownership of computer hardware and subscription to Internet services falls dramatically. Ethnic-based programming on DBS uses a market model and is targeted at fairly affluent members of various diasporas. Mainstream companies are increasingly interested in ethnic media, with corporations like Shaw Communications buying a stake in the Telelatino network in Canada, CBS acquiring TeleNoticias, and Rupert Murdoch's empire expanding to reach South Asian audiences in the U.K. As ethnic broadcasters become successful, they will increasingly become targets for takeovers by global media conglomerations.

CASE STUDY: ETHNIC BROADCASTING IN CANADA

Ethnic media have grown significantly in Canada over the last decade. They range from small newspapers run from home basements to well-established and professionally run broadcast stations. Most of them have substantial diasporic content. Third-language media are also the only source of information on matters such as public health, education, training, job-seeking, and business opportunities for many newcomers who have not yet obtained proficiency in an official language. There are hundreds of ethnic newspapers across the country, most of which publish on a weekly or monthly cycle. Some larger dailies are the Chinese-language *Ming Pao*, *Sing Tao*, and *World Journal*, and the Italian *Corriere Canadese*. Ethnic print organs are becoming increasingly sophisticated in terms of operation and content, and in some cases compete directly with non-ethnic newspapers.

A unique approach to ethnic broadcasting has developed in Canada under official multiculturalism. The Multiculturalism Act proclaims the federal government's policy to recognize the diverse cultures of Canadian society. In the same vein, the Broadcasting Act asserts that the Canadian broadcasting system should reflect the diversity of the country's cultures. The Canadian Radio-television and Telecommunications Commission (CRTC), which introduced an ethnic broadcasting policy in 1985 (revised 1999), specifies the conditions under which the dissemination of ethnic and multilingual programming can be carried out.

Ethnic radio programming is present in most Canadian cities of significant size. This includes time slots acquired at mainstream stations, community radio, and campus radio, as well as 24-hour multilingual broadcasters such as CHIN in Toronto and Ottawa. The CRTC has granted a number of ethnic AM and FM licences in metropolitan areas, as well as a number of Aboriginal station licences. Subsidiary Communications Multiplex Operation (SCMO) technology has allowed several third-language stations operating on sub-carrier frequencies to emerge in various cities. However, subscribers need to acquire specialized radio equipment to hear this programming. Besides on the multicultural channels OMNI (Ontario), CJNT (Montreal), and Channel M (Vancouver), ethnic and multilingual television content can be found in various time slots on community cable, commercial stations, and a national network (Vision TV). Various services in languages including Arabic, Chinese, Farsi, Greek, Hindi, Italian, Korean, Polish, Portuguese,

Punjabi, Russian, Spanish, Tagalog, Tamil, Ukrainian, Urdu, and Vietnamese are available on a national basis via satellite and digital cable services. These Canadian channels carry a blend of programming produced in this country and in other parts of the various diasporas. Growing numbers of foreign-based services are available in some specialty cable packages.[1] The national network of the Aboriginal Peoples Television Network was established in 1999.

Some ethnic media provide extensive coverage of Canadian current affairs and other information that can help members of minorities remain informed about the larger Canadian society (Karim, 2002). However, not all ethnic media offer such information. The smaller the publication or broadcast production, the less likely that civic discourse relating to Canada will be carried. A primary goal of most ethnic media seems to be to provide cultural and informational programming related to the respective community, that is, programming that is generally unavailable in Canadian mass media. Once this goal is met, the medium is able to use any additional available time or space for discussions about Canada-related public affairs.

CONCLUSION

Transnational communication is a key aspect of globalization. However, it is not only carried out by international bodies and large corporations but also by smaller organizations and groups. Diasporas may be strung out in small settlements in various countries, but together they form communicative and other links that contribute to globalizing tendencies. Nevertheless, they are dependent to a large extent on the global infrastructures built and operated by states and corporations. They are also subject to the international regulations that govern the applications of these networks. Diasporas use the transnational communications systems innovatively, and are often early adopters of new technologies. In some cases, diasporas participate in global capitalist structures. But even though some diasporic cultural products have been able to make cross-cultural breakthroughs, they largely flow along transnational routes that are distinct from those starting in Hollywood, London, Paris, and Toronto. Frequently they run in counter-parallel directions, that is, from developing to developed countries; but they also run from one Southern continent to another and from one Northern continent to another. This form of globalization-from-below is creating networks that are genuinely alternative to those that were created under European colonialism.

The NWICO debate underscored some of the fundamental problems that underlie disparities between North and South. It helped to uncover the basic inequalities perpetuated by the global communications structures. Some of these inequities have become worse over the last decade even though the availability of telephones and television has grown in many developing countries. The widespread communications facilities enjoyed by the West continue to provide it with economic advantages over the rest of the world. However, the supporters of NWICO largely failed to recognize the internal divide within developing countries, where rich, urban members of their populations had a level of access to communications that was generally comparable to that in industrialized states. The development of the concept of cultural imperialism provided a popular framework for analyzing the relative communications positions of and influences between countries. But in presenting the idea in terms of a **hypodermic needle model,** its proponents did not account for differing interpretations that people bring to cultural products such as films and television programs. Recent research has provided more nuanced analyses. NWICO supporters also failed to see the ingenuity of Southern communicators who have been successful in countering North-South flows with their own cultural productions. Diasporas have given us a world with multilateral flows of communication, although developed countries remain predominant. Finally, despite the many advances over the last decades, there remain deep divides in the access to and use of communication technologies around the world.

QUESTIONS

1. What is the difference between economic and cultural globalization? How are they related?
2. What are diasporas and how are they layered over time and space?
3. What are globalization-from-above and globalization-from-below? Give some examples of each.
4. What were the principal claims of (a) supporters of NWICO and (b) opponents of NIWCO?
5. In light of recent technological developments, increased media concentration, and globalization, do you think that we need to revisit NWICO today? Give reasons for your answer.

NOTE

1. Canadian audiences also watch many other externally based DBS networks, which are unlicensed in Canada by the CRTC.

REFERENCES

Berfield, Susan. (1997, February). Global TV: Still local after all. *World Press Review*, p. 31.

Bhabha, Homi. (1994). *The location of culture.* London: Routledge.

Cohen, Robin. (1997). *Global diasporas: An introduction.* Seattle, WA: University of Washington Press.

Collins, Glenn. (1996, May 14). Advertising: Information resources takes aim at the ethnic market, and Nielsen. *New York Times*, 3/3.

Dàvila, Arlene. (2001). *Latinos Inc.: The marketing and making of a people*. Berkeley, CA: University of California Press.

El-Nawawy, Mohammed, and Adel Iskander. (2002). *Al-Jazeera*. Cambridge, MA: Westview.

Falk, Richard. (1993). The making of global citizenship. In Jeremy Brecher, John Brown Childs, and Jill Cutler (Eds.), *Global visions: Beyond the new world order* (pp. 39–50). Boston: South End Press.

Gillespie, Marie. (1995). *Television, ethnicity and cultural change*. London: Routledge.

Gunter, Jonathan F. (1978, Autumn). An introduction to the great debate. *Journal of Communication*, 142–156.

Hamelink, Cees J. (1994). *The politics of world communication*. Thousand Oaks, CA: Sage.

Hargreaves, Alec G., and Dalila Mahdjoub. (1997, December). Satellite television viewing among ethnic minorities in France. *European Journal of Communication*, 459–477.

Hassanpour, Amir. (2003). Diaspora, homeland and communication technologies. In Karim H. Karim (Ed.), *The media of diaspora* (pp. 76–88). London: Routledge.

ITU. (1998). *World telecommunication development report: Universal access—world telecommunications indicators*. Geneva: ITU.

Karim, Karim H. (2002). Public sphere and public sphericules: Civic discourse in ethnic media. In Sherry Ferguson and Leslie Regan Shade (Eds.), *Civic discourse and cultural politics in Canada* (pp. 230–242). Westport, CT: Ablex/Jai.

———— (Ed.). (2003). *The media of diaspora*. London: Routledge.

MacBride, Sean. (1980). *Many voices, one world: Communication and society today and tomorrow*. Paris: UNESCO.

Mishra, Vijay. (2002). *Bollywood cinema: Temples of desire*. London: Routledge.

Mowlana, Hamid. (1996). *Global information and world communication: New frontiers in international relations*. Thousand Oaks, CA: Sage.

Riggins, Stephen Harold. (1992). The media imperative: Ethnic minority survival in the age of mass communication. In Stephen Harold Riggins (Ed.), *Ethnic minority media: An international perspective* (pp. 1–20). Newbury Park, CA: Sage.

Rohter, Larry. (1996, December 15). Broadcast news: In Spanish, it's another story. *The New York Times*, 4/1, 6.

Seagrave, Sterling. (1995). *Lords of the rim*. New York: G.P. Putnam.

Shohat, Ella, and Robert Stam. (1994). *Unthinking Eurocentrism: Multiculturalism and the media*. London: Routledge.

Sinclair, John. (1997). The decentring of cultural imperialism: Televisa-tion and Globo-ization in the Latin world. In Kenneth Thompson (Ed.), *Media and cultural regulation*. London: Sage.

Sun, Wanning. (2002). *Leaving China: Media, migration, and transnational imagination*. New York: Rowman & Littlefield.

Thussu, Daya Kishan. (2000). *International communication: Continuity and change.* London: Arnold.

UNDP. (1999). *Human development report 1999.* New York: UNDP.

UNESCO. (2000). *World culture report 2000.* Paris: UNESCO.

Winseck, Dwayne. (2002). Wired cities and transnational communications: New forms of governance for telecommunications and the new media. In Leah Leivrouw (Ed.), *New media handbook* (pp. 393–409). Thousand Oaks, CA: Sage.

18

Race(ing) the Nation: Media and Minorities

Yasmin Jiwani
Concordia University

> The media are not only a powerful source of ideas about race.
> They are a place where these ideas are articulated, worked on,
> transformed and elaborated.

—Stuart Hall (1990, p. 11)

Race and representation are increasingly topical areas of research. The last decade saw a proliferation of studies documenting the qualitative and quantitative representation of racialized minorities in the media. There are four main reasons for contesting media representations.

First, the media play an important role in creating a sense of imagined community, but if that community is never represented in the media landscape, it can be a form of "symbolic annihilation" (Gross 1991).

Second, the media can further the creation of a public sphere in which citizens discuss the shape of society. However, one must first have access to the public sphere, and for minorities such access has historically been limited by structural and social barriers.

Third, the media are formidable agents of socialization. Some (Hall, 1990) claim that they provide us with our very categories of thought. For racialized minorities, this means that their children may be socialized into the dominant culture without ever seeing traces of their own cultures. They do not see themselves reflected in the media but are confronted with images of an "ideal" attainable only through assimilation.

Finally, the mass media influence social policy. Hence, if particular groups are consistently underrepresented, or are misrepresented as criminals, as un-assimilable immigrants, or as simply not belonging, then measures may be enacted that effectively curtail their rights.

Representations of racialized minorities therefore tell us not just how the nation perceives groups within it but also how it perceives itself. Such representations depend upon the invisible consensus that shapes the boundaries of acceptability. The media's messages and constructions not only inform the public imagination but also influence the lives of minorities. According to Hall, "the 'white eye' is always outside the frame—but seeing and positioning everything within it" (1990, p. 14).

Racialization and "racialized minorities" refer to the process whereby a minority is understood first and foremost through race, as though race were the self-evident, primary, or exhaustive definer of the minority. It is the "process or situation wherein the idea of 'race' is introduced to define and give meaning to some particular population, its characteristics and actions" (Miles, 1989, p. 246). Often, the meanings attached to physical and cultural differences imply inferiority. The importance of "race" lies in the fact that "in a white dominated society, the colour of your skin is the single most important factor in determining life chances, as well as your dignity, identity, and self-esteem" (Henry and Tator, in Fleras and Elliot, 1996, p. 35).

CONTEXT—THE CANADIAN SITUATION

Besides the 1986 Multiculturalism Act, numerous government reports have dealt with media representation of racialized minorities in the nation's media. In 1984, the *Equality Now!* report documented the proceedings of the Special Committee on Participation of Visible Minorities in Canadian Society. Such reports have usually recommended measures to enhance the participation and representation of racialized groups in the mass media.

Additionally, numerous briefs and interventions have been presented to the CRTC and to various other commissions. Many of these have focused on exclusion— the lack of representation of people of colour in the mainstream Canadian media, the stereotypical nature of existing representations, and concerns about the accountability of media institutions in redressing these issues. In some cases, these interventions have argued for more adequate representation both in terms of mainstream media and through the use of ethnic media. The Task Force on Cultural Diversity on Television (**Canadian Association of Broadcasters (CAB),** 2004), composed of industry representatives, consultants, and academics, has followed this line of inquiry by presenting empirical evidence underscoring the underrepresentation and lack of diversity within Canadian television programming, and offering "best practice" models for broadcasters to follow.

Academic studies have sought to demonstrate the ways in which the Canadian mass media have systematically excluded and/or stereotypically represented racialized groups (see Mahtani, 2001, for an overview).

Fleras and Kunz (2001, p. 140) categorize existing representations into five different themes: minorities as invisible, as stereotypes, as problem people, as whitewashed, and as adornments. The invisibility of racial minorities has been underscored in the previously mentioned studies that focus on underrepresentation. The stereotypical nature of minority portrayals is linked to historically inscribed images of "others" as repositories of all that is negative in society. These stereotypes are particularly apparent in coverage dealing with minorities as "problem people." Representations of minorities as whitewashed or assimilated are those that fail to reference historical exclusions or that erase the impact of these differences on the lived realities of racialized groups. Finally, representations of minorities as adornments are inherently linked to their role as exotic others whose differences can be periodically celebrated.

Stereotypical representations are the currency through which the media communicate the categories of race and racism. In light of this, it is worth noting that while stereotypes are generally considered to be negative, "positive" stereotypes are also highly problematic. In fact, stereotypes in general tend to embrace an ambivalent structure—the upstart, arrogant, and demanding slave versus the docile, obedient, and subordinate slave; the "jezebel" versus the "mammy" figure; the barbaric versus the noble savage, and so forth (Hall, 1990; Jewell, 1993). "Positive" representations, like their negative counterparts, still serve the function of reinforcing the superiority of whites by re-inscribing the inferiority of peoples of colour (see also Wynn Davies, Nandy, and Sardar, 1993).

REALITY, UNREALITY, AND IDEOLOGY

Many of the above studies focus on the issue of misrepresentation and suggest that the media holds up a mirror to society (Miller and Prince, 1994). Hence, if minorities were misrepresented or not represented at all, then the mirror was "distorted." However, this argument presupposed that the world consisted of one empirical reality "out there" on which we could all agree and which the media merely reflected. Furthermore, this implied that the media were democratic, since everyone had an equal chance of being reflected. Such, however, is not the case.

The media are also profit-based institutions. They tend to reflect elite interests or the interests of those who control them. In fact, their power resides in the ability to select the issues considered worthy of public attention and in how they explain those issues.

Yet, in a democratic society, the media must also try to convince us that they also represent "our" interests (Hackett and Gruneau, 2000; Hackett and Zhao, 1998). Thus, rather than debate the reality or unreality of particular representations, the key questions to ask are these: Whose interests are served by particular kinds of representations? What do the representations tell us about the social status ascribed to specific groups or individuals? How do these representations make sense of social reality, and what kind of actions do they legitimate?

Inferential Racism

In the current climate, it is difficult (but not impossible) for media to espouse racist views openly. However, there are strategies—notably the claim to exercise free speech—through which they may.

For example, limits to offensive speech—such as that of Howard Stern or other "shock jocks"—are often seen not as limits on offensive speech but as an attack upon the very right to free speech. This, therefore, raises the question: for whom is the speech free?

"Freedom of speech" is one of the key means by which mainstream media may camouflage racism. By permitting racist talk under the banner of free speech, the media in effect render such talk more acceptable, thereby naturalizing it. Whether such talk leads to action is another matter. But the normalization of racism becomes increasingly problematic, especially for racialized minorities who bear the brunt of it. Stuart Hall calls this "inferential racism," which occurs in "those apparently naturalized representations of events and situations relating to race, whether 'factual' or 'fictional,' which have racist premises and propositions inscribed in them as a set of unquestioned assumptions. These enable racist statements to be formulated without ever bringing into awareness the racist predicates on which these statements are grounded" (1990, pp. 12–13).

The potentially racist implications of "freedom of speech" are linked to the fact that freedom of speech is rarely discussed in its historical context. Most media coverage assumes that "freedom of speech" is absolute and untouched by social norms and values. However, freedom of speech is actually deeply rooted in the ethical premises of liberal democracy and in the status of groups within it. It is not absolute; rather, it is tempered by concerns about the moral and ethical dimensions of social life.

Aside from masking inequality, the media also advance inferential racism by using coded language. Thus, immigrants become synonymous with foreigners, illegal immigrants, and bogus refugees; diversity becomes a way to communicate racial differences (Karim, 1993; Li, 2003); tolerance is similarly unquestioned and presented as a kind of benevolent forbearance of difference (Mirchandani and Tastsoglou, 2000); and culture becomes a way of talking about race (Razack, 1998).

The Discourse on Immigration

The discourse on immigration and immigrant groups has itself become racialized. For example, the term "immigrant" is popularly understood to mean a person of colour. According to Roxana Ng, the "term conjures up the image of a woman who does not speak English or who speaks English with an accent; who is from the Third World or a member of a visible minority group; and who has a certain type of job (e.g., a sewing machine operator or a cleaning lady)" (cited in Lee, 1999, p. 16).

Immigration also connotes inferiority. This stereotype is reinforced by images that consistently represent developing nations as impoverished, war-torn, and famine-stricken, with little or no law and order (Dahlgren, 1982; Fleras and Kunz, 2001; Hackett, 1989; Kleinman and Kleinman, 1996). Additionally, advertising usually portrays women of colour as subordinates serving the needs of white tourists (Kunz and Fleras, 1998).

The flip side is the stereotype of the demanding, arrogant, undeserving immigrant woman. Here, portrayals border on overt racism when women of colour are perceived to challenge the status quo and question governmental policies. The media's treatment of Sunera Thobani, former president of the National Action Committee on the Status of Women, is instructive in this regard. Immediately upon assuming the NAC leadership, Thobani was criticized for not being an authentic Canadian (Jiwani, 1998). In October 2001, *The National Post* and *The Globe and Mail* criticized her for urging the government not to support intervention in Afghanistan. The media questioned her credentials as a "Canadian," her position as a professor, and her lack of gratitude to Canada (Thobani, 2002, 2003). One of the messages from this coverage, when combined with advertising and entertainment images, is that women of colour are tolerable, even alluring, provided they "stay in their place." However, should they step out of this place, they become targets of hostility and threats of violence.[1]

"Immigrants" are also understood as being not quite part of the nation and yet contained within it. They are never "real Canadians," as revealed through such daily questions as "where are you from?" (Kelly, 1998). Typically, the confusion of people of colour with immigrants emphasizes their difference from an assumed norm (physical, cultural, religious, and political). These differences are communicated in several strategic ways, the most obvious being culture and cuisine. Ethnic restaurants, festivals, costumes, and exotica are often celebrated as signs of difference but also as ways in which differences can be rendered more palatable as commodities to be consumed at leisure. However, more often than not, immigrants and immigration have become associated with crime. This both racializes crime and criminalizes racial groups (Fleras and Kunz, 2001; Henry and Tator, 2002, 2003; Jiwani, 2002).

In his analysis of racist talk, van Dijk (1987) found that immigrants tended to be framed as threats—to the social order due to their presumed proclivity to crime and deviance; to the cultural order by adhering to cultural traditions and resisting assimilation; and to the economic order by draining vital services, manipulating the system, and/or stealing jobs.

Threats to the Social Order—Immigrants as Moral Panic

In their study of the media coverage of the arrival of nearly 600 Chinese migrants on the coast of British Columbia in 1999, Hier and Greenberg (2002) trace the development of a moral panic through the media's amplification of the issue and call for public response:

> As soon as the first boat arrived off the coast of British Columbia, the migrants were racialized in the news media, prematurely branded as "illegal," and lumped into a homogenous category: the Chinese/Asian "other." Once further boats began arriving, and once rumours of still more boats began to circulate, the migrants were objectified within a racialized discourse of illegality through the use of terms such as "boat people," "human cargo," "aliens," "detainees," and "illegal

Chinese." This did much to amplify the "problem" among the Canadian public: fewer than 600 people arriving on four boats over two months came to epitomize "waves" of illegal Chinese/Asian refugee claimants. (p. 145)

While the media fomented hysteria, their most critical role was in reinvigorating anti-immigrant and anti-Asian sentiment. Media coverage inflamed sentiments rooted in such economic issues as the cost of real estate, high unemployment, and increases in property taxes (Ley, 1997). Anti-Asian sentiments have been an integral part of British Columbia's history. The earliest race riots, grounded in the fear of a "yellow peril," occurred in Vancouver at the turn of the 20th century and were aimed at expelling Asians from the city (Anderson, 1991; Li, 1994).

The historically entrenched view of immigrants as inferior and as perpetual foreigners has been extensively documented by Indra (1979, 1981). She not only found evidence of overt racism but also showed how a system of moral stratification governed the representations of various groups. Her analysis shows how the Scottish, British, and English ranked at the top, while Americans, Germans, Russians, and French Canadians occupied the middle range. In contrast, the Chinese, South Asians, Italians, and Aboriginal groups scored the lowest.

The way we talk about immigration also relies on the strategic use of statistics. According to van Dijk (1993), the "numbers game" is a strategy that elicits fear of invasion. Consequently, when the media report on immigration, they invariably cite figures indicating how many of "them" are out there, and how many more are trying to get in (see Dunn and Mahtani, 2001). The flip side of the "numbers game" is often used by well-meaning advocates who use population statistics to encourage media to become more diverse—in order to attract the growing numbers of well-to-do immigrants with purchasing power. In either case, the image is of invasive "hordes" that need to be contained or used for the benefit of the nation.

THE DISCOURSE OF DIFFERENCE: THE CULTURAL/RACIAL OTHER

Inferential racism also works through the language of cultural differences. As Lalvani (1995) has pointed out, women's bodies are the site of multiple and competing discourses. Representations of racialized women tend to cluster around the following axes: the exotic, erotic, and alluring "other"; the repressed, oppressed victim of ultra-patriarchal cultures; and the militant, demanding upstart.

Popular films tend to focus on the exotic other—either as the hypersexual feline (*Catwoman*, 2004), the decorative sidekick of the James Bond films, or the docile lotus blossom (*The Last Samurai*, 2003). Women of colour as evil and manipulative have also been a stock in trade of Hollywood films. The subtext—and in some cases, the main text—in these films is the emphasis on the superiority of white, Western culture. Whiteness represents a homogenized Western culture characterized by rationality, economic wealth, cultural sophistication, and technological superiority (see also Shohat and Stam, 1994).

The same white, Western culture forms the backdrop to representations of racialized women in the news. For example, immediately after September 11, 2001, images of Muslim women veiled in burqas were frequently used as a backdrop for the horrors of the Taliban. In contemporary Western media, the veil remains a symbol of the oppression of Muslim women by conservative, primitive, and tribal upholders of Islam (Ahmed, 1992; Jafri, 1998; Hoodfar, 1993). As Anouar Majid (1998, p. 334) remarks, "For the Western media, the picture of the veiled woman visually defines both the mystery of Islamic culture and its backwardness." Yet, the absence of any mention of the Afghan women's resistance movement results in an unbalanced portrayal—these women are just victims never involved in resistance or mobilization.

In the case of Afghanistan, the constant and repetitive portrayal of Afghan women as victims served to legitimize their "rescue" by the progressive, humanitarian, and benevolent West. By portraying Muslim women as victims, the media are able to reinforce the stereotypical notion of all Muslim women as targets of barbaric Islamic practices and savage Muslim men (Bullock and Jafri, 2001; Jafri, 1998). In contrast, Muslim women living in the West were portrayed as having privileges that their counterparts in Afghanistan did not enjoy. These privileges—the right to attend university and the right to work outside the home—strategically underscored the egalitarian and democratic nature of Western societies (Jiwani, 2004).

The assumption that particular cultures and religions are inherently violent is a theme that underpins much of the media coverage dealing with violence against women in racialized minority communities. The focus on culture serves to position these women as somehow trapped within a system that not only makes them more vulnerable but also naturalizes violence as an innate cultural trait. As Razack (1998, p. 60) notes, "Culture becomes the framework used by white society to pre-empt both racism and sexism in a process that I refer to as culturalization."

We can observe the process of culturalization in the media's account of a case of murder in Vernon, British Columbia. This example highlights the intersecting influences of racism and sexism in the portrayal of racialized immigrant women and girls.

The Discourse of Culturalization

On April 5, 1996, Mark Chahal drove to the Vernon, B.C., home of his estranged wife, Rajwar Ghakhal. There, he shot her father in the driveway, entered the house, killed eight other family members, and also wounded two. He then killed himself. The murders hit the headlines the next day. *The Vancouver Sun* said: "Killer had threatened family: Nine die in Canada's second-largest mass murder on the eve of a Vernon wedding, and the murderer commits suicide. Killer apologizes in suicide note."(Bocking and Bolan, 1996). The front-page article described the murders in detail, with recurrent references to the family's background.

In addition to noting the family's ethnic and religious background, the article also said that the estranged wife's father had been an immigrant: "Harjinder Singh Brar headed to Karnail Gakhal's home seconds after he heard of the shooting. Brar and Gakhal had been friends for 20 years since they both immigrated from India's Punjab state to B.C.'s Interior in search of a better life."

A subsequent article opened with, "The blood on the aggregate concrete was that of Karnail Gakhal, the head of a quiet Sikh family who lived at the home." (Balcom, 1996). Two days later, the victims are described as "all members of a prominent Indo-Canadian family." (Bell, Kines, Bocking, and Fong, 1996). The same story also raises the question of arranged marriages as a possible motive for the tragedy, stating that, "According to people who know the family, Chahal was abusive to his arranged bride from the day they were married; on their wedding night he allegedly called her a 'slut' and beat her."

Within three days, the media had offered explanations of the tragedy that coalesced around a culturalized interpretation. References to the family's immigrant background, Sikh religious tradition, and the custom of arranged marriage served not only to locate the murders on a cultural terrain, but may also have suggested that the custom of arranged marriage, close-knit community life, and religious belief were to some extent responsible for the violence.

Interestingly, less than two weeks after the Vernon tragedy, a comparable story came to light. Sharon Velisek had been shot in November 1995 by her ex-boyfriend, who then shot himself. However, prior to these shootings, Velisek had frequently complained to the Vernon RCMP but said she never received an adequate response. The media reports on the Velisek case did not mention her cultural background, her ethnic community, or her religious affiliation. Rather, the stories concentrated on the events leading up to her attempted murder and highlighted the lack of police action.

The absence of a cultural explanation in the Velisek case may be related to her "unmarked" appearance—she does not belong to a racial minority or to a community or religious background traditionally recognized as "other." Rather, she embodies the dominant culture that remains invisible to scrutiny.

However, if we were to culturalize this episode, we would have to conclude that the violence suffered by Sharon Velisek is an inherent trait of Canadian culture. That the media did not do so is indicative of how, within the dominant gaze, only certain groups are seen as being culturally marked.

The Discourse of Erasure

The coverage of the Kelly Ellard trials reflects another dominant discourse in the media, the discourse of erasure or of indifference and invisibility (Jiwani, 1999). Ellard had been accused of murdering 15-year-old Reena Virk in 1997. Rather than culturalizing racism, erasure means that the media simply omit any mention of racism or racial identity although these factors may be crucial in understanding an event. On July 18, 2004, Ellard's second trial ended in a mistrial; a third trial began in February 2005. It concluded with her conviction and, in July 2005, a sentence of life in prison. Coverage of the earlier Ellard trials, however, may illustrate a continuing erasure of both race and racism as contributing factors in Virk's death.

On the night of November 14, 1997, Reena Virk, of South Asian Indian descent, was attacked by a group of seven girls and one boy in a small suburb of Victoria, B.C. After being beaten, Virk staggered across a bridge in an attempt to get home. She was allegedly followed by Warren Glowatski and Kelly Ellard, told to remove her shoes and jacket, and beaten again to the point of unconsciousness. Virk's body was then dragged to a waterway known as "the Gorge." Ellard was accused of placing her foot on Virk's head until she drowned. Glowatski admitted his guilt and was convicted of second-degree murder.

Neither Ellard nor Glowatski knew Reena Virk. They had met her only that night. According to the pathologist who testified in the first trial, the injuries suffered by Virk would have killed her even if she had not been dragged to the water and drowned.

As the events leading to Virk's murder unfolded, the horror of what "girls do to other girls" was highlighted and quickly overshadowed the issue of male violence or racism. In contrast to the numerous deaths of women at the hands of their spouses or ex-spouses, Virk's death was held up as a symbol of how girls may also commit violence. Story after story covered the issue of teen girl violence, quoting research to support the contention that girls can be just as dangerous as boys.

Although existing research links teen girl violence to the *internalization* of a dominant, patriarchal culture that values sex and power (Artz, 1998; Joe and Chesney-Lind, 1995; Reitsma-Street, 1999), this connection was trivialized. Additional evidence showing that only 3.83 percent of violent crimes are committed by girls (Schramm, 1998) did not hit the headlines with the same intensity. Instead, the media focused on Virk's weight and lack of "fit" with her peer group.

Subsequent coverage of the court appearances and sentencing of the six girls who were also charged focused on Virk's inability to find acceptance in her peer group. Despite her physical difference—as a racialized girl—there was no mention, save one, that the motive might have been racism. Rather, the stories stressed her lack of fitness and overweight condition. In other words, the coverage implied that, had Virk met normative standards, she might have found acceptance.

The issue of racism as a motive is absent in early media coverage and only surfaces two years later in the coverage of the trial of one of her attackers. But even here, the issue is sidestepped and never fully explored.

At the trial of Warren Glowatski, racism was mentioned by one witness, his girlfriend Syreeta Hartley. As one journalist stated, "Syreeta Hartley said her former boyfriend told her that his involvement was partly motivated by racism. Virk was Indo-Canadian" (Hall, 1999, p. A5). However, aside from the brief reporting of Hartley's testimony, the issue itself was not taken up by the media.

The absence of racism as a perceived motive not only minimizes the violence of racism, but also highlights the fact that it is taken for granted as an unrecognizable element. As Hall (1990) and Essed (1990) point out, everyday racism is ingrained in the daily interactions of people of colour with the dominant society—it structures commonsense reality and is thereby naturalized in insidious ways. Part of its naturalization arises from its taken-for-granted nature and embeddedness. The media's denial of racism then corresponds with and reinforces hegemonic definitions of racism as an activity confined to extremist groups, rather than as a system and structure of domination inherent in the very fabric of society and its institutions.

CONCLUSION

As the above examples show, the discourses of racism are multiple and intersecting. They intersect with discourses on gender, immigration, culture, and with values such as freedom of speech. This complicates the analysis of racist rhetoric in the media, especially when considering that the very nature of the "commonsense" knowledge that informs media producers and audiences is itself saturated and textured by racism (Hall, 1982).

A genealogy of racism, as Cornel West (2002) has shown, reveals that it mutates over time in response to changing social conditions. Thus, while the old, or traditional, racism evident in the biological attribution of inferiority is no longer overtly present, the new racism is more complex and utilizes various discourses such as culture, erasure, and national identity (Hall, 1990). Therein lies the continuity. That basic, foundational grammar of race continues a theme inherited from colonialism: the opposition between "us" and "them," which reinforces the boundaries of the nation, preserving hegemonic power and indicating sanctioned pathways toward a sense of belonging and acceptance. It comes to seem, therefore, that racism is simply the act of a "few loonies" out there; that racialized minorities can make it in this land; and that we are a "tolerant" nation— so long as "they" don't overstep their boundaries.

That the boundaries are transgressed by those who are *not* similarly racialized merely highlights the ways in which racialization works to demarcate particular groups in society, making them more vulnerable to a host of unwanted and unwarranted experiences.

A common response to the line of argument developed above could be to conclude that given the systemic nature of racism, there is nothing we can do. Alternately, some may respond that not all media producers are racist. However, Stuart Hall's comments are particularly insightful here as he suggests:

> If the media function in a systematically racist manner, it is not because they are run and organized exclusively by active racists; this is a category mistake. This would be equivalent to saying that you could change the character of the capitalist state by replacing its personnel. Whereas the media, like the state, have a *structure*, a set of *practices*, which are not reducible to the individuals who staff them. . . . what is significant is not

that they produce a racist ideology, from single-minded and unified conception of the world, but that they are so powerfully constrained—"spoken by" a particular set of ideological discourses. (1990, p. 20)

The very act of decoding these ideological discourses may provide one avenue of change. In so doing, it may open spaces that may allow us to tell the story in another way—that is, to change both the subordinate and the dominant discourses over time. Another avenue for change is to intervene in the very practices that shape media production, offering alternatives in both telling the story and organizing media production. A third is to transform the structure itself. This is where the success of alternative media becomes important as they broaden the field of contestation.

QUESTIONS

1. What does the author mean by "racialization"?
2. What does the term "culturalization" mean? Provide an example.
3. Can you identify a recent newspaper or television story that illustrates how some groups are considered "part of the nation" whereas other groups are not?
4. Why does the author claim that media representations should be an object of concern? Where does their power lie?
5. What other groups may be similarly typecast when it comes to their representations in the public sphere of the media?

NOTE

1. Thobani received death threats, anonymous messages, and hate e-mails.

REFERENCES

Ahmed, Leila. (1992). *Women and gender in Islam: Historical roots of a modern debate.* New Haven, CT: Yale University Press.

Anderson, Kay. (1991). *Vancouver's Chinatown: Racial discourse in Canada, 1875–1980.* Montreal: McGill-Queen's University Press.

Artz, Sibylle. (1998). *Sex, power, and the violent school girl.* Toronto: Trifolium Books.

Balcom, Susan. (1996, April 6). Small-town Vernon in shock over massacre. *The Vancouver Sun*, p. A3.

Bell, Stewart, Lindsay Kines, Mike Bocking, and Petti Fong. (1996, April 8). How did killer get gun permit?: Family and friends ask that question, saying police already knew Mark Chahal had made threats to his estranged wife: Wife "was too terrified" to press charges. *The Vancouver Sun*, p. A1.

Bocking, Mike, and Kim Bolan. (1996, April 6). Killer had threatened family: Nine die in Canada's second-largest mass murder on the eve of a Vernon wedding, and the murderer commits suicide: Killer apologizes in suicide note. *The Vancouver Sun*, p. A1.

Bullock, Katherine, and Gul Jafri. (2001). Media (mis)representations: Muslim women in the Canadian nation. *Canadian Woman Studies*, *20*(2), 35–40.

CAB (Canadian Association of Broadcasters). (2004). Task Force for Cultural Diversity on Television Report. Retrieved July 8, 2005, from http://www.cab-acr.ca/english/social/diversity/taskforce/report.shtm

Dahlgren, Peter (with Chakrapani, Sumitra). (1982). The third world on TV news: Western ways of seeing the "other." In W.C. Adams (Ed.), *Television coverage of international affairs* (pp. 45–65). Norwood, NJ: Ablex.

Dunn, Kevin, and Minelle Mahtani. (2001). "Adjusting the colour bars": Media representations of ethnic minorities under Australian and Canadian multiculturalisms. *Working Paper Series*, Vancouver Centre of Excellence, Research on Immigration and Integration in the Metropolis, No. 01-06.

Essed, Philomena. (1990). *Everyday racism: Reports from women of two cultures* (Cynthia Jaffe, Trans.). Claremont, CA: Hunter House.

Fleras, Augie, and Jean Leonard Elliot. (1996). *Unequal relations: An introduction to race, ethnic and Aboriginal dynamics in Canada* (2nd ed.). Scarborough, ON: Prentice Hall.

Fleras, Augie, and Jean Lock Kunz. (2001). *Media and minorities: Representing diversity in a multicultural Canada*. Toronto: Thompson Educational Publishing.

Gross, Larry. (1991). Out of the mainstream: Sexual minorities and the mass media. In M.A. Wolf and A.P. Kielwasser (Eds.), *Gay people, sex and the media* (pp. 19–46). New York and London: Harrington Park Press.

Hackett, Robert A. (1989). Coups, earthquakes and hostages? Foreign news on Canadian television. *Canadian Journal of Political Science*, *22*(4), 809–825.

Hackett, Robert A., and Richard Gruneau (with Gutstein, Donald, Timothy A. Gibson, and NewsWatch Canada). (2000). *The missing news: Filters and blind spots in Canada's press*. Ottawa: Canadian Centre for Policy Alternatives.

Hackett, Robert A., and Yuezhi Zhao (with Repo, Satu). (1998). *Sustaining democracy? Journalism and the politics of objectivity*. Toronto: Garamond.

Hall, Neal. (1999, April 15). Virk's killing motivated by racism, witness says. *The Vancouver Sun*, p. A5.

Hall, Stuart. (1982). The rediscovery of "ideology": Return of the repressed in media studies. In M. Gurevitch, T. Bennett, J. Curran, and J. Woollacott (Eds.), *Culture, society and the media* (pp. 56–90). London: Methuen.

———. (1990). The whites of their eyes. In M. Alvarado and J.O. Thompson (Eds.), *The media reader* (pp. 9–23). London: British Film Institute.

Henry, Frances, and Carol Tator. (2002). *Discourses of domination: Racial bias in the Canadian English language press*. Toronto: University of Toronto Press.

———. (2003). *Racial profiling in Toronto: Discourses of domination, mediation and opposition*. Submitted to the Canadian Race Relations Foundation, March 20. Available on the CRRF website. Retrieved May 2004 from http://www.crr.ca

Hier, Sean, and Joshua Greenberg. (2002). News discourse and the problematization of Chinese migration to Canada. In Frances Henry and Carol Tator (Eds.), *Discourses of domination: Racial bias in the Canadian English language press* (pp. 138–162). Toronto: University of Toronto Press.

Hoodfar, Homa. (1993). The veil in their minds and on our heads: The persistence of colonial images of Muslim women. *Resources for Feminist Research, 22*(3/4), 5–18.

Indra, D. (1979). South Asian stereotypes in the Vancouver press. *Ethnic and Racial Studies, 2*, 166–189.

————. (1981). The invisible mosaic: Women, ethnicity and the Vancouver press, 1905–1976. *Canadian Ethnic Studies, 13*, 63–74.

Jafri, Gul Joya. (1998). *The portrayal of Muslim women in Canadian mainstream media: A community-based analysis*. Afghan Women's Organization, Ontario, Canada. Retrieved May 19, 2005, from http://www.education medias.ca/english/resources/research_documents/reports/diversity/muslim_women_media.cfm

Jewell, K. Sue. (1993). *From mammy to Miss America and beyond: Cultural images and the shaping of US social policy*. London: Routledge.

Jiwani, Yasmin. (1998). On the outskirts of empire: Race and gender in Canadian television news. In V. Strong-Boag, S. Grace, A. Eisenberg, and J. Anderson (Eds.), *Painting the maple: Essays on race, gender, and the construction of Canada* (pp. 53–68). Vancouver: University of British Columbia Press.

————. (1999). Erasing race: The story of Reena Virk. *Canadian Woman Studies, 19*(3), 178–184.

————. (2002). The criminalization of race/The racialization of crime. In W. Chan and K. Mirchandani (Eds.), *Crimes of colour: Racialization and the criminal justice system in Canada* (pp. 67–86). Peterborough, ON: Broadview Press.

————. (2004). Gendering terror: Representations of the orientalized body in Quebec's post–September 11 English-language press. *Critique: Critical Middle Eastern Studies, 13*(3), 265–291.

Joe, Karen A., and Meda Chesney-Lind. (1995). "Just every mother's angel": An analysis of gender and ethnic variations in youth gang membership. *Gender & Society, 9*(4), 408–431.

Karim, Karim H. (1993). Reconstructing the multicultural community in Canada: Discursive strategies of inclusion and exclusion. *International Journal of Politics, Culture and Society, 7*(2), 189–207.

Kelly, Jennifer. (1998). *Under the gaze: Learning to be black in white society*. Halifax, NS: Fernwood Publishing.

Kleinman, Arthur, and Joan Kleinman. (1996). The appeal of experience; the dismay of images: Cultural appropriations of suffering in our times. *Daedalus, 125*(1), 1–23.

Kunz, Jean Lock, and Augie Fleras. (1998). Women of color in mainstream advertising: Distorted mirror or looking glass. *Atlantis, 22*(2), 27–38.

Lalvani, Suren. (1995). Consuming the exotic other. *Critical Studies in Mass Communication, 12*(3), 263–286.

Lee, Jo-Anne (with Harrison, Cheryl). (1999, June). Immigrant settlement and mul-
ticulturalism programs for immigrant, refugee and visible minority women:
A study of outcomes, best practices and issues. A report submitted to the BC
Ministry Responsible for Multiculturalism and Immigration.

Ley, David. (1997). The rhetoric of racism and the politics of explanation in the
Vancouver housing market. In E. Laquian, A. Laquian, and T. McGee (Eds.),
The silent debate: Asian immigration and racism in Canada (pp. 331–348).
University of British Columbia: Institute of Asian Research.

Li, Peter. (1994). Unneighbourly houses or unwelcome Chinese: The social construction of race in the battle over "monster homes" in Vancouver, Canada.
International Journal of Comparative Race and Ethnic Relations, 1(1), 14–33.

Li, Peter S. (2003). Social inclusion of visible minorities and newcomers: The articulation of "race" and "racial" differences in Canadian society. Paper prepared
for the Conference on Social Inclusion, Canadian Council on Social
Development, Ottawa, March 27–28.

Mahtani, Minelle. (2001). Representing minorities: Canadian media and minority
identities. *Canadian Ethnic Studies, 33*(3), 99–133.

Majid, Anouar. (1998). The politics of feminism in Islam. *Signs, 23*(2), 321–361.

Miles, Robert. (1989). *Racism*. London and New York: Routledge, Key Idea Series.

Miller, John, and Kimberly Prince. (1994). *The imperfect mirror: Analysis of minority pictures and news in six Canadian newspapers* (Toronto: School of Journalism, Ryerson
Polytechnic University, 1994). [Report online] Retrieved April 15, 2002, from
http://www.media-awareness.ca/eng/issues/minrep/quick /miller.htm

Mirchandani, Kiran, and Evangelia Tastsoglou. (2000). Towards a diversity beyond
tolerance. *Studies in Political Economy, 61*, 49–78.

Razack, S.H. (1998). *Looking white people in the eye: Gender, race, and culture in courtrooms and classrooms*. Toronto: University of Toronto Press.

Reitsma-Street, Marge. (1999). Justice for Canadian girls: A 1990s update. *Canadian
Journal of Criminology, 41*(3), 335–363.

Schramm, Heather. (1998). *Young women who use violence: Myths and facts*. Calgary,
AB: Elizabeth Fry Society of Calgary.

Shohat, Ella, and Robert Stam. (1994). *Unthinking Eurocentrism: Multiculturalism
and the media*. London and New York: Routledge.

Thobani, Sunera. (2002). Controversies: War frenzy. *Atlantis, 27*(1), 5–11.

———. (2003, May–June). War and the politics of truth-making in Canada.
Qualitative Studies in Education, 16(3), 399–414.

van Dijk, Teun. (1993). *Elite discourse and racism*. Thousand Oaks, CA: Sage Publications.

van Dijk, Teun. A. (1987). *Communicating racism: Ethnic prejudice in thought and talk*.
Newbury Park, CA: Sage Publications.

West, Cornel. (2002). A genealogy of modern racism. In P. Essed and D. Theo
Goldberg (Eds.), *Race critical theories* (pp. 90–112). Maiden, MA and Oxford,
England: Blackwell.

Wyn Davies, Merryl, Ashish Nandy, and Ziauddin Sardar. (1993). *Barbaric others:
A manifesto on western racism*. London: Pluto Press.

19

First Peoples' Television in Canada's North: A Case Study of the Aboriginal Peoples Television Network

Lorna Roth[1]
Concordia University

Of all the First Peoples around the world, those in Canada have led the way in establishing legislatively based, nationwide television services reflecting their cultural perspectives and languages. The negotiation of an infrastructure for First Peoples television in Canada occurred between 1970 and 1999. During that time, the federal government shifted from attempting to assimilate First Peoples (1969) to recognizing First Peoples as a national constituency group with collective broadcasting rights and a special status.

For most of this period, federally funded broadcasting undertakings were located north of the 55th latitude. This region includes one third of Canada's land mass and encompasses the Northwest Territories, Nunavut, Yukon Territories, Labrador, and the northern parts of all of the central and western provinces. After consistent successes with pilot experiments and more permanent undertakings, Northern broadcasters sought to integrate Southern First Peoples into their established services and convinced the federal government of the viability of a national indigenous service. They subsequently gained federal, territorial, provincial, and a broad range of institutional support through legislation, regulation, and financial assistance to operate an **Aboriginal Peoples Television Network (APTN).**

In 1991, the federal government passed the current Broadcasting Act, which enshrined multiculturalism, multiracialism, and Aboriginal broadcasting:

> Through its programming and the employment opportunities arising out of its operation, [the Canadian broadcasting system should] serve the needs and interests, and reflect the circumstances and aspirations of Canadian men, women and children, including equal rights, the linguistic duality and multicultural and multiracial nature of Canadian society and the special place of aboriginal peoples within that society. (Government of Canada, 1991, S. 3[d][iii])

AN OVERVIEW OF KEY PHASES IN NORTHERN TELEVISION HISTORY

The history of Northern television can be divided into six phases separated by shifts in representational practices, improved technological infrastructures, and corresponding expansions of target audiences (Roth, 1994, 1998).

Phases I and II: Pre–Northern TV Context and (de)Romancing the North

Phase 1 (Pre–Northern Television) is well documented in the literature (Roth, 1994; Alia, 1999) and covers the period in which Southern-produced imagery of First Peoples consisted of stereotypical misrepresentations, when they were presented at all. This period precedes the entry of television into the Canadian North, but provides important background information. When television was parachuted into the North, its initial impact was to underscore the absence of First Peoples from media texts.

This is followed by Phase II, in which First Peoples became aware of the potential of televisual media to record themselves and their concerns. This phase coincided with the late-1960s, when Parliament debated the Telesat Act (1968) whose purpose was to introduce the first domestic satellite in the world. Concurrent with these debates and the passing of the Telesat Act (1969), discussions around Aboriginal Northern television also began. At that time, federal policy advocated the assimilation of First Peoples (Government of Canada, 1969). Consequently, First Peoples began to realize the power of the media to erode their culture, to serve as a tool for self-development/empowerment in their efforts to resist conformity to the mainstream values of Canadian society, and to serve as a vehicle for mediating and repairing historical tensions in their social and race relations.

By 1975, all Northern communities with populations over 500 were equipped with television receiving dishes. From First Peoples' perspectives, the main activity of this period was the use of television as an experimental medium through which to explore interactive communications and community development practices. Simultaneously, the federal government wanted First Peoples to "modernize" and to become familiar with new technologies as a possible substitute for travel (expenses were prohibitive at the time), especially in relation to education and health matters. They also wanted First Peoples' feedback on alternative uses of satellite technology for community development, and on viable forms of inter-community communications. In other words, various interests and objectives converged in such a way that it became worthwhile for the government to invest in field tests and for First Peoples to undertake project work. Consequently, between 1978 and 1981, the Department of Communications established a competition among field groups in Nunavut (formerly the central and eastern lands of the Northwest Territories) and Nunavik (Northern Quebec) for access to the Anik B satellite. Several groups received monies as part of the competition but the most prominent was the Inuit Tapirisat of Canada (the Eskimo Brotherhood), which was given over $1 million to conduct interactive experiments in exchange for providing relevant data. As a result of two successful projects—"Inukshuk," in the Northwest Territories and "Naalakvik" in Northern Quebec—the Inuit were able to negotiate the licensing of the Inuit Broadcasting Corporation in 1981. At the same time, the CRTC licensed **Cancom** (Canadian Satellite Communications Inc.) to deliver Southern programming into Northern and remote communities and to carry Northern-produced broadcasts. The CBC was "expected" to carry Native-language programming as part of its public service mandate.

Phase III: Policy-ing the North

This phase runs from 1981 to 1991, when the current Broadcasting Act was amended to enshrine Aboriginal broadcasting. It was a period in which *broadcasting policy* was re-shaped in light of evidence provided by field experiments. But the path that led to this Parliamentary decision was rough and winding.

Essentially, during this period, experiments in the field were carefully monitored and used as evidence in support of granting constituency groups access rights and of providing fairer and more equitable distribution services for the North. Eventually, the work of lobbyists from the North and the South, academics, and historians, resulted in the amended Broadcasting Act of 1991.

Phase IV: Consolidation and Expansion of Broadcasting Infrastructures

Phase IV began around 1983. By this time, 13 regional Native communications societies had developed "North of 60" and had organized a lobby campaign directed toward the establishment of a distinct Native broadcasting policy.

On March 10, 1983, the Government of Canada announced a Northern Broadcasting Policy that recognized the importance of Native participation in both media programming and the regulatory process (Government of Canada, 1983, p. 2). The Northern Broadcasting Policy consisted of the following five principles:

a) Northern residents should be offered access to an increasing range of programming choices through the exploitation of technological opportunities.
b) Northern native people should have the opportunity to participate actively in the determination by the CRTC of the character, quantity, and priority of programming broadcast in predominantly native communities.
c) Northern native people should have fair access to northern broadcasting distribution systems to maintain and develop their cultures and languages.
d) Programming relevant to native concerns, including content originated by native people, should be produced for distribution on northern broadcasting services wherever native people form a significant proportion of the population in the service area.

e) Northern native representatives should be consulted regularly by government agencies engaged in establishing broadcasting policies which would affect their cultures. (Government of Canada, 1983, p. 2)

An accompanying program called the Northern Native Broadcast Access Program (NNBAP) was also established, and $40.3 million was earmarked for the long-term goal of producing 20 hours per week of Native-language radio programming and 5 hours per week of Native-perspective television. The initial funding was for four years, but the program has continued to exist, albeit under considerable financial strain.

In 1983, therefore, there was cause for celebration, but problems soon became apparent. For example, while both the CBC and Cancom did effectively deliver indigenous programming as part of their licensing conditions, they did so at rather unpopular hours. Hence, while the CBC Northern Service carried Inuit Broadcasting Corporation (IBC) programming for five hours per week, the programs were often broadcast around 3 a.m. Furthermore, national programming often preempted Native programming on the CBC.

First People came to believe, therefore, that the demand for carriage of their programming could not be left merely to the goodwill of other agencies.

In 1985, interested parties began to discuss the establishment of a dedicated Northern transponder to avoid the above-mentioned problems. In January 1987, Aboriginal and Northern broadcasters formed a consortium with the goal of establishing a Pan-Northern distribution service. In 1988, the federal Department of Communications approved monies to explore the feasibility of a separate Northern channel. In 1990, $10 million was approved to prepare an application for a Pan-Northern distribution service. Meanwhile, there were severe budgetary cutbacks in NNBAP program funding as the federal government responded to pressures to privatize the cultural industries. This led to a bizarre problem. On the one hand, First Peoples were getting distribution money; on the other, they could not afford to produce programs to distribute. There was subsequently a scramble to find ways to diversify their funding sources. Some hired fundraisers; others increased efforts to find a stronger advertising base. This brings us to the next period.

Phase V: Crossing Cultural, Racial, and Territorial Borderlines

During the early part of the fifth period, beginning around 1990, several Native communication societies initiated contracts to produce programming for Southern viewers (Inuit Broadcasting Corporation, Northern Native Broadcasting, Yukon (NNBY), WaWaTay Native Communication Societies). This was organized partly in response to the cutbacks, partly as an effort to reach a broader audience and see how they would be perceived, and partly to overcome the historical dependency of First Peoples on the federal government. In the case of NNBY, a weekly program, *Nedaa (Your Eye on the Yukon)*, was negotiated with CBC Newsworld. This was the first ongoing national channel commitment to broadcast First Nations programming to a countrywide audience and caused both celebration and minor criticism around the issue of regional versus national audiences. But no one stopped the initiative.

In programming for a national audience, NNBY had to develop a culturally hybrid approach targeting at least two distinct audiences (Native and non-Native) that were already highly diverse. Given that federal funding was disseminated for the purpose of developing regional media, the secondary, non-Native audience was considered somewhat outside the criteria of the Northern Native Broadcast Access Program. Nonetheless, NNBY's contractual arrangement was significant because it crossed social, racial, territorial, and cultural borders and opened a space—albeit small—for Aboriginal broadcasting within the mainstream of Canadian media. NNBY programming acquired a loyal following in the South, which provoked some interesting discussions in the North about how to build cross-cultural alignments for political ends. Though bold, NNBY's national project did little to solve the challenge of Pan-Northern distribution.

After the Broadcasting Act was amended in 1991, the CRTC approved the application for TVNC, a Native television network licensed to serve Northern Canada "for the purpose of broadcasting cultural, social, political and educational programming for the primary benefit of aboriginal people in the North" (Canadian Radio-television and Telecommunications Commission, 1991). By granting the TVNC licence, the Commission recognized the importance of Northern control over the distribution of Native and Northern programming. TVNC was to become the vehicle through which First Peoples would represent themselves and their concerns to the entire North. They would no longer be restricted by geography or technology to local or regional self-representation and identity-building. In this sense, TVNC constituted a de facto recognition of the communication rights of First Peoples in the North.

TVNC began broadcasting on January 21st, 1992. Spanning 5 time zones and more than 4.3 million kilometres, TVNC broadcast approximately 100 hours per week to 96 communities (in English and multiple Native languages).[2] TVNC was not a programmer, but a distributor of its members' programming, which consisted of

- 38 hours per week of Aboriginal language and cultural programming;
- 23 hours per week of formal and informal educational programming;
- 12 hours per week of produced and acquired children's programming, over half of which is in Aboriginal languages. (Television Northern Canada, 1993, p. 4)

The rest consisted of wraparound programming from Broadcast News and Environment Canada forecasts, and reruns.

TVNC was the only Aboriginal television network in the world to broadcast such a high volume of programming from indigenous sources. CAAMA (the Central Australian Aboriginal Media Association) has a remote commercial television service licence, awarded in 1987. Its "Imparja" service broadcasts mostly to non-Aboriginal viewers, such that its programming tends to be more European-oriented (Browne,

1996, p. 38). TVNC and CAAMA programming had little in common besides both being Aboriginal-controlled.[3]

As a Pan-Northern distribution undertaking, TVNC was theoretically able to forge connections (via program exchanges and uplink/downlink satellite arrangements) with Inuit and Aboriginal groups in other countries, such as Greenland, Alaska, Finland, and Siberia, as well as Australia, New Zealand, Brazil, and Bolivia (among others). In reality, it did not do much of this because of both technical and financial barriers. What it did offer to Northern viewers was limited access to programming about the "activities of indigenous people from around the globe," when this was feasible (Television Northern Canada, 1993, p. 4). For example, the network aired a half-hour weekly current affairs program called *Heartbeat Alaska*, which originated in Anchorage, Alaska, and was supplied for the cost of one-way shipping.

TVNC's ambition to be picked up by Southern cable operators on a voluntary basis did not work out well. The CRTC permitted TVNC to be listed for carriage by cable companies, but very few availed themselves of the opportunity. Furthermore, piecemeal distribution of the TVNC signal would not be an appropriate route for extension into the South. The challenge was to become a Canada-wide network. This, however, posed further unanticipated cross-cultural questions. For example, what kinds of programming would meet the information and entertainment needs of both Native/non-Native Northerners *and* Native/non-Native Southerners? What considerations and constraints would be imposed upon or voluntarily assumed by programmers in order to please a hybrid audience?

Of even greater concern were program subjects which might generate controversy when they were removed from their original context. Consider the programs that stem from the Eastern Arctic in which details of animal killings are central to the visual presentation. The culturally sensitive issue of the hunt might stir protest from members of animal rights organizations.

Finally, the cost of acquiring broadcasting rights in the South would raise costs because the target audience would be larger. Northern rights were extremely inexpensive because TVNC was a non-profit, public broadcasting distribution organization. Indeed, program distributors, who recognized TVNC's special financial conditions, virtually subsidized the rights. These are just a few of the programming considerations that TVNC would have to address if and when it negotiated a broadcasting arrangement with the South.

Phase VI: The Aboriginal Peoples Television Network—Going National

> There are some 600 First Nations. We are always fighting for this right or that right. But we are one people. This [channel] would bring us together. (Focus group participant)
>
> I am very excited by the opportunity the aboriginal people of Canada have been given. This historic decision will be a major step in building bridges of understanding between

> aboriginal and non-aboriginal people in Canada. (Abraham Tagalik, former APTN chairman, quoted in TVNC Newsletter March 1999, p. 1)

As of June 1997, TVNC undertook to become a nationwide network ("APTN Milestones," 2003). It was supported in this endeavour by the Assembly of First Nations (AFN) and began to make regular submissions to national Aboriginal organizations and to the CRTC.

In January 1998, TVNC hired Angus Reid (a public-opinion consulting firm) to conduct a survey regarding the desirability of establishing a national Aboriginal broadcasting undertaking. Results indicated that 79 percent or "two out of three Canadians supported the idea of a national aboriginal TV network, even if it would mean displacing a currently offered service" ("APTN Milestones," 2003).

In February 1998, the CRTC called for a licence application from TVNC and, in June 1998, TVNC submitted one. To be economically viable, it had to be a mandatory service, available to the nearly eight million households with cable and to those with direct-to-home and wireless television service, including ExpressVu, StarChoice, and Look TV ("APTN Fact Sheet," 1999, p. 1). To assure consistent and secure funding, TVNC requested that cable operators charge 15 cents per month per household, thereby generating an anticipated revenue stream of $15 million in the first years, although APTN expected the budget to increase with rising advertising revenues (Ibid.). In exchange for the small charge of 15 cents, subscribers would receive a service aimed at both Aboriginal and non-Aboriginal audiences with programming to interest all viewers: children's animation, youth shows, cultural and traditional programming, music, drama, dance, news and current affairs, as well as live coverage of special events and interactive programming (Ibid.). APTN promised 90 percent Canadian content with the remaining 10 percent consisting of indigenous programming from around the world (Ibid., p. 2). It has subsequently decreased its Canadian content percentage to 86 percent, due to the high production cost of Canadian original programming.

The CRTC received approximately 300 letters of support from the general public. This was not a large number, but along with the Angus Reid results, it was enough to reinforce the political will of the CRTC commissioners to make a decision in TVNC/APTN's favour. Support for the network was fairly consistent among the existing Native communication societies in the North; however, there were some expected challenges around issues of the Board of Directors' organization and control during the transition from a Northern to a national network, which indicated a need for a period of negotiation, clarification, and resolution. Primary among these challenges was one raised by the Northern Native Broadcasting, Yukon (NNBY) group involving the question of guaranteed Northern representation on the Board. NNBY was concerned with shifting power relations and the possible "systemic changes that might undermine the interests of the Aboriginal peoples of the North" and demanded guarantees for the "unrestricted right of continued distribution of their programs to support their languages, dialects, and cultures" (Northern Native Broadcasting, Yukon, 1998, pp. 5–6). There were other considerations of a more technical and administrative nature, but this one was of primary significance in terms of the discourse it generated. In response to NNBY's concerns, TVNC assured them in writing that these issues would be appropriately addressed and that it was planning a professional workshop focused on board structure and selection, as well as some administrative training (Television Northern Canada, 1998, p. 11). Eventually, these issues were worked out, and a 21-member Native Board of Directors was selected from all regions of Canada.

However, strong and organized resistance to APTN came from some cable operators and from several existing broadcasters to whom the idea of a *mandatory* national channel seemed antidemocratic. There were some exceptions (Cancom and WETV, among others), but most cable operators would have preferred APTN to be licensed "on the same optional distribution basis as all other fee-based Canadian services" (Canadian Broadcasting Corporation, 1998). Underlying their concern was the view that TVNC/APTN was a specialty service targeted to a particular audience. TVNC/APTN's perspective was that it was *not* a specialty service, but one with a special status, based on First Peoples being one of the three founding nations of Canada. That APTN should be carried on a mandatory basis as a parallel service to CBC or Radio-Canada raised the political/historical stakes in Canada's national debate about confederation.

The **Canadian Cable Television Association (CCTA)** took a position in favour of greater customer choice, complaining that the signal would be forced upon subscribers if they had to pay 15 cents for an unrequested service. This argument was framed in terms of economic competition and choice and grew out of the assumption that APTN *should* be a *specialty service*. Beyond the monthly subscriber fee, the CCTA also protested the "one time costs associated with forcing a service on basic. These included expenses related to informing customers of the change in the line-up through channel line-up stickers and explanatory letters, and in order to receive the signal, additions to headend equipment" (Canadian Cable Television Association, 1998, p. 3). Finally, it would be expensive to shift channel allocations and, in some cases, an existing channel would no longer be offered or would be bumped from one of the basic tiers to a more expensive package.

The cable industry's basic preoccupation was cost recovery for its investments. Most cable operators resisted the argument that First Peoples, only 3 percent of the population, should have either a special status or a mandatory national channel. The CCTA said that it "supported the concept of the network but not the insistence that it be offered as part of the basic cable service" (Cobb, 1999).

On February 22, 1999, the CRTC approved TVNC's application and granted mandatory carriage on basic cable throughout Canada with a 15-cent cost per subscriber per month in the South—to be used as a Program Production Fund for APTN. In the North, residents of the 96 communities would continue to receive the service free of charge (Television Northern Canada, 1999, p. 1). To provide continuity of service to Northerners, a separate Northern feed was established.

"This will ensure that special northern programming, including legislative coverage and special events will be broadcast in the North on an on-going basis" (Ibid.).

The time between the date on which the licence was granted and the actual launch was a mere six months and a few days. This was highly unusual but necessary because APTN wanted to launch on the same day as several other specialty services. This meant that APTN expenses could be included within the one-time costs for publicity and head-end equipment incurred by the other service launches (Personal Interviews).

APTN began broadcasting, as planned, on September 1, 1999. Until programming surpluses could be created, there were three programming cycles per day; that is, each day, programs were repeated three times—once every six hours. There are still repetitions on APTN. Broadcast languages include 60 percent English, 15 percent French, and 25 percent in a variety of Aboriginal languages.[4]

INITIAL IMPACT OF APTN

First Peoples television did not go through the hearing/licensing process and launch without some controversy within the Canadian press. For a few days after APTN was licensed and for about a week before and after it actually went on the air, APTN generated a fair amount of editorial comment, mainly about it being "the first in the world" and about the political context for the CRTC decision. A sense of the conflict in Canadian public opinion concerning APTN can be captured by comparing editorial perspectives published in several representative newspapers.

On the day after the CRTC decision, the *National Post* published a single article on the subject, titled "COMING SOON TO YOUR LIVING ROOM: The CRTC is forcing a new aboriginal TV channel—and its cost—on most Canadian cable viewers" (Chwialkowska, 1999). Despite its attempt to *look* objective, the overall impression was that the *Post* supported the cable operators.

On the other hand, *The Globe and Mail* noted in its February 24 editorial how important it is for non-Native audiences to have access to television produced by indigenous peoples:

> Television is so confusing. At the same time that it isn't reality, it is authenticity. Just to be seen on TV makes people genuine in a way that almost nothing else in 20th-century culture does. . . . Not only will the Aboriginal Peoples Television Network be a place for native people to present themselves to one another in English, French and 15 native languages, but it will be an electronic arena in which many Canadians will encounter aboriginals in ways they might never do otherwise. . . . That's why we support the CRTC's decision to make this channel a part of the basic cable package. Not only will it provide a secure source of funding

for the APTN's programs, but it will make the network
something people will chance upon as they click their way
along the TV dial. . . . Their relation to other Canadians isn't
tangential; it is inevitable. ("The Native Media," 1999)

The Globe and Mail editorial raises a very important issue about the relationship
between absence and presence, (in)visibility, and (in)audibility of an important national
community in Canada. It is easy to pretend liberal tolerance when a subject/
person/community is absent from our visible and conscious world. What remains
unseen can be faded out of our social relations. Moreover, it is relatively easy to circulate a discourse of tolerance and "multiculturalism" in an era of political correctness.

On a deeper level, it becomes harder to mask intolerance when an "unpopular"
constituency group gains a notable presence in a highly visible and audible media
form. At the very least, if audiences take time to focus on the programming, it might
stimulate them to recognize First Peoples as integral citizens of the country and the
airwaves.

The launch of the Aboriginal Peoples Television Network service took place at
8:00 p.m. on September 1, 1999. The live broadcast wove together commentators,
members of Native communication societies that had been involved in television
production since at least 1983, entertainers, clips of key events in First Peoples
history, and landscape images. It was a celebration of the opening up of mainstream
Canada to the lives of First Peoples. Since the launch, APTN's regularly scheduled
programming has become a centre of information and entertainment for First
Peoples and for those interested in Native perspectives on the world.

However, at the time of APTN's launch, not all Canadians were in the same
celebratory mood. In an editorial titled "Consumers should decide what they want
to watch," the *Vancouver Province* said:

> The CRTC decision was another in a long line of loopy
> broadcast regulations that amounts to political correctness
> disguised as social engineering. We wish APTN the best of
> luck. But, while Ottawa can make consumers pay for the new
> channel, it can't make them watch it. It's a good job APTN
> won't have to rely on Vancouver ratings to pay its way. (1999)

However, writing in the *Winnipeg Free Press*, arts commentator Morley Walker
evaluated the way other newspapers had been covering APTN: "the tenor of commentary in the white man's press surrounding the fledgling aboriginal cable TV
channel" is "skeptical, if not outright hostile" (1999). He adds:

> Fifteen cents a month today is a small price to pay as a cable
> subscriber to support a voice that is both indigenous to our
> country and vital to offering role models for a dispossessed
> minority. It seems to me that a first nations TV channel is an
> excellent addition to the Canadian television landscape.

Disappointed with those elements of the press that framed APTN as a project of social engineering and kept pointing out that "CRTC documents show that only 300 Canadians asked the CRTC for the channel," Walker also raises the issue of APTN's remote location on the channel grid (1999). This is a subject that symbolizes the issue of First Peoples' social placement—slightly outside of the centre of things—in a most concrete way.

APTN: ON THE MARGINS OF MAINSTREAM TELEVISION

APTN is competing with a sophisticated technological and broadcasting infrastructure put in place in the 1950s. Although it benefits from these technologies, APTN's underfunding, difficulties in finding sponsors, and lack of national experience do have consequences in terms of its need for a transitional period in which to build human resource capacity, program surpluses, financial stability, and broad public support.

To watch the network, one has first to find it on the channel grid, and that is another challenge for APTN. First Peoples have supported its development and have seen the value of television for the building of the Aboriginal community in Canada. But its reach outside of the Native communities is limited.

A key technical issue that relegates APTN to the equivalent of a "media reservation" is its usual location in the high end of the analog channel grid on most systems. These channels are often less visited by channel grazers, and it is the only national analog channel for which cable subscribers must pay.

Committed viewers will not care where it is located. But recruiting new audiences is a bigger challenge. If APTN is located so far from the centre of most popular analog television programming, how many potential new viewers will even remember its presence on the airwaves or bother exploring the high end of the grid?

APTN AS A PUBLIC MEDIUM IN CANADA

Despite its special status in Canada's broadcasting system, the case of APTN is a prototype for other states in which diverse constituency groups compete for service access in order to address and construct alignments across racial, social, economic, and territorial lines. Over the years, First Peoples have been granted political opportunities to build a nationwide mediaspace to heal the historical communication ruptures within their societies and between their communities and other Canadians. These community-building opportunities have been the result of First Peoples' persistence in overcoming challenges and demonstrating skills to develop and manage new broadcasting infrastructures. With the convergence of a strong political will on the part of the federal cabinet and the CRTC, amiable negotiations among all key parties, and the policy savvy which First Peoples have demonstrated publicly, APTN has evolved from idea to fully operational television network. It is moderately secure in terms of funding and distribution, although like most new constituency-based services, it has definitely faced financial challenges and still needs to build human resource capacity, program surpluses, and broader cross-cultural audience support. Significantly, though, its existence is enshrined in national legislation. This regulatory support is a highly important and symbolic demonstration of our collective will to include First Peoples' media/voices/images as integral to the national broadcasting system. It furthermore represents a consolidation of new power relationships among Canadian media institutions, policy bodies, and audiences.

APTN has enabled indigenous messages to be heard by constituency groups that might never have had access to a live person of Aboriginal descent; it provides an opportunity to share national imageries and histories, to build bridges of understanding, and to bridge cultural borders. Equally important, however, is that it *exists*: it is on the air, is one of many services competing for audience attention, is now a performer on the electronic power grid, and, to a great extent, has transformed the roles that were anticipated for public media since its early days.

This is important to recognize. APTN provides access only to cable and satellite subscribers. It attracts niche, not mass audiences. It is not free. In trying to figure out how to maintain secure funding over long periods of time, the CRTC has introduced a social cost to cable operators for carriage of APTN.[5] Subscriber costs of 15 cents per month are paid to cable operators who then transfer the money to APTN to be used for television production in communities that are not economically viable enough to sustain media economies. This may be a model by which states can assure the sponsorship and sustenance of public service programming that might be otherwise unaffordable.

APTN is a hybrid between what have traditionally been defined as public and private broadcasting. It carries advertising, yet it addresses public issues and models itself after public-service television. It is multilingual, multicultural, and multiracial in content, production staff, and management. It attempts to be both local and global. It does very little original production on its own; it distributes locally and regionally produced cultural programming to a national audience. The fact that APTN is already integrating international programming and is considering expanding its service to become an international First Peoples television network comparable to CNN and the BBC World Service indicates clearly its global objective of international constituency group–building across national borders.

The look of APTN's national programming closely resembles the look of U.S. public access television or Canadian community television. Its quality is uneven. APTN still replays some programs simply because of budgetary constraints. However, indigenous programming that originates in the North is now complemented by an expanded range of programs derived from Southern Canada and international sources. These include documentaries, dramas, comedy shows, variety shows, talk shows, a cooking show, and children's programming. Beginning in 2000, APTN introduced live news and current affairs programming that provides an Aboriginal lens through which to view (inter)national news and public affairs. Its *Bingo and a Movie (BAAM)* program is very popular. Shown on Friday nights, it consists of film segments broken up by bingo games, as well as interviews with guests who usually have something interesting to say about the film (although the conversation is not limited to this content). The program provides a uniquely Aboriginal perspective on the film while at the same time mobilizing indigenous communities' interest in electronic bingo (a popular means of raising funds for Native community radio across the country).

Despite the practical reality that APTN's program mandate to serve all Aboriginal and Canadian communities, North and South, is extremely complex and difficult to manage, my sense is that the network has served its constituency groups well in that it has Northernized and indigenized Canadian programming. In 2004–2005, APTN's television network licence is up for renewal by the CRTC. It will be most interesting to observe and monitor the extent to which APTN will claim to have met its central programming and audience objectives from both its own and the CRTC's perspectives.

From my point of view, APTN has indeed delivered distinct imagery from coast to coast to coast with perspectives that express what it is like to "live the difference." I believe that in our age of the 500-channel universe and the World Wide Web, APTN offers a symbolic meeting place for indigenous and non-Native peoples to communicate their common interests. If APTN can widely stimulate reflections, deliberations, and conversations about First Peoples' cultures and issues, then it will have succeeded in providing a starting point for very necessary cross-cultural and international dialogues.

QUESTIONS

1. What are the six phases of Native broadcasting history discussed in this chapter?
2. Do you think it is important to have a service such as APTN? Give reasons for your answer.
3. Are there other populations in Canada that you feel should have their own broadcasting system?
4. How does APTN serve as a model for other indigenous communities?
5. Do you feel it is important that Natives in Canada have a presence on the Internet?

NOTES

1. This chapter was adapted from Lorna Roth (2000) "Bypassing of Borders and the Building of Bridges: Steps in the Construction of the Aboriginal Peoples Television Network in Canada," *Gazette: International Journal of Communication Studies, 62*(3–4), pp. 251–269; and from the forthcoming "(re)Colouring the

Public Broadcasting System in Canada: A Case Study of the Aboriginal Peoples Television Network," in Linda K. Fuller (Ed.), *Community Media: International Perspectives (Aboriginal/Indigenous Experiences, Current Case Studies, Virtual Community Visions* (London: Sage Publications).

2. TVNC's network members consisted of the Inuit Broadcasting Corporation (Ottawa, Iqaluit); the Inuvialuit Communications Society (Inuvik); Northern Native Broadcasting, Yukon (Whitehorse); the OkalaKatiget Society (Labrador); Taqramiut Nipingat Incorporated (Northern Quebec); the Native Communications Society of the Western N.W.T. (Yellowknife); the Government of the Northwest Territories; Yukon College; and the National Aboriginal Communications Society. Associate Members included CBC Northern Service; Kativik School Board (Quebec); Labrador Community College; Northern Native Broadcasting (Terrace); Telesat Canada; and Wawatay Native Communications Society (Sioux Lookout).

3. For further information on the Australian Aboriginal broadcasting situation, see Michael Meadows (1993a, 1993b, among others) and Faye Ginsburg (1992, 1993, and others).

4. To view a current schedule, visit the APTN Web site at http://www.aptn.ca:8080/strands/news_currentaffairs/Schedule/schedule_html.

5. A recent example: as part of their social benefits package offered in exchange for taking over CTV, a national private network, Bell Canada Enterprises has agreed to give $3 million to APTN to establish several news offices across the country.

REFERENCES

Alia, Valerie. (1999). *Un/Covering the north: News, media, and Aboriginal people.* Vancouver: UBC Press.

APTN fact sheet. (1999). Aboriginal Peoples Television Network. Retrieved from http://www.aptn.ca:8080/corporate/about/profile_html

APTN milestones. (2003). Aboriginal Peoples Television Network. Retrieved from http://www.aptn.ca:8080/corporate/about/milestones_html

APTN schedule. (1999). Aboriginal Peoples Television Network. Retrieved from http://www.aptn.ca:8080/strands/news_currentaffairs/Schedule/schedule_html

Browne, Donald R. (1996). *Electronic media and indigenous peoples: A voice of our own?* Ames, IA: Iowa State University Press.

Canadian Broadcasting Corporation. (1998, October 19). Intervention Letter to CRTC. Ottawa: Author.

Canadian Cable Television Association. (1998, November 12). Intervention Letter to CRTC. Ottawa: Author.

Canadian Radio-television and Telecommunications Commission. (1991, October 28). Decision CRTC 91-826. Television Northern Canada Incorporated. Ottawa: Author.

———. (1999, February 22). Decision CRTC 99-42. Ottawa: Author.

Chwialkowska, Luiza. (1999, February 23). Coming soon to your living room. *The National Post*, p. A3.

Cobb, Chris. (1999, February 23). Aboriginal TV goes Canada-wide. *Gazette*, p. F5.

Consumers should decide what they want to watch. (1999, September 2). *The Vancouver Province*, p. A36.

Ginsburg, Faye. (1992). Indigenous media: Faustian contract or global village? In George E. Marcus (Ed.), *Rereading cultural anthropology* (pp. 356–376). Durham, NC: Duke University Press.

———. (1993, Spring). Aboriginal media and the Australian imaginary. *Public Culture 5*, 20.

Government of Canada. (1969). Statement of the Government of Canada on Indian policy presented to the first session of the twenty-eighth Parliament by the Honourable Jean Chrétien, Minister of Indian Affairs and Northern Development. Ottawa.

———. (1983, March 10). The northern broadcasting policy. Federal government news release.

———. (1991, June 4). Broadcasting Act. Ottawa.

Meadows, Michael. (1993a). Voice blo mipla all ilan man: Torres Strait Islanders' struggle for television access. In J. Craik, J. James Bailey, and A. Moran (Eds.), *Public voices, private interests: Australia's media*. Sydney, Australia: Allen & Unwin.

———. (1993b, July). *Indigenous media responses to racism*. Paper delivered to Post Colonial Formations Conference. Nathan, Australia: Griffith University.

The native media. (1999, February 24). *The Globe and Mail*, p. A16.

Northern Native Broadcasting, Yukon. (1998, October 19). An intervention of conditional support of application 199804068 to the CRTC. Whitehorse, YK: Author.

Roth, Lorna. (1994). Northern voices and mediating structures: The emergence and development of First Peoples' television broadcasting in the Canadian North. Doctoral dissertation. Montreal: Concordia University.

Roth, L. (1998). Television broadcasting north of 60. In L. d'Haenens (Ed.), *Images of Canadianness: Visions on Canada's politics, culture, economics* (pp. 147–166). Ottawa: University of Ottawa Press.

Television Northern Canada. (1993, March 10). Response to CRTC Public Notice 1992-13, 4.

———. (1998, October 30). Replies to interventions submitted with respect to an application by TVNC Inc. for a national aboriginal television network application #199804068. TVNC Letter to the CRTC. Ottawa: Author.

———. (1999 March). *North Link* [TVNC Newsletter]. Ottawa: Author.

Walker, Morley. (1999, September 4). Aboriginal TV deserves better spot on dial. *Winnipeg Free Press*, p. B7.

WETV. (1998, November 12). Intervention transcript from CRTC hearing of application #199804068 to the CRTC.

Personal Interviews:

At APTN:
Patrick Tourigny, Director, Regulatory Affairs and Industry Relations
Jennifer David, Director of Communications
Abe Tagalik, Chairman of the Board of Directors
Gerry Giberson, Operations Manager
Dan David, News Director

20

Boundaries Blurred: The Mass Media and Politics in a Hyper-Media Age

Jonathan Rose and Simon Kiss
Queen's University

The media, we are told, are a vital link between citizens and government. Traditional ideals of the media see them as having a pivotal role in keeping government accountable and providing information to citizens about the health of the body politic. The centrality of the media is evident in the metaphors we employ in discussing their functions. When we speak of the media as a barometer of the citizenry or a watchdog over government, or even when we talk of muckraking journalism, we are suggesting that the media are an important link to how citizens get political information and how they understand the world around them. Canadian media scholar David Taras (1990) discusses the mass media through a number of different metaphors: media as watchdog, but also media as mirror and as distorted mirror. The former suggests that the media can be accurate reflectors of objective phenomena in the world; the latter grants more latitude to the interpretation of political life. All of these metaphors, however, assume a clear division between the mass media and the state. In this chapter we suggest that the metaphor of blurred boundaries provides us with useful insights into contemporary developments in the news media. In terms of structure, we see a blurring of boundaries between different media; between insiders and outsiders; between media and government; and between news and entertainment.

The media are, arguably, one of the most significant institutions in modern society. Timothy Cook goes so far as to suggest that newsmaking is now a central way for governmental actors to accomplish political and policy goals. "In that sense, the news media may well be an unwitting adjunct to power. . . . Making news, in other words, is not merely a way to get elected or reelected, to boost one's own ego or to be a show horse instead of a work horse; instead, it is a way to govern" (1998, p. 164). Other authors are equally emphatic in their claims about the centrality of the media in public life. Robert Hackett and Yuezhi Zhao suggest that "journalism is arguably the most important form of public knowledge in contemporary society. The mass media . . . have become the leading institutions of the public sphere" (1998, p. 1). Canadian media scholar Paul Nesbitt-Larking (2001) makes a compelling case that the media are conduits for the creation of our culture. For him, the media shape and are shaped by our social practices, norms, and values. It is clear that conventional scholarship on the mass media sees a critical role for the news media in their support of liberal democratic values.

Democracy is premised on the ability of citizens to deliberate and reflect on issues. Early democratic theorists decried the fact that citizens did not have enough access to information. John Dewey, for example, argued that it was not that the public lacked ability but rather they lacked resources to have a public conversation (Dewey, 1927). The media, he believed, could be this conduit between the public and the governed. In the early days of the 20th century, the solution to the problem of creating an informed public was found in the mass media.

When one examines the media today, we find that few of these democratic obligations are met. Robert McChesney has called the current situation "a disaster for anything but the most superficial notion of democracy" (2000, p. 59). Ownership and the concentration of power has attenuated the public conversation. The news media's obsession with celebrity and the inane has not provided the fuel for the democratic fire. News is now virtually subsumed by entertainment so that discerning the boundary between the two is like drawing lines in the sand at the water's edge: boundaries are temporary, regularly wiped out, and continually shifting. Where we once could discuss separate spheres of news, politics, and entertainment, we argue that these are supplanted by boundaries that are increasingly porous, so that fulfilling important democratic functions is difficult if not impossible. This carries with it significant implications for the state of democratic debate. Despite the explosion in the type and number of media sources, there has not been an increase in their quality. Moreover, this explosion has not resulted in a better-informed public. This chapter explores the paradoxes of the modern media environment and raises questions about the relationship of the media to politics. Serious questions of accountability are also raised, given the relationships between journalists and their sources. The fact that the modern media have been marked by an adaptation of the codes, narratives, and styles of entertainment raises serious questions about the relationship between politics and mass media.

THE BLUR OF SPEED

In contemporary political life, the problem is not that we need greater access to information but arguably that we have access to too much information. For most of North America, where television sets reach over 90 percent of the population and, in Canada, where more than 70 percent of people have cable-TV access and 15 percent subscribe to pay TV (Statistics Canada, 2002), the issue is less one of access than of sheer volume. Some time ago Bruce Springsteen wrote a song where he lamented that there were "fifty-seven channels and nothing on." Now, in the age of satellite television, the choices are virtually infinite. One can choose sports channels, comedy channels, lifestyle channels, and channels for seniors, women, or children. David Taras (2001) calls these fragmentation bombs the biggest threat to national communities and the ability to create a public space. Each one of these speaks to a particular community defined by gender, age, hobby, interest, or any number of categories. The fragmentation of the public creates markets for advertisers rather than enabling a conversation of government with the people. The media have become vehicles for producing specialized audiences of consumers rather than for producing debate among citizens.

Despite the explosion in the production of information, there is evidence that citizens are no better informed. In the United States, the world's most media-literate society, citizens lack basic knowledge of political issues. For example, a study at the University of Maryland (Kull, 2004) found that those tending to support President Bush were more likely than Democratic supporters to believe that Saddam Hussein had weapons of mass destruction and that the Iraqi government played a role in the terrorist attacks on September 11. This study *followed* the Congressional 9/11 commission, which categorically refuted these widely held beliefs. In Canada, the Dominion Institute regularly chronicles Canadians' lack of basic political knowledge. One poll found that Canadians were worse informed about basic historic facts than were Americans (Dominion Institute, 2001), suggesting that this lack of knowledge is not confined to the United States.

Todd Gitlin sees the proliferation of media not, primarily, as having a fragmentation effect—though he acknowledges that component—but rather as a flood, or an aural and visual tsunami. As the subtitle of his recent book suggests, this "torrent of images and sounds overwhelms our lives" (2001). Raymond Williams, the great cultural critic, was probably the first to observe this when he said, "What we have now is drama as habitual experience: more in a week, in many cases, than most human beings would previously have seen in a lifetime" (cited in Gitlin, 2001, p. 15). For Gitlin, the mass media torrent is indivisible. It is not that media fragmentation atomizes us but rather that the flood of media does not allow any critical reflection. The much discussed effects of the media are not to cultivate a more violent society (Gerbner, Gross, Morgan, and Signorielli, 1986), nor to create a bored society, as Neil Postman (1985) argues. Rather "media are . . . themselves the main products, the main transactions, the main effects of media" (Gitlin, 2001, p. 10).

Faced with this continuous flood of images and ideas we are forced to erect dams to protect ourselves. There is evidence to suggest that despite the plethora of media sources, we seek out media that merely confirm our own views rather than media that might challenge us. According to a Pew Research Center study, in the United States if you are Republican you will likely watch Fox, while if you are Democrat you will watch CNN (Kohut, 2004, p. 5). Apparently, your partisanship dictates what you watch. While some might point to the phenomenal success of Michael Moore's documentary film *Farenheit 9/11* as a counterexample, the National Annenberg Election Study found that virtually all Americans who saw the film were Democrats. They were therefore already convinced of the movie's main contention that George W. Bush acted improperly after the events of September 11. According to the study, "only a handful of Republicans saw the movie; they were too few for their attitudes to be measured with confidence" ("Farenheit 9/11 Viewers," 2004). Far from a free marketplace of ideas envisioned by early democratic theorists, modern media, though more plentiful and accessible than ever, have narrowed choices precisely because of their ineffable size and scope.

The speed and volume with which the torrent floods us also creates other problems besides the creation of filters. Susan Moeller (1999) argues that the flood of grisly images of disease, famine, death, and war has created "compassion fatigue," where the frames of the story result in a inured public whose sympathy and compassion are dulled. The media, in their attempt to deliver powerful images that pack a punch and speak to the audience, rely on formulas for these sorts of stories. They focus on stereotypical characters, the economic or cultural connection to the United States, and, of course, vivid and powerful images. This might explain the apparent rationale of newspapers around the world that on April 4, 2004, published pictures of the charred bodies of four Americans hanging from a bridge in Fallujah, Iraq. Such photos and styles of reportage do no service to informing the public but merely reinforce low levels of public efficacy and trust in elite institutions. The photos and the blur of speed reinforce the idea that with traditional media, citizens are mere observers. Having been forced to respond to a 24-hour news cycle and having to interest a public that treats political information like any other commodity, the media may have been creators of this media flood.

THE BLURRING BETWEEN GOVERNMENT AND JOURNALISTS

Historically, the media have viewed themselves as an independent watchdog on government power (Donohue, Tichenor, Olien, 1995). However, there is evidence to suggest that this role is changing. The relationship between political journalists and those they cover in the government has come under some scrutiny in Canada. A number of journalists have given up their role as supposedly independent political observers to become highly paid public relations practitioners for governments and cabinet ministers. Could it be that the watchdog has become the lap dog? One of the more high-profile examples is that of senior CBC radio correspondent Susan Murray, who left the press gallery to become the spokesperson for the Liberal Minister of Public Works, Scott Brison. A further example is the case of Drew Fagan, *The Globe and Mail*'s senior parliamentary bureau chief, who left the newspaper to become a senior advisor to the Department of Foreign Affairs and International Trade (Martin, 2004, p. A18). Jim Munson, who was a reporter for CTV, moved to the Prime Minister's Office as Director of Communications under Jean Chrétien, after which he was appointed to the Senate in 2003.

Given the increasing complexity, intensity, and speed of contemporary political media, governments (and other institutions) require highly specialized knowledge that professional political journalists can often provide. The explosion of the hyper-media environment has also made the media more integral to government operations. In his exhaustive study of the centralization of Canadian political power in the office of the Prime Minister, Donald Savoie consistently cites the mass media as a cause:

> For the most part, [the media] is no longer just a narrator or an independent observer reporting and commenting on political events. It has become an important political actor in its own right. Television and its tendency to turn a thirty-second clip on the evening news to sum up major policy issues or, much more often, to report on something gone awry in government, have had a profound impact on government operations. The centre [of government], broadly defined, has become extremely sensitive to potential media-inspired developments it cannot control and to surprises, which can give rise to political problems and embarrassments. (1996, p. 39)

Although there has always been a crossover between the professions of journalism and public relations, it is worth asking whether or not this trend is increasing or becoming more problematic. There is no straight, empirical investigation of the claim that there are journalists who are leaving the profession in greater numbers to join the ranks of elite public relations firms. However, employment growth in the public relations profession has far outstripped that of journalism. The Statistics Canada census indicates that there were 13,470 journalists in the nation in 1991; this declined to 12,960 in 2001, for a decrease of 4 percent. The same survey, however, notes an increase of 16 percent in the number of Canadians practicing public relations, from 23,780 to 27,465 (Statistics Canada, 2001). While these data are stark, it should not be entirely surprising, given widespread public debate about strapped-for-cash newsrooms in institutions such as the Canadian Broadcasting Corporation. What makes the situation even more compelling is that it takes place against the backdrop of an exploding media environment that has resulted in a 500-channel universe. If the mass media are expanding at a rapid pace, but the professionals who work in that industry are experiencing severe cutbacks, then we must ask ourselves, who is producing the content that we consume in our daily lives? Perhaps public relations officials— whether they are government, industry, or otherwise—are gaining the upper hand in the production of political information.

This trend does raise other concerns about the potential reliability of political news media. Most news organizations have a segment of their staff on the political beat, working in close proximity to those in government. If some of those journalists are seeking to join the PR ranks of those they are supposed to cover, might it not colour their coverage? Don Martin, a senior columnist with the *National Post*, has raised questions about the practice of parliamentary correspondents joining the ranks of governments. He suggests a number of steps that could be taken to re-establish boundaries between governments and the journalists who cover them; for example, governments should institute a ban on hiring journalists for one year following an election campaign, as well as outright prohibitions on offering journalists patronage appointments to the Order of Canada and the Senate until a suitable cooling-off period has elapsed (Martin, 2004, A18).

A further example of this blurred boundary is the inevitable mixing of journalists, politicians, and commentators after election campaign debates. In the first minutes following live debates, the candidates, their political allies, their political staff, third-party observers, and supposedly neutral journalists all engage in a verbal brawl as they fight for a single news frame: "my candidate won." Watching this commentary, it is legitimate to ask: Who are the journalists? Who are the politicians? Who is independent and who is not? And, most importantly, who is accountable to whom for what they say? Instead, these situations appear to be a collective free-for-all, a ritual of producing political information engaged in by actors from all sides of the process.

Perhaps the most dramatic and controversial case of the blurred line between press and government was the use by the United States military of "embedded" journalists during the invasion of Iraq. In this case, journalists from Western media outlets were attached to specific military units to travel with them, even into extremely dangerous combat situations. In order to gain access to the front, journalists were required to sign an agreement with the Pentagon, foregoing their rights to sue the government in case of damages, and, perhaps more importantly, to agree to the military's standards of censorship, including not identifying "specific number of troops," "information regarding future operations," "rules of engagement," or "information on effectiveness on enemy electronic warfare," among other blanket categories (U.S. State Department, 2003).

The ethical implications of embedded journalists are a matter of significant debate. Some suggest that this practice guarantees biased coverage, pointing to the extraordinary sense of camaraderie that develops between embedded journalists and the military units they are stationed with (Laurence, 2003). On the other hand, there are those who argue that by embedding journalists, viewers and readers get a far clearer picture of the destruction caused by war. For example, John R. McArthur, publisher of *Harper's Magazine*, noted in an interview that embedded journalists with *The New York Times* and ABC News went so far as to display pictures of dead Iraqis. "Compared to the last war, that's 100 per cent more corpses. If you measure good war journalism by the extent to which it shows the violence and death, we are ahead of where we were 12 years ago" (quoted in Bedan, 2003, p. 34).

What is certain, however, is that the United States military considers media relations and the projection of images integral to the success of its operations. The guidelines issued by the Office of the Assistant Secretary of Defense for Public Affairs regarding embedded journalists are quite clear on this point:

> Media coverage of any future operation will, to a large extent, shape public perception of the national security environment now and in the years ahead. This holds true for the U.S. public; the public in allied countries whose opinion can affect the durability of our coalition; and publics in countries where we

> conduct operations, whose perceptions of us can affect the
> cost and duration of our involvement. . . . We need to tell
> the factual story—good or bad—before others seed the
> media with disinformation and distortions, as they most cer-
> tainly will continue to do. Our people in the field need to tell
> our story—only commanders can ensure the media get to the
> story. (U.S. State Department, 2003)

These examples indicate one important trend in contemporary political communications: in many ways, the media are no longer an independent institution.
Instead, they are integral to the political process, and they are inherently political
actors. The United States military has guidelines that emphasize the importance of
the media and communication strategies to their operations. Political journalists are
crossing boundaries to work for governments. These contradict traditional conceptions of journalists and how journalists view themselves. In fact, journalists will most
often recoil at the allegation that they are "political." But if we are right and today's
media are inherently political, then a major question best expressed by Timothy
Cook must be asked: "If the media are now a key intermediary institution, who
elected reporters to represent them in politics and how well is their power popularly
checked?" (1998, p. 16).

THE BLURRED LINE OF POLITICAL JOURNALISM

In the realm of hyper-media the very definition of what constitutes journalism is now
in question. No longer can we understand news media as simply news that appears
on television or radio, in print or over the Internet. But even the Internet with its
evolving structure and shifting modes of communication (i.e., from text to pictures to
video) is creating new forms of news dissemination. If every U.S. presidential election
brings with it a new innovation in political campaigning, then surely the story of
the 2004 presidential election was the growth of Web logs, the stripped down Web sites
known as "blogs." Essentially on-line diaries, blogs can also chronicle the musings,
gossip, and news of any political actor. Because they are not constrained by editors,
owners, or any pretense of balance, and because of the immediacy with which stories
can be published, blogs are a challenge to traditional media. So, when mainstream news
outlets refused to publish stories of Bill Clinton's affair with an intern, Matt Drudge in
his Drudge Report (http://www.drudgereport.com), had no hesitation. Another leading
blog, "Wonkette" (http://www.wonkette.com), caters to Washington insiders. It uses
the format of listing links to mainstream media sources as well as creating its own
stories. The blog has become not just a filter in the media torrent but also another
source of journalism and another source for journalists. In Canada, Warren Kinsella,
who was a top Chrétien aide, uses his blog (http://www.warrenkinsella.com) to influence current political debates.

Blogs became an important part of the election cycle in the role they played in propelling Howard Dean from outside populist candidate to front-runner for the U.S. Democratic Party's presidential nominee. In this case, blogs supposedly enabled Dean's campaign to raise extraordinary amounts of money—$5 million per month in the second half of 2003, more than any other Democratic contender in history (Edsall, 2004)—and helped grassroots activists connect with each other, communicate with each other, and plan campaign events from the ground up.

Blogs also play an important role, not just in grassroots political organizations, but as alternate news sources. One prominent case in point occurred during the 2004 presidential election campaign, when CBS News mistakenly reported the existence of documents that supposedly proved President Bush had shirked his duties as a member of the National Guard during the Vietnam War. Within hours of the story being broadcast on the CBS nightly newscast, conservative bloggers had downloaded copies of the documents and raised serious questions about the documents' veracity. Forty-eight hours later, the controversy had spilled from the "blogosphere" into the mainstream media and quickly led CBS News to apologize and launch an internal inquiry into how the story had passed internal checks.

The importance of this incident lies in the increasing ability of bloggers to hold the mass media to account. Whereas the traditional media have often understood themselves to be the primary watchdog of government power, blogs allow citizens to hold the media to account in their political coverage. A common complaint levied against the political media is that they cannot be held accountable. Traditional means (letters to the editor, ombudsmen, etc.) are often too weak or too slow to respond to biases, slants, or outright errors propagated by the mass media.

Simple errors or biases within prominent newscasts in the midst of a campaign can quickly take on the status of what has been called congenial truths, a concept that William Fox applies to Canadian politics. Congenial truths are "a pact between the reporter and the reader, an understanding of reality that is mutually acceptable" (Fox, 1999). Fox discusses one Canadian congenial truth as our belief in Jean Chrétien as "le petit gar de Shawinigan"—we are willing to believe this as a congenial truth despite any evidence that might contradict it. In the case of the CBS newscast, above, the news story was a product of the congenial truth that President Bush had inappropriately avoided his military service; unchallenged, it would have substantially contributed to the strength of that truth within public debate. The interdiction by conservative bloggers was able to substantially alter the progress of the story. In this case, at least, blogs gave citizens a potentially powerful entry point into the 24-hour news cycle, subjecting mainstream journalists to real-time scrutiny, commentary, and accountability.

Blogs are important in other ways as well. Drezner and Farrell (2004) emphasize the role that political blogs played in United States Senator Trent Lott's political troubles in 2002. In that instance, videotaped comments made by Lott, in which he expressed sentiments sympathetic to segregation, were prominently discussed throughout the blogosphere, with liberal-minded bloggers expressing their outrage.

The debate on-line became so fierce that the traditional media were forced to pick up the story, generating enough political pressure that Lott, at that time the Senate Majority Leader, was forced to resign. Moreover, Drezner and Farrell argue that blogs have significant advantages in the opinion-formation process, often shaping important political events early on. Whereas members of the traditional media must go through some basic processes of vetting and editing before their accounts can be put forward, these constraints are nonexistent for bloggers. It might be that blogs are the 21st-century version of the penny press in the 19th century (Tucher, 1994). In the Canadian context, bloggers could serve as early interpreters of key political events such as debates, throne speeches, budget speeches, or Question Period debates.

THE BLURRING OF ENTERTAINMENT AND NEWS

U2 singer Bono appears at the federal Liberal Party leadership convention that elects Paul Martin in 2004; Bruce Springsteen appears with U.S. Democratic candidate John Kerry in the last few days of the 2004 campaign. In both cases the photos and stories are front-page news. Just after the bombing of the World Trade Center, *Politically Incorrect* host Bill Maher is publicly chastised by White House spokesman Ari Fleischer for calling American politicians cowardly. In his rebuke, Fleischer says Americans "need to watch what they say, watch what they do. This is not a time for remarks like that; there never is" ("The *Salon* Interview," 2002). In 2003, country music stars The Dixie Chicks are pilloried in the press and have their music pulled from radio stations when they criticize George Bush's policy on Iraq. In all of these examples, the political views of celebrities become grist for the media mill. Our society has a longstanding fascination with the power of celebrity. That the potent combination of the mass media and capitalism has accelerated the growth of celebrity is not new (Gitlin, 1980). What has changed is that celebrities are now being sought out—or targeted—for their political views. In becoming the new pundits, they have demonstrated how news and entertainment cannot be separated.

One of the most significant political challenges to President Bush's reelection effort and to democratic debate came not from the traditional political media but from Michael Moore's feature film *Fahrenheit 9/11*. The impact of the film should not be underestimated. For example, the Saudi Arabian ambassador to the United Kingdom took the extraordinary step of publicly refuting claims made in the movie in an exclusive interview with BBC News. The movie is the highest-grossing documentary ever made, grossing approximately $119 million (U.S.) in ticket sales (Smith, 2004, p. 98). Shortly after the film's release, MoveOn.org organized thousands of private screenings of the film, offering private groups the opportunity to hear the filmmaker address the groups over telephone links. Moore was explicit in urging participants to support Democratic presidential nominee John Kerry (Gilgoff and Tobin, 2004, p. 38).

A similar story is found in the phenomenal growth of the satirical comedic news show, *The Daily Show with Jon Stewart*. This nightly comedy program mocks political actors and the political media simultaneously. The high point of Stewart's political influence, perhaps, came with a much publicized appearance on CNN's daily debate show *Crossfire*. On that show, Stewart publicly chastened the show's hosts and, by extension, the broader political media. On the American election night, many networks (CNN and CTV being two examples) seemed to throw in the towel and embrace celebrity/journalism when they broadcast Stewart's comedy show in the middle of electoral returns. Viewers who tuned in during the comedy show would find little difference between *The Daily Show*'s news-style presentation and a regular newscast. Both had attractive anchors sitting behind a desk and reporters filing stories about who might win, routinely interrupted by any electoral results that emerged. It was difficult to determine if comedy was co-opting the election or the election was simply material for a comedian. Either way, the line between entertainment and news was completely blurred.

Should the political warnings of a comedian be taken seriously? Perhaps in this case, there is little to fear. A study of over 19,000 respondents during the presidential campaign found that viewers of *The Daily Show* had higher levels of campaign information than did those who did not watch late-night comedy or those who watched other shows such as *The Late Show with David Letterman* ("*Daily Show* Viewers," 2004). There are no data to suggest that the show is a cause of increased political information; rather, it is more likely that the show's content requires a certain amount of political awareness on the part of its viewers to be successful. There are other, more general reasons to be cautiously optimistic about this development. First, in an age where youth voting is abysmally low, there may be positive benefits in seeing spokespeople more representative of that generation. Second, a poll of Canadians in 2000 suggests that 61 percent of Canadians have not very much or no confidence in the media (Canadian Opinion Research Archive, 2004). Hearing alternative voices might offset the apparently low esteem in which the media are held.

The theme of the blurring between news and entertainment has been addressed perhaps most successfully by Neil Postman (1985) in his book *Amusing Ourselves to Death*. In that work, Postman argues that the trend toward treating entertainment as news and news as a form of entertainment represents a powerful threat to democratic debate. He suggests that the threat to modern democracies is not from Big Brother, but from ourselves through our collective ennui. Though he did not live long enough to see the emergence and growth of reality TV, there is no doubt that Postman would see it as proof that television, in particular, is a medium completely unsuited for deliberation.

The growth of reality TV programming around the world is a strong testament to this idea. In the U.K., the final two candidates in the reality program *Pop Idol* "polled more votes than the Liberal Democrats in the general election" (Corner and Pels, 2003, p. 1). Each episode had more viewers than did the 10 o'clock news during the real election campaign. In Australia, more people watched the final episode of *Australian Idol* than the election debate. Even the treasurer acknowledged that "a lot of people would have turned on [the debate] to see how it was going then they'd start wavering with their finger on the remote control" (Symonds and Schultz, 2004). In the United States, the Showtime network had a reality TV show called *American Candidate* where viewers were invited to select the people's candidate. While candidates were not voted off the island *à la Survivor*, they were subjected to the same sort of competition where two individuals faced off to see who was the victor and who the vanquished. Lest anyone doubt the seriousness of this, the prestigious University of Virginia Center for Politics held an all candidates' debate with both entertainer Montel Williams and noted academic, Larry Sabato. The program was neither entertainment nor news but, with its blurred boundaries, a new hybrid of infotainment where you could not discern the expert academics from the talk-show host.

The growth of non-traditional media, whether in the form of blogs or as a response to why citizens are flocking to entertainment/news, gives us reason to examine what needs these other forms of communication are filling. Their popularity stems from a craving for substantive political debate, alternative narratives, and news frames that are simply not being provided by traditional media. Instead, the traditional political media have become part of the political process, themselves political insiders. Rather than frowning on the intrusions of Jon Stewart and Michael Moore into the political process, we need to ask why they—and not traditional news—are capturing the imagination of viewers.

IS PUBLIC JOURNALISM THE ANSWER?

If the new forms of media are no longer able to provide the kind of information required in a democracy, then what ought to be done about these new blurred boundaries? Jay Rosen, one of the most vocal adherents of "public journalism" (sometimes called civic journalism) argues that what is needed is a new way of doing journalism that recognizes these blurred boundaries and uses them to construct a dialogue with the public. For Rosen, public journalism sees a radical transformation of the role of journalists in society. Public journalism asks journalists to address citizens as participants, not spectators; to help the public act on its problems, not just learn about them; and to improve the climate of public discussion (1999, p. 262).

It maintains some elements of impartiality while abandoning others. For example, the Canadian Association of Journalists has a "Statement of Principles" that lists fairness, freedom of speech, diversity, privacy, balance, and public interest as guiding principles. While public journalism would not abandon these ideals, it would recognize that journalists have an obligation to address compelling social problems and that often means taking sides in a public conversation. While this notion might subvert our traditional understanding of what journalists do, under public journalism the media provide a platform for meaningful deliberation and debate. By using newspapers as forums for public discussion, by allowing the public to frame issues put before political elites, public journalism changes the media from watchdog to participant. Newspapers (through on-line discussion boards) and television news (through town hall meetings) have begun to adopt some of the central tenets of this movement, but these are the exception, not the rule. Public journalism may offer a solution, as it respects citizens and sees the role of journalists as facilitating this great conversation with government rather than providing bite-sized and intellectually unfulfilling nuggets of news.

We have tried to show in this chapter that the mass media are undergoing tremendous structural changes. Since the boundaries surrounding media have become more open, this should be taken as an ideal opportunity to illuminate what media do and in doing so, shine a light on what that shows us about our own democratic practices and habits. A vibrant media is a necessary precondition for a vibrant democracy.

QUESTIONS

1. What are the ethical issues surrounding the military practice of embedding journalists?
2. Can you think of recent examples of "compassion fatigue" in the media?
3. According to the authors, how has entertainment media and news become increasingly blurred? Provide a recent example.
4. Why do you think there has been such an increase in the popularity of blogs and blogging?
5. What other forms of entertainment media can inform youth about political and news events?

REFERENCES

Bedan, Audin. (2003, April 7). More skewed, very biased. *Maclean's*, 34.

Canadian Opinion Research Archive. (2004). Retrieved November 2, 2004, from http://www.queensu.ca/cora/trends/tables/Confidence-Media.htm

Cook, Timothy. (1998). *Governing with the news: The news media as political institution*. Chicago: University of Chicago Press.

Corner, John, and Dick Pels. (2003). The restyling of politics. In John Corner and Dick Pels (Eds.), *Media and the restyling of politics*. London: Sage.

Daily Show viewers knowledgeable about presidential campaign, national Annenberg election survey shows. (2004). Annenberg Center for Public Policy. Retrieved November 5, 2004, from http://www.annenbergpublicpolicycenter.org/naes/2004_03_late-night-knowledge-2_9-21_pr.pdf

Dewey, John. (1927). *The public and its problems*. London: Allen.

Dominion Institute. (2001). 5th annual Canada Day history quiz. Retrieved November 2, 2004, from http://www.ipsos-na.com/news/pressrelease.cfm?id=1255

Donohue, George. A., Phillip J. Tichenor, and Clarice N. Olien. (1995). A guard dog perspective on the role of media. *Journal of Communication, 45*, 115–132.

Drezner, Daniel, and Henry Farrell. (2004). The power and politics of blogs. Paper presented at the 2004 Annual Meeting of the American Political Science Association. Retrieved May 19, 2005, from http://www.utsc.utoronto.ca/~farrell/blogpaperfinal.pdf

Edsall, Thomas. (2004, January 7). Dean fundraising sets party record: Goal of matching Bush is still far off. *Washington Post*, A4. Retrieved November 7, 2004, from http://www.washingtonpost.com/wp-dyn/articles/A60457-2004Jan6.html

Farenheit 9/11 viewers and Limbaugh listeners about equal in size even though they perceive two different nations, Annenberg data show. (2004. August 3). National Annenberg Election Study 2004. Retrieved November 2, 2004, from http://www.naes04.org

Fox, Bill. (1999). *Spin wars: Politics and new media.* Toronto: Key Porter Books.

Gerbner, George, Larry Gross, Michael Morgan, and Nancy Signorielli. (1986). Living with television: The dynamics of the cultivation process. In Jennings Bryant and Dolf Zillmann (Eds.), *Perspectives on media effects* (pp. 17–40). Hillsdale, NJ: Lawrence Erlbaum.

Gilgoff, Dan, and Michael Tobin. (2004, July 12). Moore or less. *U.S. News & World Report*, 38.

Gitlin, Todd. (1980). *The whole world is watching: Mass media in the making and unmaking of the new left.* Berkeley, CA: University of California Press.

————. (2001). *Media unlimited: How the torrent of images and sounds overwhelms our lives.* New York: Metropolitan Books.

Hackett, Robert, and Yuezhi Zhao. (1998). *Sustaining democracy: Journalism and the politics of objectivity.* Toronto: Garamond Press.

Kohut, Andrew. (2004, July 11). More news is not necessarily good news. *The New York Times*, section 4, p. 5.

Kull, Steven. (2004, October 21). The separate realities of Bush and Kerry supporters. The PIPA/Knowledge Networks Poll, The American Public on International Issues. College Park, MD: Program on International Policy Attitudes, and Menlo Park, CA: Knowledge Networks. Retrieved from http://www.pipa.org

Laurence, John. (2003, March–April). Embedding: A military view. *Columbia Journalism Review*. Retrieved November 11, 2004, from http://www.cjr.org/issues/2003/2/embed-laurence.asp

Martin, Don. (2004, October 19). From media hack to ministry flack. *The National Post*, p. A18.

McChesney, Robert. (2000). The global media giants. In Robin Andersen and Lance Strate (Eds.), *Critical studies in media commercialism* (pp. 59–70). Oxford, England: Oxford University Press.

Moeller, Susan. (1999). *Compassion fatigue: How the media sell disease, famine, war and death*. New York: Routledge.

Nesbitt-Larking, Paul. (2001). *Politics, society and the media: Canadian perspectives*. Toronto: Broadview Press.

Postman, Neil. (1985). *Amusing ourselves to death: Public discourse in the age of show business*. New York: Penguin.

Rosen, Jay. (1999). *What are journalists for?* New Haven, CT: Yale University Press.

The *Salon* interview: Bill Maher. (2002, December 11). *Salon*. Retrieved November 5, 2004, from http://archive.salon.com/people/interview/2002/12/11/maher

Savoie, Donald. (1996). *Governing from the centre*. Toronto: University of Toronto Press.

Smith, Sean. (2004, October 24). Will Oscar listen? *Newsweek*, 98G.

Statistics Canada. (2001). *2001 census of Canada*. Census. Cat. No. 97F0012XCB01018.

———. (2002, December 2). Television viewing, Fall 2001. *The Daily*. Retrieved from http://www.statcan.ca/Daily/English/021202/d021202a.htm

Symonds, Emma-Kate, and Jane Schultz. (2004, September 14). Idol moments defending PM. *The Australian*, p. 6.

Taras, David. (1990). *The newsmakers: The media's influence on Canadian politics*. Toronto: Nelson.

———. (2001). *Power and betrayal in the Canadian media*. Toronto: Broadview.

Tucher, Andie. (1994). *Froth and scum: Truth, beauty, goodness, and the ax murder in America's first mass medium*. Chapel Hill, NC: University of North Carolina Press.

U.S. State Department. (2003, February). Public affairs guidance (PAG) on embedding media during possible future operations/deployments in the U.S. central commands [*sic*] (CENTCOM) area of responsibility (AOR), Sections, 4G1, 4G6, 4G9, 4G14. Retrieved November 7, 2004, from http://www.defenselink.mil/news/Feb2003/d20030228pag.pdf

21

O Canada: Media (De)Convergence, Concentration, and Culture

Leslie Regan Shade
Concordia University

This final chapter revisits some of the themes and trends discussed in earlier chapters, particularly as they relate to the issue of Canadian "identity" and culture. It will consider the notion of **cultural sovereignty** and its importance for Canada. It will describe some of the issues arising from culture and trade debates, and the role of Canadian culture within the global context. Finally, it will look at media ownership and related issues such as technological convergence, the future of the CBC, and the role of the CRTC.

THE FUTURE OF CANADIAN MEDIA INDUSTRIES

Culture and trade issues are just one among many challenges facing the Canadian communication industry in the 21st century. There are four main trends in world communication: (1) convergence; (2) conglomeration and concentration; (3) globalization; and (4) deregulation.

Convergence refers to the manner in which digital technologies alter the traditional distinctions between print and broadcasting media. It is a contested arena for policymakers and for media industries themselves; indeed, former CRTC Commissioner David Colville once observed of Canadian convergence strategies, "I am still left wondering how these businesses are going to add value in the public interest as well as in their own interests" ("Mediasaurus Wrecks," 2001).

Convergence was heavily promoted in the 1990s as the ownership of cross-media platforms and assets, coupled with the integration of digital technologies, produced both vertically- and horizontally-integrated conglomerates. Promoted as "one-stop" shopping for consumers, media behemoths envisioned themselves as providers of information and entertainment, content and distribution, telephone and cable, subscriptions and advertisements. In Canada, some of the mergers that characterized convergence included the following:

- *Bell Globemedia.* Bell Canada (phone company, Internet portal Sympatico-Lycos, satellite distributor Bell ExpressVu) bought CTV (the Canadian Television Network), and *The Globe and Mail* newspaper.

- *Rogers Communications* (owner of cable TV, cell phones, and radio stations) bought Maclean Hunter Publishing, Astral Media (specialty and pay-per-view TV, radio, and outdoor advertising) and the Toronto Blue Jays baseball team.
- *Shaw Communications* (cable TV) bought cable-TV owner Moffat Communications, Nelvana (animation house—*Babar*), and created StarChoice satellite distributor. It dominates Western Canada.
- *Quebecor* (newspaper and printing group) bought Sun Media (newspapers), TVA (French-language television network), and Videotron (cable TV, Internet services).
- *CanWest Global Communications* (Global TV) bought Western International Communications (TV stations), Southam (newspapers), Hollinger's Canadian Internet properties, and the *National Post*.
- *Indigo Books* purchased the Chapters bookstore chain. Indigo is controlled by Onex Corporation, which owns Loews Cineplex (movie theatres), Galaxy Entertainment (megaplex theatres in small- to medium-sized markets), and Phoenix Pictures (feature-length filmed entertainment).

However, the exalted visions of convergence have since faded, as many media companies have failed to reap anticipated financial revenues.

Conglomeration and concentration are structural features of the global media system, whereby a small number of media firms own the majority of media products. There are basically two forms of concentration: horizontal concentration and vertical concentration. **Horizontal concentration of ownership** occurs when a firm in one line of media buys a major interest in another media operation not directly related to the original business, or when it takes a major stake in a non-media company. This form of conglomerate ownership is exemplified by the $19 billion (U.S.) merger of ABC and Disney in 1996, which gave Disney control over 10 television stations and 29 radio stations in the United States. **Vertical concentration of ownership** is characterized by a concentration of firms within a single line of business in order to extend a company's control over the process of production and/or distribution. This form of ownership is illustrated by Disney's TV production and distribution through Touchstone, Miramax Films, and Buena Vista. As will be seen, a high level of **cross-media ownership** characterizes Canadian media companies.

Globalization (see Chapter 17) refers to the transformation of communication spaces and social relations occurring across national borders. It is characterized by economic globalization, or the integration of the global economy through free-trade mechanisms and international bodies such as the World Trade Organization (WTO); and by cultural globalization, or the absorption and integration of global cultural forms into other cultural products and services.

Finally, deregulation occurs when governments and international trade bodies try to foster a more competitive environment by not regulating the media. Governments are particularly loath to impose restrictions (relating, for example, to content and foreign ownership) on the media. Deregulation has been fostered by neoliberalism, which promotes the idea that the marketplace and the accrual of profits should be allowed in all facets of social, economic, and cultural affairs. But, as Robert McChesney comments, particularly referring to the United States, "while the rhetoric extols small government, free markets, competition, and entrepreneurial risk-taking, the reality is that a large government is doling out crucial contracts, monopoly licenses, and subsidies to huge firms in highly concentrated industries" (2004, 51).

WHAT IS "CULTURAL SOVEREIGNTY"?

Cultural sovereignty can be defined as the ability of a country to enact laws and policies that protect and promote its culture and cultural industries. In Canada, cultural policies on heritage, film, television, and now multimedia are instituted through legislation, regulation, program support, or taxation measures. Legislation enacted by the federal government has created or modified cultural institutions such as the CBC. Cultural rights were established through the Copyright Act, and regulations have also established the governance of Canada's broadcasting, cable, and telecommunications sectors. For instance, the Broadcasting Act requires that television and radio stations air a predominant amount of Canadian content (CanCon) and the CRTC enforces this regulation. Program support includes grants and contributions for Canada's cultural industries; agencies such as the Canada Council, Telefilm Canada, and the National Film Board administer many of these programs. Specific programs for targeted cultural industries include the Feature Film Fund and the Book Publishing Industry Development Program. Taxation measures include tax credits for corporations that support Canadian cultural industries. The Income Tax Act, for instance, allows Canadian advertisers to claim expenses on advertising placed in periodicals and on television stations that are Canadian-owned.

Why is there such a concern about making sure that Canadian content is allowed to thrive? Many feel that measures are needed to protect us from American culture. For almost a century, Canadian nationalists have attempted to assert Canadian cultural sovereignty in order to counterbalance the American newspapers, films, television, magazines, comic books, videotapes, and music flooding across the border. Although American cultural products flow continually into other countries (both industrialized and developing) as well, Canada's situation is unique in that its exposure is mediated by its geographical proximity to the U.S. border (about 80 percent of the Canadian population resides within 100 kilometres of the U.S. border) and the considerable distances between communities (Thompson, 1992, p. 189).

As early as the 1920s, Graham Spry and, later, members of the Canadian Radio League recognized and advocated the importance of establishing a public broadcasting system distinct from its commercial counterpart to the south. "It is a choice between the State and the United States," Spry said, calling for government support of a communications policy that would foster "Canada as a nation, as a community, as a social organism" (cited in Babe, 2000, p. 41). This sense of broadcasting as a social and non-commercial utility (i.e., related to and encompassing the concerns of the community) is, as Marc Raboy has argued, one of the strengths of the Canadian "identity" (Raboy, 1990), and it has been discussed in this book with particular reference to radio (Chapter 8), film (Chapter 9), television (Chapter 11), and Native communications (Chapter 19). Whereas U.S. public broadcasting depends on a mix of foundational, corporate, and individual donor support (Ledbetter, 1998), public broadcasting in Canada—principally in the form of the CBC—has been and remains a stalwart institution since it is still dependent on state funding (although increasingly it is becoming dependent on advertising).

Debates over Canadian content have centred on the cultural imperialism thesis: Are Canadians swamped by an intrusion of American monoculture? Will the Canadian identity be eroded if Canadians are not able to consume and produce their own media products? For instance, many Canadians were upset when the Walt Disney Company signed an agreement with the Mounted Police Foundation— which is affiliated with the Royal Canadian Mounted Police (RCMP)—to license and control the promotion of Mounties merchandise. How could such a revered Canadian icon join hands with "the Mouse"? The Police Foundation contended that the move was designed to stop the production of "tasteless merchandise . . . everything from Mountie swizzle sticks to porn flicks . . . and to raise funds for some of the Mounties' community projects" (Wasko, 2001, p. 65). Although the licensing agreement with Disney has expired, critics fear that similar agreements will be struck with other Canadian cultural icons.

International sales of U.S. software and entertainment products were estimated at $60.2 billion (U.S.) in 1996 alone, "more than any other U.S. industry" (Farhi and Rosenfeld, 1998, p. 6). In 2001 in English Canada, 95 percent of feature films and 80 percent of prime-time television watched were from the United States (DePalma, 1999). American scholars Benjamin Barber and Herbert Schiller have documented the strength and power of the American cultural and media industries, expressing concern about the erosion of democracy in light of huge media consolidation, technological convergence, and the decline of public broadcasting. Schiller (2000) criticizes the American "free flow of information" doctrine as an attempt to establish a new world information and communication order. Barber describes "McWorld" as "an American push into the future animated by onrushing economic, technological, and ecological forces that demand integration and uniformity and that mesmerize people everywhere with fast music, fast computers, and fast food, MTV, Macintosh, and McDonalds" (1998, p. 1).

In order to meet the requirements of the Broadcasting Act, which stipulates that broadcasting is a public service essential to Canadian culture and sovereignty and that a diversity of programming reflecting the spectrum of Canadian "attitudes, opinions, ideas, values and artistic creativity" be created, the CRTC has created Canadian content quotas. These "CanCon" rules regulate the amount of Canadian content broadcast on television and radio. Some Canadian critics who take issue with the

notion that American culture is a threat to Canadian sovereignty deride the establishment of Canadian content requirements for radio and television broadcasting:

> [The regulations] have become intolerable. They restrict the
> choices of viewers/listeners and raise the price of cable TV
> services. Worst of all, the CanCon policy involves the coer-
> cion of the many (including taxation) to provide benefits to a
> few, notably the producers of CanCon and the few people
> who enjoy consuming it. (Stanbury, 1996)

David Taras (1999), on the other hand, makes a case for *stronger* CanCon regulation: "The result of an unregulated market would be even greater control by the
Hollywood entertainment conglomerates. Ted Turner and Rupert Murdoch have
no interest in telling Canadian stories or reflecting Canadian realities" (p. 223).

CULTURE AND TRADE DEBATES[1]

> [Culture] cannot be treated like just another thing to be
> bought and sold, subject to the vagaries of market demand.
> American pop culture is so pervasive. . . . Obviously, we can't
> prevent that, but we need to make certain our own culture has
> a chance. (Jean-Louis Roux, former chair of the Canada
> Council for the Arts, cited in Gauthier, 2000, p. E4)

Many Canadian nationalists fear that the global sweep of networked technologies,
coupled with a climate of growing open competition, could result in the commercialization and Americanization of Canada. Will Canadians have the same access to
the channels of production and distribution as their southern neighbours? Culture
and trade debates have exacerbated these concerns. The MAI (Multilateral
Agreement on Investment) debate in 1997 raised new questions about cultural
rights. The MAI followed in the wake of other global agreements such as the North
American Free Trade Agreement (NAFTA), which included an exemption for
cultural industries; the General Agreement on Tariffs and Trade (GATT); and the
World Trade Organization (WTO) (Clarke and Barlow, 1997).

With the Free Trade of the Americas (FTAA) and General Agreement on Trade
in Services (GATS) deliberations, debates over trade and culture have become more
controversial. According to Ted Magder, Canada's cultural industries suffered
"a devastating blow" (1999, p. 12) when the WTO overturned legislation designed
to block the sale in Canada of U.S. split-run magazines through the imposition of
an 80 percent excise tax on the accrual of Canadian advertising revenues.

Split-run magazines are Canadian editions of magazines originally published in
another country. These magazines contain the basic content of the original, but
advertisements targeted at Canadians replace more than 5 percent of the original ads.

Sales and advertising in Canada cover the cost of producing split-run magazines. Split-run magazines and Canadian-produced magazines compete for advertising revenue needed to cover production costs.

The dispute over split-run magazines arose in the 1990s, when *Sports Illustrated* (owned by Time Warner) began to transmit the magazine electronically in order to evade physical borders. The Canadian government's response was to impose an 80-percent excise tax on advertising in split-run magazines and to provide lower postal rates and subsidies to Canadian magazines. The WTO ruling, settled through the WTO Dispute Settlement Body (DSB), made clear that Canadian cultural policies are not sacrosanct. *Canada—Certain Measures Concerning Periodicals* challenged the cultural aspect of a "good" and failed to acknowledge the cultural distinction of "goods." A clear victory for the United States, this ruling exemplifies how the free-flow-of-information doctrine—first enunciated in the New World Information and Communication Order (NWICO) debates of the 1970s (see Chapter 17)—has become "the doctrine of free trade" (Magder, 1999, p. 14).

The role of the WTO has raised many concerns about the future of global democracy. The WTO, established in 1995 as part of the Uruguay Round of the General Agreement on Tariffs and Trade that was designed to formulate a set of rules governing international trade, consists of 137 member countries committed to pursuing a free trade agenda (Ellwood, 2001). Carmody contends that the "dominant gaze of WTO decision-making is so fixedly economic that it is in some ways blind to context" (1999, p. 25). In the case of the split-run magazine decision, the WTO did not recognize or accept cultural justifications for regulation and legislation. A cultural waiver under WTO agreements is one remedy that could ameliorate future cultural disputes. However, because of the WTO ruling, the Canadian government has opened its market to U.S. split-run magazines, relaxed foreign ownership controls in the Canadian publishing industry, and abolished the postal subsidy. In compensation, the government has promised more subsidies to the Canadian publishing industry.

Will the FTAA further undermine the role of cultural sovereignty? The FTAA, considered by government leaders at the Summit of the Americas in Quebec City in April 2001 and in Miami in November 2003, has as its goal the integration of the General Agreement on Trade in Services (GATS) with the powers of the defunct Multilateral Agreement on Investment (Lee, 2001). Canadian critics fear that such integration would "create a new trade powerhouse with sweeping new authority over every aspect of life in Canada and the Americas" (Barlow, 2001).

Maude Barlow (2001), speaking for the Council of Canadians, argues that culture will be either fully included in the pact or exempted using language similar to that used in NAFTA Annex 2106. There, articles dealing with the cultural industry (Art. 2005:2) give the United States "the right to retaliate against Canada with measures 'of equivalent commercial effect' and to do so using sectors unrelated to culture" (Barlow, 2001, p. 36). In effect, this agreement would allow the United States to decide if Canadian cultural measures are "inconsistent" with NAFTA and to retaliate against Canada, which would have no legal recourse in the event of an unfavourable ruling.

The fear is that cultural services will be included in the definition of services under the General Agreement on Trade in Services. GATS is "a multilateral agreement that restricts government actions affecting services through legally enforceable constraints backed up by trade sanctions" (Sinclair, 2000, p. 29). Services commercialized and regulated could include broadcasting (even public broadcasting) and telecommunications. If GATS is implemented, then the principles of national treatment and most-favoured nation will apply to cultural services. The national treatment principle accords the same status to imported goods and foreign services as to locally produced goods, domestic services, local **trademarks, copyrights,** and **patents.** The most-favoured nation principle states that countries are to grant equal treatment (neither favourable nor discriminatory) to goods and services produced by all WTO members (UNESCO, 2000).

These principles challenge government subsidies to cultural industries, including those to the CBC and Canadian book publishers. The principles also call into question legislation limiting foreign investment in broadcasting, telecommunications, and cable companies, as well as regulations governing Canadian content. The Canadian government would not be able to restrict its arts and culture subsidies and grants to Canadian individuals and organizations; moreover, it would have to award funds to American and other corporations within the FTAA hemisphere. The threat here is that "Canada's domination by the U.S. entertainment industry would be written into international law" (Council of Canadians, 2001).

The November 2003 FTAA meetings in Miami reinforced the proposed broad sweep of such trade agreements, which are not restricted to Canadian cultural industries. "Trade violations" could consist of U.S. rules that limit media ownership and consolidation. "The American determination to bring culture within the ambit of national treatment and most-favoured nation remains undiminished," Grant and Wood write (2004, p. 371), but by treating cultural goods as products like any other, they argue, "their *public-good* characteristics lead to *market failure*" (p. 417) and lead to a reduction of cultural citizenship.

Former Minister of Canadian Heritage Sheila Copps took an international role in the debates on cultural globalization. Arguing that "world institutions must see culture as more than merely entertainment or merely an afterthought of decision-making" (Copps, 1998, p. 17), she enlisted the support of other ministers of culture to form the International Network for Cultural Diversity (INCD). The INCD builds on work initiated at the UNESCO Intergovernmental Conference on Cultural Policies for Development in Stockholm with a mandate "to build increased awareness and support for cultural diversity in an era of globalization and technological change" (see http://www.incd.net). Seventy countries and 500 members consisting of non-governmental organizations and individuals comprise the network, whose objectives include strengthening cultural and linguistic diversity, supporting local and national cultures, and ensuring that culture is accounted for in international negotiations. The INCD *Proposed Convention on Cultural Diversity* (2003) established a multilateral framework of principles, rules, and disciplines for preserving cultural diversity within and among nations, securing appropriate freedom of expression rights for artists and creators, and providing means for dispute settlement within the Convention.

CONCENTRATION OF MEDIA OWNERSHIP

Ben Bagdikian, former dean of the Graduate School of Journalism at the University of California at Berkeley, was one of the first media critics to write a full-length study of media ownership concentration. In the first edition of *The Media Monopoly*, published in 1983, he documented 50 major corporations that controlled the media; by the time of the seventh edition, 21 years later, there were only 5 major media corporations. "The leaders of the Big Five are not Hitlers and Stalins. They are American and foreign entrepreneurs whose corporate empires control every means by which the population learns of its society. And like any close-knit hierarchy, they find ways to cooperate so that all five can work together to expand their power, a power that has become a major force in shaping contemporary American life" (Bagdikian, 2004, p. 4).

The five major transnational corporations that make up the current global media-entertainment complex are Disney, Bertelsmann, Time Warner, Viacom, and News Corp. Concentration and conglomeration, interlocking boards of directors, mutual promotion and synergy among their media products, as well as a surprising and often bland homogeneity of content characterize each corporation. The Disney Corporation exemplifies the power and reach of these companies, illustrated by the following chart delineating some of its holdings. A pioneer in cross-licensing agreements, in 1996 Disney entered into a 10-year estimated $100 million (U.S.) partnership with McDonald's, wherein it licensed its "classic" characters (e.g., Mickey Mouse, Snow White) for use as toys in McDonald's Happy Meals, and in film, television, and theme-park products (Graser, 2004).

The Walt Disney Company

CEO: Michael D. Eisner
Employees: 120,000
Revenues: $1,267,061 million (U.S.)

Television Holdings

ABC TV and radio networks; 10 television stations; 64 radio stations (U.S.)
International holdings include The Disney Channel in the U.K.; channels in France, Italy, Spain, Taiwan, Australia, Malaysia, and Middle East; ESPN Inc. International; Sportsvision Australia; ESPN Brazil; ESPN STAR; Net STAR; The Sports Network of Canada

(continued)

Studio Entertainment
Walt Disney Pictures, Touchstone Pictures, Walt Disney Feature Animation, Disney Toon Studios, Miramax, Buena Vista Theatrical Group, Buena Vista International, Buena Vista Home Entertainment, Buena Vista Music Group

Television Production and Distribution
Touchstone Television, Buena Vista Television, Walt Disney Television, Walt Disney Television Animation (including production facilities in Canada)

Media Networks: Cable
ESPN, Disney Channel, Toon Disney, ABC Family, SOAPnet, Lifetime Entertainment Services, A&E Television Networks, E! Networks, Buena Vista Television, ABC Radio, Radio Disney, Hyperion Books

Magazines and Newspapers
ABC Publishing Imprints; Disney Publishing Inc.; Diversified Publications Group; Miller Publishing Group; four daily U.S. newspapers; magazine titles include *Disney Adventures, Disney Magazine, Family Fun, Automotive Industries, Video Business, Discover, Institutional Investor*

Book Publishing
Hyperion (Miramax, ESPN Books, Theia, ABC Daytime Press, Hyperion Audiobooks, Hyperion East, Hyperion Books for Children); Disney Publishing Worldwide; Disney Global Children's Books

Internet and Electronic Services
Buena Vista Internet Group, ABC Internet Group, ABC.com, ABCNEWS.com, Oscar.com, Mr. Showbiz, Disney's Daily Blast, Disney Online, Disney.com, Family.com, ESPN Internet Group, ESPN.sportszone.com, Soccernet.com, NFL.com, NBA.com, NASCAR.com, Go Network, Infoseek, Toysmart.com, Disney Interactive, Wall of Sound

Music
Buena Vista Music Group, Hollywood Records, Lyric Street Records, Mammoth Records, Walt Disney Records

Theatre
Walt Disney Theatrical Productions (stage versions of *The Lion King, Beauty and the Beast,* and *King David*)

Sports
Franchises in Anaheim Sports Inc., Mighty Ducks of Anaheim, Anaheim Angels

Theme Parks
Disneyland, Anaheim Disney, MGM Studios, Disneyland Paris, Walt Disney World, Disney's Animal Kingdom (Orlando, Florida), Walt Disney's World

Sports Complex, California Adventure Park, Disney Vacation Club, Epcot, Tokyo Disneyland, Disney-MGM Studios

Consumer Products
Classic Properties (Mickey Mouse, Disney Princess), Movie Merchandising, New Entertainment Properties, Disney Publishing, Disney Toys, DisneySoftlines, Disney Hardlines, Buena Vista Games, Baby Einstein, Disney Direct Marketing, Disney Store

Other Properties
Disney Cruise Line, The Disney Institute, Celebration (a planned community in Orlando, Florida), TiVo (partial ownership)

Source: Adapted from *Columbia Journalism Review*. Who Owns What? Retrieved from http://www.cjr.org/tools/owners/disney.asp and the Disney Corporate Web site at http://www.disney.com.

CANADIAN MEDIA COMPANIES

Canada's mediascape is characterized by one of the most consolidated media systems in the world, with a high degree of cross-media ownership. Indeed, what is new about today's media ownership concentration is the dramatic increase in such cross-media ownership that has resulted from frenzied takeover activity. Cross-media ownership occurs when a firm owns properties in two or more kinds of media. The four dominant players in Canada are BCE, CanWest Global, Quebecor, and Rogers.

The following chart outlines the holdings of these major corporations as of October 2004. This current media configuration, it should be noted, will inevitably change with future buyouts and mergers.

Bell Globemedia Inc. (http://www.bce.ca)

BCE is best known for Bell Canada, which boasts 26 million customer connections for local and long-distance telephone services, wireless services, high-speed Internet access through Bell Sympatico, data, and satellite television through Bell ExpressVu. Specific holdings through Bell Globemedia include

- Broadcasting: 21 CTV affiliates, a satellite-to-cable network, ASN, specialty channels (17, including CTV Newsnet, Discovery Channel, Outdoor Life Network, Report on Business Television, Les Réseau des Sports, the Comedy Network, talktv, the Sports Network, ARTV, and Viewers Choice Canada), and digital specialty channels (Animal Planet, CTV Travel, Discovery Civilization, ESPN Classic Canada, and NHL Network)

(continued)

- Print: *The Globe and Mail*, a national daily newspaper with a weekly circulation of about 2,000,000; *Report on Business Magazine;* and Globe Television
- Internet: sites include spinoffs from print and broadcasting holdings—globeandmail.com, globeinvestor.com, globalfund.com, globetechnology. com, globemegawheels.com, Workopolis.com, robtv.com, ctv.ca, discoverychannel.ca, animalplanet.ca, ctvtravel.ca, and degrassi.tv
- Other properties: include Agincourt Productions, Command Post and Transfer, Exploration Distribution, Exploration Production, Dome Productions, CTC Music, Maple Leafs Sports and Entertainment, and Megawheels Technologies

CanWest Global Communications Corp. (http://www.canwestglobal.com)

Owned by the Asper family, CanWest Global Communications, under CanWest MediaWorks, is best known for the private TV broadcaster Global Television Network, CanWest Entertainment, and CanWest Interactive. The largest daily newspaper provider in Canada, in 2000 it acquired from Hollinger 14 daily newspapers, 126 community newspapers, and a 50-percent stake in the *National Post*. (Hollinger sold its remaining stake in the *Post* to CanWest in 2001.) It now owns 11 major daily newspapers in Canada (including the *National Post, Montreal Gazette, Ottawa Citizen,* and *Calgary Herald*), Global Television Network (11 television stations in 8 provinces, which reach 94 percent of English-speaking Canada), 8 specialty cable networks (including Prime TV, Men TV, Mystery, and Fox Sportsworld Canada), and 2 Canadian radio stations. Under CanWest MediaWorks International, it owns broadcasters in New Zealand, Australia, and the Republic of Ireland. Other holdings include the Canada.com Internet portal; Fpinfomart, an aggregator of Canadian business news; the Financial Post DataGroup; CanWest Studios, an Edmonton-based film and television centre; and Toronto-based Fireworks Entertainment, which finances, develops, and produces film and TV projects.

Quebecor Inc. (http://www.quebecor.com)

Quebecor is organized into two operations: Quebecor World is one of the largest commercial printers in the world, and Quebecor Media includes a range of companies. In 1999, Quebecor became the second-largest newspaper group in Canada when it purchased Sun Media Corporation, with 8 metropolitan dailies, (including *Le Journal de Montréal, Le Journal de Québec,* and *Sun* newspapers in Ottawa, Toronto, London, Winnipeg, Edmonton, and Calgary), 180 local dailies, and other publications in Canada and Florida. Other holdings include

- Groupe Vidéotron, the largest cable provider in Quebec and a major Internet provider
- TVA, Quebec television network

- Netgraphe, operator of CANOE networks of Internet properties
- Nurun, a global Web agency
- Magazines, entertainment weeklies, and alternative newspapers
- Archambault music chain (11 megastores in Eastern Canada)
- Le SuperClub Vidéotron (170 video rental stores)

Rogers Communications Inc. (http://www.rogers.com)
Holdings include cable television, Internet access, and video retailing. Rogers Cable is the largest cable operator in Canada, reaching approximately 30 percent of cable subscribers in the country. Rogers Wireless has 4.1 million customers and over 3.9 million wireless voice and data subscribers. Broadcasting holdings include 43 radio stations, 2 Ontario multicultural television stations, an 80-percent interest in Rogers Sportsnet, The Shopping Channel, minority interests in Canadian specialty television service (Viewers Choice Canada, Outdoor Life Network (OLN), Tech TV Canada, The Biography Channel Canada, MSNBC Canada), and a partnership with CTV Specialty Television

Other large media firms include:

Torstar Corporation (http://www.torstar.ca), publisher of the *Toronto Star*, the *Hamilton Spectator*, the *Kitchener-Waterloo Record*; the CityMedia Group consisting of three metro dailies; Metroland Printing consisting of 70 community newspapers; an alliance with Sing Tao media group, publisher of Chinese-language newspapers in Canada; and Harlequin Enterprises, the world's largest publisher of romance novels.

Astral Media Inc. (http://www.astralmedia.com), Canada's largest English- and French-language specialty, pay, and pay-per-view television network, including 24 radio stations and outdoor advertising. Television networks include The Movie Network, Super Écran, Canal Indigo, Viewers Choice, Canal Vie, Canal D, Teletoon and MusiquePlus.

CHUM Limited (http://www.chumlimited.com), owners of 30 radio stations, 8 television stations (including Citytv in Toronto and Vancouver, the New RO in Ottawa), 18 specialty channels (including MuchMusic, Bravo!, FashionTelevisionChannel, and SexTV) and a music distribution division.

Shaw Communications Inc. (http://www.shaw.ca), a large cable operator and telecommunications and Internet provider.

Concerns about media ownership concentration in Canada are not new. In 1970, the Davey Senate Committee on the Mass Media warned that daily newspapers were owned by fewer and fewer owners. The Royal Commission on Newspapers (Kent Commission) reiterated this concern in 1981, at which time the 3 largest chains controlled 57 percent of the daily circulation. Today, 3 corporations dominate newspaper ownership as a percentage of total circulation; in 2003 CanWest comprised 28.5 percent of the total **market share**, Quebecor, 21 percent, and Torstar, 13.8 percent, for a total of 63.3 percent (Senate of Canada, 2004, p. 8). In television, 2000 statistics show that 5 Canadian corporations owned 68 percent of all private television stations, a 40 percent increase from 1970 (Ibid., p. 18). 2002 figures show that Bell Globemedia/CTV, CanWest, and CHUM dominated 41.5 percent of television viewership (Ibid., p. 20). Commercial radio in 2002 was dominated by 10 companies that accounted for 63 percent of the revenues (an increase of 12 percent since 2000) (Ibid., p. 14).

Cross-media ownership (when a firm in one discrete industry acquires a firm in another industry, such as a broadcaster buying up a newspaper) increasingly characterizes the Canadian mediascape. The media industry has rationalized why this is good for Canadians. Quebecor CEO Pierre Karl Péladeau argued before the CRTC that his takeover bid for cable and broadcast giant Groupe Vidéotron went beyond economic imperatives: "[The proposed takeover] is a project of considerable interest to the greater collectivity because its success will secure a preponderant place for French-speaking Canada in the digital and multimedia universe" (cited in Marotte, 2001). Then BCE Chairman Jean Monty exulted that the $4-billion merger between BCE and Thomson Corp. would create "a true gem in the Canadian content field," and that "the Internet facilitates the possibility of cross-selling, cross-promotion and repurposing" (cited in Damsell, 2000, B1).

Media executives boasted about the benefits of convergence for shareholders and consumers. Said Leonard Asper of CanWest, "What we have really acquired is a quantum leap in the product we offer advertisers and a massive, creative, content-generation machine [where] journalists will wake up, write a story for the Web, write a column, take their cameras, cover an event and do a report for TV, and file a video clip for the Web" ("Mediasaurus Wrecks," 2001).

However, economic downturns in the telecommunications and Internet sector in the late 1990s led to lacklustre results for many Canadian companies. Television viewing demographics (with fewer people watching TV networks but instead turning to specialty cable channels or Internet downloading) and stalled newspaper circulation led many media companies to sell off their holdings in order to reduce debt. Convergence strategies thus morphed into de-convergence. For instance, Quebecor purchased Groupe Vidéotron for $5.7 billion just as the market collapsed. It posted a fourth-quarter 2002 loss of $173.5 million on revenue of $622 million ("Quebecor Ekes Out Slim Profit," 2003). The Aspers of CanWest bought the Southam chain of newspapers and the *National Post* for $3.2 billion in 2001, but in order to get out of debt, they cut jobs, eliminated sections of the newspaper, and reduced bulk sales. In October 2004 they announced a shakeout of their senior management team, hiring five "convergence-savvy American executives" (Blackwell, 2004, p. B17), which had analysts speculating that their new strategy would be to "repurpose" their convergence strategy and seek broader international expansion. And, under Jean Monty, BCE emerged as one of the poster companies for convergence, with its phone, Internet, television, and print services. Monty boasted that the convergence services would "expand available commercial inventory, create multiple platform stories and offer channels of distribution that put your clients within inches of closing the deal" (Gray, 2001). Now, however, under CEO Michael Sabia, BCE is being reorganized under its core business, a near-monopoly telephone utility (Pitts, 2002).

Convergence strategies have also shifted from multimedia content convergence for consumers to cross-media opportunities for advertisers. An example of this is Time Warner's $1 billion expenditures for cross-platform ad deals with companies including Burger King, Kellogg, and Kraft Foods (Powell, 2002). Typical packages include newspaper and television ads coupled with Internet ads, product placements, and even "virtual ads," wherein products are digitally placed into programs or on-air promotions. Another example is CTV's *Canadian Idol* series, where the integration of makeup and hair products provided by L'Oréal Paris and voting via text messaging (SMS) services provided by wireless companies including Bell Mobility, Microcell, Rogers Wireless, and SaskTel Mobility have become an integral component of the programming.

Others are appropriately concerned about the decline of public interest imperatives amid such rampant media ownership concentration and privatization (Hackett, 2000). The Campaign for Press and Broadcasting Freedom, undertaken by an assembly of academics, activists, and labour/community groups, has raised awareness about Canadian media ownership and promoted the need for a greater diversity of media ownership, pressuring the government to enact legislation aimed at addressing the problem of media ownership concentration through three broad goals: (1) limiting and eventually reversing the current level of media ownership concentration; (2) providing measures that will promote a diversity of media ownership; and (3) encouraging the media to more effectively "live up" to their social responsibility and provide a more diverse range of coverage and content.

Journalistic freedom is threatened by media ownership concentration. The choice and quality of news can be undermined as controversial topics are deemed too sensitive to explore (Hackett and Uzelman, 2003). Naomi Klein, addressing the ethical implications of journalistic self-censorship, argued that under conglomeration, "the zones where journalists are expected to tread cautiously are also stretching. It becomes awkward to cover not only one's parent company, for fear of being accused of boosterism, but all of their holdings, and their competitors' as well, for fear that it will seem like sour grapes" (Klein, 2000, p. A15). CanWest has come under intense criticism from local citizens and national and international newspaper unions for its centralization of content (particularly a national editorial policy) reflecting an autocratic attitude toward journalists—and revealing, for many, a disturbing pattern of censorship. Their actions have galvanized local citizens to debate the notion of editorial freedom and media democracy (Shade, 2005).

The Canadian Heritage Standing Committee on Broadcasting, whose mandate was to provide an in-depth study of the Canadian broadcasting system in meeting the objectives of the Broadcasting Act of 1991, paying particular attention to cultural diversity, technological developments, globalization of media and information, and new trends in convergence and conglomeration, released its final report in June 2003. Commenting on the concerns of cross-media ownership, the Committee acknowledged the intense concentration of ownership since 2000, and created specific recommendations to ensure citizen access to a plurality of viewpoints, without jeopardizing the financial stability of Canadian media industries. Recognizing that media ownership concentration poses a threat to public broadcasting, the Committee recommended long-term and stable funding for the CBC (Canadian Heritage Standing Committee, 2003). As many have argued, public-service broadcasting is "a necessary democratic agency" (McChesney, 1999) which needs to be invigorated through sustained public support.

The Committee also recommended a review of the Canadian Radio-television and Telecommunications Commission (CRTC), an independent agency responsible for regulating broadcasting and telecommunications by reporting to Parliament through Canadian Heritage. Although its motto is "Communications in the Public Interest," throughout the 1990s wave of media and telecom deregulation, CRTC decisions were criticized by many for encouraging cross-media ownership and lessening Canadian content and sovereignty, thus muting the public interest.

CONCLUSION

Foreign ownership of Canadian media is hotly debated. Currently, cable companies have been pushing the federal government to lift the 47-percent limit on foreign ownership, arguing that such restrictions are stifling their competitiveness. The Broadcasting Act of 1968 established that Canadian media should be owned and controlled by Canadians in order to "enrich and strengthen the cultural, political, social and economic fabric of Canada." To that end, Order in Council 1968–1809 directed the CRTC to reduce foreign ownership of Canadian broadcasting to no more than 20 percent of the voting shares. Amended in 1991, the Broadcasting Act reaffirmed that the Canadian broadcasting system "should be a single system, effectively owned and controlled by Canadians." However, defining what is "Canadian" is tricky. Given the interlocking ownership of so many Canadian media companies, holding companies (those that own all or a portion of the company) may also circuitously own other companies. Most of the largest media firms are closely held, which refers to the numbers of voting shares held by the founder or founder's family. For instance, the Asper Family Trust controls 89 percent of the voting shares of CanWest, while the Péladeau family controls 64 percent of Quebecor (Senate of Canada, 2004, p. 38).

Media concentration and cross-media ownership raise important questions in relation to the public interest: Does this lead to a lack of diversity in news content, a lessening of local coverage, and paucity in the diversity of sources? Are Canadian media providing quality news coverage of international political and social issues? How have economic pressures in Canadian media companies influenced the autonomy and professionalism of journalists? Do convergence and globalization create opportunities for the Canadian media industry, or do they threaten Canadian sovereignty and cultural diversity?

Communication studies in Canada has never been more exciting. There are great opportunities for engaging the public with the salient issues concerning the fate of Canadian media, culture, and identity in a globalized world. The development of new technologies, rapid convergence, and the porous nature of national boundaries are also creating stimulating challenges. One of the more endearing and lasting traits of Canadian communication scholarship is the notion of communication as a common good. We hope that the wide-ranging chapters in this book will inspire our readers to continue to engage with these pressing issues.

QUESTIONS

1. Explain why cultural sovereignty does or does not matter in the Canadian context.
2. Do you believe that cultural diversity is threatened by international trade agreements? Why or why not?
3. Should Canadians fear the dominance of American media content? Give reasons for your answer.
4. In what ways could regulators and citizens respond to the increasing concentration of media ownership?
5. Should we be concerned about threats to public-service broadcasting? Give reasons for your answer.

NOTE

1. An earlier version of this section by Leslie Regan Shade appeared as "Who's Afraid of Canadian Culture?" in Sherry Devereaux Ferguson and Leslie Regan Shade (Eds.), *Civic Discourse and Cultural Politics in Canada: A Cacophony of Voices* (Westport, CT: Ablex Books, 2002), pp. 15–23.

REFERENCES

Babe, Robert. (2000). *Canadian communication thought: Ten foundational writers.* Toronto: University of Toronto Press.

Bagdikian, Ben H. (2004). *The new media monopoly.* Boston: Beacon Press.

Barber, Benjamin. (1998). Democracy at risk: American culture in a global world. *World Policy Journal, 29*(13), 1–9.

Barlow, Maude. (2001). *The Free Trade Area of the Americas and the threat to social programs, environmental sustainability and social justice in Canada and the Americas.* Ottawa: Council of Canadians.

Blackwell, Richard. (2004, October 5). CanWest shakes up its ranks with U.S. recruits. *The Globe and Mail,* p. B17.

Canadian Heritage Standing Committee. (2003). *Our cultural sovereignty: The second century of Canadian broadcasting.* Ottawa: Canadian Government Publishing. Retrieved from http://www.parl.gc.ca/InfoComDoc/37/2/HERI/Studies/Reports/herirp02-e.htm

Carmody, C.C. (1999). When "cultural identity was not an issue": Thinking about Canada—certain measures concerning periodicals. *Law and Policy in International Business, 231*(1), 1–62.

Clarke, Tony, and Maude Barlow. (1997). *The Multilateral Agreement on Investment (MAI) and the threat to Canadian sovereignty.* Toronto: Stoddart.

Copps, Sheila. (1998). Céline Dion: Made in Canada. *New Perspectives Quarterly, 15*(5), 17–18.

Council of Canadians. (2001). *Stop the FTAA!: Democracy before trade/Non à la ZLEA—La démocratie d'abord!* [Pamphlet].

Damsell, Keith. (2000, September 16). BCE, Thomson converge into titan. *The Globe and Mail,* p. B1.

DePalma, Anthony. (1999, July 14). Tough rules stand guard over Canadian culture. *The New York Times.*

Ellwood, Wayne. (2001). *The no-nonsense guide to globalization.* Toronto: New Internationalist and Between the Lines.

Farhi, Paul, and Megan Rosenfeld. (1998, November 30). Exporting America. *The Washington Post* (National Weekly Edition), pp. 6–7.

Gauthier, Natasha. (2000, November 30). Ottawa, the world's cultural stage. *Ottawa Citizen,* p. E1.

Grant, Peter S., and Chris Wood. (2004). *Blockbusters and trade wars: Popular culture in a globalized world.* Vancouver: Douglas & McIntyre.

Graser, Marc. (2004, June 28). Downsizing a super-sized deal. *Variety.*

Gray, John. (2001, May 14). Waiting for the wave: BCE and CanWest Global bet big on convergence, counting on a surge of revenue. But it might turn into one long drought. *Canadian Business, 74*(9), 30–36.

Hackett, Robert A. (2000, Autumn). Taking back the media: Notes on the potential for a communicative democracy movement. *Studies in Political Economy, 63,* 61–86.

Hackett, Robert A., and Scott Uzelman. (2003). Tracing corporate influences on press content: A summary of recent NewsWatch Canada research. *Journalism Studies, 4,* 331–346.

Klein, Naomi. (2000, September 13). One person's synergy is a columnist's nightmare. *The Globe and Mail,* p. A15.

Ledbetter, James. (1998). *Made possible by . . .: The death of public broadcasting in the United States.* London: Verso.

Lee, Marc. (2001, April). *Inside the fortress: What's going on at the FTAA negotiations.* Ottawa: Canadian Centre for Policy Alternatives.

Magder, Ted. (1999, August). Going global. *Canadian Forum,* 11–16.

Marotte, Bertrand. (2001, March 27). Quebecor pitches to CRTC. *The Globe and Mail,* p. B11.

McChesney, Robert W. (1999). Graham Spry and the future of public broadcasting: The 1997 Spry Memorial Lecture. *Canadian Journal of Communication, 24*(1). Retrieved from http://www.cjc-online.ca/viewarticle.php?id=504&layout=html

———. 2004. *The problem of the media: U.S. communication politics in the 21st century.* New York: Monthly Review Press.

Mediasaurus wrecks: as media companies become bigger by taking over each other, the choice they offer diminishes. . . . (2001, October). *Canada and the World Backgrounder, 67*(2), 4–9.

Pitts, Gordon. (2002, June 29). BCE reaches out, touches its past. *The Globe and Mail,* p. B1.

Powell, Chris. (2002, February 25). Putting it all together. *Marketing, 107*(8), 15–16.

Quebecor ekes out slim profit. (2003, February 14). *The Globe Investor.* Retrieved from http://www.globeinvestor.com/servlet/ArticleNews/story/GAM/20030214/RQUEB

Raboy, Marc. (1990). *Missed opportunities: The story of Canada's broadcasting policy.* Toronto: University of Toronto Press.

Schiller, Herbert. I. (2000). *Living in the number one country: Reflections from a critic of American empire.* New York: Seven Stories Press.

The Senate of Canada. (2004, April). *Interim Report on the Canadian News Media.* Ottawa: Standing Senate Committee on Transport and Communications. Retrieved from http://www.parl.gc.ca/37/3/parlbus/commbus/senate/come/tran-e/rep-e/rep04apr04-e.htm

Shade, Leslie Regan. (2005, forthcoming). Aspergate: Concentration, convergence and censorship in Canadian media. In David Skinner, James Compton, and Mike Gasher (Eds.), *Converging media, diverging politics: A political economy of news in the United States and Canada.* Lanham, MD: Lexington Books.

Sinclair, Scott. (2000). *GATS: How the World Trade Organization's new "services" negotiations threaten democracy.* Ottawa: Canadian Centre for Policy Alternatives.

Stanbury, William T. (1996, October). CanCon rules should be canned. *Policy Options.* Retrieved from http://www.media-awareness.ca/english/resources/articles/sovereignty_identity/cancon_rules.cfm

Taras, David. (1999). *Power and betrayal in the Canadian media*. Peterborough, ON: Broadview Press.

Thompson, J.H. (1992). Canada's quest for cultural sovereignty: Protection, promotion, and popular culture. In Helen Holmes and David Taras (Eds.), *Seeing ourselves: Media power and policy in Canada* (pp. 188–201). Toronto: Harcourt Brace Jovanovich Canada.

UNESCO. (2000). *Culture, trade and globalisation: Questions and answers*. Retrieved from http://www.unesco.org/culture/industries/trade

Wasko, Janet. (2001). *Understanding Disney: The manufacture of fantasy*. Cambridge, England: Polity.

CONTRIBUTORS

Paul Attallah Paul Attallah teaches in the Mass Communication Program of Carleton University. From 1991 to 2005, he was the Associate-Director of the School of Journalism and Communication. He is the author of three books and numerous articles on television, communication theory, and contemporary culture. He is a former president of the Canadian Communication Association.

Bart Beaty Bart Beaty is an associate professor in the Faculty of Communication and Culture at the University of Calgary. He is the author of *All Our Innocences: Fredric Wertham and the Critique of Mass Culture* (University Press of Mississippi, 2005), and has published widely on film, television, and comic books.

Pierre Bélanger Pierre C. Bélanger is a professor in the Department of Communication at the University of Ottawa. He specializes in Canadian media industries and the psycho-sociology of technological innovations. From June 1998 until September 2001, he worked at Société Radio-Canada, first as Head of New Media and then as Chief Advisor–New Media Development. He is a member of the Board of Directors of TVO/TFO. He has published numerous articles on issues pertaining to the uses of traditional and emerging media in domestic and learning contexts. As a recipient of a research grant from the Social Sciences and Humanities Research Council of Canada, he is currently studying various federal initiatives fostering the development and promotion of Canada's national memory on the Web.

Paul Boin Paul D. Boin is an assistant professor of Media and Communication Studies (University of Windsor). He teaches courses on media democracy, social movements, alternative media, media and communication policy, the political economy of media and communication, and media analysis techniques. He is also an investigative journalist and founder of the Real News Network (www.RNNnews.info). A media democracy activist, he cofounded Media Democracy Day. Paul's forthcoming book is entitled *Reclaiming Our Minds: Towards a Democratic and Informative News Media*, to be published in the spring of 2006 by Fernwood Press.

Daniel Downes Daniel Downes is an assistant professor and coordinator of the Information and Communication Studies Program at the University of New Brunswick at Saint John. He is the author of *Interactive Realism: The Poetics of Cyberspace* (McGill-Queen's University Press, 2005).

Charlene Elliott Charlene Elliott is an assistant professor in the School of Journalism and Communication at Carleton University. She has published various articles on law and communication, colour communication, and the politics of consumption.

Derek Foster Derek Foster holds a Ph.D. in Communication from Carleton University. He has taught at Carleton University, the University of Ottawa, and Wilfrid Laurier University. His research interests span mediated and popular culture, with a concentration on television and the rhetorical construction of social issues.

Josh Greenberg Josh Greenberg is an assistant professor in the School of Journalism and Mass Communication at Carleton University. His research interests fall in the broad area of political communication, with a focus on the role of news media in public policy debates, the relationship between journalism and PR, critical news analysis, and social movement activism and media strategies.

Sheryl N. Hamilton Sheryl N. Hamilton is the Canada Research Chair in Communication, Law and Governance at Carleton University, where she is also an associate professor in the School of Journalism and Communication and the Department of Law. Her current research is exploring the ways in which active citizens, the media, and the courts are coming together to shape social policy on moral issues in Canada. She has published in journals such as the *Canadian Review of American Studies, Convergence: The Journal of Research into New Media Technologies, Science Fiction Studies,* and *Communication Inquiry.* She teaches in the areas of gender and technology, intellectual property, communication theory, and cultural studies of law.

Yasmin Jiwani Yasmin Jiwani is an associate professor in the Department of Communication Studies at Concordia University. Prior to her move to Montreal, she was the executive coordinator and principal researcher at the B.C./Yukon Feminist Research, Education, Development and Action Centre (FREDA). Her interests lie in mapping the intersections of institutional, structural forms of violence and intimate, interpersonal forms of violence as refracted through the language of race and gender. Professor Jiwani has recently completed a book manuscript entitled *Discourses of Denial,* which is forthcoming from the University of British Columbia Press, and has also published numerous articles and book chapters. Her work ranges from a critical examination of violence against women and girls of colour to representations of women of colour in the popular and news media.

Russell Johnston Russell Johnston is associate professor in the Department of Communications, Popular Culture, and Film at Brock University. He is a cultural historian whose research explores the Canadian media and culture industries. In particular, he has documented the emergence of the modern advertising industry between 1860 and 1930 in *Selling Themselves* (University of Toronto Press, 2001), and examined the impact that advertising has had upon the press, magazines, and radio broadcasting. His work has appeared in *Canadian Historical Review; Historical Journal of Film, Radio, and Television;* and *Media, Culture, & Society.*

Karim H. Karim Karim H. Karim is the associate director of Carleton University's School of Journalism and Communication. He is the author of *Islamic Peril: Media* *and Global Violence* (Black Rose, 2000; 2003), for which he won the inaugural Robinson Book Prize in 2001. He is also the editor of *The Media of Diaspora* (Routledge, 2003), which examines the use of traditional and new communication technologies by diasporas around the world.

Anne-Marie Kinahan Anne-Marie Kinahan is an instructor in the School of Journalism and Communication at Carleton University, where she teaches courses on media and moral panic, media and gender, and television. Her articles have been published in the *Canadian Review of American Studies, Pop Can: Popular Culture in Canada* (Prentice-Hall, 1999), and *Feminisms and Womanisms: A Women's Studies Reader* (Women's Press, 2004). Her research interests include the history of the Canadian women's movement, communication and the public sphere, and contemporary feminism and popular culture.

Simon Kiss Simon Kiss is a doctoral student at Queen's University studying Canadian politics, with an emphasis on processes of political communication as well as the impact of technology on political life. He has previous experience working for a provincial political party.

Martin Laba Martin Laba is the director of the School of Communication at Simon Fraser University. He has researched and published widely in the areas of popular culture and media, applied communication for social issues, media advocacy, and international communication/education for social change. He is a prominent contributor to local and national media on issues and controversies in media culture.

Jonathan Rose Jonathan Rose is Associate Professor of Political Studies at Queen's University, where he teaches courses in political communication, mass media, and Canadian politics. He is the author of *Making Pictures in Our Heads: Government Advertising in Canada*.

Lorna Roth Lorna Roth is an associate professor and past Chairperson of the Department of Communication Studies, Concordia University in Montreal. She has been involved in broadcasting policy development and analysis, and has consulted with First Peoples and multicultural/multiracial groups since the late seventies on issues of technology access, fair portrayal practices, infrastructure and human resource diversity, and minority representation at the level of employment. She is the author of *Something New in the Air: The Story of First Peoples Television Broadcasting in Canada* (McGill-Queen's University Press, 2005) and is currently working on her second book, *The Colour-Balance Project: Race and Visual Representation*. She has a longstanding interest in minorities in public and private broadcasting sectors and has written extensively about the construction of cultural and racial diversity in the media.

Eileen Saunders Eileen Saunders is an associate professor at Carleton University. She has served as the associate dean of the Faculty of Public Affairs and Management since 1997 and is also the director of the Arthur Kroeger College of Public Affairs. Her research interests are in the field of media institutions and policies, social inequality and gender, and children and the media. She is the author of numerous publications concerning such topics as regulatory guidelines on questions of gender representation in the media, the role of violence in the media, sex-role stereotyping in popular culture, public opinion and social inequality, and access of visible minority groups to news media.

Valerie Scatamburlo-D'Annibale Valerie Scatamburlo-D'Annibale is an associate professor in the Department of Communication Studies at the University of Windsor. She also currently serves as the Chair of the Graduate Program in Communication and Social Justice. Her first book, *Soldiers of Misfortune: The New Right's Culture War and the Politics of Political Correctness*, earned her the American Educational Studies Association's Critics Choice Award in 2000. Additionally, she has published widely on topics ranging from critical pedagogy and contemporary social theory to Indymedia and critical media analysis.

Leslie Regan Shade Leslie Regan Shade is an associate professor at Concordia University's Department of Communication Studies. Her research focus since the mid-1990s has been on the social, policy, and ethical aspects of information and communication technologies (ICTs), with particular concerns toward issues of gender, globalization, and political economy. She is the current president of the Canadian Communication Association (2004–2006).

David Skinner David Skinner is an assistant professor in the Communication Studies Program at York University. He was the founding chair of the Bachelor of Journalism at the University College of the Cariboo in British Columbia and has written a number of articles on broadcasting and alternative media in Canada. Along with James Compton and Mike Gasher, he is co-editor of the forthcoming book, *Converging Media, Diverging Interests: A Political Economy of News in the United States and Canada*, to be published by Lexington Books in 2005.

Valerie Steeves Valerie Steeves is an assistant professor in the Department of Criminology at the University of Ottawa. She has written and spoken extensively on privacy and is the author of a number of award-winning educational games designed to teach children about protecting their human rights in cyberspace. Professor Steeves is also active in the policymaking process. She has appeared as an expert witness before a number of parliamentary committees regarding privacy legislation, is a member of the Canadian Standards Association's Technical Committee on Privacy, and is the chair of the National Privacy Coalition.

Rebecca Sullivan Rebecca Sullivan is an associate professor of Communications at the University of Calgary, specializing in feminist media and cultural studies. She specializes in the relationship between discourses of religion, science, and sexuality. Her book, *Visual Habits: Nuns, Feminism and American Postwar Popular Culture*, was published by University of Toronto Press in 2005. She is completing a team project on biotechnology and culture, contributing work on feminist politics of reproductive technologies. Her new research project is about Natalie Wood and the Sexual Revolution.

Brian Wilson Brian Wilson is an assistant professor in the School of Human Kinetics at the University of British Columbia. His expertise is in the general area of cultural studies, with a focus on youth subcultures, the use of alternative media by youth, youth interpretations of media messages, and representations of youth in the news.

G L O S S A R Y

A

Aboriginal Peoples Television Network (APTN).   A television network launched in 1999, with headquarters in Winnipeg. APTN is devoted to the stories and culture of Canada's First Peoples and is available nationally on basic cable and satellite. See http://www.aptn.ca.

ACNielsen Inc.   A leading global market research firm, best known for its ratings of television shows. It has operated in Canada since the mid-1990s. See http://www.acnielsen.com or http://www.acnielsen.ca.

Administrative research.   A term first used by Lazarsfeld (1941) to describe the type of research he himself conducted and frequently also called "dominant," "mainstream," or "non-critical." This approach is more characteristic of U.S. research, which produces knowledge useful to media corporations and state agencies. It is often funded by the media industry, uses primarily quantitative and empirical methods (such as opinion polling), and seeks to answer clearly defined problems (e.g., who watches TV, how effective are messages, etc.).

Advertising.   Commercial speech whose function is to place products and attitudes in the mind of the public with the eventual goal of persuading members of the public to buy products. Advertising is organized industrially on a large scale.

Alternative media.   Media that provide a range of perspectives and/or modes of communication that aren't readily available through the corporate, profit-driven media that dominate the Canadian mediascape.

AOL (America Online).   An on-line service created by Steve Case in 1985 as Quantum Computer Services. In 1991, it changed its name to America Online and changed its corporate structure. Throughout the 1990s AOL pursued aggressive marketing, which made it the world's leading on-line service. In January 2000, AOL merged with Time Warner in a deal worth $166 billion (U.S.) to become the world's largest media conglomerate. See http://www.corp.aol.com.

Audience.   Derived from the Latin word *audire* (to hear), the word refers to any group of people united around a common experience. The experience usually offers itself as pleasurable and worthy of repetition. Some audiences—such as those for sporting events, movies, concerts, etc.—are physically co-present. Other audiences—such as those for novels, television, radio, etc.—are not physically co-present. Additionally, audience members need not undergo the experience at the same time (i.e., not everyone reads the book or sees the movie at the same time).

Audience competence. The body of knowledge that audience members build up around their object of interest. Often the knowledge is latent, but all audience members eventually become more sophisticated in their own tastes and how to gratify them. The ability to recognize and pursue rationally individualized taste is audience competence.

Audience fragmentation. Refers to the fact that audiences are increasingly splintered into ever narrower segments and niches such that the mass audience, with which television was initially associated, is now the exception rather than the norm. Audience fragmentation is accompanied by increasing audience sophistication as audience members gain knowledge of, and seek out, ever more specialized interests. In response, television targets audiences by tailoring content to market niches and by using new technologies in order to enhance and to regain some measure of control over the overall television experience.

B

Behaviourism. A theory of human behaviour most closely associated with the work of Ivan Pavlov (1849–1936) in Russia and John B. Watson (1878–1958) in the United States. Behaviourism views the mind as a bundle of nerves that can be stimulated in order to bring about desired actions and responses. The stimulus-response theory of communication (also known as the "hypodermic needle" or "magic bullet" theory) is the classic example of behaviourism.

Berne Convention. An international agreement for the "protection of literary and artistic works." Originally adopted in 1886, it has been frequently revised, most recently in 1971. It provides the international framework for the protection of intellectual property, copyright, patents, and trademarks. See http://www.cerebalaw.com/berne.htm.

Board of Broadcast Governors (BBG). Created by the Broadcasting Act of 1958 to serve as the regulatory agency for all Canadian broadcasting. It was replaced in 1968 by the Canadian Radio-television Commission (CRTC). See *Canadian Television Policy and the Board of Broadcast Governors, 1958–1968*, by Andrew Stewart and William H.N. Hull.

Branding. The process by which an organization associates a symbol—a word, colour, sound, smell, etc.—with a product in the hope that the sight of the symbol triggers a recollection of the product in people's minds.

Broadband.   A term dating from the 1950s that describes a type of connection in which a single wire can deliver many channels simultaneously. Cable TV uses broadband, and so do many computer connections. For home computer users, broadband is most often associated with the ability to surf the World Wide Web with greater speed than would be possible with a telephone connection.

Broadcasting Act.   In 1932 the Government of Canada introduced the first Broadcasting Act. It was revised in 1936, 1958, 1968, 1988, and 1991. The Broadcasting Act sets out objectives for Canadian broadcasting generally and for the Canadian Broadcasting Corporation (CBC) specifically. It specifies the composition of the CBC's board of governors, the creation of the broadcasting regulatory agency (CRTC), content rules, and so on. See http://laws.justice.gc.ca/en/B-9.01/index.html.

Bulletin board system (BBS).   A computer or computers on which messages are stored. Users can access the messages by calling the computer via a modem. Most bulletin boards are devoted to particular interests. The messages are usually organized thematically. Computers share their messages when one computer calls another and downloads its messages to the new computer. This process could be repeated several times until computers all around the world had downloaded their messages to one another. With the launch of the World Wide Web in 1993, bulletin board systems went into decline.

Bureau of Broadcast Measurement (BBM).   Created in 1944 at the urging of the Canadian Association of Broadcasters (CAB), it was originally known as the Bureau of Broadcast Measurement. Its board consists of members drawn from both broadcasting and advertising industries. It provides audience measurements for both radio and television. See http://www.bbm.ca and *Channels of Influence* (1994), by Ross A. Eaman.

C

Cable television.   A system for distributing television signals over coaxial cable that was invented by Bell Labs in 1937. The advantages of cable are clarity of signal and the distribution of distant signals. Canada is one of the world's most heavily cabled countries; penetration rates often exceed 90 percent in major metropolitan areas. The first cable television system is usually attributed to John Walson, an appliance store owner in Mahanoy City, Pennsylvania, who in 1948 constructed the first such system to bring distant signals to his store so that he could display television to potential customers. The first cable system in Canada is attributed to Ed Jarmain and Harry Anderson of London, Ontario, in 1951. From the 1970s to the 1990s, cable television grew into a major player in Canadian broadcasting. Cable systems are represented by the Canadian Cable Telecommunications Association. See http://www.ccta.ca.

Canadian Association of Broadcasters (CAB).   Created in 1926 as a lobby group for private radio broadcasters. It expanded to include private television broadcasters in the 1950s. It is concerned with all aspects of broadcasting and specialty services and has long demanded a separate regulatory agency for public and private broadcasting in Canada. See http://www.cab-acr.ca.

Canadian Cable Telecommunications Association (CCTA).   Founded in 1957 as the National Community Antenna Television Association of Canada (NCATAC). The name was changed to the Canadian Cable Television Association in 1968 and to the Canadian Cable Telecommunications Association in 2004. A powerful lobby group, the CCTA has worked successfully in cooperation with the CRTC to protect and advance member interests. Cable expanded exponentially in the 1970s and industry profits kept pace. The association represents over 800 members.

Canadian Film Development Corporation.   Created in 1967 with a $10 million endowment, the CFDC was charged with developing a feature film industry in Canada by lending money to private companies engaged in film production. In 1984, the organization's mandate expanded to include television, and it was re-named Telefilm Canada. It is a Crown corporation of the federal government.

Canadian Journal of Communication (CJC).   Founded in 1975, the leading English-language scholarly journal devoted to communication in Canada. Currently edited by Kim Sawchuk at Concordia University. See http://www.cjc-online.ca.

Canadian Radio-television and Telecommunications Commission (CRTC).   Federal regulatory agency created by the Broadcasting Act of 1968 as the Canadian Radio-television Commission. Its name was changed in 1975 when its mandate was expanded to include telecommunications. Its first and best known chairman was Pierre Juneau. The CRTC grants and may revoke licences for radio, television stations, television networks, cable companies, specialty and pay channels, satellite distribution systems, and multi-point microwave distribution systems. Since 1975 it has also overseen the telephone and telecommunications industries. The CRTC has established Canadian-content rules for both radio and television and has set forth numerous regulations on such issues as sex-role stereotyping, television violence, editorial independence, etc. While the CRTC has been activist with regard to broadcasting, it decided in 2000 not to regulate the Internet for the foreseeable future. The CRTC consists of up to 13 full-time and 6 part-time commissioners appointed by order in council. Cabinet maintains the right to give directions to the CRTC, to set aside its decisions, and to refer decisions back to it.

CANARIE (Canada's Advanced Internet Development Corporation).   A nonprofit organization created in 1993, with headquarters in Ottawa, consisting of industry, government, community groups, and individuals concerned with research and development for the Internet in Canada. See http://www.canarie.ca.

Cancom (Canadian Satellite Communications Inc.).   A corporation providing satellite services to industry and end users. Cancom is a wholly owned subsidary of Shaw Communications Inc., which also owns StarChoice Satellite Television. Besides satellite-delivered television programs, Cancom also provides tracking services to allow companies to control truck fleets, and so on. See http://www.cancom.ca.

CanCon.   Canadian content. This refers to content that satisfies the various quotas and content rules enacted for different cultural industries by the CRTC and other regulatory agencies. The best known CanCon rules concern the percentage of Canadian records that must be aired on Canadian radio stations and the percentage of Canadian programs that must be broadcast on TV. Supporters of Cancom claim that without the rules, little Canadian content would be seen by Canadians, thereby damaging their sense of cultural identity as well as the quality of life in Canada. Opponents argue that the rules create artificial markets in which content is traded not because audiences demand it but because the rules require it.

Chicago School.   A school of philosophical inquiry at the University of Chicago between 1894 and 1904. Founded by John Dewey, its notable members included George H. Mead, James H. Tufts, James R. Angell, Edward Scribner Ames, and Addison W. Moore. The Chicago School sought to apply the principles of pragmatism to social inquiry. As such, it rejected strictly empirical approaches and attempted to understand the ways in which human groups shaped meanings collectively and interactively. This implied a systematic questioning of received notions and standard explanations that makes the Chicago School a representative of critical inquiry. A leading modern-day exponent of Chicago School pragmatism is philosopher Richard Rorty.

Communication.   Refers to the exchange of ideas and symbols between people, and later between institutions or between machines. It is linked etymologically to such words as "community" and "common," and in its oldest acceptance means "to make common," therefore to share, to exchange, or to make public. It was often associated with means of transportation, and prior to the 20th century the railway, waterways, and public roads were often thought of as means of communication. After the 20th century, communication was increasingly used to refer to media of communication, such as film, radio, television, and the Internet. In this more modern meaning, the word is often pluralized (communications) to underline clearly that it refers to media or systems or technologies of communication. As a field of study, communication refers to the way in which the various phenomena of communication (i.e., the fact of interpersonal exchange, the existence of technologies, their social and cultural uses) came into being, have evolved in various contexts, have affected or been affected by the circumstances of their use and development, have been constrained or encouraged, and have been understood, misunderstood, theorized, and thought about.

Conglomeration. A term that refers to the process by which one company in a field buys up other companies in the same field. For example, when one newspaper or newspaper chain buys other newspapers, the press industry is undergoing conglomeration. The process is characterized by fewer and fewer owners and larger and larger corporations. Supporters of conglomeration claim that it is a desirable business practice that protects jobs and brings stability to the marketplace. Opponents claim that it confers too much power on dominant owners who can shape our knowledge of events to suit their interests.

Convergence. The process by which formerly separate technologies such as television and the telephone are brought together by a common technological base (digitization) or a common industrial strategy. The Internet is the most outstanding example of technological convergence, because it can deliver digitized print, images, sound, voice, data, etc., equally well. Large corporations such as CanWest Global, AOL, and Bell Globemedia are examples of industrial convergence, because they bring together under a single corporate umbrella television broadcasting, telephony, newspapers, etc., and use each to cross-promote and to provide content for the others.

Copyright. An exclusive right held by the creators of original works to reproduce, distribute copies of, perform publicly, or display their original work, or to create derivative works based on the original. The duration of copyright is the author's life plus 50 years (in Canada), plus 70 years (in the European Union), or plus 75 years (in the United States).

Corporate media. Generally, these are large, privately owned media corporations that are operated on a for-profit basis.

Critical research. A term first used by Lazarsfeld (1941) to describe research that (a) takes as its proper object of study the relationship between communication and power, (b) sees power as unequally distributed, (c) believes theory (social critique) is more important than method (objective knowledge), (d) argues that researchers must acknowledge their own value orientations, (e) is inspired by European Marxist (Frankfurt School) or American radical (pragmatism) approaches, and (f) seeks to bring about positive social change. It is often assumed that communication study in Canada is naturally or spontaneously critical.

Cross-media ownership. Cross-media ownership occurs when a firm in one industry acquires a firm in another similar but not directly related industry; an example is when a television broadcaster purchases a newspaper.

Cultural imperialism. The process whereby the cultural artifacts of a politically and economically dominant power—usually the United States—enter into another country and eventually dominate it, thereby spreading the cultural, political, and other values of the dominant power, to the exclusion of indigenous values and voices.

Cultural industries. In the Frankfurt School specifically, and political economy generally, cultural industries refers to the fact that culture has been debased by being turned into a commodity controlled by profit-making enterprises. In this view, the function of culture is not to enrich or enlighten but to manipulate and indoctrinate. Since roughly the 1970s, a new and more optimistic definition has arisen, which sees culture as an occasion for economic expansion, employment opportunities, and the development of individual preference.

Cultural nationalism. This perspective aims to strengthen and protect Canadian culture (and Canadian television) by (a) creating a strong public broadcaster independent from market pressures and American programming; (b) funding distinctive Canadian productions; (c) establishing Canadian content regulations; (d) forming activist citizens groups to lobby for Canadian broadcasting; and (e) creating a strong regulatory structure to correct perceived market imbalances and exclude foreign ownership. Proponents of the "Canadian nationalist" perspective argue that the size of the Canadian market compared to the American market make these government protective measures necessary.

Cultural sovereignty. The ability of countries to enact laws and policies to protect and promote their culture and cultural industries. These can include legislations, regulations, program support, or taxation measures.

Cultural studies. An approach to the study of culture developed in Britain in the 1960s and 1970s and most closely associated with the work of Hoggart, Williams, Hall, and that of the Centre for Contemporary Culture Studies at the University of Birmingham. It draws inspiration from both Marxism and semiotics and tends to view cultural artifacts—popular music, television programs, advertising, fashion, etc.—as texts that express social relations of power. Perhaps the best-known examples of cultural studies are Dick Hebdige's study of subcultures and Stuart Hall's examination of Thatcherism.

D

DBS. Refers to direct broadcast satellites, relatively powerful spacecraft operating in geostationary orbit about 33,000 kilometres above the earth. They are capable of transmitting hundreds of information channels across very large footprints. The word is commonly associated with satellite-delivered television, whose signals are picked up by small receiving dishes provided by such companies as DirecTV, Bell ExpressVu, and StarChoice. In the early 1990s, when cable companies realized that DBS posed a serious competitive threat, the satellites were briefly dubbed "death stars." In Canada and in many other countries, DBS is also known as DTH (direct-to-home).

Dialectical. A position on social determination that suggests that historical change is produced through the coming into conflict of oppositional forces. Key scholars exploring a dialectical approach are G.W.F. Hegel and Karl Marx.

Diaspora. A group of geographically dispersed people united by ethnic, cultural, religious, or other ties. For example, there are people of South Asian, Middle Eastern, South American, etc., descent in almost every country of the world, and their cultural, ethnic, religious, and other ties naturally lead them to an interest in the cultural artifacts of their homelands. As such, they constitute diasporas that both consume artifacts from the homeland and create their own hybrid artifacts, which are research-related to the homeland and to the rest of the diaspora.

Digital divide. Refers to the fact that socioeconomic factors including income and educational levels, geographical location, gender, and age influence participation in the new media environment. As a result, richer people and countries have greater access to, and make greater use of, new media and the Internet than do poorer people and countries, a situation that has led to the creation of the categories of the "information-rich" and the "information-poor." This term also refers to the view held by many that digital technologies not only confer benefits but also contribute to social inequalities. For example, not everyone has equal access to digital technology and, even among those who do, not everyone is equally competent in using it.

Digitization. Refers to the process, applicable to any medium, whereby the content of that medium is converted into computer-readable format and can be manipulated and transmitted electronically. This allows the content of formerly separate media— for example, newsprint, radio sound, television images, and hypertext links—to exist side by side on the Internet in a way that was previously impossible. Digital media also possess greater storage capacity and higher transmission speeds and permit infinite non-degraded reproduction of the original content. They tend also to be more user-friendly and to heighten the opportunity for individual creation, manipulation, storage, and transmission of content. In so doing, digitization has raised questions about copyright control and the ownership of intellectual property that have pitted individuals against corporations.

Discourse. An ongoing set of communicational processes through which we try to maintain order and continuity in our social and cultural environments.

E

Empirical. An approach to research that focuses on the analysis of social phenomena through their observation and analysis in accordance with accepted principles and methods. For empirical scholars, observation precedes theoretical analysis.

Entertainment.   A term that describes most—though not all—of the content of the mass media. Entertainment is therefore a mode of contact with an audience. It seeks to provide an experience that is sufficiently pleasurable that audiences will want to come back for more. However, simply by making itself available, entertainment teaches audiences to become familiar with it. Entertainment is therefore characterized by a constant search for novelty, a fear of overexposure, the possibility of offending or alienating important audience segments, and the necessity to express itself in a way that is universally accessible without being formulaic or condescending. The other major content category of the mass media is news.

Epistemology.   An element in the construction of knowledge that focuses on the question: how is it that we know what we know? Epistemological debates ask whether we can produce objective truth about our reality or whether or our knowledge is always subjective.

F

Fair dealing.   Refers to the fact that under some limited conditions—private study, research, criticism, review, or newspaper summary—individuals may make copies of copyrighted material without seeking the permission of the copyright holder. Instead, institutions that hold the material (universities, libraries, etc.) buy blanket copyright licences that allow their members (students, library users, etc.) to copy the material. However, the copying must fall into one of the categories that make it "fair." It is similar to the U.S. concept of fair use.

Fan.   A term derived from "fanatic." It refers to a person with a strong liking for or interest in some aspect of modern culture. Fans, by definition, acquire knowledge about the object of their interest. However, the term is often used in a derogatory sense, as when it is used to suggest that fans have no ideas of their own and are easily amused by any product thrust at them. Their absorption in their object of interest is often seen as a sign of immaturity.

First/Second/Third-Wave Feminism.   The historical categories assigned to the feminist movement. The first wave was the suffragette movement to give women the right to vote. The second wave occurred in the 1960s and 1970s and fought especially for women's sexual and labour rights. The third wave does not have an explicit political agenda but is more about the representation of feminism in the media.

Fragmentation.   A term that describes the process by which a formerly unified or mass audience undergoes a process of breakdown into components. For example, the availability of specialty television channels has resulted in the fragmentation of the television audience. However, some audiences, such as those for books and magazines, have been highly fragmented for a very long time. Radio underwent a process of fragmentation in the 1950s with the introduction of television.

Fragmentation makes it difficult to assemble mass audiences and may threaten the economic survival of media that depend on mass audiences. However, it also allows for the expression of specialized tastes and subcultures.

Frankfurt School (Institute for Social Research). A school of critical inquiry founded at the University of Frankfurt in 1922. It was the world's first clearly Marxist institute of social research, and its leading members included Theodor Adorno, Max Horkheimer, Herbert Marcuse, Erich Fromm, and Leo Lowenthal. Its aim was to understand the way in which human groups create meaning collectively under the impact of modern technology, instrumental or means–ends rationality, authoritarian social structures, and the increasing absorption of the formerly autonomous individual into the culture industries. The Frankfurt School was highly pessimistic about the possibility of genuine individuality under modern capitalism and condemned most forms of popular or mass culture as a type of incessant propaganda that indoctrinated the masses and disguised genuine social inequalities.

Functionalism. A view of society and human interaction that sees relations as adaptive to each other and to their environment. In this context, media are not primarily industries or strategies of manipulation but rather tools used by people in order to gain knowledge of the world. Functionalism holds that if there were no need for the media, the media would not exist. The media, therefore, are adaptations to our needs. In the functionalist view, all elements of society tend to form an integrated whole that works toward equilibrium or consensus. Functionalists ask, therefore, how the media contribute to social equilibrium, how the media system constitutes an integrated whole, and what needs the media answer or fulfill.

G

Gender hegemony. A dominant belief system in which gender roles are limited.

Globalization. A term that refers to the process in which formerly separate, discrete, or local phenomena are brought into contact with one another and with new groups of people. This contact generates the idea that the world is a single place. Supporters of globalization claim that it liberates populations from local or particularistic rules, generates wealth, makes possible the movement of people and ideas, and contributes to the development of human rights by putting all people in touch with all other people. Critics of globalization claim that it flattens out cultural differences, spreads a single culture (usually American culture) to all areas of the world, and strengthens capitalism and unequal property relations.

H

Hegemony.   A term most closely associated with the Italian Marxist Antonio Gramsci (1891–1937). It is similar to ideology in that it refers to a system of ideas or beliefs that are widely held, but it is different in that hegemony involves active effort on the part of the dominant to gain the consent of the dominated. Hegemony, therefore, refers both to (a) the fact that there are commonly accepted ideas and values and (b) the process by which the dominant sectors of society convince subaltern sectors to go along with these ideas and values. The instruments of hegemony range from outright coercion (e.g., incarceration, secret police, threats, physical elimination, etc.) to gentler and more "managerial" tactics (e.g., education, religion, processes of socialization, control of the mass media, etc.). The concept of hegemony has found widespread use in *cultural studies.*

Horizontal concentration of ownership.   When a firm in one line of media buys a major interest in another media operation not directly related to the original business; or when it takes a major stake in a non-media company.

Hypertext.   A word that was coined by Ted Nelson in the early 1980s to describe nonlinear writing, in which users follow links and jump about within a text or around the World Wide Web.

Hypodermic needle.   See *behaviorism.*

I

Ideology.   A frequently used word with two main definitions. From Marx, ideology refers first to false consciousness, the fact that people fail to understand their genuine interests and instead adopt values and ideas that are opposed to their interests. Second, it refers to a system of ideas and values, specifically those of the ruling classes. The ideas of the ruling classes are contained within and reproduced by the dominant social institutions (the law, the family, religion, education, etc.). Ideology is that which appears to be common sense, unchallengeable, natural, good, and desirable but which is actually socially constructed and contingent.

Information Highway Advisory Council (IHAC).   A study group created in 1994 by the minister of Industry Canada to provide advice on developing the information highway. Its final report (1996) was titled *Preparing Canada for a Digital World.*

Instant World.   In 1971, the former Department of Communication struck a "telecommission" that issued a report titled *Instant World: A Report on Telecommunications in Canada.* This was one of the first studies of computers and communication, and it championed the notion of a "right to communicate."

Institutionalization of communication. The process, involving government, universities, and individual scholars, by which the field of communication came to be recognized as an autonomous field of study, with its own departments, research agendas and funds, scholarly publications, debates, etc. In Canada, this process largely occurred in the 1960s and 1970s and involved the coming together of administrative research, political economy, and cultural studies.

Intellectual property. Intellectual or creative work that can be owned by an individual, institution, or company. The thing owned can be an actual artifact (e.g., a machine or device), an artistic or intellectual expression (e.g., a novel, a painting, a film, a mathematical formula, etc.), a process (i.e., a specific method of producing that artifact), and so on. The main methods used to protect intellectual property are trademarks, patents, and copyright.

Intelsat (International Telecommunications Satellite Organization). The world's first commercial satellite operator. Its first satellite was EarlyBird (1965). It now operates over 20 satellites, which provide voice and data transmission, television broadcast, corporate networking, etc. See http://www.intelsat.com.

Interactivity. The ability to participate in the production and consumption of on-line material; the feeling of interchange and interaction.

International co-production. International co-productions are films that are financed by companies in a number of countries at once. For example, Canada and France may jointly fund a film, with stars and production crew drawn from both countries. This method of production reduces risks by spreading costs and expands distribution possibilities for films.

Internet. The Internet is a "network of networks" that connects millions of computers around the world. Networks connected to the Internet use a common protocol, TCP/IP (Transmission Control Protocol/Internet Protocol). This allows networks to have unique addresses and to communicate seamlessly with one another. Internet services include e-mail, e-mail lists, Usenet, gopher, FTP, WWW, Telnet, and chat. The origins of the Internet are found in the late 1950s and early 1960s, when it was decided to construct a communication system that could withstand thermonuclear attack. The goal was to build a decentred system that could continue to operate and route messages even if part or parts of it were destroyed. This involved devising a method for splitting messages into smaller parts (packet switching) so that each part could find its own path to its destination, where all the parts would be reassembled. Much credit is often given to Paul Baran, Vinton Cerf, the Rand Corporation, and DARPA (Defense Advanced Research Projects Agency), but the true list of contributors is extremely long. Virtually identical efforts were undertaken at the same time in the Soviet Union, Britain, and Australia. See http://www.isoc.org/internet/history/brief.shtml.

M

MAPL system.   Refers to the four elements by which Canadian content is determined in musical selections broadcasting by Canadian radio. The acronym stands for Music, Artist, Production, Lyric. See http://www.crtc.gc.ca/eng/INFO_SHT/R1.htm.

Marginality.   The fact of being on the margins, not being at the centre, not being the focus of attention. It is sometimes claimed that marginality affords perspective, distance, and the luxury of contemplation. As such, it is sometimes claimed marginal thinkers can discover insights that thinkers at the centre of things could never attain.

Market-driven television policy.   This perspective is built upon the belief that a free market (and not government imperatives) should determine the content of television. It is often recognized by proposals to (a) deregulate broadcasting, including allowing foreign ownership; (b) abandon content requirements; (c) encourage market/audience-driven private sector production; and (d) open the airwaves to all competitors. Proponents of a market-driven approach argue that cultural nationalism has failed and that only a genuine connection with audience tastes can build a cultural industry.

Market share.   That part of an audience that attends to a particular medium. If 33 percent of an audience reads a particular magazine, then the magazine's share of the market is 33 percent.

Mass.   One of the most frequently used words in communication. Its meaning is most often pejorative. First, a mass designates any large group of anonymous individuals, often a mob, a crowd, a herd. It is usually claimed that the members of the mass tend to lose their individual identity and assume a group or collective identity. As such, members of a mass are likely to do things as a group that they would never do alone (e.g., engage in riots or illegal activity). It is often said that masses are moved by simple yet strong emotions. Consequently, the terms mass society, mass audience, mass media, etc., tend to indicate that the phenomenon under consideration draws on base instincts rather than more elevated and rational thoughts. A mass society is one in which individuals are lost in a sea of anonymity; mass audiences are audiences easily amused; mass media are media that use tired formulas and aim at the lowest common denominator. The mass is usually distinguished from both the public and the audience.

Mass society.   A term frequently used to describe contemporary society, especially in the West, especially after the 1920s. The main characteristics of mass society are usually said to be (a) agglomerations of very large numbers of people, (b) a sense of individual alienation or isolation (anomie), (c) industrial and highly formulaic types of culture (mass media) used to distract rather than enlighten the masses, (d) forms of government whose inner workings are obscure and tend toward authoritarianism, and (e) a generalized sense of dullness, repetitiveness, and sameness. One of the most frightening and evocative images of mass society can be found in Orwell's *1984* (1948).

Media power.   The ability of media to represent reality, particularly the reality of others.

Methodology.   An element in the construction of knowledge that focuses on the processes through which questions are framed and research is conducted. Examples of methodologies include ethnography, science, and discourse analysis.

Methods.   An element in the construction of knowledge that involves the actual techniques through which knowledge is produced. Examples of methods include interviews, surveys, narrative analysis, content analysis, and focus groups.

Modernity.   Refers to a type of society in which individuals are deemed to be fundamentally rational and therefore capable of determining their own forms of social organization. Societies that are modern, therefore, also tend to value freedom of speech and of association, democratic forms of government, increasing knowledge, variety of cultural forms, and so on. They reject the notion that forms of social organization and individual behaviour are predetermined or unalterable. As a result, in modern societies, norms of behaviour are the object of constant debate. Societies that place less emphasis on the individual and more on divine transcendence (the view that social forms are given by a divinity outside of human society) are often called pre-modern, or traditional, societies. Societies that value the individual but also doubt the value of rationality are often called postmodern societies. The fundamental characteristic of modernity, therefore, is the central role granted to reason or rationality in the determination of norms for individual and collective behaviour.

Moral panic.   A media-induced fear that some aspect of modern culture is leading people, especially children and youths, astray, into deviance, delinquency, and criminality. Also known as social crisis. An example: the belief that raves are, at best, generally dangerous and at worst, havens of criminality, drug use, and promiscuity.

Motion Picture Bureau.   The predecessor of the National Film Board of Canada (NFB). Created in 1923 and terminated in 1941, it produced travelogues, scenic shorts, industrial films, etc.

MTE.   Refers to **m**edia **t**elecommunications and **e**lectronic companies, horizontally and vertically integrated enterprises that control information (content), the channels through which information flows (carriage), and the electronic systems (platforms) on which content is accessed.

▬
N

Napster. An on-line peer-to-peer music-trading company developed in 1999 for the MP3 format by Shawn Fanning, then a freshman at Northeastern University. It enabled users to trade files directly without going through a central server. In 2000, most of the major record labels—Universal Music, BMG, Sony Corp., Warner Music, and EMI—filed a lawsuit against Napster for encouraging the illegal duplication of musical recordings. The lawsuit was successful, and Napster was eventually taken over by Bertelsmann AG, which owns BMG. In 2001, BMG introduced a user fee for Napster, but its user base had largely defected to other peer-to-peer services such as Kazaa, Morpheus, and Aimster, Napster's greatest legacy may have been to introduce the idea of peer-to-peer sharing for video, film, text, and other files, in addition to music files.

National Film Board (NFB). A film-production unit established by the federal government in 1939, originally to make wartime propaganda films. Its first and most famous commissioner was John Grierson (1898–1972). After the Second World War, the NFB abandoned propaganda in favour of documentaries, trave-logues, social issue films, scenics, etc. In the 1950s and 1960s, it spawned the *Cinéma direct* movement and was instrumental in launching the Quebec film industry. The NFB was intended to serve as a foil to American film distribution and production. NFB films have won 11 Academy Awards and numerous other international awards. It has served as a training school for some of Canada's most successful film directors.

NCIT. Refers to **n**ew **c**ommunication and **i**nformation **t**echnology, the electronic technologies based on digitization and associated with the computer.

Neoliberalism. Economic and social movement that promotes policies for a free and open marketplace. In the communication sector, it is characterized by privati-zation, commercialization, and the deregulation of media industries.

New media. Refers to communicative forms that are interactive, digital, related to the Internet, and characterized by a convergence of "old" and "new media." The result of social, political, economic, and technical forces, they can engender changes in everyday practices, our experience of reality, and our experience of ourselves.

New television disposition. The new television disposition refers to the entire array of new technologies (HDTV, PVRs, VOD), industrial alignments (signal distribu-tors and content manufacturers), content types (digital and/or pseudo-interactive), and contact strategies (timeshifting, multiple windows, cross-platform tie-ins, repurposing) that characterize the current experience of television viewing. The new experience of television is one of heightened personalization, individualized control, particularistic content, advanced technology, concentrated ownership, and strategies of audience seduction that use the new technologies both to appeal to the audience and to track its movements.

NWICO (New World Information and Communication Order).   In 1980, UNESCO (United Nations Educational, Scientific, and Cultural Organization) published a report titled *Many Voices, One World*. The report was produced by a committee chaired by Sean McBride (1904–1988) and is often called the McBride Report. The authors of the report advanced the notion of a new world information and communication order. Its goal was to view communication as a right integral to individual and cultural development rather than as a commodity or an industry. The report also advocated building communication capacity in poorer and less developed countries in an attempt to rectify the global flow of communication. See http://www2.hawaii.edu/~rvincent/mcbcon1.htm.

O

Ontology.   An element of the construction of knowledge that focuses on the question: what is the nature of being? Ontological debates ask whether reality exists outside of our perceptions of it.

P

Patent.   A patent gives inventors the exclusive right to demand payment (royalties) for the manufacture, use, or sale of their "inventions." Patents therefore are not concerned with words and symbols (the domain of *trademarks*) but with inventions (processes, machines, and combinations of matter). Patents protect an invention for up to 20 years.

Payne Fund Studies.   Between 1929 and 1933, Rev. William Short, head of the Motion Picture Research Council, convinced the Payne Fund of Cleveland, Ohio, headed by Professor W.W. Charters, of Ohio State University, to undertake one of the first major studies of media impacts. The team of researchers, which included a roster of eminent scholars, published their findings in eight volumes. These findings were known as the Payne Fund Studies. The best-known volume is *Movies, Delinquency and Crime*, by Herbert Blumer and Philip M. Hauser, of the Department of Sociology, University of Chicago. As its title suggests, that volume purports to show a link between movies and crime.

Piracy.   The unauthorized duplication of copyrighted material for profit.

Positivist.   A stream within an empirical approach to research that is highly indebted to science. It seeks to produce verifiable data through the application of strict scientific methods to any social phenomenon.

Privacy.   The right to be let alone, to be free from surveillance by the state, institutions, or one's fellow citizens; the right to control the disclosure of personal information; the right to determine the use of information disclosed; respect for the dignity of the person.

Q

Queer Theory.   A type of theory that claims gender is a fluid category and people are not limited to just masculinity/femininity or homosexuality/heterosexuality.

R

Radical alternative media.   Media that explicitly challenge dominant institutions, ideas, and values.

Reversible Resistance.   The ironic negotiation of American popular culture by Canadian audiences. Canadians create their own popular culture through an engagement with and response to the presence of American popular culture in Canada.

Royalties.   Money paid to an inventor, creator, or copyright holder for use of the creation.

S

Scientific method.   A method of inquiry aimed at producing empirically verifiable certainty. To be scientific, a method must be (a) objective (it must not depend on the nature or status of the person conducting the experiment, and it must not be influenced by ideology, personal preference, desire for gain, etc.); (b) reproducible (it must not be the result of chance and must therefore be infinitely repeatable); and (c) falsifiable (it must be stable in a way that allows it to be subjected to experimentation; hence, statements concerning parapsychology, for example, are not scientific because they are not subject to experimentation). Further, various experiments must be internally consistent and work together in support of an overall hypothesis.

Semiotics.   The study of signs or signifying practices, also known as semiology. Semiotics attempts to explain the meanings of objects, actions, images, etc., in the world around us by showing how they fit into, and express, larger systems and patterns of belief and meanings of which we are frequently unaware. For example, semioticians will attempt to explain the success (or failure) of an advertising campaign by showing how its imagery or musical theme or catch line, etc., fit into and draw on older patterns of meaning and symbolism with which we are all familiar but whose far-reaching nature might be unknown to us. For years, the leading exponent of semiotics was Roland Barthes (1915–1980).

Stimulus-response theory.   See *behaviourism.*

T

Technological nationalism.   The Canadian government's reliance on the communications industry to materially and symbolically unify the Canadian nation. Ironically, it is through this industry—the mass media in particular—that Canadians are routinely exposed to American popular culture.

Telecommunications.   The general term for all electronic communications at a distance, and more specifically for telephony, data transmission, computer networking, satellite transmission, undersea cable, and the like.

Telecommunications Act.   In Canada, the Telecommunications Act of 1993 (see http://laws.justice.gc.ca/en/T-3.4/text.html), which covers the provision of services and rates charged. In the United States, the Telecommunications Act of 1996 was a major attempt to extend telecommunications legislation to the Internet; see http://www.cato.org/pubs/regulation/reg19n3d.html.

Telefilm Canada.   Formerly the Canadian Film Development Corporation (CFDC), the agency was renamed Telefilm Canada in 1984 and given expanded responsibilities for both film and television production. It administers the Canadian Broadcast Program Development Fund (CBPDF), the Canadian Television Fund (CTF, $250 million), the Canadian Feature Film Fund (CFFF, $100 million), the Feature Film Distribution Fund (FFDF), the Canada New Media Fund (CNMF, $9 million), and the Music Entrepreneur Program (MEP). Telefilm can invest in all stages of production, pre-production, and postproduction. See http://www.telefilm.gc.ca.

Trademark.   A legal protection allowing the holder to take advantage of commercial symbols or designations. Trademarks are territorial and depend on local trademark use or reputation. For example, Atlas Van Lines is the only moving company that can call itself Atlas. But other companies not in the moving business could use the name Atlas to represent their product or service, e.g., Atlas Catering. A trademark merely protects the holder of the trademark against the use of the same trademark by other people.

U

UNESCO (United Nations Educational, Scientific, and Cultural Organization).   Established in 1945, with headquarters in Paris, to "contribute to peace and security by promoting collaboration among the nations through education, science and culture in order to further universal respect for justice, for the rule of law and for human rights and fundamental freedoms which are affirmed for the peoples of the world, without distinction of race, sex, language or religion, by the Charter of the United Nations." See http://www.unesco.org.

Universal Copyright Convention.   First adopted in 1952, revised in 1971, this convention is an agreement of the member states of UNESCO "to provide for the adequate and effective protection of the rights of authors and other copyright proprietors in literary, scientific and artistic works, including writings, musical, dramatic and cinematographic works, and paintings, engravings and sculpture." See http://www.unesco.org/culture/laws/copyright/html_eng/page1.shtml.

V

Vaudeville.   The principal form of popular entertainment in North America before the advent of film. Vaudeville—also called burlesque, variety, or music hall—refers to a series of unrelated acts (singer, juggler, magician, dancer, dog act, etc.) presented in a theatre (the vaudeville house or venue) to a paying audience. With the advent of film, radio, and television, vaudeville effectively died as a form of entertainment, although its main features were incorporated into the Hollywood musical and the radio or television variety show.

V-chip.   A device invented by Tom Collings, an engineering professor at Simon Fraser University, to be installed in television sets in order to make the screen go blank or switch to another channel whenever the content exceeds certain limits of violence, bad language, sexual content, and so on, as set by the user. In 1996, the U.S. Congress in collaboration with the Clinton administration determined that all new television sets with screens larger than 33 cm (13 inches) must have a built-in V-chip. It is often assumed that the V stands for "violence," when in fact it stands for "viewer choice."

VCR (videocassette recorder).   Although prototypes of the videotape recorder were in development as long ago as the early 1950s, the first commercially successful VCR for home use was the Sony Betamax, launched in 1975. The Betamax used a cassette rather than a spool of tape and allowed for timeshifting. It was joined in the marketplace by the incompatible VHS format, launched by JVC in 1976, which grew to dominate the market. The heyday of the VCR was the 1980s. In recent years its market share has dwindled in the face of competition from digital recorders and the DVD player.

Vertical concentration of ownership.   A concentration of firms within a line of business that extends a company's control over the process of production and/or distribution.

—
W

Walled garden.   In cyberspace, a controlled-access area that attempts to keep users within its confines. For example, AOL is a walled garden in that it attempts to provide users with everything they may need within its own services. This undermines a user's inclination to look elsewhere and allows the operator to stream users toward content it may control.

World Intellectual Property Organization (WIPO).   Established in 1970, with headquarters in Geneva, WIPO is a specialized agency of the United Nations. It currently has 179 member states and administers and develops policy on intellectual property, such as the Patent Cooperation Treaty, the Protocol to Madrid Agreement, the WIPO Copyright Treaty, and the Patent Law Treaty. WIPO is currently concerned with extending intellectual property protection to digital media. See http://www.wipo.org.

World Trade Organization (WTO).   Created in 1995 as the successor to the General Agreement on Tariffs and Trade (GATT), the WTO has 147 members and has its headquarters in Geneva. It sets global trade rules between nations in order to ensure smooth and predictable trade flows. It also provides a dispute settlement body (DSB) in case of disagreements between members. See http://www.wto.org.

World Wide Web (WWW).   In the late 1980s, Tim Berners-Lee of the Centre européen de recherche nucléaire (CERN), in Switzerland, sought a way to make information more manageable within the internationally dispersed community of high particle physics researchers. With some colleagues, he devised the hypertext markup language (html) and the first Web browser, Mosaic. The system was up and running in 1993. It has since become the main way to explore, or surf, the Internet.

COPYRIGHT ACKNOWLEDGMENTS

I N D E X